THE
FIRST
LIBERTY

RELIGION AND THE
AMERICAN REPUBLIC

William Lee Miller

PARAGON HOUSE PUBLISHERS

New York

TO WILLIAM F. MAY

First paperback edition, 1988.
Published in the United States by
Paragon House Publishers
90 Fifth Avenue
New York, New York 10011
Copyright © 1985 by William Lee Miller

Published by arrangement with Alfred A. Knopf, Inc.

Grateful acknowledgment is made to the following for permission
to reprint previously published material:
Macmillan Publishing Company: Excerpt from *Roger Williams,* by Perry Miller.
Copyright 1953 by Macmillan Publishing Company, renewed 1981 by Elisabeth
W. Miller. Reprinted with permission of Macmillan Publishing Company.
Russell & Russell, Inc.: Excerpt from "Essay in Interpretation" by Perry Miller,
from *The Collected Writings of Roger Williams,* vol. VII. Copyright © 1963 by
Russell & Russell, Inc., a division of Atheneum Publishers, Inc.
Sheed & Ward: Excerpt from *We Hold These Truths,* by
John Courtney Murray. Used with permission of Sheed &
Ward, 115 East Armour Boulevard, P.O. Box 281, Kansas
City, Missouri 64141-0281, (800) 821-7926.

Library of Congress Cataloging-in-Publication Data
Miller, William Lee.
The first liberty.
Reprint. Originally published: New York : Knopf, 1986.
Includes index.
1. Religious liberty—United States—History—19th century.
2. Religious liberty—United States—History—20th century.
3. United States—Church history—Colonial period, ca. 1600-1775.
4. United States—Church history—19th century.   I. Title.
[BR516.M545 1988]   323.44'2'0973   87-21103
ISBN 1-55778-007-2 (pbk.)

CONTENTS

FOREWORD

The new nation that our fathers brought forth, to quote Abraham Lincoln, on this continent has rightly given itself much praise as the leader among the peoples of the world in working out the ancient tangled matter of religion and state: of Religious Liberty, as we would put it, often like that, with capitals. We "secured" it—our forefathers did—among the other blessings of liberty for ourselves and our posterity, and on the whole it has stayed secured. We are proud of that, and we ought to be. The most terrible old issues of religious persecution—not so old, in other parts of the world—are really not issues any longer here, though from some shrill statements one might think they were.

But the unique liberty in which the American nation was "conceived" included more than personal religious liberty, as it would be understood worldwide; it includes also the full institutional independence of the federal union from all churches and of those churches from the national state. The mother country, and some other democracies, would come in time to have a religious liberty equal to, perhaps in some informal ways surpassing, that in the United States, but without this constitutional separation.

That was a new idea, that there did not have to be any link between religion and the state, between ultimate convictions and the power of the law. The unity of the state did not require any unity of religion. A great nation-state could exist, and hold together, and walk upright upon its legs among the nations of the world, without the spinal column of an official religious institution. The variety of religious beliefs and nonbeliefs could be altogether voluntary; in the eyes of the state they could be equal and free. The mixture of beliefs in the nation could be whatever the people would decide upon.

The new nation, of, by, and for the people, was, or came to be, distinctive in yet another regard, to the considerable puzzlement of the world: That full formal independence of the state from all religious beliefs and nonbeliefs did not represent, and did not entail, hostility to the traditional religious beliefs of Western civilization. On the contrary.

The American arrangements, like the American nation itself, had been to a marked extent shaped by those beliefs, and as the nations touched by the civilization of the West rolled on into the modern world of the city and science and the machine, and of new universalistic creeds, the United States was almost unique again in the persistence of these older beliefs.

Some beginnings of this unusual combination went back to the first coming of English settlers to this continent, and further back into European history. But the "securing" of America's religious liberty came in the great founding moment for the new Republic itself, as part of the new nation's essential self-definition. What follows in these pages is an account of, and a commentary on, some important episodes in that original formation, beginning in Virginia in 1776.

PART ONE

Bill Number 82

1776

In May of the year the thirteen colonies were jointly to declare their independence from England, their representatives mutually pledging their "lives, their fortunes, and their sacred honor," Virginia had had its own convention, declared *its* independence, called upon the other colonies to do the same, and shaped its independent government. And as in Philadelphia, so also, some weeks earlier, in Williamsburg: While the convention carried out these noteworthy deeds it also set forth, in the fashion of the eighteenth-century Enlightenment, the universal philosophical underpinnings, declaring to the world, as their fellow Virginian was soon to write in Philadelphia, out of a "decent respect to the opinions of mankind," the moral convictions on which they acted.

This philosophical explanation to the tribunal of humankind was the Virginia Declaration of Rights, soon to be famous and influential throughout the colonies and even beyond, and indeed to have at its core a very considerable resemblance to Mr. Jefferson's July 4th Declaration, shortly to be set before "a candid world" from Philadelphia: all men free, equal, and endowed with rights that cannot be taken away by the societies into which they enter. There was in it more than an echo of John Locke, and of later Scottish thinkers as well; it was an outgrowth of many centuries of European history and thinking and rights-declaring and declaration-making, especially in England.

In the Virginia case, however, as not yet in Philadelphia, the "patriots" not only declared their independence from Britain and specified the nugget of the philosophy of equal liberty on which their action was grounded, but also expanded that nugget to a full list of rights—the first in the series of such lists, or "bills," of rights in the several states that would culminate fifteen years later in the first ten amendments to the U.S. Constitution. George Mason, the Northern Virginia planter who was an expert on the history of these matters—of what would today be called human rights—was the chief author, for a committee, of this Virginia Declaration. When he came to the last item, the very weighty one on religious rights—Article Sixteen, as it was to become— Mason, a conventional Anglican in religious matters, wrote that since reason and not force should govern belief, "all men should enjoy the fullest Toleration in the Exercise of Religion according to the Dictates of Conscience." To most of the delegates to the convention, that sounded, presumably, fine: Mason was using what had become the accepted, conventional word, following upon John Locke's *Letter Concerning Toleration* and the legislation built upon it in 1689, in which the mother country, after decades of revolution, uproar, and regicide all linked to religion, had at last wiped her collective brow and more or less settled things: "toleration."

But for one man across the water in Williamsburg eight decades later, that was not enough. In fact, we may infer, the very word gave him intellectual heartburn. This was the youthful delegate from Orange County, James Madison, Jr., making his first appearance in the great world of public affairs. He was shy and short and new and diffident, and his voice was weak, and he did not play a visible role in this convention, but he was not going to let pass mere "toleration."

He had been to college, not, as might be expected of an Anglican planter's son, to William and Mary, but rather up north, to the College of New Jersey. That college—later to be called Princeton—had been founded by the "New Side" wing of the Presbyterians that came out of the torrent of religious revivals that had rained upon the colonies in the 1740s and afterward; the college had become a lively center for revolutionary political and religious ideas. The president of the college when Madison studied there, John Witherspoon, had but recently come to that post from Scotland, where he had had his own troubles with the Scottish Kirk. Mere "toleration" (implying condescension—implying some institution or belief in the superior position from which to do the tolerating) had regularly been disdained and dismissed by Witherspoon and by others with whom Madison had studied and talked and argued in the lively Whiggish prerevolutionary atmosphere of the College of New Jersey.

Moreover young Madison had gone on to his own researches and reflection on the subject of religion in civil society. In the years after college, rattling around in his home in Orange County, teaching literature to his younger siblings, wondering what to do with his life, he had got hold of books on the subject of religion and civil society— rationalistic, Enlightenment books, French and English. He had written his best friend from college, William Bradford, up in Philadelphia, to learn the laws and practices in *that* colony, which he wistfully admitted to be much superior in regard to religious freedom to his native Virginia. In addition he had had a concrete experience of the evil—state oppression of religious conscience—about which he was developing strong convictions. That eighteenth-century torrent of religious revivals (called the Great Awakening) had left many pools of new believers in Orange and Culpeper counties, around Madison's home. (Coming from God as the rains from heaven is the way Jonathan Edwards, and other leaders of the Great Awakening, saw those astonishing revivals.) In 1773–74 there had been a new shower, with Baptists meeting unauthorized in homes, preaching without a license, and disporting themselves evangelistically in a way that gave pain to the old order in church and state. There were persecutions, arrests, imprisonments. Madison, the son of a chief squire of the region, had argued and agitated—as he wrote to his friend "Billey" Bradford—against this noxious persecution. Legend has it that he actually heard one of the Baptists, continuing his preaching unsquelched, from the jail. So Madison had his youthful theoretical position confirmed by experience. In contrast to the other chief participants in the great events that were to come, James Madison was first moved to revolutionary ardor by the issue of religious liberty.

So now here he was in Williamsburg in June of 1776, only twenty-five years old. Here was a formidable draft of a Declaration of Rights, admirably rooted in the sound republican language of liberty—which when one read through to the article on religion asserted not "liberty," but only "toleration." We might say that the events that were to culminate almost exactly ten years later (1776–86) with the most unusual of all the accomplishments of the American Revolution had their beginning at this moment in Williamsburg.

For Madison drafted an amendment to the offending portion of Mason's draft of Article Sixteen, eliminating "toleration" and putting in its place that "all men are equally entitled to the full and free exercise of religion, according to the dictates of conscience." That word *equally* was important, and survived into the final result. It would mean, presumably, that the unlearned Separate Baptists of Culpeper had rights of religious conscience equal to those of well-educated Anglican priests and powerful Anglican squires, and in the longer history it would set in motion it would mean that heathens, pagans, and nonbelievers had rights equal to those of believers, although that point would not be emphasized in Williamsburg, Virginia, in June of 1776. One did not even emphasize that it placed the established church in jeopardy.

As a novice in public affairs, Madison did not stand upon his own legs to offer his amendment. What he did (and would do again on other occasions) was to persuade a more prestigious and commanding presence, please, sir, to offer it for him—in this case, at first, none other than the great Patrick Henry himself, of whom Madison was still at this point an admirer.

In addition to the clause quoted above, however, Madison had also included in his first effort to amend Article Sixteen the following: "that no man or class of man ought on account of religion to be invested with peculiar emoluments or privileges." Apparently somebody in the convention read the language of the amendment carefully—that does not always happen in conventions—and asked Patrick Henry whether that clause meant the end of the established church. Henry—not one to go far beyond public opinion, a master indeed of a strictly *safe* boldness—backpedaled fast and answered, "No," and the amendment as originally constituted was not passed. But then a revision by Madison that omitted that sentence—offered now by the conservative statesman Edmund Pendleton—*did* pass, and did get rid of the word "toleration," and did start on its long and potent course through subsequent American history the concept of the "free exercise" of religion as a human right.

Thus, though he did not get all he wanted, Madison did achieve the declaration that freedom of conscience is an equal right for all, which made the resulting document a marked advance on the English law and the arguments of John Locke (Locke's toleration had not extended to atheists, implicitly not to Roman Catholics, and not to some others; of course, it left the established church in place). Although it is not clear that the members of the Virginia convention knew that they were doing it, they had, by Madison's amendment, removed freedom of religion from the purview of what lawyers today call "legislative grace"— with the implicit assumption that what is thus given can be withdrawn by the power that grants it—by making the fundamental philosophical claim that freedom of "conscience," or belief, is not a matter of toleration, forbearance, or gift, but rather what the Declaration of Independence, issued a little over a month later in Philadelphia, would call an inalienable right, equally possessed by all. That was new.

One may add that Madison had also proposed, in the draft that failed of passage, the essentials of the rest of the tradition that was now to develop in the New World. By writing that "no man or class of man ought, on account of religion, to be invested with particular emoluments or privileges," he did anticipate the full-fledged disestablishment of all religion and the "separation" of church and state. So one could say that everything that was to come in the American arrangement of these matters was already present in Williamsburg, Virginia, in June of 1776, in the proposals of young James Madison.

When the Virginia Declaration of Rights spread out across the colony—or independent state, as it now was, in the summer of 1776—it brought forth a more pungent and excited response than most of the members of the convention that passed it—most of them members of the established church—probably intended. Especially out in the Shenandoah Valley and the piedmont, among the evangelicals, the amended Article Sixteen claiming full freedom of religion as an equal right for all aroused a most embarrassing enthusiasm—a disconcerting inclination on the part of many to take it seriously, and to apply it to themselves and to the restrictions and disadvantages imposed on them by the established church in Virginia. If the convention members had not meant that article to imply the end of the established church, many dissenters who read it nevertheless took it that way—and the Declaration was now part of the fundamental law of the state. The tinder was already there, among the dissenters; they had been petitioning since at least 1772 against requirements that they pay taxes to support the Anglican church, that their preachers apply for licenses, that their meetings be authorized. They had asked that their clergy, like the Anglicans, be allowed to perform marriages. Now the Declaration of Rights cut through all these issues to proclaim full freedom and equality, and the winds of Revolution—this was '76 after all—fanned the flames.

So when the mostly Anglican legislators of Virginia reassembled the following autumn—now as an independent government, under the new constitution they had composed in Williamsburg in May, with the old House of Burgesses now become the new House of Delegates—they found heaped upon their tables all the trouble they had inadvertently asked for. There was petition after petition asking the end of the established church and the equality of all religions: from German Lutherans in Culpeper; from Presbyterians in Frederick County; more carefully argued, from the famous Hanover Presbytery; from Baptists in many western counties. One petition had 10,000 signatures, an astounding number in that setting. Almost all of these petitions appealed for their authority to the Virginia Declaration—usually called "Bill"—of Rights that young Madison had managed to get amended six months before.

.   .   .

Now the new House of Delegates that faced this inundation of petitions against the established church had as an important member a lawyer from Albemarle County who had not been able to be present at Williamsburg the previous May, being then otherwise engaged, in Philadelphia. This was Thomas Jefferson, who, having written the Declaration of Independence for a new country, was now to set about remaking from the ground up his—so to speak—old country, Virginia.

Thirty-three years old, he had been, since 1769, a member of the Virginia House of Burgesses—the colonial parliament—and though young had become an important political leader in the state—not as important, then, as Patrick Henry or Peyton Randolph or a few others, not to mention General Washington, who was already in a class by himself, but sufficiently highly regarded to have been chosen, as Randolph's substitute, to be a member of the Virginia delegation to the Congress of all the colonies that met in Philadelphia in 1775. He had had to return to that duty in the spring of 1776, but though he did his work conscientiously, including in it the most important piece of draftsmanship in the nation's history, "his heart," according to his biographer Dumas Malone, "was always in Virginia," and he found time to submit in absentia to the convention in Williamsburg, through his friend and teacher George Wythe, a proposed new constitution for the new state. (In addition to announcing their independence, and issuing their Declaration of Rights, the Virginians in May–June '76 framed a new government—the first of such new state constitutions.) But then, as later, Jefferson was unsuccessful, and a generally more conservative frame of Virginia government was adopted in place of his proposals. "Several times during the next fifty years," wrote his interpretive biographer Merrill Peterson, "Jefferson rode full tilt against [the Virginia constitution], each charge more democratic than the last, and each time he retired in defeat." But, in 1776, "if he could not revamp the Constitution"—to continue quoting Peterson—"he might, for the present, turn one of its most vicious principles, the unfettered power of the assembly, to virtuous ends, and endeavour to achieve by ordinary legislation those fundamental reforms in Virginia law and customs he had hoped to accomplish at one stroke by a liberal constitution."

These efforts by Jefferson reflect his conception of the meaning of the Revolution: not independence alone (this was the point at which the more conservative colonial patriots stopped) but the building, after independence, of something new on the globe, a complete, fresh, and large-scale republican form of government. "In truth it is the whole object of the present controversy," Jefferson had written to a friend, with his characteristic moral sweep, "for should a bad government be instituted for us, in future it had been as well to have accepted at first the bad one offered us from beyond the water without the risk and expense of contest."

So in the autumn of 1776 Jefferson resigned his seat in the Continental Congress and returned to Virginia, declining election as one of the joint commissioners who were to negotiate a treaty with France. He took up a seat in the Virginia House of Delegates, and set about making sure that in Virginia a good government, a republican government, a reformed government be instituted.

In October he proposed, and the Assembly enacted, a bill for the wholesale revision of the state's laws. Jefferson was himself then appointed, with four eminent and older Virginians, two of whom later resigned (one who remained was Wythe), to a Committee of Revisors, to remake Virginia—at least this was Jefferson's intent.

The euphoria of freedom plainly was particularly heady for a born reformer like Thomas Jefferson. He later wrote about this effort at revisal, with something of the heroic naïveté that was to be part of his legacy to the new nation, that "our whole code must be reviewed, adapted to our republican form of government, and, now that we have no negatives of Councils, Governors, and Kings to restrain us from doing right, it should be corrected, in all its parts, with a single eye to reason, and the good of those for whose government it was framed." Now that we do not have those negatives to restrain us from doing right—let's do it. Redo the whole system. Redo the system "in all its parts" with "a single eye" to reason and the public good.

One aspect of the old Virginia that particularly needed such redoing, in Jefferson's view, was the established church. And there on the tables were all those petitions attacking it, asking for religious freedom, on the basis of Article Sixteen in the new state's new Declaration of Rights.

Jefferson was to become the foremost advocate of that freedom, in its most thoroughgoing interpretation, in the House of Delegates and indeed in Virginia. Though ordinarily a man more of pen and committee than of speeches, he did rise to give an exposition of his position in that session of the fall of 1776. He had worked up a list of all the old restrictions on religious freedom from British or Virginia law that were still on the books—"heresy" still a capital offense, denial of the Trinity or the divine authority of the Scriptures punishable by imprisonment, profanity a crime, Roman Catholics excluded from civil posts, freethinkers and unitarians subject to being declared unfit and having their children taken away from them (he had quite a catalog of antique horrors)—and that though admittedly not now enforced, should be abolished. He offered a series of resolutions that not only took care of that task of cleaning up the law but also, much more important, proposed a radically new conception of religion and the state: complete freedom of religion; equality of all beliefs before the law; an end to all control, support, or linkage between religion and the state. In sum, Jefferson's proposals and arguments in the fall 1776 session of the Virginia House of Delegates first developed fully the ideas on this subject for which one day he would be known throughout the world.

The Assembly in response to Jefferson's resolutions and those waves of petitions did take some important steps in their direction, but certainly did not go all the way. There was a good deal of struggle within the committee of the whole and between the House of Delegates and the Senate—Virginia's new upper house—and, in the manner of legislatures everywhere, the outcome was a compromise. Dissenters were relieved of taxes for the established church, and taxes on other citizens—all assumed to be Anglicans—for the support of the church were *suspended* for a year (and later, another year, and another until finally ended). But the established church still stood, perhaps a little shakily, and the Assembly kept in its hands power over the Anglican clergy and churches and over the licensing of preachers and meeting houses—law and order issues, as the old Virginia legislators saw them. Until the end of the century there would be pushing and pulling over issues having to do with the reorganizing, or the dismantling, of that established church, and about the old, or new, religious situation, including what to do about the glebe lands and other church property.

But up through the smoke of this first heavy skirmish, in the collection of compromises the Assembly finally passed, there appeared a new idea, a proposal from worried churchmen, presumably, opposed to the radical resolutions of the delegate from Albemarle, an idea that would float up over the Virginia battles for the next ten years and leave a faint shadow, perhaps, in the United States in the twentieth century: the novel notion of a tax on the citizens of the state, not for the support of a *single* church "by law established," but rather "for the support and maintenance of several Ministers and Teachers of the Gospel who are of different Persuasions, and Denominations. . . . " This General Assessment, as it came to be called, was not enacted into law, but was set forth as a possibility, to be sorted out by some later Assembly. The Virginia Assembly of 1776 resolved, in an act of unusual deference for a legislative body, that whereas great varieties of Opinions have arisen touching the Propriety of a general Assessment or whether every religious society should be left to voluntary Contributions... this Difference of Sentiments cannot now well be accommodated, so that it is thought most prudent to defer this matter to the Discussion and final Determination of a future assembly when the Opinions of the Country in General may be better known....

The Assembly certainly got the public comment it asked for: resolutions, sermons, petitions, pamphlets, articles, and even poems in the newspapers... a stream of contending commentary continuing through the years, part of the larger stream of American revolutionary pamphleteering. As has regularly happened in American politics ever since—as generations of public officials, editors, and political commentators have discovered, often to their surprise and usually to their dismay—a "religious" issue provoked a public response going beyond that accorded to any other issue, both in passion and in quantity. Dumas Malone wrote that "of all contests in which Jefferson engaged as a member of the Assembly of Virginia the one on the subject of religion was the most bitter." Jefferson himself was to write years after it was over that this contest over religion in Virginia was the severest in his entire lifetime, which if you consider the career of Thomas Jefferson is quite a statement.

VIRGINIA

Virginia, the oldest of the colonies, it will be remembered—and, despite the early subtraction of what would become Maryland and the Carolinas, at this time still the largest, richest, and most populous—had been founded as a mercantile venture. Although its charter made conventional provision for the conversion of the Indians, it was not, like Massachusetts Bay, intended by its original English settlers to be any godly city on a hill, showing forth to the world a beacon of biblical righteousness. The Harvard constitutional lawyer Lawrence Tribe recalled in an essay on these matters the cartoon showing two Puritans on a ship approaching the New World, one saying to the other: "Religious freedom is my immediate goal . . . but my long-range objective is to go into real estate." Much of our country's history, Mr. Tribe observed, is encapsulated in that brief exchange. In the same facetious mode we can say that such a capsule of early Virginia history, in which there was no such distracting duality of purpose, can be even shorter: Religious freedom had nothing to do with it.

The Church of England, as a matter of course, came with the settlers and became an arm of the colonial government. During the ages of Puritan religious intensity in England and the colonies in the seventeenth century, and of the Great Awakening's religious intensity in the colonies in the first half of the eighteenth, the Anglican vestrymen and clergy in Virginia in general avoided it: they were not guilty of any such intensity.

One can read a full panoramic account of this Anglican Virginia in the decades before the Revolution in a superior book called *The Transformation of Virginia* by the Australian scholar Rhys Isaac, published in 1982. What Mr. Isaac presents is a kind of ethnography of a society located in the past. He examines with loving or at least noncommittal care the whole fabric of the colony: architecture, dress, food, fun, and games. Horses were very important, of course; one of the games was a particularly unruly contest of horsemen and riders called the quarter race. Another regular entertainment was the cockfight, and dancing figured large in Virginia life.

The older Virginia—the Old Dominion—Isaac presents, built around order, hierarchy, community, and rank, was given its shape by the dominance of the landed gentry and by the ideal (not altogether gone even yet) of the Virginia gentleman, borrowed of course from the English version but much changed in its transatlantic migration. In Virginia that dominance and that ideal did not, of course, have the solid layers of history beneath them that the English gentry had been provided; the Virginians built not upon centuries of accumulated civilization but upon the peninsulas, rivers, hills, and forests of a new country. Theirs was a sparsely populated plantation society with no great cities or even towns, and an enormous open western expanse—real estate, indeed. Most important, this colony named for the Virgin Queen rested on human slavery, which among its many other effects must have sharpened the importance of domination and deference.

The shared values, the pattern of gentry domination, the ideals of gentlemanly "honor" and "liberality" and of hierarchy, were inculcated in the rituals of communal gatherings in communal places: on election day, when there certainly was no secret ballot; at the mustering of the militia; in the courthouse on Court Day; in the drinking bouts at the ordinary; at the great balls in the great houses.

And, inextricably interwoven with these others, in the churches. The Anglican church in each parish was state property, built and maintained by taxes. Every person not formally a dissenter—there was a scattering of Quakers, but very few other "dissenters" before 1740—was assumed to be a member of "the church of England by law established," and was required to attend divine services (a requirement not enforced) at least one Sunday in four. The Book of Common Prayer was, by law, the liturgy of the churches. Only Anglican clergymen, by law, could perform marriages; if you were a besotted Scotch-Irish Presbyterian in the Shenandoah Valley, you could not go with your beloved to your Presbyterian preacher to be married, and of course not to a justice of the peace; you had to find an Anglican parson, which in that sparsely settled region might not be easy to do. This annoying issue of the right to perform marriages stretched right through the controversy that was to come, and gave a strong push to the result. Each Anglican church was governed by a vestry, which consisted of twelve gentlemen—the squires, as it were—who chose their own successors by cooptation, administered poor relief, could levy taxes to repair and build churches, and picked the parsons. One prerevolutionary dispute—the famous and complicated "Parson's cause"—dealt with, among other things, the independent tenure and, especially, pay of parsons, who were discontented with the degree to which they were, in Virginia, subject to the squires. It was this case that brought fame to the aspiring young lawyer-politician-orator Patrick Henry.

The vestries thus were an arm of the government, because their church was an arm of the government—perhaps it is better to say, of the social order, or ruling elite. They rested not upon democratic choice or fervent belief but upon aristocratic succession. The fathers of both Thomas Jefferson and James Madison—large landowners—served on vestries; a gentleman did so, as part of the duty of his station.

As one might guess, the Virginia Anglican churches were not particularly strong in piety and devotion. "Church-going in colonial Virginia," wrote Rhys Isaac, "had more to do with expressing the dominance of the gentry than with inculcating piety or forming devout personalities." Isaac demonstrates how this hierarchical atmosphere expressed itself throughout: in the precedence of entry into and exit from church; in the vestry's governance; in the architecture, liturgy, and use of space in the churches; in the criteria for selecting parsons.

These Virginia parsons had to present evidence that they were ordained by an English bishop, thus maintaining formal link both to the apostolic succession and to the mother country. (Another prerevolutionary controversy had to do with the possibility of an American bishop. These complicated struggles in Anglican Virginia reflected in part the effort of the squirarchy to maintain its power with respect to the clergymen. In another part they reflected the pulling and tugging between mother country and colony.) But the requirement did not entail any showing of excessive piety. An Anglican parson sent out to Virginia was not surrounded by the immediately present structure of a church hierarchy, of universities, of old family connections that he would have had in England to support him against the laymen. He lacked what today would be called a power base. And his patrons the squires generally wanted their parsons to have some—but not too much—fervor. The services, social gatherings in part, mingled the sacred and the profane without strain. Isaac serves up this sample: An agent for a Virginia squire, in this very horsy country, "without revealing any sense of incongruity... informed the baronet that a blood stallion of his had been taken to church so that the people might look the proud creature over with a view to having him cover their mares."

The Anglican church of colonial Virginia was thus no concentrate of otherworldly piety but a ritual flavoring running through the whole of the social, legal, political, geographical arrangement, inseparable from it, vindicating it. Just how this old Anglican colonial Virginia was able to produce Thomas Jefferson, James Madison, George Washington, John Marshall, George Mason, Edmund Randolph, Richard Henry Lee, Patrick Henry, Edmund Pendleton, and others, less well known now, of considerable distinction, is certainly a question worth asking. There must have been something there beyond horse racing and dances. First among the answers may be that the education for the few who benefited from it—Jefferson and Madison among them—must sometimes have been very effective. So perhaps may have been the experience in civic responsibility of the gentleman as vestryman, and perhaps the military experience in colonial wars.

However that may be, the mid-eighteenth century struck against the older Virginia of the Anglican gentry not just one blow but two, and at that weakest point, the established church.

The first was the religious eruption, already mentioned, that rocked all the colonies in the 1730s and 1740s and has come to be called the Great Awakening. The aftershocks and the outpouring of "enthusiasm" from this large event did not stop at Virginia's boundaries. Far from it. Virginia was prime territory. "Enthusiasm," evangelical religion, "New Light" views spread, even in the Anglican church, even in the clergy; some former members of the established church formed the new congregations of dissent.

There were already some non-Anglicans of foreign origin in Virginia—the Scotch-Irish Presbyterians in the southwest and in the Shenandoah Valley, some Lutherans and Reformed in the Valley, a few Quakers. These settled and cohesive groups, bringing their dissenting religion with them from elsewhere, were not too troublesome to the Anglican establishment, which granted them legal dissenter status and licenses to preach without much strain. But the New Side Presbyterians, converted out of the nominally Anglican population in Hanover County and elsewhere in the 1740s and 1750s, were another matter. They came to their religion not by inheritance and custom, as a gentleman ought to do, but by Bible reading, revivalist preaching, and conversion.

Moreover, their preachers did not stay put in one parish, as a gentlemanly parson ought to do, but traveled about, preaching now here, now there, now the other place, often in "revivals," like those that had brought on the volcanic eruption in the first place. This "itineracy" of preachers was to be a persistent issue, and a revealing one, throughout the decades leading up to the Revolution. The old Anglicans felt a parson should be tied to a particular parish and a particular flock in a particular place. He should be a learned man who would instruct the people of his parish in Christian learning, and, at least implicitly, in the proprieties of the social order. But these "New Lights" from the revivals seemed to regard religion as something portable, detachable from the social order in a most unsettling way. (New Light was the term applied across the board to evangelical enthusiasts produced in all denominations by the Great Awakening of the 1730s and 1740s, and its aftermath; New Side, describing the same thing, was contrasted to the resistant Old Side, in the conflict within the Presbyterian denomination.)

As if the new "Presbyterians" were not bad enough, in the 1760s and '70s there came another and bigger wave, much worse from the Anglican gentleman's point of view, the Separate Baptists. They spread even more rapidly than the Presbyterians had done, especially in the piedmont counties. They would not even apply for licenses to preach or hold meetings. The New Side Presbyterians attained comparative respectability with the old Anglicans when upstaged in outrageousness by the more numerous, more plebeian, more emotionally insistent Baptists. And then, just before the Revolution, there was a brief but intense period of Methodist evangelism as well, particularly galling to the old order in yet another way: As in England, so in Virginia, the "people called Methodists" arose at first as a movement within the Anglican church itself.

Isaac presents these Awakening New Lights as being a "counterculture" to Anglican Virginia. And indeed they represented a sharp contrast and a threat to the whole social structure. Thomas Jefferson was to write, in his *Notes on the State of Virginia*, that by the time of the Revolution a majority of the state's population had become dissenters from the established church. That may have been too high an estimate, but it reflects the feeling of a tide.

The second blow to the Anglican church in Virginia was, of course, the Revolution itself, and the ideas it generated. When the revolutionary period came, with the Stamp Act in 1765 and the remarkable decade leading up to 1776 and beyond, the established church in Virginia was not, to put it mildly, in a very good position. The first problem was simply that it was Anglican: Obviously it is a little awkward politically to be an outpost and epitome of British rule when British rule itself is repudiated and opposed with force of arms. And there was the matter of loyalties. An Anglican clergyman took an oath to support the king, the supreme head of the church, as part of his ordination. Almost a third of the Anglican clergy, we are told, were outright loyalists; many more had little sympathy with the "patriots."

Finally there was the domain of ideas (all of these, of course, were bound together). The "contagion of liberty," as the Harvard historian Bernard Bailyn called it, included not only civil and political liberty but also religious liberty and badly infected the old gentrified, stratified body of Anglican Virginia.

In the patriot cause, unlike the cause of religious enthusiasm a generation earlier, the squires of Virginia, surprisingly united, were not in the opposition but in the lead. In the battles they were to fight against the British they needed the support of hunters and farmers and mechanics—many of them dissenters, many from the piedmont and from across the mountains—the "heroes in hunting shirts." After collaborating with them in battles for liberty against the British it was hard to deny the religious liberty they asked for.

1779

For two and a half years, while the war was going on mostly in the North, the Committee of the Revisors in the Virginia Assembly, with Jefferson as the chairman and mainspring, worked away at reforming the state by reforming the laws. They finally brought in their report in June of 1779 with a full new code, "the whole adapted," in James Madison's words, to "the Independent and Republican form of Government."

This last was the important point. What the Revisors had undertaken was not simply the gathering together and codifying of preexisting laws; it was the wholesale reform and recasting of the law, "adapting" it to the invigorating new condition of independence and the exhilarating possibility of full-fledged republican government.

The 126 proposed new or warmed-over laws included, as law codes must, and despite Jefferson's grand intentions for the whole project, many that were of quite minor importance. But they included also bills of far-reaching significance. One of these was bill number 82, Jefferson's radical bill for religious freedom. Probably drafted in 1777, it gathered up the ideas its author had expressed in the 1776 assembly, going the whole way to move religion outside the public realm and over into the domain of private affairs, with strictly voluntary support. After a trenchant preamble, the bill made unmistakable in its enacting clause what some had found implicit in the "free exercise" article of the Virginia Declaration, what young Madison had even then tried to spell out, that "no man shall be compelled to frequent or support any religious worship, place, or ministry whatsoever"—there went the established church, and all forms of general assessment—and, moreover,

> none shall be enforced, restrained, molested, or burthened in
> his body or goods, nor shall otherwise suffer, on account of his
> religious opinions or belief; but that all men shall be free to

profess, and by argument to maintain, their opinions in matters of religion, and that the same shall in no wise diminish, enlarge, or affect their civil capacities.

Unfortunately there proved to be, in Virginia in 1779, additional impediments to right and to reason beyond those that had theretofore been presented by the now deposed British rule. The Virginia Assembly in 1779 declined to enact bill number 82. Despite the atmosphere of revolutionary ardor, and the eloquence of the preamble and the growing eminence of its author, it went too far. And while Jefferson was in Virginia to observe this first presentation of his remarkable production before the public, observe was all he could do, because he was no longer a member of the House of Delegates.

Just before the revisors reported, Jefferson was elevated (if that is the word) to the governor's chair—the Assembly chose the governor, under the new constitution—and thus was lifted up out of the legislative battle. The same thing would happen to Patrick Henry—Jefferson and Madison *wanted* it to happen, as a strategem to get him out of the way—later in this story. But now it was Jefferson having to be merely governor at one end of Williamsburg while the House of Delegates declined to consider most of his revisal, and specifically rejected his religion bill, at the other end. The bill had to be presented by another member, and although it survived two readings it was then consigned to that limbo that legislatures reserve for those bills they are not quite ready exactly to reject, but do not want to pass, either.

That was June. There was another session of the Assembly in October of 1779, and in the interval the tides of public opinion not only washed Jefferson's bill ashore—this time it was not even to be considered—but brought into the main legislative current what had become its chief competition, the idea of a General Assessment. A number of petitions specifically asked for some such plan to rescue the churches, and public virtue, from the plight that had been theirs since tax support had been suspended. A select committee, with George Mason as one member, was directed to bring in a bill "concerning religion."

This committee of Anglican laymen, unaccustomed no doubt to efforts at doctrinal formulation—not a strong suit perhaps with the Virginia gentry, who had lived their lives to that point taking for granted the formulae of the Church of England—obtained a copy of the new 1778 constitution of the state of South Carolina, which did their doctrinal formulating for them.

That South Carolina constitution—adopted two years *after*, it will be noted, the Virginia Declaration of Rights and the Declaration of Independence—is one of the more remarkable documents in the protracted effort of the former English colonies, now by their own declaration independent, to straighten out their religious life. It made *Protestant Christianity*—not any one church or denomination, but *Protestantism*—the established religion of the state with a specificity that probably cannot be matched in American history and would be hard to match even in the multitudinous variations of Christendom since the Reformation. It provided that *only Protestants* could sit in the two houses of the state legislature. Then it put the point as forthrightly as anyone could ask: "The Christian Protestant religion shall be deemed, and is hereby constituted and declared to be, the established religion of this State."

It went on to say that all denominations of "Christian Protestants" were equal. The formerly established Church of England was to retain its property, its incorporation, its established condition. But it was now to be joined by others. Whenever "fifteen or more male persons, not under twenty-one years of age, professing the Christian Protestant religion" united to form a religious body, and gave themselves a name, they could become "a church of the established religion of the state." In petitioning for that status they would have to subscribe to these five articles—South Carolina's 1778 definition of the "Christian Protestant religion":

> 1st. That there is one eternal God, and a future state of rewards and punishments.
>
> 2d. That God is publicly to be worshipped.
>
> 3d. That the Christian religion is the true religion.
>
> 4th. That the holy scriptures of the Old and New Testaments are of divine inspiration, and are the rule of faith and practice.
>
> 5th. That it is lawful and the duty of every man being thereunto called by those that govern, to bear witness to the truth.

The fifth of these is particularly intriguing. The South Carolina constitution-makers went on to say: "And that every inhabitant of this State, when called to make an appeal to God as a witness to truth, shall be permitted to do it in that way which is most agreeable to the dictates of his own conscience." Toleration—within severe limits.

There then followed a series of paragraphs, even more singular for

an American state constitution, about what clergymen shall do, believe, and subscribe to, in order that "the State may have sufficient security for the due discharge of the pastoral office." The document even included a long quoted declaration that ministers in any of the branches of the established Protestant religion would be required by the state to make, in addition to their adherence to the five articles. This declaration turns out to be taken, almost word for word, from the answers an Anglican priest gives to the bishop in his ordination service, as contained in the Book of Common Prayer. Like the rest of the South, South Carolina had had an established Anglican church; obviously Anglicans played a large role in writing this extraordinary constitution.

Having got the ministers straightened out by a state-required testimony to their good intentions, the South Carolina constitution proceeded to take care of any interference with the flow of Protestant truth: "No person shall disturb or molest any religious assembly," the constitution-makers said, "nor shall use any reproachful, reviling, or abusive language against any church, that being the certain way of disturbing the peace, and of hindering the conversion of any to the truth, by engaging them in quarrels and animosities, to the hatred of the professors, and that profession which otherwise they might be brought to assent to." Finally, with the path of religious truth thus cleared, the South Carolinians turned to the interests of the state: "No person whatsoever shall speak anything in their religious assembly irreverently or seditiously of the government of this State."

When in October of 1779 the select committee on religion of the Virginia House of Delegates got hold of this composition—this fundamental enactment—by their brethren to the south, they decided that it represented what Virginia needed, too. They took over its provisions almost completely in the bill they reported.

The Virginians did go through and take out "Protestant," so that in their bill it was simply the "Christian Religion" that was deemed established, and simply the Christian religion that the requisite number of free male persons, not under twenty-one, should subscribe to in order to be esteemed a Church of the Established Religion of the Commonwealth. But they took over the five doctrinal articles undisturbed, so that the High Reformation flavor of number four—scripture as the only "rule of faith"—might in fact have ruled out even the Old Dominion's toleration of groups with a ground of authority beyond the Bible—the pope, tradition, reason, the Inner Light—such as Roman Catholics and Quakers, and later on Unitarians. Item three would already have taken care of Jews.

The Virginia committee, perhaps embarrassed by the contrast to the ringing libertarian statements they had made three years before, did remove that interesting South Carolina prohibition against "hindering the conversion of any to the truth by engaging them in quarrels and animosities." And they began their bill by a preliminary little belch of, perhaps, bad conscience: "For the encouragement of Religion and Virtue; and for removing all restraints on the mind in its inquiries after truth...." But after that they proceeded to lay down almost the same restraints on the mind, and almost the same predetermination of what truth was to be found, as South Carolina had. One wonders about the role of George Mason, the chief author of the Virginia Declaration of Rights, in this remarkable episode. As to Jefferson—Governor Thomas Jefferson, in the Governor's Palace at the other end of Williamsburg— he must have been beating his elegant head against his desk at what his former colleagues were now proposing.

One wonders also about the other delegates, the conventional ones, who, in June, had been stunned by Jefferson's proposal that religion ought to be entirely separated from the state and given no tax money whatever, with none established at all, and that truth was mighty enough to prevail by reason alone, without any help at all from the state; and who then in October were stunned from the opposite direction by this bill that would give truth all *kinds* of state help, and unmistakably establish a quite specific set of doctrines, and make all sorts of specific connections of the government with religion, including quizzing clergymen on their prospective performance of their duty. Surely they were soaked by crossing waves of petitions, editorials, resolutions, letters. It is hard to live in revolutionary times.

And there was one more thing. Whereas the Virginia committee had taken over almost in toto the provisions as to doctrine and establishment from South Carolina, they had their own idea about tax support. The South Carolina constitution, after all of those specifications, had left the established Protestants to support their churches entirely by voluntary gift. If fifteen males professed Protestantism there might be in it the glory of truth in heaven and "establishment" on earth, but there was no tax money, not in South Carolina. The Virginia committee, however, joined to all the borrowings from South Carolina their own Virginia idea of a General Assessment. The bill the committee reported included quite elaborate provisions for how much tobacco's worth of support should go to the established Christian churches that met the test.

The phrase "multiple establishment" was to be used fairly often in the subsequent history of the new nation of which Virginia was to be a part to describe a variety of relationships of church to state, somewhere between one "Church by law established" and complete separation. But here in this Virginia bill in 1779 there really was proposed a multiple establishment, with no element of metaphor in the second term and no undefined open-endedness in the first. A quite specific Christianity, in more than one actual church, would have been quite specifically established.

But the conflicted House of Delegates did not do that, either. Some must have sensed how contradictory the bill was to Article Sixteen of the Virginia Declaration of Rights. The delegates debated it, but finally put it in limbo, too, and, unlike Jefferson's, it was never to be taken out.

They did take just one little action, after all this turmoil about religion. They had been *suspending* the tax provision of salaries for the established—formerly established?—clergy from session to session since 1776. Now they finally ended it. They did not know it, but that also ended all direct tax support for religion in Virginia.

As to the rest of those 126 bills in the revised code, the Assembly passed a few lesser ones of immediate application, but the scheme as a whole, and all the most important bills, were, as they say in legislative bodies, "laid over" for a future Assembly.

1779–83: REVOLUTION

They stayed laid over for a very long time. The years immediately after the revisors' report were the years of active fighting in the Revolutionary War in Virginia: a British raid on Portsmouth, the invasion of the state by Benedict Arnold, heavy fighting in the Carolinas, the invasion of Virginia from the south by a large British force under Cornwallis. The state government was forced to flee from Richmond to Charlottesville, and then again over the Blue Ridge mountains to Staunton, almost dissolving in the process. These events understandably served to distract attention from the matter of legal reform.

The fabled surrender of Cornwallis at Yorktown took place in October of 1781, but technically the war lasted, with the British continuing to fight the colonists' ally France, and France's ally Spain, and with the diplomats scurrying across the water, for almost another two years. The peace treaty between the Americans and the British was signed in Paris in September 1783, and made known in Virginia in December.

Meanwhile, what of the chief author of those reforms stored up on the table by the interruption of the war? Life and history had forced upon Thomas Jefferson, too, some other preoccupations. His term as governor of Virginia, which had begun in June of 1779 just before the revisors reported, was war-troubled and unhappy. The colonials, with bitter memories of royal governors, had often made that rather a feeble office in their new constitutions; Virginia had done so in its constitution written in Williamsburg. Jefferson served in the office through most of the time of invasions, and of hasty and embarrassing governmental removals, and after he got himself out of the job in 1781, a resolution proposing "an inquiry into the conduct of the executive" was introduced in the Assembly. It did not go anywhere, and the Assembly later extended him a formal apology, but it stung him nonetheless. This was the low point of Jefferson's remarkable career, and he resolved (not the only time) to leave public life, and declined several possibilities of public office. Then, in September of 1782, there came a terrible blow of another kind, when his wife died. That helped to change his mind about public life, and in November of 1782 he accepted appointment, which he had earlier declined, to represent the American Confederation in Paris.

He arrived in Philadelphia in December to prepare to leave for France, but for complicated international reasons he could not actually go until a year and a half later. In the meantime he accepted election, in June of 1783, as one of Virginia's delegates to the Congress of the Confederation. It tells you a good deal about that feeble body that when he first went to join it in Philadelphia, in the words of Dumas Malone, "he did not even know where he should find it." And it tells a good deal, too, that when he had chased it down from Philadelphia to Princeton to Annapolis (Merrill Peterson, borrowing a phrase from Jefferson himself, calls this episode "the vagabond congress"), he had a difficult time getting together delegates from enough of the newly independent states to accept the peace treaty.

And who was chairman of the congressional committee to accept the treaty with Britain? Thomas Jefferson, of course. The author of the Declaration of Independence at the start of the war turned up again at the end of it to get the peace treaty ratified. Reading about him, one is reminded of Lanny Budd, the fictional character Upton Sinclair maneuvered through all the big events of twentieth-century history; one has a little the feeling that Malone, Peterson, Julian Boyd, et al., have invented such a character for the founding period of the American nation. But this Thomas Jefferson, it seems, was real, and finally was able to leave for Paris in July of 1784, where he was to remain for five on-the-whole happy years.

Meanwhile his reforms to remake Virginia "with a single eye to reason" were left behind on the legislators' table for others now to deal with.

1783–84: PATRICK HENRY
AND A NEW PROPOSAL

When, after the fighting was over, the Virginia Assembly began to sort out the meaning of the state's newly independent condition—quite a moment—there came, along with fierce financial and other troubles, all those pending, suspended, laid-over matters tumbling back into their legislative laps: the revised code, including Jefferson's bill for religious freedom, and also that "idea," now detached again from specific legislative form, of a General Assessment for religion.

But history moves along, especially in times of revolution, and one year is not like another. The landscape of religion after the war appeared to many Virginians to be a shambles. Many church buildings were in ruins. Religious observance had markedly declined. The merely voluntary method of supporting churches after tax support had been suspended in 1776 and then ended in 1779 had not worked at all well for a religious institution wholly unaccustomed to it, and the cutting off of public support for the Anglican clergy had left many without a livelihood. Many had departed. (Some of course, had been Tories, and had returned to England, or fled to Canada.)

There was, moreover, a widespread conviction that during and after the war the moral condition of the state had deteriorated. There were articles in the newspapers, and resolutions by church bodies, and even petitions to the Virginia Assembly in 1783 and 1784, deploring the unraveling of the fabric of public virtue in Virginia, the spread of Lewdness, Wickedness, and Vice—often thus with capitals.

And as the General Assembly gathered its strength to approach once more these difficult questions, the General Assessment received a tremendous boost. It had not been known just where on these religion bills the most popular political leader in the state would take his stand. But now, returning to the House of Delegates in 1783 after three one-year terms as governor, Patrick Henry himself came out for a General Assessment in support of religion.

Both Jefferson and Madison started their public careers in Virginia as admirers of Henry, and were associated loosely with the vaguely defined tendency—the more radical patriots—to which Henry had given a strong early push. Jefferson while still a student had met Henry, seven years his senior, in Hanover County, and then had been spellbound, as everyone seems to have been, by Henry's oratory against the Stamp Act in Williamsburg. He had even heard Henry's famous speech, with its perfectly timed pause, and its quick recovery, and its quick response to the cries of "treason."

Though Jefferson was later to have severe differences with Henry, and sharp criticisms of him, he always acknowledged Henry's important role at the outset of the Revolution. And Jefferson was to say, of Henry's gift of oratorical power, that he spoke as Homer wrote. Others were to say, decades afterward, that whenever they called to mind the mighty events of the 1760s and '70s, they would hear again Henry's voice.

Rhys Isaac regards Henry's oratorical prowess as derived from the style of New Light preachers; although he was an Anglican, his mother had Presbyterian connections and for years had taken young Patrick to hear the preaching of Samuel Davies, the leading dissenting preacher in Virginia, the preacher who had persuaded the born-again Hanover County converts in the time of the Awakening that they were Presbyterians. Young Henry had imitated the revivalist's style and carried it over into the law courts, and then into politics: the repetitions, rhythms, sharp sense of audience response, pauses and variations for effect. Generally speaking, his hearers could not afterward recall with precision what he had said, but could remember forever how moved they were by his performance.

Many of Henry's early law cases and speeches had involved religious issues, and he had generally been regarded as a friend of dissenters. He dressed simply, lived in the piedmont and the woods, affected a common man's manner, associated with the common folk, played the fiddle, quoted no Greek or Latin authors. His speeches, his actions, his legend had made him enormously popular. And, already a popular hero, he had been more of a success in the rather empty office of governor than Jefferson. Neither Jefferson nor Madison, though of course they came to be much respected, would ever have the broad popularity with the Virginia populace that Patrick Henry enjoyed. And now—he supported the assessment.

Perhaps he was swayed by public opinion. The petitions that came into the Assembly in those postwar years deploring the decline of virtue did ask, or seemed to ask, for a General Assessment for religion. In 1783 the idea, at Henry's insistence, was discussed; in 1784 the committee of the whole voted, 42–36, that the idea be given form as a specific bill. Patrick Henry was appointed chairman of a ten-man committee to draft it.

Henry wrote a much more palatable bill than the 1779 effort (or perhaps it was his harder-working colleagues; in the mature view of Jefferson and Madison, and their biographers, Henry was not one to do much of the actual work once speechmaking time was over). In 1779 the measure, as we have seen, had come complete with the specific establishment of Christianity and specific requirements of doctrine and worship. Now, in 1784, there were no such requirements—nothing about creed or form of worship. The short bill provided for a property tax, with the taxpayer determining the denomination to which his money would be given. It allowed for those who made no choice of denomination just to support the building of schools in their county, a particular point about this bill that Madison appears to have overlooked in his famous *Memorial and Remonstrance* against it (there were not any such schools yet, though). Although the money otherwise thus raised was to be used to pay the clergy (in their role as "Christian teachers") and to keep up church buildings, in the case of the Quakers and "Menonists," who had no clergy, the bill specifically provided that the money should go into the general fund "to promote their particular mode of worship." Madison, in his *Memorial and Remonstrance*, was to refer to this special treatment for these denominations as giving them an unfair *advantage* over others, but that would seem to be reaching a long way for a debating point. The purpose of the provision would seem rather to have been to include these clergyless denominations, too, in the interests of fairness and political appeal.

To its supporters this version of the General Assessment provided full equality among all religious groups, and full religious liberty. It was not, if we want to make distinctions, really an *establishment* of religion; it was, rather, direct aid to whatever religions the people had chosen and existed in the state, in order that they might serve the *state's* purpose, the inculcation of virtue. The bill even specifically asserted that it did not "counteract" the "liberal principle heretofore adopted," that is, Article Sixteen of the Virginia Declaration of Rights.

THE SUPPORT OF VIRTUE

Because it was to lose out—and because its historical role has proved to be merely that of a foil for one of the signal accomplishments in American history—this General Assessment idea, and the bill embodying it that Henry and his cohorts produced, have not received a very good press in subsequent American interpretations of our national beginnings. It may be useful, therefore, to stop a minute to ask why so many of the patriots, whose deeds otherwise are framed in glory, supported it.

For it was not, as it sometimes is allowed to appear, an aberrant proposal made forceful simply by the eloquence of the Forest Demosthenes. Many of the other great figures in Virginia politics, and in American politics, supported it, or were tempted to: Richard Henry Lee (otherwise Patrick Henry's rival), the future chief justice John Marshall, even, perhaps rather tepidly, George Washington. Mr. Virginia Human Rights George Mason himself wrote some worried paragraphs about the state's moral condition that encouraged Henry; and Edmund Pendleton, Jefferson's colleague on the Committee of Revisors, a more conservative man than Jefferson but an honorable and conscientious statesman and good friend, was a leading supporter. It was by no means a proposal put forward by "clerics" seeking some "clerical" control of the state, as a certain kind of twentieth-century interpretation presents it: All of the Virginians so far named were laymen.

Neither was the General Assessment a program merely of the old elite. The Assembly divided along unusual lines on the religion bills, allies on other matters being opponents on these. And the populace divided, too. In 1783 the Assembly had been flooded with a wave of petitions and resolutions in favor of the General Assessment, and there were newspaper articles and broadsides for it.

In the view of the proassessment forces throughout this decade-long battle, such an assessment was a measure to support the state, not the church. Many citizens of Virginia in 1783–84, like vast numbers of Americans in the new country Tocqueville examined fifty years later, believed that the kind of society now being formed—a republic, an experiment in self-government, a "democracy" as it would later be called—required a moral foundation in the citizenry, "public virtue," a phrase of the founding patriots to which modern American political thinkers sometimes look with a certain wistfulness. Most believed— as Tocqueville discovered the Americans of a half century later over-whelmingly to believe—that public virtue required religion as its foun-dation and nurturing source. To put it in the terms of Tocqueville's day: Democracy requires public morality, and that morality requires religion. And many Virginians took another step. Religion needed and deserved public support because, as the Presbyterian memorial put it, "whatever is to conduce equally to the Advantage of all, should be borne Equally by all." An article asked the Virginia Assembly to support "public virtue, being the public care."

Citizens of this now very liberated country may find it stunning and amusing that once upon a time some of their forebears thought of religion as a kind of public utility like the gas or water works, but they did. One county's petition in 1784 said Virginia should operate on "the principle of public utility" in supporting religion, which was the bul-wark of government: As it conduces to the public happiness and well-being, so should it have public support. The General Assessment bill itself began this way: "Whereas the general diffusion of Christian knowledge hath a natural tendency to correct the morals of men, re-strain their vices, and preserve the peace of society..."

These arguments were cast in terms applicable to the immediate situation of post-revolutionary Virginia, but they carried the heavy weight of fourteen hundred years in Christendom: All sides in all the religious battles for centuries, the whole stream of the tradition since Constantine, had assumed that the social order required a shared re-ligious belief as its system of nurture and sanction, and that religion was both a public good and a public responsibility. (All sides, except the little trickle of sectarians on the left, who were now, in this New World, for the first time to become the main current.) These events in Virginia may be seen, to continue the fluvial metaphor, as coming now to a great historical fork in the river of Western history: For the first time in a responsible government in a "Christian" state it was proposed (by Jefferson's bill in the Revisal) that religion be diverted out of the main current of public things—the roads everyone travels upon, the common land that all use, the army that defends the whole society—and flow wholly over into the other realm of the "private," and "voluntary," like domestic arrangements and family life. Education was soon to make something like the opposite journey, and from these crossing currents would come many of the conflicts two hundred years later.

The contest in Virginia may be seen to reflect not only a fork in the great river of Western civilization—to invest this moment with sufficient grandeur—but also a more immediate dispute about the requirements of the form of government the patriots, victorious in their revolt, were just now constructing. For Jefferson and Madison, of course, religious liberty as they understood it—not "toleration" merely but a completely voluntary arrangement—was a central feature of the reformed and republican government that was to them the whole purpose of the Revolution.

The pro-assessment people, on the other hand, saw public virtue—and therefore the publicly supported nurturing of the institution, religion, that had always been assumed to nurture that virtue—as being still more important for a free republic, a self-governing society, than for the tyrannies and monarchies of old, because the shaping of the public was everything.

THE ACTION OF
THE HANOVER PRESBYTERY

In the autumn of 1784, arguments like these about the state's need for public virtue joined with considerations of a more mundane kind to produce an event that was a sharp blow to the opponents of the assessment, the Jefferson forces, as we may call them. The famous Hanover Presbytery, the first denominational deposit of the Great

Awakening, in social position much the strongest of the dissenters, and hitherto counted on by the antiassessment forces as an ally, passed a cautious resolution endorsing, under carefully specified conditions, a General Assessment.

That deeply annoyed Madison and Jefferson. Madison said there was a "shameful contrast" between the Presbyterian memorials to the Assembly in 1776 and in 1784; the Presbyterian clergy, he wrote, were "as ready to set up an establishment which is to take them in as they were to pull down that which shut them out."

One can find in the writings of Thomas Jefferson more acid comments about the Presbyterians than about the clergy of the established Anglican church he did much to disestablish, or the Catholic clergy whose "priestcraft," he would often write, had for centuries held the mind of men in "shackles." "The Presbyterian clergy are the loudest; the most intolerant of all sects, the most tyrannical and ambitious," he wrote, for example, in a private letter. The about-face (as Jefferson saw it) by the Hanover Presbytery plainly did not recommend that denomination to the Apostle of Reason.

But the Presbyterians had their own story. By theology and heritage they had a more corporate sense both of the church and of society than did either the individualist Baptists and other sectarians or the new Enlightenment people of the stripe of Jefferson and Madison—corporate, but with a representative principle, too.

The Calvinist/Reformed tradition, of which they were a branch, led to widely varying political applications, from stirring statements of opposition to tyranny, and John Knox's opposition to Scottish monarchy, and solid support by most of the Colonial Presbyterian clergy for the patriotic cause in the American Revolution—John Witherspoon vigorously among them—to the oppressive regimes that prevailed in the home base of Calvin's Geneva and other places. The Virginia Presbyterians in the late 1770s and early 1780s appear to have reflected some of these differing strains. They were divided between two strong leaders, and roughly between a separationist spirit in the Valley and an outlook more sympathetic to some corporate connection in the piedmont. The Presbyterian memorial was by no means an unequivocal endorsement of tax support for churches. It specified carefully the conditions under which the Presbyterians would support an assessment: full equality of religious bodies and full freedom for everyone, above all. And no state interference with creeds, with internal church affairs, or with forms of worship—all points that were violated by the bill of 1779, to which the Presbyterians had not given their endorsement.

Though religion as such should not be an object of "human legislation," it might nevertheless be seen in a civil view to preserve and promote "the happiness of society." Public worship and "public periodical Instructions" to the people might therefore, with full freedom and equality preserved, be supported by a tax. It was a carefully guarded statement, but still, in the political context, it gave enormously important support from a powerful swing group to the General Assessment bill.

And so it came about that the General Assessment almost passed... or rather, it *did* pass, as an *idea*. On November 11, 1784, the committee of the whole of the Virginia House of Delegates resolved by a vote of 47 to 32 that "the People of this Commonwealth, according to their respective abilities, ought to pay a moderate tax or contribution annually for the support of the Christian religion." A ten-man committee, chaired by Patrick Henry, was appointed to draft a bill embodying the principle the resolution stated, to "reduce to writing," as they say in legislatures, the general proposition. For the moment the side favoring the assessment had won.

The story was not over, however. The opposition was gathering strength. Fifty-five members of the House of Delegates—not always the most diligent of bodies during the social season, and horse races, that accompanied their biennial sojourn in Richmond—had not been present or had not voted for the resolution (the Virginia Assembly had moved from Williamsburg to Richmond four years earlier). And—most important—in the session of the previous spring, in May 1784, a formidable opponent to the whole idea had joined the fray. Before it would be over he would carry off one of the most striking political achievements of American history.

1784: JAMES MADISON'S POLITICAL TACTICS

James Madison had come back from service in the Continental Congress in Philadelphia to take his place as the leader of the younger group, the "children of the Revolution" in Edmund Randolph's phrase, in the

Assembly of the newly independent state. A great deal of revolutionary and Virginia history, and of Madison's life, had intervened in the eight years since young Madison made his trip over to Williamsburg and drafted his amendment to the Virginia Declaration of Rights. The some-time colonies were now independent states, joined together in Articles of Confederation, operating with their new governments.

Madison, now thirty-four, had become a respected Virginian and national statesman. He had served in the Virginia House of Delegates, where he must have met Thomas Jefferson, and then in the Virginia Council of State (in a sense a small upper house, advising the governor), where he had come to know the then Governor Jefferson very well, beginning that remarkable friendship and collaboration with him that would last through all their lives. Then Madison had been four years in Philadelphia as an increasingly influential member of the Continental Congress—typically, its most diligent member. So when he came back to Virginia politics, in the spring of 1784, he was a seasoned legislator and politician, expected to be a younger leader, standing in some woodwind counterpoint to the stereophonic contrast between the two older rival oratorical brass bands, Patrick Henry and Richard Henry Lee.

Given an opening, Madison tried again to have the Assembly enact the revisal of the laws—Jefferson, the chief revisor, was by then on his way to Paris—but was blocked by the opposition of the conservative forces, led by the one-time radical Patrick Henry. (In 1784 the Assembly did, however, order that the revisal be printed, although, in what Madison called a "frivolous economy," it limited the number of copies to 500.) And, as one would expect, he led the forces opposing Henry on the great matter of tax support for religion ("general assessment" was of course one of those euphemisms that legislators of all ages devise to avoid the sensitive word *tax*), giving one of his rare speeches on the floor in answer to Henry's resounding assertions on the "decay" of civilizations when religion wanes. He appears to have said—the Madison papers reproduce the notes he used—that civilization had not always done so well when religion flourished either, if it was state-supported religion. And as to the purity of religion itself: Christianity was purest in its primitive moment, before it got entangled with the state. Madison gave explanations for the moral condition of Virginia other than the decline of religion; the war itself was the main one. He made a thorough case, anticipating what he would write the next summer in his *Memorial and Remonstrance*. He then finished, according to his notes, with a "panegyric" on "it" (Christianity) "on our side."

The amusing note to himself to give a "panegyric" on Christianity from *his* side began, among the strict opponents of projects like the General Assessment, a long tradition of assuring their hearers that they are no less devoted to religion than the proponents of such projects: They oppose only *compulsion* in its alleged behalf.

Madison was, of course, no match for Henry as an orator. They were opponents on many other issues in 1784, and Henry generally prevailed. But Madison had other weapons to defeat the General Assessment, just as it appeared that a specific bill might pass.

One action he took may have been a surprise to his colleagues: He gave his *support* to a companion religion bill that incorporated the "formerly established church"—the Episcopal church in Virginia—under the civil law.

Many of the churchly forces that supported the General Assessment also supported this incorporation bill; most of the forces opposed to the General Assessment opposed the incorporation, too. The two bills were linked in the minds of the legislators and the public—the religious leaders especially. The assessment would provide money for all groups, to be sure, but de facto most importantly for the former Anglicans. And the incorporation of this one church by the act of the legislature would put it back into business with its property holdings intact. The Baptists, for example, condemned in one sweep both bills.

Madison's action, supporting the one bill while opposing the other, may be seen as the work of a wily politician. Passage of that incorporation bill accomplished two purposes at once: It partially satisfied the old Anglican forces, and at the same time it frightened the Presbyterians and others about an Anglican resurgence. (The politics of this affair, to a degree that may be difficult for a modern American to comprehend, revolved around the debates within, and rivalries among, the denominations out in the state; Madison's experience in this battle must have been a principal source of that outlook on politics—on power—to which he was shortly thereafter to give memorable and historically potent expression. It was an important day for American history when "Jemmy" Madison discovered the value of dividing, balancing, and limiting power.)

But Madison also employed—or joined in using—another, very different strategy against the powerful pro-assessment forces: He got Patrick Henry out of there; at least, historians seem to agree that he played a role in doing so. Jefferson and Madison had exchanged some rather pungent comments about the great desirability of Henry's removal from the scene. Now came an opportunity. The governor's chair was vacant; the incumbent could not succeed himself; Henry had been a popular and successful governor for three years during the war, and had loved it, and was now eligible again. The Assembly chose the governor. So now, in the late fall of 1784, Henry was proposed for the governor's chair again, and was elected unanimously by the Assembly. Thus, smack in the middle of the fight over the assessment its leading proponent—one gathers one should use stronger words than that about the electricity of Patrick Henry's influence—was neatly lifted up out of the fray. (Henry, not one for details, may have felt he had won the General Assessment battle with the vote of the committee of the whole.)

Finally Madison did what legislators in his position always do: With the Episcopal incorporation bill already passed as a kind of sop, he persuaded the Assembly, now late in its session (in December 1784) and anxious to go home, to postpone the General Assessment bill in order that the populace might once again express itself (which with his considerable help, it certainly was to do).

So all the controverted matters—the revisal, now printed into 500 copies and ready to go, with Jefferson's religious freedom bill in its middle, and the General Assessment, now in a more tempting and palatable legislative form—were laid over yet one more time. The next session would surely be the showdown.

1785–86: CLIMAX

A year later, on January 22, 1786, James Madison—or James Madison, Jr., as he regularly signed himself—wrote from Richmond a very long letter to Jefferson, then in Paris serving as the minister to France from a rather wobbly new country. Madison's letter touched on several of the topics that appeared regularly in the correspondence between these two Virginia politicians—the trunks of books that Jefferson shipped to Madison from Paris, the care that Madison was taking of the education of Jefferson's young nephews back home—but its main subject was a thorough report on the ninety-seven-day session of the Virginia Assembly that had brought itself to an end the night before Madison sat down to write the letter.

For the most part Madison, who played a major role in that Assembly of 1785–86, had to give one of those untidily complex, somewhat frustrated, inconclusive, plus-and-minus lists that legislative sessions usually generate. He took up a large part of the letter filling in Jefferson, in detail, on the mostly minor bills the Assembly had enacted—new bills, about which Jefferson had not known: Act for safekeeping land papers of the Northern Neck, Act for postponing the tax of the present year and admitting facilities in payment, Act for disposing of waste lands on eastern waters, Act for reforming county courts ("It amounts to nothing"), and so on. In addition he appended a little list of the "promotions"—the shifts in role of major characters—in Virginia's political life, and a list of the prices of tobacco, wheat, corn, and pork. On reading all this, one is impressed with the tireless specificity with which these two allegedly visionary statesmen followed the concrete detail of Virginia life, even while the senior friend was happily, despite his alleged dislike of great cities, enjoying the bookstalls, salons, and theaters of Paris. Jefferson, on leaving for France, had asked Madison to give him such a report of the bills and events and people at the end of each Assembly session. His friend, the soul of conscientiousness, was now providing, in fullest measure, just what he had asked.

But there was one enormous cluster of bills that had come before that Assembly about the substance of which Jefferson did not need to be told; he had long ago written those bills himself, or helped to write them. These were the proposals in the wholesale revisal of the laws of Virginia, and Madison had to inform him that the Assembly, though it *could* have done it, had not by any means enacted, or even considered, the entire set of 126 bills. But it had enacted nearly a third of them, and about one of these the two friends could be unequivocally enthusiastic, could write to each other in the most far-reaching terms, going well beyond the current price of pork.

Madison reported the "very warm struggle for the chair," the bringing forward of the revised code and its referral to committee, the overcoming of early procedural and substantive difficulties, and the allocation by the assembly of three days of each week to the consideration of the code. "We went on slowly but successfully," Madison wrote, "till we arrived at the bill concerning crimes and punishments." This was bill number 64, Jefferson's humane revision of the law with respect to the punishment of capital crimes. As Madison wrote to Jefferson,

> Here the adversaries of the code exerted their whole force, which being abetted by the impatience of its friends in an advanced

stage of the Session, so far prevailed that the prosecution of the work was postponed until the next Session. The operation of the bills passed is suspended until the beginning of 1787, so that if the code should be resumed by the next Assembly and finished early in the Session, the whole system may commence at once.

To run ahead of the story, the next Assembly, again, did not perform altogether in accord with right and reason, and although many individual items were plucked from the pack and enacted into law, the "whole system" never was enacted and never did commence as one comprehensive entity. Nevertheless the reformers were to get more than they might once have expected. "I found it [the code] more popular in the Assembly than I had formed any idea of," Madison continued. But there was also bad news, reflecting again the perennial frustration of conscientious legislators. "Though it [the revised code] was considered by paragraphs and carried through all the customary forms, it might have been finished at one Session with great ease—if the time spent on motions to put it off and other dilatory artifices, had been employed on its merits." Madison then named the chief opponents, noted that he had enclosed a list of the bills adopted, and explained about minor alterations and minor bills passed over. At last came the major item. "After the completion of the work at this Session was despaired of," Madison wrote, "it was proposed and decided that a few of the bills following the bill concerning crimes and punishments should be taken up as of peculiar importance." Here, one reads between the lines, James Madison made an enormously important strategic decision about which bill to select and to push. And here the preceding summer's outpouring of petitions against the General Assessment, which were to doom that bill, created an atmosphere favorable to Madison's purposes. He reached down through the list on the revisal, past some other important ones, to bill number 82. "The only one of these which was pursued into an Act," he went on, "is the bill concerning Religious freedom."

LARGE POLITICS:
WHY IN VIRGINIA?

How had it been possible to enact so radical a document in conservative Virginia? An American academic, reading it 200 years later, remarked that he did not see how it could have been enacted back then in Virginia or, for that matter, how it could be enacted today in the United States. On the second point his implication, that it could not be enacted, may be right. But Virginia in those years had provided a uniquely favorable political environment for a ringing endorsement of religious liberty. There was an extremely vulnerable establishment, still resented, still a threat, on the one side, and a host of dissenters, outnumbering the establishment's supporters, on the other. And Virginia had the New World's most distinguished Enlightenment statesmen, including two of the foundingest of the founding fathers, for leadership.

The Congregational establishment in Massachusetts and Connecticut, by contrast, did not have the awkward political and social difficulties of the Virginia Anglicans. They were not tied to the patriots' enemy. To the contrary, with their Puritan heritage they could support a Revolution against the English Crown without embarrassment... indeed, with enthusiasm. Neither were those once-Puritan establishments marked by excessive resort to the card table, rum, or horseback riding, nor by a too-tight containment within an aristocracy. Nor were their members outnumbered by restive sectarians outside the fold: The Congregational churches of Connecticut and Massachusetts comprehended large majorities of their states' religious populations. A founding father in Massachusetts—John Adams—not only supported a kind of establishment (a very mild one) but even participated in designing it.

The middle colonies did not offer a solid opportunity for a striking defense of religious liberty for the opposite reason: They had already attained it, or something close to it. Pennsylvania, the weightiest of them, had been from its beginning not far from the ideal that Madison wanted, through the courtesy of its Quaker founder William Penn. It had come to be populated with a motley 300 kinds of Continental sectarians among whom it would have been impossible to reinvent an ecclesiastical establishment in order for it to be overthrown in the name of liberty. The other middle colonies had mixtures, too, without oppressive establishments. Indeed, the experience of these middle colonies provided a practical base for the arrangement the new nation would adopt.

But the new nation was to go further than simply to decide that there would be no one church "by law established." It was also to reject the intermediate possibilities and go all the way to the separation of church and state. The first institution of that radical possibility—"utterly without precedent in the Atlantic World," in Rhys Isaac's words— was in Virginia, through this bill that Madison had managed finally to have extracted from the pile of proposals in the revisal.

1785: THE SMALLER POLITICS

Madison's letters to his great friend in Paris—from the legislative manager to the author of the bill, as it were—tell something about the politics behind its enactment, having mostly to do with that other bill, the General Assessment, with the fate of which Jefferson's bill had become inextricably entwined. Madison had written to Jefferson back in April of 1785, that "the Bill for a general assessment" had produced "some fermentation below the Mountains and a violent one beyond them. The contest at the next session on this question will be a warm and precarious one." And then in his letter of the following January, after the next session's contest, warm and precarious indeed, was completed, he went back and described the developments that had made possible its result.

"The steps taken throughout the Country to defeat the General Assessment," Madison wrote to Jefferson, "had produced all the effect that could have been wished." He does not need to say, for Jefferson knew, that he—Madison—was a leader among those who took those steps. "The table was loaded with petitions and remonstrances from all parts against the interposition of the Legislature in matters of Religion." It was this load on the table that sank the assessment, and gave a corresponding lift to Jefferson's bill.

One of the remonstrances on the table, as Jefferson already knew (Madison had sent him a copy), was the one that Madison himself had written, anonymously, in June, at the urging of other opponents of the assessment. This was the *Memorial and Remonstrance* that was later to attain—partly because he wrote it—a continuing fame. It was to be compared to the great libertarian productions of Locke, Milton, and Mill; to be reprinted in toto in opinions of two justices of the United States Supreme Court (so far); and to be quoted as a definitive argument for the arrangement the United States was to construct. In Virginia in the summer of 1785, however, it was simply one anonymous broadside circulated along with others in the campaign to defeat the General Assessment. The headnote in the Madison papers reports that there were at least thirteen copies of Madison's remonstrance, garnering 1,552 signatures; another petition, however, oriented distinctly to an evangelical point of view—it described the General Assessment as, along with its other faults, contrary to the "spirit of the gospel"—had on its 20 copies 4,899 signatures. In other words, Madison's was not the only, or the most widely supported, petition.

In addition to these and other remonstrances and newspaper articles attacking the assessment—in the spring and summer of 1785 the opponents were carrying on an active, highly motivated campaign—there were developments adverse to the bill in the 1785 elections for the Assembly. A few pro-assessment delegates lost their seats. So the Assembly that convened in Richmond in October of 1785 had a somewhat different flavor from its predecessor: Patrick Henry had departed for the governor's office, and now some supporters of his bill had disappeared as well.

But the most potent politics of this episode was, again, the politics within and among the religious groups. The act of the 1784 Assembly incorporating the Anglicans—now the Episcopalians under the civil law—and the threatened General Assessment, when put together looked as if they might represent the reemergence of the Anglicans into a position of domination, and that rang the alarm bells in the fervent hearts of the dissenters. Madison and Jefferson had shrewdly guessed that this would be so—that an act by the civil government incorporating the Episcopalians would remind the dissenters that the old established church might try for a comeback. When the Episcopal clergy had asked to be incorporated, Jefferson had written to Madison that he was glad they had "shown their teeth and fangs" to remind dissenters of the threat.

In the summer of 1785 the Baptists, who never needed to be reminded about the teeth and fangs of established churches, weighed in with resolutions not only against the General Assessment but also against the incorporation of the Episcopal church. They reiterated their historic position, now with added fervor: The assessment would be "opening the door to religious tyranny"; the incorporation act was "inconsistent with American freedom." (These quotations, and the other quotations from denominational petitions and resolutions, and many other items in these pages, are taken from the leading history, *Church and State in Revolutionary Virginia 1776–1787*, by Thomas E. Buckley, S.J.)

The Baptists were joined now by a newly independent group, the Methodists. At Christmas 1784 the Methodist movement in the New World gathered itself together and pulled out of the Anglican/Episcopal church, making itself into a new religious body. That subtracted zeal and New Light energy from the Episcopalians, and set up an additional source of petitions and resolutions against both incorporation and assessment.

But the major political development had to do with the Presbyterians. They switched. Again. One reason was their confrontation with the laity, in a setting in which the opposition to the religion bills was particularly strong. The Hanover Presbytery met in May 1785, beyond the mountains, in the Valley wherein the "fermentation" was violent. The Scotch-Irish in the Valley had pursued their migrations in part for religious freedom, had fought with established churches elsewhere, and had long supported their own clergy by voluntary subscription. There had been a shift in the balance of leadership in the Presbytery.

But in addition there were philosophical, or theological, reasons of the Presbyterians' own kind. Though they had earlier given carefully qualified support to the *idea* of a General Assessment, the particular bill in which it was now embodied went against their Presbyterian grain. They did not like the idea of a tax subsidy for the sole purpose of paying the *clergy*—which would disengage the clergy from the laity and increase the clergy's separate power. Such an arrangement was contrary to a Presbyterian polity—that is, representative church government, with laymen and clergymen, lay Elders and teaching Elders, in an equal mixture of power. The Presbyterians did not want to give separate independent (state-based) financial standing to their own Presbyterian clergy—and even less to the Episcopalian clergy.

This last may have been the most potent point. Madison had written once that he feared an Episcopalian-Presbyterian alliance as the one combination that could endanger the colony's religious liberty; now he wrote to Jefferson that he did not mind at all the "jealousy" and "mutual hatred" between the two groups that the religion bills had provoked. (Of such materials are great monuments to liberty made!)

The Presbyterians, as a climax to that summer's politics, not only passed a resolution at Presbytery but also called a special convention just to consider, and denounce, the religion bills. They did not any longer insist that "religion" should be supported by the state because the virtue it produced was to the public benefit. Their fear now was, apparently, that the Episcopalians would be the ones chiefly empowered to produce it. The petition from the extraordinary Presbyterian convention attacked both the assessment and the incorporation as violating the Declaration of Rights and favoring the Episcopalians. In his letter from Richmond in January 1786, Madison reported to Jefferson how far they had gone: "A general convention of the Presbyterian church prayed expressly that the bill in the revisal might be passed into law, as the best safeguard of their religious rights." In other words the Presbyterians now not only rejected the assessment bill but specifically asked that Jefferson's bill for religious freedom be enacted.

So the Virginia Assembly, which at the fall session of 1784 had voted in principle for a General Assessment to give direct tax aid to clergymen, faced at its next session a firestorm of protest against it—remonstrances, petitions, editorials, and the opposition, now unanimous, of the dissenting denominations. The Assembly was presented, in addition, with the specific request by the strongest group after the Episcopalians that Jefferson's bill in the revisal be enacted.

As the assessment was sunk under that load of objections on one end of the scale—it simply dropped out of sight—the bill in the revisal, the one present alternative, rose at the other. And so it happened that Jefferson's bill, out of principle and politics, out of hope and fear, out of love of liberty and denominational jealousy, came to be passed.

OCTOBER 1785–JANUARY 1786:

VERY SMALL POLITICS

There were, as always, complications in the legislative endgame. "The Bill was carried thro the House of Delegates," Madison wrote to Jefferson, "without alteration. The Senate objected to the Preamble"— Jefferson's pungent argument, the body of the document as it was to achieve worldwide fame—"and sent down a proposed substitution of the 16th article of the Declaration of Rights."

There was a certain nicely rounded irony in this counterproposal by the more conservative Virginia Senate. That Article Sixteen, as amended, had been a big stroke for liberty in its time, ten years before, and Madison himself had been, as we have seen, the source of the amendment that had provided its particular libertarian punch. But one decade's bold advance becomes another decade's line of defense. In this later context, in 1785, Article Sixteen represented a defensive falling back on generalities already enacted and celebrated. And these were capable, as events had proved, of differing interpretations. That was not true of the stinging explicitness of Jefferson's preamble. "The house of Delegates disagreed," Madison went on (he was himself of course the leader in the House of Delegates). "The Senate insisted and asked a Conference. Their objections were frivolous indeed."

Madison then tried to explain, partly in shorthand, the further adventures of his friend's composition at the hands of the two Virginia houses. There were, in deference to the Senate, "one or two verbal alterations in the preamble." It was thought better to agree than to run further risks, especially as "it was getting late in the Session and the House growing thin"—such are the trials of a legislative manager. "The enacting clauses were passed without a single alteration...." (In this Madison's reporting was, in a very minor way, inaccurate, as we shall see.) Out of the struggle in December–January of 1785–86 the preamble was retained with the few small changes conceded to the Senate, the enacting clauses emerged unscathed, and the whole bill then passed the Virginia Assembly on January 16, 1786.

Although James Madison, Jr. was a quite different sort of a person from the ebullient floor manager of another bill more than a century and a half later, and the Virginia House of Delegates different from the U.S. Senate, one may be pardoned for imagining Madison in fact feeling at the moment Jefferson's bill at last had the votes something of what Hubert Humphrey exhibited in June 1964, after all the years of trying to pass a civil rights bill, when the clinching vote for closure was cast: sitting at a front desk, suddenly holding both his arms stretched toward the Capitol dome in a gesture of rejoicing.

So now at the end of his account of these complicated doings, Madison, writing his letter six days after the clinching of *his* triumph, drew himself up to his full sense of the importance of what they had done and let fly with a claim about the result, which claim rises up out of the details of daily legislative life to the universals to which he and his correspondent both aspired. Madison was a tad more realistic than Jefferson, but he could deal in the large Jeffersonian sweep when it was appropriate. "I flatter myself," Madison wrote, that the enacting clauses of this now-enacted bill 82 "have in this country extinguished forever the ambitious hope of making laws for the human mind."

THE OLD DOMINION
SORTS THE POSSIBILITIES

So at last they had won. We may say that the new state of Virginia, in these ten years, without knowing it, had passed in review the main choices for religion's place in the republican governments of the New World, and had come up with this startling result. It may not be stretching too far to say that the "Old Dominion" (a "much caressed phrase," as Edmund Wilson once wrote—much caressed particularly in the

"Commonwealth" itself) had sorted the possibilities not only for itself but for the new continental nation that its sons and daughters were soon to have a very large role in building.

First there had been, at least in theory, the possibility of a restoration of an established church. Theoretically one can picture the lay members of what had been the Church of England in Virginia regrouping after the Revolution to form out of its remnants a new established Church of Virginia. Unlike many of their Anglican counterparts in the northern and middle colonies (and unlike many of their own clergy), these Virginians had supported—indeed not only supported but vigorously led— the "patriot" revolt against England. They were therefore the opposite of discredited. And they had all been nurtured in—in fact had managed, as members of vestries—Virginia Anglicanism. Perhaps they could even have made a compromise with the only other large Virginia group with a social elite and an uncongregational church government, the Presbyterians—exactly the alliance James Madison feared—to create a broader established church. Suppose Virginia had worked out what we might call a "Washingtonian" settlement, comparable to the English Elizabethan settlement, in honor of Washington's support for the General Assessment and of the sentiments favoring a more or less uniform national religion that the Father of his Country would express in his Farewell Address. The vestrymen of Virginia were accustomed to running churches, and accustomed to running the government and society, too, and were certainly interested in a church that served the civil state and the continuities of the social order, as well as in liberty.

Or, if a single church is too difficult to imagine, there is the second, stronger possibility. The bill actually proposed in Virginia in 1779— the borrowing from South Carolina—was, as we have said, truly a "multiple-establishment" bill in a literal sense of both of those words: Christianity would have been specifically established, with five state-endorsed points of doctrine and tax support for all groups that adhered to them. But the Virginia Assembly in 1779, with Article Sixteen in their memory and liberty in the air and Jefferson's bill staring at them, so to speak, from the table, did not do that, either. (South Carolina was to change its constitution in 1790, after a twelve-year experiment with their version of this program, and to adopt instead, partly under the influence of Virginia, a libertarian constitution. Had Virginia gone the other way in 1779, presumably South Carolina's history would have been different, too.)

Though that 1779 possibility still included a doctrinal commitment on the part of the state, the third of the choices, the 1784 bill—Patrick

Henry's bill—did not. That the proponents of a religion bill had quietly given up on that ancient requirement—a religious commitment by the state—was already, one might say, a big step in the history of the West. At this juncture even the conservatives were conceding that free and independent Virginia should not be a "confessing" state—it should have no official commitment or belief, no collective religious affirmation—and if not Virginia, then probably, as events would unfold, not the other new republican governments, either. Often history passes over a great Continental Divide in this scarcely noticed way: Long-held positions are silently and implicitly given up without a fight when the line of battle moves down the mountain on the other side, and the resistant forces have to dig in at another spot.

So they did now, defending just some tax aid to religion—*all* religions—in order to serve the state, not the church, in its task of providing the virtuous citizenry the state requires. That proposal almost passed, as we have seen—did pass, as an idea.

Suppose it had passed as law? If any of these possibilities had been enacted back then in Virginia, one can picture a quite different result elsewhere. The Old Dominion with a new Church of Virginia, or more probably a multiple establishment or General Assessment, might have made a rapprochement with the Standing Order of Connecticut, and the establishments elsewhere, and changed the balance of forces enough for there to have been constructed some kind of a Church of America, or a linkage, for the colonies as a whole.

There were, indeed, as we have noted, "establishments" of Protestant Christianity of various weights and kinds, in some colonies—if "establishment" is defined loosely, in most of them—and all had at least a remote Anglican heritage by being English. A budding Church of America would have found at least six state establishments in place, depending on what you count and when: New Hampshire, Connecticut, New Jersey, Georgia, and North and South Carolina.

Massachusetts, according to a broad definition, might have been included, too. Most of the newly independent "states" of course were writing their constitutions in the late 1770s and 1780s, and influencing one another as they did it; that Virginia production at Williamsburg in 1776 had been the first. Massachusetts included in its 1780 constitution, largely written by John Adams (this is the design mentioned above), a religious policy, liberal for its time and particularly for that state: There were to be "public" Protestant teachers of "piety, morality, and religion" in each locality, but these localities would then *choose* whether to support such "teachers" (preachers) voluntarily or by taxes.

It was this decentralized quasi-establishment that John Adams later told the leading Baptist fighter for radical separation, Isaac Backus, was too "benign" to bother overthrowing, and that would last as long as the solar system (it lasted until 1833).

The Church of America could have made an arrangement with that state, before or after that convention, and with New York before it altogether undid its establishment—and so on through the colonies. There was some test oath for officials and/or voting citizens in every state except Rhode Island—even in otherwise libertarian Pennsylvania (one eternal God; heaven and hell) and Delaware (the doctrine of the Trinity).

With a Virginia initiative the United States conceivably might have developed a formally established national church with a patchwork of state forms. It would clearly be necessary in that case to grant full religious toleration to "dissenters," as they would then be, in some states. The result could have been a more complicated version of the situation in England, Germany, or the Scandinavian countries.

If some doctrinally specific multiple establishment had been worked out, in law, for the nation as a whole, then there really would have been what thousands of preachers, some judges of the courts, and a great many religious Americans down to the present day have insisted either does exist or should be made to exist: "A Christian America."

But that did not happen. Virginia moved from having one of the most solidly established churches all the way to join little Rhode Island on the side of full religious liberty and the separation of church and state.

CIVIC REPUBLICANISM
REJECTED

Madison and Jefferson had brought the world—or at any rate Virginia—partway around to right, reason, and republican government. But had they brought it the whole way? Had they put in place Jefferson's full vision of the free mind and virtuous citizen in an empire of liberty? Not quite.

The bill for religious freedom was only a part of Jefferson's program—very important, of course, but essentially a first step: the liberation from the old order necessary before construction of the new. The constructive part of the program—Jefferson's provisions for the nurture of citizens in the knowledge and virtue that a republic requires—was not enacted. When at the weary end of the 1785–86 session of the Virginia Assembly the machinery ground to a halt on bill number 64 and James Madison rescued what he could—the bill on religious freedom—the leapfrog over other bills included those numbered 79, 80, and 81 in the revisal. They are, respectively, the famous Bill for the More General Diffusion of Knowledge, and the closely related bills for amending the constitution of the College of William and Mary and for establishing a public library. Taken together these three bills represented Jefferson's program for a system of education that would nurture a republican citizenry. Whereas Patrick Henry and company wanted to provide for the "diffusion" of Christian teaching, Jefferson wanted to provide for the "diffusion" of secular republican knowledge. The Virginians decided not to diffuse either one.

Jefferson's bills provided not only for a public elementary-school system, like the common schools already then existing in New England, but also for a state college—William and Mary—republicanized and split off from the Anglican church. This thoroughgoing educational reform—this "systematical plan" for general education supported out of public funds—embodied Jefferson's famous notion of a "natural aristocracy" of virtue and talent. A note in the edition of Jefferson's papers quotes the contemporary appraisal by Jefferson's friend William Wirt: " . . . the bill proposes a simple and beautiful scheme, whereby science . . . would have been 'carried to every man's door.' Genius, instead of having to break its way through the thick opposing clouds of native obscurity, indigence, and ignorance, was to be sought for through every family in the Commonwealth. . . . "

These education bills, and a few other bills in the revisal, comprised Jefferson's scheme to care for features of the common life that had hitherto been the responsibility, more or less, of the vestries and the clergymen of the established church. The Bill for the General Diffusion of Knowledge included his system of "hundreds" or "wards"—a kind of rural Virginia equivalent of New England towns, or modern school districts, into which each county would be divided. These were to have been of a size appropriate to the maintenance of an elementary school, and would have provided free public education for all children through the elementary grades—for all Virginians the beginning of the education that wealthier Virginians like Jefferson and Madison had received, for a fee, from tutorials or schools run by Anglican clergymen. Moral instruction and education in civic responsibility were explicitly to have been a part of the curriculum. The old churches, for all their faults, had been the central carriers of such education as had been provided in Anglican Virginia, not only because many clergymen ran schools or served as tutors but also because the church's own ritual life was conceived to have a nurturing and instructional function beyond anything a twentieth-century U.S. citizen is likely to conceive a church to have. "Learning" blended with Christian learning; parsons could be called, as they were in the assessment, Christian teachers; for all its acculturation and perhaps sometimes superficiality, the established church was the moral center of the social order.

In the full Jeffersonian program, there would have been a substitute for this churchly nurture in the system of state-supported schools, with training in civic virtue grounded in the reason all men share. The religious groups would have been left to the private realm, essentially outside this public system, free to carry on their voluntary religious activities but no longer the primary nurturing agents for the citizenry and social order. Thus would a nonreligious "republicanism" have been fully developed as the core commitment of the state. Jefferson and Madison, though insisting that there be no official state commitment to religion, made no such insistence with respect to political ideas. When they came to form the University of Virginia, they reserved the right to specify the professors of government in order that no wrong-headed Federalist should undo sound republican principles. Madison even drew up an essential reading list.

Other functions, besides education, of the vestry-run state church would also have been reassigned in Jefferson's revising of the laws. Each hundred was to have aldermen, and if one looks at bill number 32 in the revisal—providing for the care of the poor, which had hitherto been the responsibility, in each parish, of the vestry—one finds that duty transferred to these aldermen. But bill number 32, on the scorecard Jefferson kept in Paris, had to be marked "passed with great alterns": The Assembly in 1786 conflated two bills, the revisors' and a new one the Assembly ordered to be prepared; and it transferred control of poor relief away from the vestries, though not to Jefferson's aldermen—who were never to exist—but rather to a new apparatus of overseers of the poor, elected by the freeholders in newly drawn districts.

Among the bills from the revisal that Madison *was* able to get passed intact before the Assembly's delaying tactics ground his legislative

engine to a halt in 1786 was bill number 20, which is Jefferson's repudiation of the old inheritance system of primogeniture and entail,
through which the great estates had been held together. It was another
progressive blow at the Virginia hierarchy. But that accomplishment,
like the statute for religious freedom, was a blow for liberation against
a now very vulnerable old order. They were not the features of the
revisal that started the construction of a new communal arrangement.

Jefferson's Bill for the General Diffusion of Knowledge, and the others
linked to it, may be interpreted as the positive and communal coun-
terpart to the negative, liberating, and individualistic effect of the bill
for religious freedom in an integrated Jeffersonian program: Where the
latter knocked out the old communal and social role of an established
religion, the former were to have put in its place this civic republican
system. But that replacement was not provided.

"When Jefferson's proposals for a secular republican establishment
were brought forward," wrote Rhys Isaac, "they were frustrated as
effectively as had been his gentry opponents' design for a Christian
one.... In the event, it was communitarianism, in secular as well as
sacred form, that was defeated. Religious privatism was overtly legi-
timated." Tax resistance, in a time of postwar depression, "was the
major consideration in setting aside the Bill for the More General Diffusion of Knowledge." It was a contributory consideration, also, to the
defeat of the General Assessment, and the subsequent enactment of
Jefferson's bill for religious freedom. The citizens did not want to pay
taxes for churches or "Christian teachers." But they did not want to
pay taxes for secular republican teachers, either.

The Jeffersonian provision for religious liberty and the separation of
church and state, cut off from his positive educational program, was
in time to be given an evangelical Protestant twist. Already in 1784
the denominational petitions against the General Assessment bill had
asked that the members of the Assembly, while rejecting any kind of
tax support for religion, at the same time display the worth of religion
by the way they lived, and by passing laws punishing the "vices and
immoralities" of the time. The same Assembly that passed Jefferson's
religious liberty bill also passed a statute requiring the observance of
Sunday as a day of rest. In the compound result, it might even be said,
the triumph in these events in Virginia did not belong exactly to right,
reason, and civic republicanism; it belonged symbolically to Baptists.

The Virginia Statute for Religious Freedom was and is, nevertheless,
one of the essential documents defining the new American civilization.
It was also, of course, one of the productions of which its author was

most proud. Jefferson, it will be remembered, omitted his having been president of the United States, not to mention vice-president, secretary of state, governor of Virginia, delegate to the Continental Congress, and minister to France, among his other posts, deeds, and honors, when he came to write his epitaph for the gravestone at Monticello; he cited only his having been founder of the University of Virginia, drafter of the Declaration of Independence, and author of the Virginia statute.

A LITTLE NOTE
ABOUT THE TEXT

But first, before we examine the statute, a curious point about the composition. (This is extracted from Julian Boyd's notes in the Jefferson papers.) Between them, Jefferson and the Virginia Assembly managed to produce, in the preamble, a stupendous sentence asserting the freedom of the human mind—which (apparent) sentence, in its usual version in English, has no subject! There must have been through the years many teachers of English composition who, setting out to diagram this famous production, were staggered to discover they could not.

In his original (of which no manuscript copy exists) Jefferson began the long preamble with the phrase "Well aware that ... " and proceeded to give an enormous sequence of clauses, each beginning with "that," of which someone—not yet named—was "well aware." He then completed the structure by finally beginning the enacting clause with "We the General Assembly do enact ... " so that the answer to the question, *who* is "well aware" that and that and that, was eventually forthcoming: "We the General Assembly." But, although Madison wrote to Jefferson that the Assembly had made no changes in the enacting clause, in fact it had dropped "We the General Assembly do enact" and substituted the standard form—the pedestrian "Be it enacted ... "—which left the well-awareness up in the air.

But the Assembly had also struck, along with "We the General Assembly" in the enacting clause, the "Well aware ... " way back at the beginning, and had put instead as the first word another standard form,

an even more pedestrian favorite of lawmakers then and now, "Whereas."
That worked well enough with "Almighty God hath created the mind
free," once the "that" was removed from in front of it. But the Assembly
did not strike all the "thats" in the other clauses. It must have been a
long afternoon on January 16, 1786. So—the act is "Whereas...that...
that...that...Be it enacted..." making of the preamble no sentence,
and of the statute no grammatical sense.

Then Jefferson, in Paris, apparently made his own contribution to
this little jumble. When he made a copy, presumably using a newspaper
version, to circulate (proudly) among the literate of Europe, he restored
the "Well aware that..." at the beginning but failed to correct the
Assembly's "Be it enacted" further down. So the most widely circulated
version of the most celebrated defense of intellectual freedom in English
is not a complete sentence at all, but one enormous dangle.

THE STATUTE EXAMINED:
REASON AND EVIDENCE

When you look at the Virginia statute itself, you find an interesting
form. It is rather like an introduction to a waltz. The actual enactment
itself is quite short. It is preceded by a long and passionate preamble,
four times as long, one full clause-crammed page, that sets forth the
argument, and is intellectually the important part of the statute. The
short paragraph of the enactment itself then is followed by a concluding
paragraph that might be said to be rather amusingly un-Jeffersonian, of
which more below.

Here's the way Jefferson, working on the revisal in 1777, had started
out:

> *Well aware that the opinions and belief of men depend on their
> own will, but follow involuntarily the evidence proposed to
> their minds; that Almighty God hath created the mind free,
> and manifested his supreme will that free it shall remain by
> making it altogether insusceptible of restraint;*

The Senate of Virginia, in those exchanges with the House of Delegates that Madison described, deleted the two clauses in italics and a later one, of the same tendency. This later deletion appears in the clause, perhaps strategic in its piety, about the "holy author of our religion" who chose not to propagate that religion by coercion, "as was in his Almighty power to do"—here comes the deleted part—"*but to extend it by its influence on reason alone....*" Surely it will come as news to some that Christianity spread across Europe and the world by that means alone.

These three deletions plainly were not stylistic only, although a stylistic case certainly can be made for them. They take out the most sweeping of Jefferson's assertions about the ineluctable sovereign sway of human reason—"follow involuntarily the evidence proposed to their minds"; the free mind "altogether insusceptible of restraint"; "extend it by its influence on reason alone." Madison wrote to Jefferson, in the letter that we have been quoting, that the amendments voted by the Senate "did not affect the substance though they somewhat defaced the composition," but one may argue that exactly the reverse is true. They *improved* the composition by eliminating some of Jefferson's cluttering effort to say too much, leaving the strong phrase "Almighty God hath created the mind free" in its ringing clarity as the beginning.

But deleting those clauses certainly did affect the substance. Dumas Malone wrote that as a result of the Senate's action—to which Madison and the House of Delegates in the tired ending of the session had to agree—"the Statute does not rest on quite so broad a base as the one its author had designed." You can say that, or you say it no longer asserts so insistently rationalistic a foundation for its program, but allows implicitly for the nonrational elements that many—certainly Madison's indispensable allies, the evangelical "enthusiasts"—see to be important, alongside "reason," in the making of human convictions.

As these suppressed clauses show, Jefferson held an intellectualistic picture of belief, grounded in the ineluctable power of *argument* and *evidence*. His friend Madison held such a view also. Madison had written in his *Memorial and Remonstrance*: "...the opinions of men, depending only on the evidence contemplated by their own minds, cannot follow the dictates of other men."

This view of religion is rather at odds with the religion of "enthusiasm," conversions, and revivals—religion that, whatever its connection with reason, argument, and evidence, was certainly linked to passion and will—that had furnished the chief popular support for the statute, and was to spill out across the country once again during Jefferson's presidency, and Madison's, and many times thereafter. These spillings were to shape a rather different kind of religion, and of religious liberty—a rather different country—than Jefferson and Madison, one may presume, expected. For the American system of religious liberty, as for the American system of government, Jefferson, Madison, and a small group of other heirs of the Enlightenment furnished much of the brain power, but the religion of revival furnished the troops.

The religious groups whose support was essential in order for Madison to get Jefferson's bill enacted into law did not share Jefferson's view, or Madison's, of religion, of belief, of the operations of the human soul; neither have most of the religious groups to which Jefferson's theory of religious liberty has subsequently been applied. It took the "rationalist" Jefferson to draft the sweeping statute, and to enlarge the issue from religious liberty to freedom of the human mind in a way that the evangelical allies would not have done. It took the diligent "enlightened" statesman James Madison to lead it through the Assembly into law. But it took the New Lights, whose understanding of religion was different from that of either of these learned gentlemen, to provide the political pressure to get it passed.

> Well aware that Almighty God hath created the mind free, that all attempts to influence it by temporal punishments or burthens, or by civil incapacitations, tend only to beget habits of hypocrisy and meanness, and are a departure from the plan of the holy author of our religion, who being lord both of body and mind, yet chose not to propagate it by coercions on either, as was in his Almighty power to do; ...

Long after these events, Jefferson wrote in his "Autobiography," a short piece composed for his family in his seventy-seventh year, that an amendment had been proposed, way back then in 1786, inserting the words "Jesus Christ" before the phrase "holy author of our religion," thus making it read "the plan of Jesus Christ the holy author of our religion, who being..." and so on. "The insertion," he added, "was rejected by a great majority, in proof that they meant to comprehend, within the mantle of [the statute's] protection, the Jew and the Gentile, the Christian and the Mahometan, the Hindoo, and infidel of every denomination." Whether or not a great majority of the Assembly meant any such inclusiveness, the older Thomas Jefferson certainly meant it, and the younger one no doubt would have liked to have meant it too, except that as he composed the bill he used a phrase, perhaps for strategic reasons, that sounds otherwise: *"the* holy author of *our* religion..."

PASSIONATE PHILOSOPHE

Let us start over. The long preamble, the argument, has a biting fervor not usually found in Jefferson's cool felicitous writing—not found even in the Declaration of Independence, except perhaps in the indictments of King George.

> Well aware that Almighty God hath created the mind free, that all attempts to influence it by temporal punishments, or burthens, or by civil incapacitations, tend only to beget habits of hypocrisy and meanness, and are a departure from the plan of the holy author of our religion, who being lord both of body and mind, yet chose not to propagate it by coercions on either, as was in his Almighty power to do; that the impious presumption of legislators and rulers, civil as well as ecclesiastical, who, being themselves but fallible and uninspired men, have assumed dominion over the faith of others, setting up their own opinions and modes of thinking as the only true and infallible, and as such endeavoring to impose them on others, hath established and maintained false religions over the greatest part of the world and through all time: That to compel a man to furnish contributions of money for the propagation of opinions which he disbelieves, is sinful and tyrannical...

In Carl Becker's book on that other great Jeffersonian production, *The Declaration of Independence: A Study in the History of Political Ideas*, there is an interesting chapter on the literary style of the Declaration, which becomes in the middle a discussion of Jefferson's style in general. Responding to a commentator who has called the great Virginian's writing "passionate," Becker wrote: "Of all words in the language, 'passionate' is the one least applicable to Jefferson or to his writings." Discussing the passage on Negro slavery that the Continental

Congress struck from the draft of the Declaration, Becker wrote that although it employs the "most tremendous words—'murder,' 'piratical warfare,' 'prostituted,' 'miserable death,'—the passage nevertheless somehow leaves us cold; it remains, like all of Jefferson's writing, calm and quiescent; it lacks warmth; it fails to lift us out of our equanimity." This is the result in some part, says Becker, of Jefferson's use of the abstract rather than the concrete to describe the evil of slavery.

But, he goes on to say, there is something more, which he can indicate by a comparison with a part of Lincoln's Second Inaugural Address. This Lincolnian passage is also an "abstract" or generalized statement; nevertheless it is invested with an emotional power quite beyond what Jefferson achieved. Quoting Lincoln ("Fondly do we hope—fervently do we pray . . . " and so on to the end of the next-to-last paragraph of the address) and then quoting beside it Jefferson's deleted passage on slavery, Becker observes:

> There is a quality of deep feeling about the first [Lincoln's], an indefinable something, which is profoundly moving, and this something, which informs and enriches much of Lincoln's writing, is rarely, almost never present in the writing of Jefferson. This something, which Jefferson lacked but which Lincoln possessed in full measure, may . . . be called a profoundly emotional apprehension of experience.

Becker later illustrates this lack with a striking reference to a familiar Jeffersonian sentence. "Sometimes, indeed," Becker wrote, "by virtue of saying disputed things in such a pleasant way, his words imply even less than they mean. When, for example, Jefferson says, 'the tree of liberty must be refreshed from time to time with the blood of patriots and tyrants,' so far from making us shudder, he contrives to throw about this unlovely picture a kind of arcadian charm."

None of this, true though it may be of Jefferson in general, applies to the Virginia statute. Becker wrote: "One might say that Jefferson felt with the mind, as some people think with the heart." But the issue in the Virginia statute touched him where heart and thought, mind and feeling, meet.

There is a kind of passion that unimpassioned, gracefully intellectual men like Jefferson can feel—feel and think, heart and mind right there together—about certain issues. A cool intellect can heat up rapidly when a cool intellect itself is threatened or violated. Becker says of Jefferson: "He had enthusiasm, but it was an enthusiasm engendered by an irrepressible intellectual curiosity. He was ardent, but his ardors were cool, giving forth light without heat." When, however, light-giving and intellectual curiosity themselves were under challenge—as in the matter of religious liberty as Jefferson understood it—then there was heat and warmth and passion after all. One can feel it in the Virginia statute: "habits of hypocrisy and meanness"; "impious presumption"; "themselves but fallible and uninspired men"; "sinful and tyrannical." The passion is conveyed not only by such strong words but also by the piling up of the sequence of clauses, with a rapid, sweeping argument running through them, mounting to a vision with organ music behind it in the last paragraph: "Truth is great, and will prevail...." This Jeffersonian production does not "lack warmth" or "leave us cold." To the contrary, it must be one of the warmest documents among the American political classics.

In Jefferson's draft, he had written, in the last clause quoted above, "that to compel a man to furnish contributions of money for the propagation of opinions which he disbelieves *and abhors*, is sinful and tyrannical...." He thus made explicit the fact, all too evident from the history of the human race, that our differing beliefs are not always the amiable companions taking different paths up the Mountain of Truth which, in the multifaith nation Jefferson helped to found, it is often prudent to pretend they are. They can *abhor* each other. The use of the strong word *abhor* betrays again a considerable warmth on Jefferson's part, and a perception about the underside of the contest of beliefs not always present in the genial and harmonious optimism of his line of intellectual descent.

The Senate of Virginia took out that word, and Madison and the House did not fight for it.

SEPARATION

Jefferson held not only to religious liberty but to the separation of church and state, and a strictly voluntary way in religion as the means to achieve it. Of course it was he who was later, in 1801, in his often quoted letter to Baptists in Danbury, Connecticut, to coin the metaphor of a "wall" of separation that has haunted this subject ever since, but though the participants in this Virginia struggle had not yet been favored with that subsequently ubiquitous term, they had arrived at the practical point of policy it described. Through the complexities of Virginia politics from 1776, when the established church effectively collapsed, down to the enactment of Jefferson's statute, the issue had been effectively reduced to these two alternatives: a "general assessment" for religion, under which citizens would pay their tax for the denomination of their choice, and a complete separation. Jefferson's bill of course was the expression of the second position. He opposed using government's power even on behalf of a religion a citizen believes in; this was the concrete point of policy to which Virginia politics had maneuvered itself at the time the statute was enacted.

> ... that even the forcing him to support this or that teacher of his own religious persuasion, is depriving him of the comfortable liberty of giving his contributions to the particular pastor whose morals he would make his pattern, and whose powers he feels most persuasive to righteousness, and is withdrawing from the ministry those temporary rewards, which proceeding from an approbation of their personal conduct, are an additional incitement to earnest and unremitting labours for the instruction of mankind; ...

He made plain that sharp division between the *civil* and the *religious* that he and the dissenters held in common. One of his assertions most often quoted puts it this way: "... that our civil rights have no more dependence on our religious opinions than our opinions in physics or geometry."

Some religious folk may draw back a little from the implication of the way that point is put: that for the purposes of the state and of society—of our living together—our religious opinions have no more significance than our opinions on physics or geometry. Not so, says the believer, and maybe others as well; "opinions" about the ultimate issues of life and death, good and evil, and the meaning of existence *do* have considerable civic significance—more than "opinions," if such there be, about right angles and squares.

> ... that our civil rights have no more dependence on our religious opinions than our opinions in physics or geometry; that therefore the proscribing any citizen as unworthy of the public

confidence by laying upon him an incapacity of being called to offices of trust and emolument, unless he profess or renounce this or that religious opinion. . . .

The orthodox interlocutor of Jefferson may find a further touch of latitudinarianism in that rather shoulder-shrugging phrase "this or that opinion" about religion. Such an outlook—the dominant modern outlook, to be sure—is more evident still in another Jeffersonian observation, perhaps the most often quoted of all he made on this subject. It comes not from the statute but from his *Notes on the State of Virginia*: "But it does me no injury for my neighbour to say that there are twenty gods, or no god. It neither picks my pocket nor breaks my leg." The orthodox have historically responded: But it does do me and my children and my neighbors and the society we all share much injury, more substantial injury perhaps than pocket-picking or leg-breaking, though of a less tangible kind, to say there is no God. Think not only of what one of our modern television evangelists might say—with his attacks on the "humanists" who "pull down God from the skies" (quite a concept, that one) and on "Godless" this and that, but also of what a G. K. Chesterton might say. Your no-Godliness affects the fabric of our shared world. But a "fastidious atheist" (to borrow a phrase from Justice William O. Douglas, who said humorously that such a one might even object to "God save this honorable court") could of course retort that your Godliness pollutes our shared world. And so we have to live together, with these counterclaims of injury. The Jeffersonians say— exactly because we disagree so directly—that the outcome should be left to free choice; it should not be determined by the power of law.

NATURAL RIGHT

Jefferson's statute mingles pragmatic with principled arguments, as advocates do in the heat of rhetorical battle. His fundamental claim however, rests on substantive human rights, as he will insist in the most extraordinary way, at the end of the statute itself. Though he believed that voluntary religion is best for all concerned, and thus may be justified by arguments from utility, his position at its foundation did not rest on a calculation about what would prove to be "best," but on an intrinsic claim of natural right, freedom of "conscience" or of "mind."

Or perhaps on two natural rights, closely interwoven. The claim of the right for every person to believe and profess whatever he does believe resounds through the whole document. Not only the many styles of believers in one God but also the believers in twenty gods or in none may rightfully claim full freedom to hold and to profess their belief. There is in addition a closely related "natural right," referred to in the passage that follows, the right of every person to full, unlimited participation in civic life—to hold office, to receive honors, to be a citizen in every particular—without regard to religion.

> ...that our civil rights have no dependence on our religious opinions, any more than on our opinions in physics or geometry; that therefore the proscribing any citizen as unworthy of the public confidence by laying upon him an incapacity of being called to offices of trust and emolument, unless he profess or renounce this or that religious opinion, is depriving him injuriously of those privileges and advantages to which, in common with his fellow citizens, he has a natural right; ...

These two rights, or two aspects of the one right, represent the two dimensions, personal and social, of civil liberty in general and of religious liberty in particular. The moral grounding of religious liberty in a democracy rests upon the recognition that the human being transcends every social order, most especially in his most fundamental convictions. But it rests also on the need of the society, and the benefit to society, of uncoerced consent of the governed.

RELIGIOUS LIBERTY
AND OTHER LIBERTIES

Jefferson did make an argument about the benefit to religion at least from the negative side: Compulsion, he pointed out, damages religion at its core. Already he has said that attempts to coerce belief "tend only to produce habits of hypocrisy and meanness." Now he adds further:

> ...that it tends also to corrupt the principles of that *very* religion it is meant to encourage, by bribing, with a monopoly of worldly honours and emoluments, those who will externally profess and conform to it; that though indeed those are criminal who do not withstand such temptation, yet neither are those innocent who lay the bait in their way; ...

Jefferson did not ordinarily exhibit a full awareness of the tendency of a man's interests to warp his thought that his friend Madison was to remark a few years later in Federalist Ten and Fifty-one. But on the subject of religion, Jefferson took for granted that any magistrate would "of course" make his own "opinions" the sole rule of his actions.

> ...that to suffer the civil magistrate to intrude his powers into the field of opinion and to restrain the profession or propagation of principles on supposition of their ill tendency is a dangerous falacy, which at once destroys all religious liberty, because he being of course judge of that tendency will make his opinions the rule of judgment, and approve or condemn the sentiments of others only as they shall square with or differ from his own; ...

Pursued further, that assertion—that any person elevated to the civil magistracy would "of course" make judgments strictly to promote his own commitment—might call into question the social functioning of Jefferson's own rationalism and optimism. Just how is it that truth is to prevail in combat with error if none of us can recognize a piece of the former that goes against our prior opinion? Or the rights of persons to hold the latter? Perhaps even "civil magistrates" can do better, even in the field of "opinion," than Jefferson here allows—or Jefferson's own world of rational argument could scarcely function.

In any case, say the Jeffersonians, the state's purposes are fully served by intervening only when an *act* occurs. The statute contains this sentence, quoted at important moments thereafter by the U.S. Supreme Court, when that body made a distinction, in the "free exercise" of religion, between "belief," which should be completely free, and "action" based on religious belief, which cannot always be so: " ... that it is time enough for the rightful purposes of civil government for its officers to interfere when principles break out into overt acts against peace and good order; ... " Jefferson put the whole point succinctly (he was not always succinct) in a straightforward sentence that was perhaps too blunt for Virginians with their establishmentarian hangover, because the Assembly struck it out: "the opinions of men are not the object of civil government, nor under its jurisdiction."

For Jefferson, religious liberty was a part of that larger liberty (larger to him—larger and also smaller to many believers), freedom of the *mind*, which it takes no search to discover to be the center of Jefferson's life: founder of the University of Virginia, most prominent early advocate of universal education, defender of freedom of the press, enthusiastic supporter of science and friend of scientists, aristocrat only in his belief in a natural—intellectual—aristocracy. That list of achievements that Jefferson chose for his epitaph showed again that freedom of the mind was central for him—more central, alas, than it was to prove in practice for the nation of which he was intellectually the most significant of the founders. His great oath, which now encircles his memorial in Washington, is: "I have sworn upon the altar of God eternal hostility against every form of tyranny over the mind of man."

The most important passage in the Virginia statute is the climax of the argument in the preamble, which spreads the claims hitherto restricted to religion out into a broader territory. The famous passage, to which we will return in a moment, might almost be presented as the quintessence of Jeffersonianism:

> ... that truth is great and will prevail if left to herself; that she is the proper and sufficient antagonist to error, and has nothing to fear from the conflict unless by human interposition disarmed of her natural weapons, free argument and debate; errors

ceasing to be dangerous when it is permitted freely to contradict them.

Jefferson's sharp condemnation of all compulsion in this domain is compressed in the enactment itself, now stated as the Law of Virginia:

> Be it enacted by the General Assembly [or: We the General Assembly of Virginia do enact] that no man shall be compelled to frequent or support any religious worship, place, or ministry whatsoever, nor shall be enforced, restrained, molested, or burthened in his body or goods, nor shall otherwise suffer, on account of his religious opinions or belief; ...

Then comes the other side of this thoroughgoing repudiation of all compulsion—the securing of unfettered freedom:

> ... but that all men shall be free to profess, and by argument to maintain, their opinions in matters of religion, and that the same shall in no wise diminish, enlarge or affect their civil capacities.

It is one of the familiar effects of a thoroughgoing social achievement that those who come afterward, and live their lives taking its benefits for granted, have a hard time believing that it ever was much of an issue. Yesterday's battle cry has become today's commonplace. But the issue of religious liberty had been of great moment, and still was (still is) elsewhere in the world. With this statute Virginia became the first state to end by law all forms of official religious persecution and exclusion and compulsion—to break with the whole ugly history of the use of state power to punish, enforce, suppress, and enact religious beliefs.

NATURAL RIGHT FOREVER

Now the final paragraph, which was described above as rather amusingly un-Jeffersonian.

> And though we know well that this assembly [has] no power to restrain the acts of succeeding Assemblies, ... and that therefore to declare this act irrevocable would be of no effect in law; yet we are free to declare, and do declare, that the rights hereby asserted are of the natural rights of mankind, and that if any act shall be hereafter passed to repeal the present or to narrow its operation, such act will be an infringement of natural right.

May we not find in this paragraph an implied wariness that error, in this field, just might make a comeback after all? And that truth, even equipped with its natural weapons, might still have something to fear? More clearly one can discover in this last paragraph the un-Jeffersonian desire, suppressed but real, to bind the future.

Jefferson is distinctive among the American founding fathers, and indeed perhaps among thinkers about politics anywhere, in the thoroughness with which he wanted to free the present from the encumbrances of the past. He was, of course, one of the purest products of the Enlightenment, a man who took the institutions of human societies intellectually in hand, put them under the clear-glassed microscope of human reason, and found many of them defective. They were defective by reason's test—the degree to which they provided for human freedom and human happiness. Therefore, repair them, for the earth belongs to the living.

This testing of human societies by the glass of reason (and the standard of human rights and freedoms and pursuings of happiness) is not, moreover, something that is to be done only once, in one time and one place, after which, perfection attained, they are to be left alone. On the contrary: The testing is to continue, and be repeated, in every generation. There is in Mr. Jefferson this bald theme covered over by the wig of his prestige, his Virginia aristocratic mien, and his gentleness, of the need for *regular* and *repeated* revolutions. One about every twenty years, in fact. He gave thorough support to the French Revolution, not only at the start but after its bloody turning. There is more than a trace of this outlook of his in the Declaration of Independence itself, though it certainly tends to be overlooked by the Daughters and Sons of the American Revolution: Governments are disposable when they fail to meet the test of securing God-given universal human rights. They are disposable not just in the American colonies in 1776 but wherever and whenever they do so fail, even presumably in some places in recent and current history.

Jefferson had a remarkable view about the discontinuity of generations: "one generation is to another as one independent nation to another," he wrote. Here is an elaboration of this view, by the historian Edmund Morgan in his *The Meaning of Independence*:

> He liked to think of generations as nations, and he sought independence not merely of Americans from England but of every generation of Americans from the preceding one. At the risk of putting words in the mouth of a man who could speak quite well enough for himself, I would say that Jefferson's public career focused on securing for Americans a right of expatriation from the past.

Expatriation from the past! *By right!* Each generation a nation to itself! Ah yes, but now when something deep and central in him is touched—freedom of religion, as he understands it—he wishes he could prevent any expatriation. On this matter he wanted with his own dead hand to reach out from the past and to shake an admonitory finger at any future Assembly, at any future American generation, that would diminish this statute. Don't do it! In his statute something final, eternal, permanent, beyond all generations, applying to all generations, had been captured: a natural right of man. Freedom of the mind.

=====

TRUTH'S ADVENTURES
BEFORE JEFFERSON

=====

Jefferson's statute contains enough echoes of John Locke's *Letter Concerning Toleration* for a twentieth-century student in Mr. Jefferson's university to wonder whether in composing it Mr. Jefferson had violated the university's honor code (Locke, in his turn, has what seem at least to be many echoes of Roger Williams). As just one example of the passages that would anticipate Jefferson, Locke wrote,

> For the truth certainly would do well enough if she were once left to shift for herself.... She is not taught by laws, nor has

she any need of force to procure her entrance into the minds of men. Errors indeed prevail by the assistance of foreign and borrowed succors. But if truth makes not her way into the understanding by her own light, she will be but weaker for any borrowed force violence can add to her.

(Locke and Jefferson—and Milton, too—discover truth to be feminine.)

One of the best-known passages in Milton's *Areopagitica*, published more than four decades before Locke, begins this way: "And though all the winds of doctrine were let loose upon the earth, so truth be in the field, we do injuriously by licensing and prohibiting to misdoubt her strength." Then, where Jefferson will use metaphors of battle, Milton uses a wrestling metaphor (both are still at some distance from the perhaps revealing modern metaphor of a "marketplace of ideas," in which truth, if it exists, becomes the presumably superior choice among competing commodities): "Let her and Falsehood grapple; who ever knew Truth put to the worse in a free and open encounter. Her confuting is the best and surest suppressing."

Earlier in the *Areopagitica* Milton produced passages with somewhat different emphases from the Enlightenment rationalism of Locke and Jefferson, sentences with their own echoes of a tradition of Saint Augustine, about how good and evil, and the knowledge of good and evil, are mixed, interwoven, grow up together in this world, so that in attempting to suppress an evil you will suppress the good entangled with it. Milton had also the theme—it appears in the well-known sentence "I cannot praise a fugitive and cloistered virtue, unexercised and unbreathed"—about how important "trial by what is contrary" is to the aerobics of virtue, the fitness of the mind, the exercise and therefore development and purification both of the conscience and of the intellect: "our faith and knowledge thrives by exercise, as well as our limbs and complexion."

Although the *Areopagitica* was, of course, an argument against censorship—specifically, against a licensing act of the Puritan Commonwealth's Long Parliament—it was an argument provoked by and applying to issues of religious toleration. The licensing act had been aimed at the publications of the dissenting divines in the Westminster Assembly, and at Roger Williams's *Bloudy Tenent, of Persecution, for Cause of Conscience*, and at publications of Milton himself in the heady first days of Puritan parliamentary government after 1640, a moment of great hope for the making of a new human society that was not unlike the other moment that was to come, across the Atlantic, after 1776.

Milton saw a positive good in the diversity of religious groups and religious opinions beyond the very limited goods explicitly recognized by Jefferson and Madison (mostly, in their cases, to fulfill the freedom of the "private" person's mind, and to allow each religious group to be a *censor morum* to the others). "Truth is compared in Scripture," wrote Milton—not the kind of thing Jefferson or Madison would be likely to write—"to a streaming fountain; if her waters flow not in a perpetual progression, they sicken into a muddy pool of conformity and tradition." This dynamic flowing-water notion of truth is then given a personal, and a personal-religious—could one say existential?—interpretation differing from a picture of truth as a static final impersonal objective absolute. "A man may be a heretic in truth," wrote Milton, "and if he believes things only because his pastor says so, or the Assembly so determines, without knowing other reason, though his belief be true, yet the very truth he holds becomes his heresy." Milton goes on to draw an amusing, and certainly still pertinent, portrait of a person busy with his "pleasure and profits" for whom religion is too complicated to worry about, who finds some "divine of note" and "resigns the whole warehouse of his religion, with all the locks and keys, into his custody; and indeed makes the very person of that man his religion."

"Truth indeed came once into the world with her divine Master, and was a perfect shape to look on.... " This is another of Milton's metaphors, with a classical allusion, and perhaps a different emphasis. Wickedness took "the Virgin Truth, hewed her lovely form into a thousand pieces, and scattered them to the four winds. From that time ever since, the sad friends of Truth ... went up and down gathering up limb by limb still as they could find them. We have not yet found them all, Lords and Commons, nor ever shall do, till her master's second coming."

Those who "perpetually complain of schisms and sects and make it such a calamity that any man dissents from their maxims" are *themselves* the disturbers, the troublers, the dividers of unity—this is an echo or reverberation of a point Roger Williams had made, too, very hard for the John Cottons of the world to understand—they who would put down the sects and schisms are the disturbers and dividers because they "permit not others to unite those dissevered pieces which are yet wanting to the body of Truth."

The pieces of the body of truth accessible to John Milton in 1644 did not include the extension of toleration beyond "neighboring differences, or rather indifferences," and specifically not to "popery and open superstition." The parts of truth available to John Locke in 1689, as we have said, also did not include extending toleration, at least we may infer, to Catholics and some others and explicitly excluded atheists. But when the streaming fountain of truth flowed on to Virginia in 1777, the young lawyer-politician working away in Monticello at revising his state's laws to make a new sort of human society, with Locke at least and perhaps Milton as well beside him, wrote into his bill on religion an understanding of the rightful claim of each person's mind and conscience, of truth's liberty and liberty's truth, that was complete. Of Locke, Jefferson wrote, "It was a great thing to go so far ... but where he stopped short, we may go on."

Liberty's truth, as we may call it, was then in the field still beset with many winds of doctrine; she grappled with Falsehood in various guises for almost ten years, as we have seen, in more or less free and open encounter, and contended with Error using her natural weapons, free argument and debate, notably in the speeches and the *Memorial and Remonstrance* of James Madison, and also in the petitions of the Baptists and other dissenters and the disputation within the Hanover Presbytery, and she made her way into the understanding of relevant Virginia legislators by her own light—with considerable help from astute politics—and at last in January 1786 this Truth did prevail, and entered the conception of full religious and intellectual liberty into the soul of a nation then being born.

> ... that truth is great and will prevail if left to herself; that she is the proper and sufficient antagonist to error, and has nothing to fear from the conflict unless by human interposition disarmed of her natural weapons, free argument and debate; errors ceasing to be dangerous when it is permitted freely to contradict them.

The metaphor of a "wall" of separation that Jefferson used in his letter to the Danbury Baptists in 1801 was to become part of the standard stock of American phrases, and many times Jefferson and the Virginia statute are quoted in support of that wall. The twentieth-century decision by the U.S. Supreme Court that is most clearly in accord with this larger aspect of Jefferson's position, however, does not have to do with breaching the wall, nor explicitly with Jefferson, nor even exclusively with religious liberty. This modern item is Justice Robert Jackson's majority opinion in the second flag-salute case, decided by the Court in the middle of World War II, in 1943. We may take it to be a modern reflection of the essence of Jefferson's view, and of the statute, setting the issue of religious liberty in the larger frame of freedom from all official requirement as to belief.

The second flag-salute case overturned the first. Despite the patriotic fervor of wartime, and powerful arguments by Felix Frankfurter against extending judicial review so far, the Court declared unconstitutional a West Virginia statute making compulsory the salute to the American flag in the state's public schools. Justice Jackson for the new majority asserted that the law "invades the sphere of intellect and spirit which it is the purpose of the First Amendment...to reserve from all official control." Jackson invoked—in the manner of Jefferson—the futility of efforts to coerce belief, with brief references to examples not only from ages past but from our time. "Compulsory unification of opinion achieves only the unanimity of the graveyard."

Efforts to compel belief also violate the particular principles of the American democratic polity. Jackson employed a phrase given widest circulation by Jefferson's pen. "We set up government by consent of the governed," he wrote, "and the Bill of Rights denies those in power any legal opportunity to coerce that consent. Authority here is controlled by public opinion, not public opinion by authority."

Jackson then produced the following thoroughly Jeffersonian paragraph, which in its turn reflected, and has evoked, a certain proud passion.

> If there is any fixed star in our constitutional constellation, it is that no official, high or petty, can prescribe what shall be orthodox in politics, nationalism, religion, or other matters of opinion or force citizens to confess by word or act their faith therein. If there are any circumstances which permit an exception, they do not now occur to us.

TRUTH PREVAILS
IN ONE ENCOUNTER

Jefferson, in understandable enthusiasm over the Virginia statute, wrote to Madison a sharply etched picture of the history of intellectual freedom: Before this enactment, the "human mind," the "reason of man," untrusted, was "held in vassalage" by kings, priests, and nobles; after this moment, with the standard of reason now in place, the mind of man was free. But truth's victories in this world are rarely that tidy or complete.

In the new nation in which Virginia became a large state and Jefferson a larger hero, the Virginian's conception of religious liberty, and complete separation of church and state, did come soon to prevail: in the constitutions of other states, in the First Amendment, in the mind of the public.

The American tradition thus built was to have a much larger meaning than could be found, two centuries later, simply by looking at issues generating heat under the headings "church and state," "religious freedom," "religion-in-politics." The American tradition built out of Jefferson's conception had effects reaching far beyond those rather narrow, though noisy, arenas; that tradition reached, instead, to issues in every arena, to the composition of the national arena itself, because that tradition helped to form the culture. Religious liberty became part of the essence of the new nation, helping to give it its shape. The United States of America would not be what it has become, would have a different moral meaning and a different composition, had the original arrangements been other than they were.

Under the "voluntary" way in religion, the new nation developed a revivalist and pietist Protestantism, permeating the culture, that was not what Jefferson and Madison had had in mind, and which generated multitudes of sects, splits, and new religions. Moreover, all the religious groups of Europe crossed the Atlantic to become a part of the new nation. Into this most "Christian" country there came the largest Jewish population in "Christendom." Into this most Protestant country there came successive waves of Catholics, making the religion of the Puritans' ancient "papist" enemy the largest religious group in the country. As this distinct product of Western civilization began its third century, there would come an increasing presence of the religions of the East. Within this most "religious" of nations there developed out of the new mind shaped by science, technology, and democracy a secular outlook with a distinct flavor, permeating even the communities of believers. Each of these communities of belief would in time have an effect upon the others.

Meanwhile, the old fiery central question of religious liberty—not so old, in other parts of the world—had been settled in this country. Citizens angered over one side or the other in current disputes, dismayed by one contemporary movement or another, may find incredible a claim that the larger issue is solved, but if they will draw back and look at it across the sweep of history and the variety of the whole globe, they should see that it is. If one makes comparison with the Western past (except for Ireland, where the past is present), or the Middle East or the Indian subcontinent today, one can see that at least the most terrible forms of religious persecution, warfare, and fanaticism have been ended in the United States. Though intense battles persist, and presumably always will, the framework of principle within which they are fought, in the United States, is rather solid ... in the law, in the realistic balance of a multitude of forces, and in the mind of the people.

═══════

TRUTH'S FURTHER
ADVENTURES

═══════

Truth's grapplings with Error do not end: The pieces of her torn body, as Milton said, will not be fully put back together until the end of time. Even if all that has happened in human thought and human history between 1786 and 1986 could be set aside—which it cannot— and his countrymen 200 years later could still see the human situation in the way Thomas Jefferson did—which we cannot—still there would be new lines of battle. He saw a primary threat to freedom of the mind in the domain of religion; two hundred years later one could certainly find it elsewhere. He saw state power as the agent of the threat; today one could discover other agents.

That Jefferson saw this freedom as a negative liberty—absence of external coercion—and saw the dangerous source of that overt compulsion in the formal power of the law and of the state is rather hard to miss in the Virginia statute: "temporal punishments, or burthens," "civil incapacitations," "coercions" of body and mind, the "impious presumption [good phrase] of legislators and rulers" who "assumed *dominion* over the faith of others," "to *compel* a man to furnish contributions," "*forcing*" one to support this or that teacher, "*proscribing* any citizen as unworthy," "laying upon him an incapacity," "*depriving* him injuriously," "*bribing*, with a monopoly of worldly honours and emoluments," "lay *bait* in their way," "to suffer the civil magistrate to *intrude* his powers," "to *restrain* the profession or propagation of principles," "no man shall be *compelled*, nor shall be *enforced, restrained, molested,* or *burthened....* nor shall otherwise *suffer*"—all these in a statute that can be printed on a page and a half.

All of this compelling and forcing and proscribing and depriving and restraining is done by magistrates and legislators; all of these burthens, punishments, and incapacitations are external and overt, and are laid on by the state, or by a priestly authoritarian church using the power of the state. That was the issue—or an issue—at the time (or in the times, recently past, to which the Enlightenment was sharply contrasting itself). The Baptists and other sectarians, different though they certainly were from Jefferson and the rather aristocratic and thoroughly rationalistic Deists on other accounts, accorded with Jefferson completely on these: Religious liberty was understood by them also to be the absence of overt compulsion by the state; and the state was viewed by them also primarily or perhaps exclusively as the instrument of coercion.

The view that perceives law and the state overwhelmingly under the aspect of coercion, neglecting its aspect of shared purpose, that conceives of the magistrate as the only enemy of the free mind and "coercion" by formal requirement as the only way the free mind is endangered, rests upon or is associated with that individualistic picture of society— the picture of the social interweaving as something added and external—that after Jefferson's time, but with a push from him, became dominant in our country. Both of the main collaborators in shaping the

American tradition of separation of church and state—Jefferson and the Baptists—held to (or held views that led to) this individualism, and contributed thereby to the overwhelming strength of that social outlook in the nation then being created.

But—let us bring that American individualism out of its American cloister, and give its truth some further exercise. We live in a more tightly knit human family than Jefferson, or the Baptists, perceived. The state is by no means the only agent of coercive power. There have always been others; but our modern social machinery multiplies and strengthens them, and turns loose in that field where Truth is supposed to slay Error a complicating collection of giants. The great value of freedom of belief and conviction—a social benefit as well as an individual right—needs defense on more communal, less rationalistic and optimistic grounds than Jefferson employed, and against perils he did not envision. Those who reject the extreme version of that social outlook need now to defend intellectual liberty on somewhat different grounds than he did.

Though as socially shaped beings we arrive at our beliefs and ideas in a less isolated and "private" way than Jefferson (and many countrymen after him) thought we do, nevertheless religious and intellectual liberty are indeed domains in which the particular human person does have a final society-transcending right—freedom of thought and conscience. And such freedom is not only an individual right but also a communal good and, for a free society, a communal necessity. What Jefferson affirmed to be fact must now be seen to be rather—and alas— only a condition to be sought: a society in which Truth, unfettered and unarmed, can prevail over Error, by reason and deliberation; a society in which Power does not constrain Liberty of thought, belief, and expression, but is instead derived from and checked by such Liberty. There remain some more pieces of the body of Truth still to be assembled.

There have come with the modern patterns and instruments of mass persuasion contests of power over "the mind" of a sort quite outside Jefferson's picture of the world. In a review of Bertrand Russell's book *Power*, and in anticipation of a theme in his own best-known book, George Orwell made an interesting use of Jefferson's phrase: "It is quite possible that we are descending into an age in which two and two will make five if the leader says so.... One has only to think of the sinister possibilities of the radio, state-controlled education and so forth to realize that 'the truth is great and will prevail' is more a prayer than an axiom."

Orwell wrote this in 1939, before the full extent of the program of the Nazis was known, or that of the Stalinists fully understood, or the distinct features of "totalitarianism" clearly identified—Orwell himself above all was later to help the general reading public in the West to identify them. He wrote it before the development, in Jefferson's own country, of commercial television, of tracking polls, of sophisticated marketing, of the domination of public discourse by the drumbeat of advertising and the blandishments of public relations. Kings, priests, and nobles were no longer to hold the human mind in "vassalage" (insofar as they ever had) but to have their place taken by prime-time sponsors and the "engineers of consent." Preserving the social conditions of liberty, under which the truth has a fighting chance, still would require the eternal vigilance that Jefferson mentioned in another connection.

But it also would require believing, as he did, that reason and conscience have a purchase upon the truth. A citizen of Jefferson's country may be pleased that he used the strong word *truth* in this resounding phrase, as he used the word *truths* at the start of the most important paragraph in the Declaration (We hold *truths* instead of, say, *ideals*, as a later generation might have said, or even, a still later generation, losing even more intellectual juice, *preferences*).

It is clearly important for us to hold to the truth that all human beings are created equal, in an age when inequalities old and new persist. It is also important to hold that "truth" can prevail by "free argument and debate," in an age when many see only "preferences" and therefore manipulation. These Jeffersonian truths stand about as near as anything one can cite to the moral core of the nation he helped to bring into being. They are anchors of the American mind and moral understanding, not weapons with which to dominate. "We hold" these truths, and, with a decent respect for the opinion of mankind, present them to the tribunal of a candid world. In the great contests of humankind it is not that "we" will prevail, but that Truth will prevail, and Truth will prevail from its greatness, not ours, by free, and only by free, argument and debate, which presumably continues forever.

1786

Thomas Jefferson in Paris did not reply to James Madison's letter from Richmond about the 1785–86 session of the Assembly until almost eleven months after it was written. By that time Jefferson had accumulated four other unacknowledged Madisonian productions and had in the meantime, in the spring, written two of his own. It was the slow progress of mail across the water that made for this rather contrapuntal correspondence: The two men were careful to list the dates of their own last letters, and of the most recent and unacknowledged from the other. (Yet another of Jefferson's many, many efforts to bring rationality to an irrational world was his attempt, while he was in Washington's cabinet, to accelerate the mails.) Jefferson, in addition, had a particular explanation for his "very long silence" on this occasion. "An unlucky dislocation of my right wrist has disabled me from using my pen for three months. I now begin to use it a little, but with great pain; so that this letter must be taken up at such intervals as the state of my hand will permit, & will probably be the work of some days." Jefferson did not explain to Madison the reason for this unlucky dislocation: Feeling frisky one day in Paris when out walking with Maria Cosway during their flirtation, he had attempted to jump a fence, and failed.

About the effort to reform the code in general, Jefferson wrote only: "I shall be glad when the revisal shall be got thro'," but he managed a more extended comment about the act for religious freedom:

> The Virginia Act for religious freedom has been received with infinite approbation in Europe and propagated with enthusiasm. I do not mean by the governments, but by the individuals which compose them. It has been translated into French and Italian, has been sent to most of the courts of Europe & has been the best evidence of the falsehood of those reports which stated us to be in anarchy. It is inserted in the new Encyclopedie and is appearing in most of the publications respecting America.

And then, with his wrist in pain but his mind presumably at peace, Jefferson let himself go, and joined Madison in a sweeping claim for what the two of them had accomplished:

> In fact it is comfortable to see the standard of reason at length erected, after so many ages during which the human mind has been held in vassalage by kings, priests & nobles: and it is honorable for us to have produced the first legislature who had the courage to declare that the reason of man may be trusted with the formation of his own opinions.

PART TWO

The Vocation of
Jemmy Madison

THE "GREAT LITTLE MADISON"
AMONG THE GIANTS

When James Madison's chief twentieth-century biographer, Irving Brant, appeared at the White House to present to its library signed copies of his six-volume biography, President John Kennedy remarked that Madison is "the most underrated of our presidents." Presumably Kennedy intended that remark to apply not to Madison specifically as president— the fourth president of the United States, 1809–17—but to the totality of Madison's role in the work of getting the United States under way. It was a very large role indeed. But whereas Washington and Lincoln have their solemn monuments on the great mall in the capital city named for the first of them; and whereas Jefferson was later provided his own monument, too, usually described as on the Tidal Basin, but in most tourists' skyline perception just off a sharp curve in the Fourteenth Street Bridge; and whereas so recent a president as Franklin Roosevelt is to displace some softball fields with a monument in his honor when the federal budget can get itself around to allowing it; and whereas even the persistent non-president Senator Robert Taft of Ohio has carillon bells in a tower on the Capitol grounds; James Madison is honored chiefly by an expensive commercial hotel filled with rich lobbyists from all countries and an ice cream named for his wife, with her name misspelled. (This exaggerates the situation slightly, of course; there is now—relatively recently—an assortment of buildings and streets with Madison's name on them, including an annex to the Library of Congress with a good staff cafeteria and the thoroughly incongruous Avenue, and Square, and Square Garden, up in New York.) All Americans can recognize the face of Abraham Lincoln, and most that of George Washington. Fewer, certainly, but still a goodly number, can recognize Thomas Jefferson. But it would be a rare American indeed who could pick James Madison, "the father of the Constitution," out of a police lineup, in the extremely unlikely event of his being found there.

All this is said, with a bit of hyperbole, to dramatize the big distance between the limited honor accorded to Madison and the limited knowledge of him in these United States, and the quite considerable place he deserves for his work in bringing them into being, making them united, and shaping the foundations on which they continue to live.

In particular, he shaped the traditions of religious liberty. But before we proceed to his doings in that regard let us shift from exclaiming about the undeserved dimness of his star to some exclamations, mainly borrowed, about the whole galaxy.

The extraordinary group of which Madison and Jefferson are a part—the founding fathers—is, for Americans, so much wrapped in a stereotyped veneration as to leave little emotional room for a more discriminating appreciation. Citizens of this country need to be reminded, despite, or even because of, the many reminders they have already had, what a remarkable group it was. The historian Edmund Morgan made the point this way, in a little book about *The Genius of George Washington*:

> ...if one were to make a list of the great men of American history, by whatever standards one chooses to measure greatness, an astonishingly large proportion would be found whose careers began or culminated in the Revolution. It would be hard to find in all the rest of American history more than two or three men to rank with Washington, Franklin, Jefferson, Hamilton, Madison, or John Adams.

John Dewey, in an essay about Thomas Jefferson, used a different criterion for exclamatory appreciation. "Considering the small size of the American population," Dewey wrote,

> we may well be amazed, as well as grateful, at the spectacle of the intellectual and moral calibre of the men who took a hand in shaping the American political tradition. The military and moral, although not especially the intellectual, repute of Washington has made him a part of the common heritage. There are also Jefferson, Hamilton, Madison, followed at some distance by Franklin and John Adams, and at a greater distance by Monroe. There were giants in those days.

One reason for the influx of giants, to be sure, was the timing, as the quotation from Edmund Morgan makes clear. The Revolution, and the bringing into being of a new nation, provided opportunities for giant-hood, and pressures toward it, not matched in the more settled days of a Republic already in motion, grinding along over the ordinary bumps and ditches of historical life. A Thomas Jefferson, one hundred years later, if he missed the Civil War, might very well have spent his life, as he regularly insisted he wanted to, in the quiet of his books, his observations of plant life and farming, his devices and his gadgets, and his correspondence with scientists and learned folk in many countries, playing the violin in the evening. Henry Adams, to reverse the times to be compared, was surely no less distinguished, at least intellectually, than his famous forebears, but he was put on this earth in much less propitious times for top-rank fame—for well-placed achievement—and seems to have been accompanied throughout a life of genuine accomplishment by a kind of brooding, regretful Miniver-Cheevy apology for not measuring up to the Adams standard. And James Madison—now to reverse the temporal comparison once again—in some future day, though he might well have been a considerable political thinker, could hardly have been the major success in practical politics that he was in his own day.

Madison was a small, slight, reserved, bookish, sickly, and/or hypochondriacal man, perhaps a little on the prim side. Jefferson liked to josh his friend by quoting the statement about him, intended as praise, made by his formidable mentor, the president of Princeton, the Reverend John Witherspoon, which has followed Madison for almost two centuries now. During the "whole time" that Madison was under his tutelage at Princeton—so went the story Jefferson would tell—Witherspoon never knew Madison "to do, or say, an improper thing." Madison's twentieth-century biographers are pleased to have found some execrable doggerel he wrote for the Whig Society of Princeton and evidence that he liked—and even participated in—slightly daring jokes in private company (some that slightly embarrassed Jefferson) to even the score on this point after all these years.

Thought by many (not all) to be uncharming, Madison was apparently not nearly so attractive to the opposite sex (as it used to be put) as was the energetic extrovert Alexander Hamilton. In the one youthful amorous interest that the biographers know about he lost out to a more forthright suitor, and did not marry the widow who became the famous Dolley of the White House until he was forty-three. Young Madison—perhaps you could say old Madison, too—was close to being what college students of a later day would call, not favorably, a "grind," our first graduate student to make it to the White House. A foreign visitor during Madison's stay there said that the president—who always wore black—looked like a schoolmaster dressed for a funeral. All of his career he was called, whether in dismissal or in praise, a "scholar." Burdened by a formidable parent as well as a formidable Princeton tutor, he signed himself "James Madison, Junior" until he was past fifty.

His voice, in that age of orators, was "inconveniently feeble," so low during his second inaugural address "that scarcely a word could be distinguished." "The members, lest they should lose a word, were accustomed to gather around him." Sometimes he would persuade a more commanding presence to offer up his proposals, as we have seen him do in Williamsburg in 1776. On other occasions there were other stratagems. In 1788, in the very important Virginia convention on the ratification of the federal Constitution, Madison, the great authority fresh from the Philadelphia Convention, was to lead the forces arguing in favor of it. Early in the proceedings, however, Patrick Henry, who was strongly opposed, seized an opportunity to spring loose from close logic and clause-by-clause analysis—the sort of thing he was not at home with—and to spread himself instead, for the better part of a day, in the full-organ oratory that had made him Virginia's best-known citizen. He echoed in his denunciation of the proposed Constitution all the speeches he had been making against governments for more than twenty years. Madison's pro-ratification colleagues—one pictures them eyeing each other uneasily as Henry rose on wings of eloquence—decided not to send him up in that spot immediately after Henry. Instead he came on with quiet intellect at a later time.

Taken all in all, "Jemmy" (as his father called him) would not in any later age have been very promising material to face the voters as a candidate for public office, high or low, or to exercise his will at the highest level in trying times—wartime—as chief executive of the nation, or to serve in all the other ways he did in the sober and realistic task of shaping the government of a great people. So you can say that, like his colleagues among the original American heroes, he received an enormous boost toward gianthood by his judicious choice of a time in which to live. Still, the occasion is by no means the whole of the making of such giants; they must rise to the occasion, as not everybody in such circumstances does, and have the moral and intellectual stuff in them to do so, as not everybody does. In this American case, perhaps to an unusual degree, the embryonic giants helped to *make* the occasion. Later Americans generally have not realized that this was as true of James Madison, in his domain, as it was of Jefferson, Washington, and John Adams, in theirs. James Madison represented the concentrate of that conscious and continuous act of deliberate intellectual formation that was this nation's unusual beginning.

Recent historians—Bernard Bailyn and Gordon Wood in particular—have shown what a flurry of writing and arguing, of pamphleteering, preaching, and correspondence led up to the American Revolution, and then to the "Creation of the American Republic": Almost every American pen was at work. An aspect of that articulate excitement was the deliberate intellectual effort by some to go back, or down, or up, to first principles, to the very core and foundation of government, and in particular of "republican" government. Madison's work was the epitome of that effort.

Jefferson's constant bookishness and lifelong exploration of the foundations of liberty are well known. John Adams read books, too, especially on government, history, politics, and law, and produced his own theoretical treatises on government. But Madison may have been the most distinctly, or most nearly exclusively, bookish, and carefully reflective, of them all.

There is something moving in the picture of the still young Madison—he was thirty-six—earnestly boning up for the Federal Convention of 1787, surveying all the examples of constitutional republics across Western history. He may not have been exactly the "Father of the Constitution"—a sobriquet already applied to him in his own later lifetime, which he of course rejected—but he crammed for the making of it, was the most fully prepared for the debates on it, drafted the initial plan that was the basis of it, endangered his health by taking full daily notes on the forming of it, missed not a session of the Convention that wrote it, was its leading defender in the most important state to ratify it, and became in his numbers in *The Federalist* the most influential interpreter of it.

Despite Henry's oratorical prowess, and the opposition of others like George Mason, Madison *did* thereafter lead to victory the forces favoring ratification in the closely balanced Virginia convention on the federal Constitution. And, despite his deficiencies in "personality," color, decibels, metaphors, and bulk, he achieved by his reasoning and his work many other such victories as well. With careful organization and strenuous exertion, he so thoroughly trounced his opposition in the fiercely contested race for a seat in the First Congress that he thereafter had an unassailably safe seat, through three subsequent elections: not bad for an unpromising politician. John Marshall, the future chief justice, who was usually an opponent of Madison's, nevertheless said of him that if eloquence included "persuasion by convincing, Mr. Madison was the most eloquent man I ever heard." He persuaded by his thorough preparation, his layers of reading, his logical powers; he made his mark not by his tongue or his throat, or by his presence, but by his pen and his brain and his diligence.

It may be the distinctly intellectual cast to his contribution to this Republic that has left Madison rather in the shade as later popular opinion, requiring more romance, developed its heroes. He did hold an immense and almost unbroken lifelong sequence of public offices; he overcame the youthful characteristics listed above to become an expert practical politician, especially within conventions, assemblies, committees of the whole, and legislative bodies. But "legislator" is not a very compelling role to Americans even though their public life depends upon it. Madison did not have the dash of Alexander Hamilton, nor did he represent so distinct an emphasis and ideology; he did not fight in the Revolutionary War, or compose many ringing phrases. He made himself into the thoughtful scholar-statesman and embodiment of single-minded and selfless public service that the Republic needs, but by and large has not known that it needs, and has not nurtured or acknowledged.

The neglect of Madison has been reflected, at least until recently, in the skimpy pile of books about him. Of course he has not been paid anything approaching the intricate, proliferating, worldwide scholarly and biographical treatment accorded Jefferson. A large mid-nineteenth-century biography by a Virginia neighbor and fellow politician of Madison's, William Cabell Rives, stood rather lonely on the shelves until Brant's twentieth-century undertaking, a six-volume treatment published between 1941 and 1961, which may not be quite as thoughtful or as careful as its subject but probably precludes any other full-dress treatment for a long time. There is now, however, a good fat one-volume biography, by Ralph Ketcham of Syracuse University, published in 1971, which in addition to its other virtues has something of the interest in political reflection that Madison had. There is also a good short biography, also from 1971, in the Twayne series on "Rulers and Statesmen of the World," by Harold Schultz of the University of Vermont, which makes a striking virtue out of the necessity of utmost compression. In his first chapter Schultz artfully arranged an impressive armload of quotations about Madison from his contemporaries at the time of his death to give a rounded, concrete, balanced—of course it should be balanced—but in the end favorable and persuasive picture of Madison as "A Good and a Great Man" (the chapter title, taken from a eulogy by a Virginia politician and friend; Madison seems to have been one of those all too rare persons in whom goodness managed to accompany greatness). But the books by Ketcham and Schultz—from which, along with Brant's biography, much in these pages is taken—are not available in paperback. If the reader will try the largest bookstore, and perhaps even library, in his town he will find multitudinous volumes about the more glamorous national heroes but probably none of these biographies of Madison. There may be more available books about Lincoln's jokes than there are about James Madison's entire career.

There is an edition of Madison's papers now under way, published by the universities of Chicago and Virginia, with valuable introductions and headnotes, which has worked its way up to the 1790s and fourteen volumes. There are still thirty-five years of Madison's life, and many volumes, to go. The editor of the papers of Alexander Hamilton once humorously remarked, according to Ketcham, that he had considered dedicating his project to Aaron Burr, without whom it could not have been completed. The editors of the Madison papers were rendered no such convenient service; their man lived on and lived on, for eighty-five years, and kept producing paper until the end, the great bulk of it dealing with public questions, more single-mindedly than with the wide-ranging Jefferson. This useful project—also drawn upon in these pages—may change the picture in specialized worlds, but one doubts that "Jemmy" will ever catch on with the broad public. One might say his wife is a larger figure in American legend than he is.

To return for a moment to the galaxy, and to the two particular stars of the most interest here: Among the Founders the closest friendship and collaboration was that between Jefferson and Madison. One good book about Madison deals with Jefferson, too, and with their joint efforts. It has the subtitle *The Great Collaboration*, and was written by the late Adrienne Koch, who wrote well about Madison in other books, too; she gave vent to the lamentations about the neglect of Madison that are echoed here. The Jefferson-Madison collaboration she describes, though it covered the gamut of government and five decades, was particularly potent on the subject of religious liberty. On this issue the names of these two Virginia friends are woven through all the subsequent history of this matter down to, and very much including, the U.S. Supreme Court cases of our own day. Their convictions overlapped almost completely, and indeed were in part formed by reciprocal interchange, with Madison by no means a junior partner (though he was eight years younger than Jefferson).

If we graph the founding giants around the center point of Jefferson, we find that Hamilton became an adversary in the starting up of American political parties and divergent ideologies. Washington, a man of an older generation, with his prestige—the highest of them all, of course—already in the bank, tried to remain aloof, but tilted away from "Jeffersonian" positions toward what became the Federalist ones. The universally respected Benjamin Franklin was much closer in spirit to Jefferson than Washington was, and in Paris overlapped with, and was succeeded by, Jefferson. ("So you are Dr. Franklin's replacement?" "No one can replace him; I am only his successor.") But Franklin died in 1790 and was also really a man of another generation. John Adams, at first a friend and collaborator of Jefferson in the heady days of the American Revolution, became then almost an enemy, so opposed were the two men in their responses to the French Revolution, the Alien and Sedition Acts and other events of Adams's own presidency, the so-called revolution of 1800 and Jefferson's succession to the presidency (Adams appointing the midnight judges and grumpily leaving town before Jefferson took office), and Jefferson's two terms. (In old age, when the flying fur from those disputes had settled, Adams became a friend of Jefferson again, in particular an epistolary friend, and even managed with incredible neatness to die on the same day as his old adversary, exactly fifty years after the Declaration, on July 4, 1826.) Madison, on the other hand, and uniquely among these original American heroes, was a steady friend and full collaborator of Jefferson's throughout the whole of their long lives, and was asked by Jefferson near the end of his life to "take care of me when dead."

The two of them, well situated, plant their conception of religious liberty in the original soil of the American Republic. They stand out from the others on this issue more clearly than they do on the broader matter of the creation of the American Republic, in all its parts and stages. On that broader matter the emphasis upon their collaboration may obscure important differences. Madison, at home in the late 1780s, was a central intellectual source of the ideas embodied in the Constitution, his version of which he stated in The Federalist. Jefferson, in Paris, and of a different cast of mind, was somewhat outside all of that, and had important reservations and criticism of it. But on religious liberty their collaboration would appear to be complete, and also distinctive.

Though of course we may be grateful that it has his stamp, in the

Declaration of Independence Thomas Jefferson, writing for a five-man committee and at the behest of a Continental Congress, produced, as Adams later grumpily remarked and Jefferson freely admitted, very much the common currency of the group. In his draft of the Virginia Statute for Religious Freedom, on the other hand, Jefferson was unequivocally calling upon his own distinct ideas, in sharp contrast with many, for a time most, others. Likewise, though Madison might be said to be the most important single figure shaping the republican political theory of the Constitution, that theory, too, was "the work of many heads and many hands" (as Madison said of the Constitution). But in the maneuvering for disestablishment of religion in Virginia in 1785, and in composing the *Memorial and Remonstrance*, Madison was opposed by many of Virginia's best-known figures, and would have been opposed by leaders in other colonies. It has already been suggested that it was not probable that the sweeping principles of the Virginia statute would have come from another colony—New England had established churches still—or from others of the major Founders. We may then dramatize the situation a little to say that on this issue, as not on others, Madison and Jefferson brought off something of an intellectual coup.

YOUNG MADISON

Let us trace something of Madison's background, since he is so much less well known than his great friend and collaborator. Madison had ties not only to the amiable Virginia Anglicanism, and the Enlightenment, as Jefferson did, but also, as already noted in these pages, to energetically dissenting Protestantism, as Jefferson did not.

He was born and raised in a moderately well-fixed and moderately old Virginia family that owned the largest spread of land in Orange County, in the Virginia piedmont. His father, James Madison, Sr., was a vestryman and his mother a devout Anglican all of her long life. (Like her son, she was sickly and perhaps hypochondriacal, and outlived most of the healthy people.) His second cousin—Madison was very well supplied with relatives and good connections, which mattered then, and matters now, in that state—who had the same name yet again, became, after the Revolution, the first bishop of the new Episcopal church in the new state of Virginia.

This James Madison—the eventual bishop—was only two years older than the other one, the president-to-be, and these cousins with the same name were friends all their lives. The ecclesiastical Madison attended the College of William and Mary, an institution of which he would eventually become president, and while an undergraduate was spokesman for the liberal side in an early conflict over religious liberty. He became a friend and admirer of Thomas Jefferson; he seems perhaps to have been more interested in scientific than in religious topics; his republicanism went so far as to produce a sermon on the *Republic* (as opposed to the *Kingdom*) of God. The political James Madison may have imbibed some liberalism from his family's version of Anglicanism, as well as from the Presbyterians up north and the Baptists next door and the French and English books from across the seas.

The tutors for the James Madison who was to be president were both Anglican clergymen. Indeed, virtually all the teachers he ever had were clergymen, which was not unusual then, and were also apparently very good teachers, which was unusual then as now. Of the first of them, Donald Robertson, a learned Scotsman who conducted a little school to which Madison was sent for five years, Madison was to say later: "All that I have been in life I owe to that man." He got from him, among other things, a grounding in Greek and Latin and classical learning. The second of these clerical teachers, Thomas Martin, who lived at the Madisons' house and was a tutor specifically for James, Jr. for two years, was a young man fresh from the enthusiasm of having been graduated from the College of New Jersey, the New Side Presbyterian stronghold. The influence of this tutor may have been one of the reasons for the important decision the Madison family made to send Jemmy north to Princeton, instead of to William and Mary.

It does not, of course, always matter where one goes to college, or whether one goes at all—thousands of Americans two hundred years later emerge from college unscathed, and not many of the other Founders were much shaped by the experience, if they went through it—but for Madison, by all reports and inferences, it mattered a great deal that he went to the College of New Jersey and went there at the time he did.

Princeton was a kind of West Point for dissenting Presbyterianism, opposed to ecclesiastical and political authority, Whiggish and then "patriot" or "rebel" in political inclination. Samuel Davies, the most famous dissenting preacher in Virginia, a founder of the famous Hanover Presbytery and a leader among the New Lights of the Awakening among Presbyterians, had briefly been a president of the New Jersey college. The new president (in 1768) was the redoubtable John Witherspoon, who had brought his forthright Calvinist but Whiggish principles and his opposition to church establishments across from Scotland to the New World, where he fitted right into the great revolutionary struggle then about to take place.

Princeton under John Witherspoon had this stated goal: "in the instruction of the Youth, care is to be taken to cherish the spirit of liberty, and free enquiry; and not only to permit, but even to encourage their right of private judgment, without presuming to dictate with an air of infallibility, or demanding an implicit assent to the decisions of the preceptor." The historian Richard Morris, reporting this, exclaims: "One might imagine that these objectives had been dictated by rebellious American college students of our own age, not by the college establishment itself!"

Witherspoon was to be not only the president of the then little college, and a pervasive influence there while Madison matriculated, but also Madison's own tutor in his senior year and in the six months he stayed on after graduation to be what today is called a graduate student. Witherspoon and Madison would continue to be intermittently associated in the events of the Revolution, serving together and collaborating sometimes—opposed to each other occasionally—in legislative undertakings; Witherspoon would become a signer of the Declaration of Independence and a potent name in the history of American Presbyterianism. Nor was Witherspoon the only influence in the anti-Tory direction at Princeton; other faculty members were to be active in revolutionary events, and Madison's classmates—the poet Philip Freneau and the novelist Hugh Henry Brackenridge among them—shared his developing republican political views.

Princeton was thus a center of intellectual and also political excitement—the excitement of a fresh intellectual movement, with practical results—of the sort that comes about now and then: Cambridge University for Puritan England, the London School of Economics for the British socialists, the Harvard Law School of Felix Frankfurter for the New Deal. These places send their missionaries out to the unenlightened reaches of the world to spread the message from the thrill and illumination that has been received in the classrooms, reading, discussions, and late-night arguments of the intellectual home base.

But these "rebels" in the sober Dr. Witherspoon's Princeton were rebels of an unusually "responsible" sort. Ketcham says that Princeton was not only a nursery for ideas undercutting the prevailing (English) government; it was also a "school for statesmen trained to seek freedom and ordered government through the pursuit of virtue." James Madison was to become such a statesman.

Madison, thus, had the best formal education of any of the major founding fathers, and made good use of it; it was more important to him than to any other. And much of it was in the context of an antiestablishment Protestantism. It gave him a knowledge of and sympathy with the tradition of dissent that Jefferson did not have and few of the other major figures in the nation's founding would have.

It is the custom in discussing church and state in the United States to presume those two traditions we have already seen in Virginia, the tradition of the Enlightenment on the one hand and the tradition of antiestablishment Protestant Christianity on the other, to be quite separate. But they were not always so separate as they appeared to be in Virginia, if one puts the Baptist-Methodist "counterculture" of "mechanic preachers" over against the educated rationalists like Jefferson. Nor were they always then as separate as they would appear later, when the secular currents had left anything too distinctly religious over on an isolated sandbar in the great river of intellectual life, and American Christianity had lost its intellectual punch. It was not always so in those days. There was a Christian Enlightenment alongside the secular Enlightenment. John Witherspoon, for example, was himself a product at once of Calvinism and of what has come to be called the Scottish Enlightenment. He was, in his own way, an opponent of established churches. Princeton itself was a mixture of these ideas.

Thus the conscientious Madison, despite the evidence of absence of a religious interest in his maturity, had acquired in his youth from multitudinous learned clergymen a knowledge of the Christian intellectual tradition such that an historian on the Madison papers project could describe him (by perhaps a not very exacting standard) as "probably America's most theologically knowledgeable President." In his retirement he was able to compose a list of books on theology for the University of Virginia library, and to show considerable knowledge still of the Church fathers and of mainstream orthodoxy, although of course with Voltaire and Joseph Priestley alongside to provide the antidote. Alas, some modern and severe interpretations of the radical separation of church and state, claiming the authority of James Madison, have made it difficult for later generations to acquire the kind of education from which James Madison himself benefited.

Madison's discussion, never extensive, of his own religion would later fall away into total silence. The only hints that come, after his career as a statesman was launched, were a couple of guarded private conversations from which his interlocutors concluded that he had sympathy with deistic, liberal, unitarian positions and was not strictly guided by "Biblical religion." But because he was silent on the subject and perhaps a little cagey, as others in something like his position have been known to turn cagey, Madison's religious attitudes did not become a known public position or a subject of argument or dispute, and he was never subjected, as his friend Jefferson repeatedly was, to attacks upon him as an unorthodox "infidel" who was a menace to the religious or moral foundations of the nation. Somewhere in the substructure of his being, however, there must have been memories of Witherspoon's Princeton. And he became, as we have seen, a hero to some passionately believing dissenters as a defender of full religious liberty.

The young James Madison—to return to him now as he was just out of college, missing its excitements and wishing he were back among them—often felt ill, even to despairing of leading a "long and healthy life," and expecting before long to exchange "Time for Eternity." He was at loose ends, rattling around at home in Orange with his father and mother and siblings, undertaking to "instruct" his brothers and sisters in "the first rudiments of literature," and wondering what he would do with his life—a situation not unknown to other young people just out of college.

He began then, in 1772, a correspondence—a lifeline to the old days—with his best college friend, William Bradford, of a Philadelphia printing family, about Life, Eternity, and Human Happiness; about their reading (Madison asked Bradford to procure for him books on religious toleration); about the writings and doings of "The Doctor" (Witherspoon); about the news of their "old Nassovian friends" (that is, Princetonians; Nassau Hall was Princeton's one building; many of these Nassovians of course were clergymen); and, of particular interest, about their choices of professions.

The earliest letters, in 1772 and 1773, had much sober, youthful philosophizing and moralizing, with traces of a piety that later disappeared—the imprint of Presbyterian Princeton and of the good doctor. When young Bradford wrote about the temptations and uncertainties of his future, young Madison responded with a gravity worthy of Witherspoon himself: "I hope you are sufficiently guarded against the allurements and varieties that beset us on our first entrance on the theater of Life.... a watchful eye must be kept on ourselves lest while we are building ideal monuments of Renown and Bliss here we do neglect to have our names enrolled in the Annals of Heaven. . . . Pray do not suffer those impertinent fops that abound in every city to divert you." About the dubious tendency of "the present State of literature" and the "choicest Books," he wrote, very much in the tones of the old doctor, "I find them loose in their principles and encouragers of free enquiry even such as destroys the most essential Truths, Enemies to serious religion." (The editors of the Madison papers felt it necessary to enter a disclaimer in a footnote saying that this sentence is at odds with the later, civil-libertarian Madison.)

Bradford asked Madison to advise him about the profession he should follow. In the view of both men, the top theoretical choice (for somebody else, anyway) was the ministry. Bradford ruled it out for himself, even though "in my opinion a divine may be the most useful as well as the most happy member of society." Madison responded: "I cannot . . . suppress thus much of my advice on that head that you would always keep the Ministry obliquely in View whatever your profession be. This will lead you to cultivate an acquaintance occasionally with the most sublime of all Sciences. . . . " Madison means theology or "Divinity," which he himself "cultivated" for a time in those postcollege years. "I have sometimes thought," he went on to say, "there could not be a stronger testimony in favor of Religion" than that able people like his friend, "rising in reputation and wealth," should "publicly . . . declare their unsatisfactoriness by becoming fervent Advocates in the cause of Christ, & I wish you may give your Evidence in this way."

When James Madison wrote this letter, in September of 1772, he was just a year out of Princeton. He was not thereafter to recommend to friends that they become "fervent Advocates in the cause of Christ"; he himself became, instead, an advocate, fervent in his unfervent way, in the cause of republican government.

Both Bradford and Madison would, while insisting on its importance, put aside "Divinity" as a vocation for themselves. They would both also resist the temptations of belles lettres. On this point—not wasting too much time on literature—one can hear again the accent of Witherspoon, very different in its purposeful and self-improving spirit from that of a Virginia gentleman. "I myself used to have too great a hankering after those amusing studies," wrote Madison, after commending Bradford for putting mere literature aside. "Poetry wit and Criticism Romances Plays &c captivated me much: but I begin to discover that they deserve but a moderate portion of a mortal's Time, and that some-

thing more substantial more durable more profitable befits a riper Age."
(Madison had by now attained the ripe age of twenty-three.)

As the correspondence moves to the end of 1773, political affairs
appear for the first time: "I enclose you an account of the Destruction
of the Tea at Boston," Bradford wrote to Madison on Christmas Day,
1773, mentioning also a "more gentle but full as effectual a method of
avoiding the duty" in Philadelphia. A few months earlier young Madison had written: "I do not meddle with Politicks." Now, however, in
January of 1774, he responds, "I congratulate you on your heroic proceedings in Philada. with respect to the Tea. I wish Boston may conduct
matters with as much discretion as they seem to do with boldness."
After several more sentences he exclaims, "But away with politicks!"
Politicks, however, did not go away.

The professions considered in the correspondence between these two
earnest young Princetonians, divinity having been praised and set aside,
included the law (full of moral dangers, they both agreed), "Merchan-
dize" (even more moral dangers), and "Physic" (neither showed much
desire to go into that).

William Bradford, helped no doubt by the sweep of history, decided
upon the law, and politics, as his profession. Though he died still young,
in 1794, he was to serve as attorney general both of the State of Pennsylvania and, in Washington's cabinet, of the new United States. James
Madison, also with the help of the times, made a similar career decision.
One can sense in his letters the forming, out of the earnest Princeton
materials, of a role in the world that has something of the high seriousness of purpose of the ministerial vocation that many of his classmates followed, transferred now to the realm of statecraft. He was to
meddle uninterruptedly with politics, with a rare and single-minded
devotion, for sixty years. "He never contrasted the pleasures of private
life with the pains of public duty," wrote Harold Schultz. "Jefferson
could think of reading, study, and philosophical conversation as very
pleasurable substitutes for the burdens of public office....No such
thought was ever put on paper by his friend Madison."

In 1774 the correspondence began to carry more and more material
about the rapidly unfolding colonial rebellion. Up in Philadelphia, Bradford was to be a good correspondent on those subjects; among other
things, his family's business printed the records of the First Continental
Congress. Even before the exchange about the Tea Party, on December
1, 1773, Madison was writing to Bradford that "the principles & modes
of Government are too important to be disregarded by an Inquisitive

mind." As an inquisitive mind himself, he asked Bradford for his reading plan on that subject, and then asked him also when he had "obtained sufficient insight into the constitution of your Country," to send him a draft of Pennsylvania's government and laws, and in particular—a harbinger of what is to come—"the extent of your religious Toleration." He propounded a query: "Is an Ecclesiastical Establishment absolutely necessary to support civil society in a supream Government? & how far is it hurtful to a dependent state?" Young Madison did not expect immediate answers, but suggested that Bradford consult "experienced Lawyers and Politicians" as well as books. Thus already, in December 1773, while still twenty-two, long before he met Thomas Jefferson, and somewhat before his encounter with the persecution of the neighbor-hood Baptists, he was starting a serious inquiry into religious toleration, the first social-political topic to engage him. Presumably that interest followed in part from the considerable presence of the subject in With-erspoon, with his strong antagonism to "sacerdotal tyranny," and in Princeton, with its atmosphere interweaving evangelical religion with religious liberty and with political liberty, too, generating in Madison's and Witherspoon's day a considerable supply of embryonic rebels, pa-triots, and, when the time came, participants in the Constitutional Convention in Philadelphia—nine from Princeton, to five from Yale and three from Harvard.

In his letter of January 24, 1774, in which Madison responded to Bradford's comment on the Boston Tea Party, he ventured a substantive political judgment of a very large kind. It appears to be his first on any of the great topics then agitating the colonies. About Boston's perfor-mance in the matter of the tea he was cautiously pedestrian and middle-of-the-road. But then he came out with a more far-reaching generali-zation in a field he had evidently thought about.

> If the Church of England had been the established and general Religion in all the Northern Colonies as it has been among us here...it is clear to me that slavery and Subjection might and would have been gradually insinuated among us. Union of Re-ligious Sentiments begets a surprising confidence and Eccle-siastical Establishments tend to great ignorance and Corruption all of which facilitate the Execution of mischievous Projects.

Madison's firmest and earliest convictions, on matters of government in a revolutionary moment, had to do with the danger of ecclesiastical establishments and of those mischievous projects; for him, as not for

Jefferson or others of the Founders, that appeared to be the beginning of his republican and revolutionary conviction.

And now, toward the end of that same letter, in January 1774, Madison referred to the episode of the persecuted Baptists, which has acquired in Madison's own legend something of the place held, in the later, mightier legend of Lincoln, by the story of his seeing slaves on a southern trip. Here is what Madison wrote to Bradford:

> that diabolical Hell conceived principle of persecution rages.... and to their infamy the Clergy can furnish their Quota of Imps for such business. This vexes me the most of any thing whatever. There are at this time in the adjacent county not less than 5 or 6 well meaning men in close Gaol for publishing their religious Sentiments which in the main are very orthodox.... I have squabbled and scolded and abused and ridiculed so long about it, to so little purpose that I am without common patience. So I leave you to pity me and pray for Liberty and Conscience to revive among us.

The Baptist preachers in Culpeper County were doing nothing more than, or different from, what a number of Madison's friends from the College of New Jersey were doing: trying to bring a religious renewal to the sleepy Anglican churches of the South. Though Madison showed no discernible temptation to do that kind of thing himself, being put off a bit even then by "enthusiasts," still he knew what it was all about from personal friendships and his exposure in New Jersey as well as Virginia. One of the topics in the Princeton graduation exercises the year before Madison graduated, for just one example, was a support for the proposition that "every religious profession, which does not by its principles disturb the public peace, ought to be tolerated by a wise state."

Madison's initiatives then and later brought him favorable notice with the Baptists and other dissenters, to the point that he became an ally of theirs—one might almost say a spokesman. Eventually an important part of his political constituency was to be furnished by these dissenting groups in Virginia, and he came to count on their support. There may therefore have come to be mixed in Madison's principles just a trace of that political realism—men, as he said, are not angels— of which he himself produced a classic analysis. In him as in the nation, on this point, expediency may have reinforced principle, while principle helped itself by pointing to necessity. But he began by working out the principle, and having it made pungent by experience.

MADISON ON RELIGIOUS LIBERTY:
THE MEMORIAL AND REMONSTRANCE

Anson Phelps Stokes, canon of Washington Cathedral and sometime secretary of Yale, produced in 1950 a comprehensive three-volume omnium gatherum called *Church and State in the United States*, giving this subject the full treatment. His volumes—which stretch from the "major old world influences," beginning with the Decalogue, the Hebrew Commonwealth, and the Prophets, in volume I, all the way to the proposed Social Security benefits for church employees, in volume III—are filled throughout with numbered lists, honor rolls, and a gentle celebratory tone. They are arranged in a complicated way that makes them hard to use and impossible to read straight through. Nevertheless, anyone who works in this field must be grateful to Canon Stokes for the prodigious labor of putting together his monumental collection of materials and facts. Though he cited long lists of persons, events, and movements contributing to the American tradition, when he reached James Madison he used a superlative: "our greatest constructive legal statesman in this field."

That sweeping encomium would not be much disputed. Madison is the most influential individual shaping this tradition, and it is a tradition that indeed has been *shaped*. It has in it less of mindless growth and inertia, and more of deliberate human contrivance, than do most human institutions.

Madison uniquely had a central role in each of four clinching points in making the American tradition:

First, as we have seen, in amending the article on religion in the Virginia Declaration of Rights, in June 1776, to assert the equal right of every human being to free exercise of religious conscience;

Second, in composing the most pungent of all American argumentative documents on this subject, the rhetorical equivalent, one might say, of *Common Sense* in this field, his 1785 *Memorial and Remonstrance Against Religious Assessments*, of which more in a moment;

Third, after the popular outcry created in part by that document, in resurrecting Jefferson's draft for the Virginia statute and steering it through the Assembly and into Virginia law, in 1785–86, as described above; and

Fourth, in proposing and drafting the first amendments to the Constitution that were to become the Bill of Rights, including the religion clauses of the First Amendment, in the first Congress under the new federal Constitution in 1789. He was a prime mover in the complicated congressional politics out of which came the language of the First Amendment, as judges and lawyers refine and distinguish and squeeze and expand and chop and blend it down to the present day.

The first three of these events have already been described in the story of the Virginia statute. Madison's public career really started when, a little over a year after the firing of the shots at Lexington and Concord, he had been chosen as one of the two delegates from Orange County to that Virginia convention in Williamsburg in May and June of 1776. He was only twenty-five years old and not yet established, apart from his father's reputation and his many good family connections. He was, however, well provided in those regards, and it was not surprising that he and an uncle of his should be picked by the folk of the sparsely populated piedmont county to make the journey over to the tidewater to this gathering. As a novice and a young and diffident man he did not, so far as we know, play much of a role in the general proceedings of the convention, except on the one point: substituting "free exercise" for George Mason's "toleration" in the way we have described. In his account Canon Stokes exclaimed, "For insistence on this point in the Virginia Declaration Madison should be remembered with gratitude by every earnest Jew, Catholic, Protestant, and member of every other sect in the United States." He could have added, every nonbeliever, too.

The theory that underlay Madison's activities in all these episodes is given its fullest expression in the second, the composition, nine years later, of his *Memorial and Remonstrance Against Religious Assessments*. Madison, now thirty-four and an experienced politician, having returned to the Virginia battles after four years at the Continental Congress in Philadelphia, felt at first, by the spring of 1785, with the tide of opinion changing and Patrick Henry out of the picture (elevated

97

to the governor's chair), that he did not need to write a petition himself as a part of that summer's exertions against the Henry bill. But his fellow opponents persuaded him that he should do it. So he retired to his home in Orange County in the summer of 1785 and there, among his books, produced his famous (now famous, then anonymous) *Remonstrance.*

To write it he drew upon arguments he had given against the Patrick Henry bill in the debate in the Virginia Assembly in December of 1784. The notes he used for that debate, as we have said, are included in the Madison papers. He drew also on his reading and thinking on this subject going back to the days of his correspondence with William Bradford, and to the College of New Jersey, and even before.

The result of his effort is now regularly accorded extravagant praise. When Anson Phelps Stokes's story comes to this potent Madisonian production it rises once again to a laudatory interjection: " ... it [Madison's *Remonstrance*] must be considered one of the truly epoch-making documents in the history of American Church-State separation; as impressive and convincing today as it was over a century and a half ago." Madison's biographer Brant was even more emphatic: "The remonstrance against religious assessments continues to stand, not merely through the years but through the centuries, as the most powerful defense of religious liberty ever written in America." Ralph Ketcham wrote that it is a statement of freedom "worthy of Locke, Milton, or Mill." And when at the start of the modern string of Supreme Court cases on the "establishment clause," Justice Wiley Rutledge wanted to dissent from the "breach," as he saw it, in the by-then celebrated "wall" of separation in the New Jersey bus case of 1947 he reprinted, as part of his dissent, the entire text of this document from Madison.

It has since then reverberated in the twentieth century a good deal more than it did in the eighteenth. Madison had not signed his name to it—that was not the way one did this remonstrating—and, according to the headnote in the Madison papers, was slow, coy, perhaps reluctant, to acknowledge his authorship until many years later, when the battle was won and the smoke had cleared. In the twentieth century, though, it is of course Madison's authorship—now much underlined—that gives it what is taken to be its particular importance. Here, it is said or implied, here in this *Remonstrance* from 1785, one can find the full expression of the views of the Father of the Constitution and the author, more or less, of the First Amendment. The document, given thus a retroactive elevation by the later activities of its author, is therefore presented as the decisive expression of the American tradition.

. . .

But let us look at it, if we can, without these twentieth-century preoccupations. What does one find when one reads it? A work of relentless advocacy, certainly, but also conceptual power.

Madison did fire away, full blast, not only at the General Assessment bill, but at anything like it and the principles behind it. He mobilized his artillery on this subject, put together across his adult lifetime. The brief preamble says that the proposed bill is an "abuse of power," and, in the Enlightenment manner of the revolutionary period, that the petition will "declare the reasons" the petitioners oppose it. Madison then proceeds to give those reasons a thorough declaring.

He sets forth the arguments in fifteen numbered paragraphs, introduced by the phrase "We remonstrate against the said Bill." Each numbered item then begins with the word "because," denouncing state support of religion in this, that, and the other way, to this audience, that one, and the other one, because..., because..., because, pouring forth a fusillade from his rhetorical battery, carrying the matter all the way to first principles and to extreme applications. The intellectual foundation of the *Remonstrance* is the philosophy of natural rights, but in a late-eighteenth-century American colonists' "republican" setting that made it differ somewhat from its English antecedents; it borrows the terms of "the late revolution," and the enthusiasm aroused by that cause, to attack all state support of religion.

The document reflects throughout the particular ideology, and the remembered fervor, of the Revolution. The colonists had come through the ideological pamphlet wars since 1763, up to the utopian moment of the seventies and independence, over the hump of wartime troubles down into the realistic complexities of trying to set up their governments, and govern. In the most quoted of all his arguments, the third, Madison specifically refers to an ideological characteristic that developed, as one discovers in Bernard Bailyn's *The Ideological Origins of the American Revolution*, in the colonists' adoption of radical Whig ideology: "...it is proper," Madison wrote,

> to take alarm at the first experiment on our liberties. We hold this prudent jealousy to be the first duty of Citizens, and one of the noblest characteristics of the late Revolution. The free men of America did not wait till usurped power had strengthened itself by exercise, and entangled the question in precedents. They saw all the consequences in the principle, and they

avoided the consequences by denying the principle. We revere this lesson too much soon to forget it.

This abrupt extrapolation from small evidence, this taking alarm, this wariness about "precedents" and emerging patterns in what "usurped power" was doing—think of the rather extravagant indictment of King George in the Declaration of Independence—was one of the features of the ideology Bailyn extracted from the revolutionary pamphlets. Now Madison applied it to the General Assessment bill and church and state. And at the end of this third argument he put in two specific echoes of the Revolution: the "three pence only" that citizens should not be forced to contribute to any religious establishment is the same amount of the duty on the tea dumped into Boston's harbor. And, in explaining at the end that an authority which can force one to contribute to an establishment may "force him to conform to any other establishment in all cases whatsoever . . . ," Madison borrowed a phrase, offensive to the colonists, that Parliament had used in 1766 in the Declaratory Act asserting its right to make laws binding the colonists: "in all cases whatsoever."

The document begins and ends with references to the Virginia Declaration of Rights, which had by that time come to be enshrined in the consciousness of the newly independent Virginians. In particular Madison cites Article Sixteen, which, as a young man, he had himself helped to shape. In "Because" number one, starting off the argument, he quotes this part of it: "Religion, or the duty which we owe to our Creator . . . can be directed only by reason and conviction, not by force or violence." And in the fifteenth argument, concluding the whole bombardment, he draws upon exactly that part of the religion article of the Virginia Declaration that he himself had written:

> 15. Because finally, "The equal right of every citizen to the free exercise of his Religion according to the dictates of conscience" is held by the same tenure with all our other rights. . . .

He went on to argue, in this concluding shot, that the fundamental rights asserted in the Virginia Declaration were bound inextricably together: Either the will of the legislature is the sole authority, and may "sweep away" all the rights enumerated in the Declaration, or it has no such authority, and may do no such sweeping, and must respect then all of the rights, including the right of religious conscience, which are "enumerated with equal solemnity, or rather studied emphasis" alongside the others. These rights, said Madison, stand or fall together; either we must say that the legislature in the "plenitude" of "authority" may "control the freedom of the press, may abolish Trial by Jury, may swallow up the Executive and Judiciary Powers of the State; nay that they may despoil us of our very right of suffrage, and erect themselves into an independent and hereditary Assembly" (Madison worked up a full head of rhetorical steam) *or* we must deny that they have the authority to enact this bill. The *Remonstrance*, of course, *does* deny that the General Assembly has the authority to do any of these things. (A whisper of skepticism may arise: Is it true that *all* those rights— trial by jury, free press, and the like—would have collapsed at once in a heap, if Henry's bill had been passed?)

Madison asserted not only that all these rights are bound in a bundle, standing or falling together, but also that the General Assessment bill violated the particular right, perhaps the weightiest in the whole bundle, of religious freedom. A tax to support religion, even without preference, is a violation of that right: In other words, already in 1785, before there was any First Amendment with its establishment clause, before there was any federal Constitution to be amended, Madison has found that the right to religious freedom entails what would later be called the separation of church and state. No tax aid to religion. No tax aid to religion, not just as a matter of *policy*, but because the legislature has no authority to enact such a bill. Such an enactment is outside its jurisdiction. As Supreme Court justices more than a century and a half later would ground that claim in the First Amendment, so Madison in 1785 grounded it in the Virginia Declaration of Rights.

And he grounded it in a theory; in the view that there are rights the society cannot properly invade. Back at the beginning of the document he set forth a fundamental jurisdictional division, by which the domain of religious belief is prior to and outside the proper reach of "civil society." That domain of "conviction and conscience" is by its *nature*, and by "unalienable" right—Madison used the word *unalienable* three times in argument number one—beyond the reach of society's proper regulation. The right follows from a duty "towards the Creator." It is "precedent, both in order of time and in degree of obligation, to the claims of Civil Society."

> Before any man can be considered as a member of Civil Society, he must be considered as a subject of the Governor of the Universe: And if a member of Civil Society, who enters into

any subordinate Association, must always do it with a reservation of his duty to the General Authority; much more must every man who becomes a member of any particular Civil Society, do it with a saving of his allegiance to the Universal Sovereign. We maintain therefore that in matters of Religion, no man's right is abridged by the institution of Civil Society and that Religion is wholly exempt from its cognizance.

All that is in Madison's first "because." Only in the second does he come to the "state": "Because if Religion be exempt from the authority of the Society at large, still less can it be subject to that of the Legislative Body. The latter are but the creatures and vicegerents of the former. Their jurisdiction is both derivative and limited: it is limited with regard to the co-ordinate departments, more necessarily is it limited with regard to the constituents." It may be worth noting that this bundle of rights is inalienable, first of all, by *society*, which is distinct from, and superior to, the *state*. Madison does not reflect the later American tendency to skip over the first step, and to see in the state *alone* the threat to human rights. *Society* threatens them, so to speak, first.

In the pattern of this *Remonstrance* there is a four-tier layer cake of rights, duties, and limits. At the first and highest level there is that domain of "duty which we owe to our Creator," in which we have the right that goes with that duty not to have that domain abridged or invaded. In this "precedent" higher realm of religion—duty we owe to the "Universal Sovereign," which is up to each of us to discern, fill in, act upon as our own conscience dictates—human beings are and remain "*equally* free and independent" (this from his point 4, quoting once again from Article One of the Virginia Declaration of Rights). "All men are to be considered as entering into Society on equal conditions, as relinquishing no more, and therefore retaining no less, one than another, of their natural rights," of which natural rights none is higher than freedom of conscience. Above all are they to be considered as retaining an "equal title to the free exercise of Religion according to the dictates of Conscience." (It was Madison, in 1776 in Williamsburg, who had put that emphasis on the *equal* freedom of human persons in the highest domain.)

So the realm of religion is superior to, precedent to "Civil Society," which in its turn, then, is superior to the legislative body. Only now, in layer three, so to speak, do we get to the state—which is the creature and agent of civil society, on a leash, "derivative." That lawmaking power is internally limited, by "co-ordinate departments," but—here is layer four—superior to "any subordinate association."

This piece of energetic advocacy from Madison's hand is not a bad spot in which to find the concentrate of a Founder's philosophy of natural rights and, to a degree, of republicanism.

The primary point is certainly the claim of each individual human person to the right—"unalienable"—that accompanies the duty in that highest realm of conscience, outside the proper reach of civil society. Madison did of course set these rights beyond the decision of majorities. "True it is," he wrote,"that no other rule exists by which any question which may divide a Society can be ultimately determined, but the will of the majority; but it is also true that the majority may trespass on the rights of the minority." Clearly, fundamental religious freedom is, for Madison, a right of each person that precedes and stands outside the claims of "Civil Society" and therefore is not subject to any official social determination, including that taken by the action of majorities. More than a century and a half later Justice Robert Jackson was to write, in the flag-salute case we have already quoted, a continuation of the position of Madison, applied now to the federal Bill of Rights:

> The very purpose of a Bill of Rights was to withdraw certain subjects from the vicissitudes of political controversy, to place them beyond the reach of majorities and officials and to establish them as legal principles to be applied by the courts. One's right to life, liberty, and property, to free speech, a free press, freedom of worship and assembly, and other fundamental rights may not be submitted to vote; they depend on the outcome of no elections.

Madison, having made the claim for equal freedom, extends it to unbelievers, "atheists" or whatever, by implication—since all are equal."Whilst we assert for ourselves a freedom to embrace...the Religion which we believe to be of divine origin, we cannot deny an equal freedom to those whose minds have not yet yielded to the evidence which has convinced us. If this freedom be abused, it is an offence against God, not against man." Thus deftly does Madison expand religious liberty all the way, beyond the limits set by John Locke.

It is not at all clear that the broad American public two hundred years later understands, or would accept if it did understand, the position on these matters taken by the founding heroes James Madison and Thomas Jefferson: that atheists and unbelievers and all sorts of non-Christians—every human being, in fact—are included in the protection of the fundamental suprasocial human rights, of religious liberty, and that that right may not be abrogated by majority vote. But because the broad public will find those two points difficult, it has proved important, as Madison did not at first believe, but Jefferson insisted, that they be specified in the written Constitution and protected by the unusual institution of judicial review.

Madison also made the strongest of the arguments that the strict "separationists" were subsequently to make, after the First Amendment came to be written and ratified and then interpreted, in behalf of including the separation of church and state somehow within those fundamental untouchable human rights: that anything less puts the individual human beings who hold to a conviction other than that of the unseparated religion below the salt—in the overworked twentieth-century phrase, makes them "second-class citizens." Madison wrote: "the proposed establishment [Henry's aid-all-religions bill] degrades from the equal rank of Citizens all those whose opinions in Religion do not bend to those of the Legislative authority."

But though in all this there certainly is a distinct insistence on the right of each separate individual "man" (as Madison would write, in those prefeminist days—"every man" four times in the first argument) Madison is nevertheless not an individualist like those who would come later. He is an eighteenth-century republican, not a nineteenth-century romantic. He did not reflect the idealistic individualism—or near-anarchism—which was to find expression, soon after his death, in Emerson and Thoreau. Neither is his view identical with that sharply individualist, antistatist, antipublic view, that invidious contrast of a "private" sector with a public sector that in twentieth-century America was to drop overboard any notion of the public good. To move "subordinate associations"—like, say, the corporate entities of economic life—up from the fourth tier, as we have put it here, up above the civil order into the first tier, with the fundamental human liberties, would be a considerable alteration of the structure that one finds in Madison. So is the derogation of the state, and the obscuring of the place of civil society *above* the state, indeed, *using* it, but still restrained by the ultimate domain of rightful human liberty, especially of thought and conscience.

Madison asserts that the preservation of free government requires not only the maintaining of the "metes and bounds" (a metaphor, from the term for the boundaries of a parish, that John Locke also used) between separate departments of power but more especially that none of these departments be allowed to "overleap the great Barrier which defends the rights of the people." (This topic is filled with barriers, walls, and boundaries.) The use of the word "People" here and elsewhere in the *Remonstrance* may suggest the communal as well as the individualist aspect to the human life protected by that great Barrier: Beyond the Barrier, for a republican, is that original entity and agent, the People. In other documents of the Revolution one finds a term like this, improbable in a twentieth-century American context: the "Public Liberty." Although one would have to strain to find in James Madison the application of this point to the field of religion—that religion is not only an individual, but also a social, matter; that religious freedom is a good not only for "every man" but also for the society, for "the People"—Madison nevertheless did provide in his larger political understanding the materials from which someone else might develop such a view.

And he does make, in addition to his arguments from principle and his practical arguments to Christians and believers dealing with the desirable effect of full religious freedom on religion itself and the undesirable effects of establishments, arguments about what happens to the social order when religions squabble among themselves and try to get a handle on the levers of power. As with the prohibition of alcoholic beverages in a later century, so with the General Assessment: Attempts to enforce such legislation on a resistant public will "tend to enervate the laws in general, and slacken the bonds of society." It will "destroy ... moderation and harmony," produce "animosities and jealousies." Perhaps the most interesting argument in the whole list anticipates the humanitarian outlook expressed on the Statue of Liberty, if not always in American history. Madison wrote that any religious establishment would be a

> departure from that generous policy, which offering an Asylum to the persecuted and oppressed of every Nation and Religion, promised a lustre to our country.... The magnanimous sufferer under this cruel scourge in foreign Regions, must view the Bill as a Beacon on our Coast, warning him to seek some other haven, where liberty and philanthrophy in their due extent, may offer a more certain repose from his Troubles.

If the ground of Madison's argument is a theory of the rights of humankind, the primary audience he needs to persuade is that of the worried believers, facing a situation new to them—and new to everybody—in which religion would have no public support. He does include references, like those of Jefferson in the Virginia statute, for example, to the "supreme law giver of the Universe," to our "duty toward the Creator," and "allegiance to the Universal Sovereign." He puts his argument for this liberty of all, as we have seen, in theistic terms: "If this freedom [of conscience] be abused, it is an offence against God, not against man. To God, therefore, not to man, must an account of it be rendered." On a different plane, in his argument to Christians, he puts the point, as Jefferson certainly did too, that the ecclesiastical establishments "instead of maintaining purity and efficacy of Religion, have had a contrary operation."

He was careful to argue, in other words, not only that full religious liberty is required by the human rights the colonists have claimed, and needed for the proper functioning of republican government, but also good for religion itself. If you want pure, effective, real, and lively belief, then do not use coercion to support it. Madison wrote that coercive religious establishments are "a contradiction to the Christian Religion itself, for every page of it disavows a dependence on the powers of this world." Madison argued—as Roger Williams had done and as Jefferson had done—that state-enforced religion had not worked and cannot work; that "torrents of blood" have been spilled in sorry days of the past to prove that it cannot. (Of "blood" we will see more when we discuss Roger Williams.) Like Jefferson, Madison argues that the mind is governed by evidence that makes it believe what it must; it cannot be changed by external force.

The petitions to the Assembly, when Madison and his colleagues went to work, had been, as we have seen, in favor of Henry's bill. Madison wrote his *Memorial and Remonstrance* to arouse opinion, and gather signatures, on the other side. There were, as noted, other petitions, including the "spirit of the gospel" petition that gathered more signatures than his.

This firestorm of response killed the Henry bill. In the aftermath of that result, as we have seen, Madison pulled out from the endangered species in the rest of the list of bills in the revisal the most important of them all, the draft bill Jefferson had written long before, and as floor leader for it, in the events already recounted, got it passed.

Thus the two most notable documentary underpinnings for what was to become the American tradition came out of a flurry of activity in this one state in this one short period—less than a year—with the still young James Madison at the center.

THE CONSTITUTION:
ITS COMPOSITION
AND DEFENSE

Although the dominant impression one gets of Madison is that of a cautious, reflective, careful man—the word *prudent* appears often in comments about him—he nevertheless was a leader in the very bold acts that secured this nation's constitutional groundwork: the Annapolis convention in September of 1786; the Constitutional Convention it led to, in Philadelphia in May of 1787; the ratification of the Constitution the Philadelphia Convention produced, in the key state of Virginia; the production of the greatest defense of the Constitution, *The Federalist*; and the proposal, in the First Congress and under the new government, of what became the first ten amendments.

Neither religious liberty nor religious matters of any kind figure significantly in any of these enormously important events except for the last one. The Constitution composed by Madison, James Wilson, Gouverneur Morris, Benjamin Franklin, and the other notables in the summer of 1787 in Philadelphia is surprisingly free from any substantive religion. It contains only three references to religion, two of them of the dimmest sort. First, it exempts Sundays from the days to be numbered in the countdown for a presidential pocket veto. Second, at the end it gives as its date "in the year of our Lord seventeen hundred and eighty-seven, and of the Independence of the United States the twelfth." The Constitution-makers did want to get away from counting years by the reign of kings. And they certainly did *not* do what the French Revolutionary Constitution was to do: set up a new calendar dated from the autumnal equinox, the day after the Republic was proclaimed. In the later stages of the French Revolution, in 1793, Sunday was abolished as the sabbath and replaced by a festival every tenth day; this was in that brief period when the Cathedral of Notre Dame, with its Christian symbols covered, or torn off the façades, became the Temple of Reason. In contrast the American Constitution-makers, after the very different American Revolution with its very different aftermath, may be said, at the least, not to have explicitly repudiated—and in these minor ways to have implicitly acknowledged—the customs, habits, and traditions that arose out of the overwhelmingly Christian heritage of the new nation.

At the same time, however, the Founders wrote into the body of the Constitution, in Article VI, a prohibition of all religious tests. The last paragraph of that article provides that officials of the United States "shall be bound by oath or affirmation to support this Constitution." (The phrase "oath or affirmation" accommodated the objections of Quakers and others who refrained on Biblical grounds from the swearing of oaths.) The Constitution-makers then added "but no religious test shall ever be required as a qualification to any office or public trust under the United States." Disallowing any "religious test" broke with the long, complicated, and not edifying history of requiring some particular belief, at least a belief in God, for the holding of office and the swearing of a solemn oath. Even John Locke's *Letter Concerning Toleration* had given as its reason for not tolerating atheists the taking of oaths: "Lastly, those are not at all to be tolerated who deny the being of a God," wrote Locke. "Promises, covenants, and oaths, which are the bonds of human society, can have no hold upon an atheist." But a century later the new United States removed that barrier and prohibited any kind of religious test for the holding of office. In the convention in Philadelphia—where North Carolina voted against this provision—there was objection that it might allow even Roman Catholics and "pagans" to hold office, as indeed it has.

The prohibition of religious tests has an importance that the overwhelming concentration on the First Amendment has tended to obscure. Candidate John Kennedy, for example, in his speech to the Protestant ministers in Houston, Texas, in the fall of 1960, could refer to the prohibition of religious tests in Article VI as a constitutional foundation for rejecting the implications of the views many of them held about a Roman Catholic in the White House. And the plaintiffs in a 1961 U.S. Supreme Court case, called *Torcaso* v. *Watkins*, could appeal to Article VI against a provision in the Maryland constitution that required officeholders—the plaintiff was a man seeking to be a notary public—to swear to their belief in God. (The provision was struck down on grounds of the establishment clause of the First Amendment.) Already, then, in the framing of Article VI of the Constitution, bearing on the decisive point of what may be required of officials—and before the addition of the Bill of Rights—the new nation was electing to be nonreligious in its civic life. (Virginia had already accomplished that end in 1786 with the passage of the statute, but that was by no means true of all the other states, as they framed new constitutions in the late 1770s and the 1780s.)

But more striking than what the federal Constitution did include is what it did not. It had no substantive religion, even of the sort that was a commonplace in documents written by the Founders: no references to "Providence," to the Creator, to nature and nature's God, to the Supreme Being. Of course the Constitution was a formal legal instrument, as, say, the Declaration of Independence was not. But other formal legal instruments—the state constitutions—often included substantive statements reflecting a collective piety: "The people of Connecticut, acknowledging with gratitude the good providence of God in permitting them to enjoy a free government, do . . . " (Connecticut, 1818); "We the people of the state of Arkansas, grateful to Almighty God for the privilege of choosing our own form of government . . . " (Arkansas, 1874). The absence of any such reference, of any reference to God, in the U.S. Constitution became a matter of dispute in the struggle over its ratification, and again early in the nineteenth century, when there was a national movement to change that. Timothy Dwight, the president of Yale, told his students that it is "highly discreditable to us that we do not acknowledge God in our Constitution." Even in the twentieth century there was still simmering the long historical effort to enact a "Christian Amendment" to the Constitution, to correct that condition. Illinois Congressman John Anderson, by heritage a Scandinavian evangelical, supported it early in his career; his perhaps rather nominal support was to prove a source of embarrassment when, transmuted from moderate conservative to liberal, he ran for president in 1980.

To go back to the writing of the Constitution: The "assembly of notables" in Philadelphia in the summer of 1787, with James Madison as a chief participant, was trying to construct a workable plan of *government*, in a volatile situation, and bent its energies wholly to that task. Its focus of attention was a long way from the subject of religion, even of religious liberty. There is, however, one episode from their days together in Independence Hall that has been lifted up out of the whole story and given currency by the pious, and sometimes the polemical, needs of later generations. We learn about it primarily from the remarkable notes he made each day after the sessions, and on weekends.

(These notes alone would be enough to guarantee a person an important place in American history.)

After the notables had been at work for over a month, it was suggested that they had got off on the wrong foot, religiously speaking. They had not provided for any chaplain, or opening prayers, or collective worship services. On June 28, when "after 4 or five weeks close attendance and close reasonings with each other"—as Benjamin Franklin put it, in Madison's notes—Franklin, who of course was the oldest as well as, next to George Washington, the most respected of all the delegates, made his famous proposal that the convention apply "to the Father of lights to illuminate our understandings." The "small progress," made so far, he suggested, was "melancholy proof of the imperfection of Human Understanding." He then presented a perhaps slightly sentimental picture of the contrasting situation in those earlier, religiously superior days of the Revolution. "In the beginning of the Contest with G. Britain, when we were sensible of the danger we had daily prayer in this room for divine protection. Our prayers, Sir, were heard." He went on to expand on the "superintending providence" that had superintended "in our favor." (A deist like Franklin could be as much inclined as any Puritan to discover a special providence working "in our favor"; the Enlightenment, as much as covenant theology, discerned a unique world role for America, and a distinctive relation of this nation to the Supreme Being—for ill and perhaps for good, a constant in American life ever since.)

Franklin wondered whether we had "forgotten that powerful friend"— distinctly a friend—and then he produced a sentence that, as Madison got it down in his notes, was destined when those notes became public to be quoted in thousands upon thousands of sermons and pious tracts in the new country: "I have lived, Sir, a long time, and the longer I· live, the more convincing proofs I see of this truth—*that God governs in the affairs of men.*" Franklin proposed that one or more of the Clergy of the City be asked to open each day's session with prayers "imploring the assistance of heaven," in order to lift the sights of the delegates above "our little partial local interests."

Roger Sherman of Connecticut seconded Franklin's motion, but the delegates seem to have regarded it as a hot potato, or a warm one anyway. They dealt with it mostly as a problem in what today would be called public relations (an anticipation of a great deal of the half-nervous, half-cynical coping of secular politicians with such matters in a religious country). Would not such a measure *now* "at this late day," since we did not do it at the start, suggest to the public that we are desperate? Would not such a measure bring "disagreeable animad-versions"? But Franklin and Sherman, not letting them off the hook, argued that "past omission of a duty could not justify a further omis-sion" and that rejecting it, now that it had been proposed, would lead to more severe "animadversions." To this Hugh Williamson of North Carolina—a man who had abandoned theology for science—made the pointedly realistic rejoinder that the public would understand the real reason for the omission: "The Convention had no funds."

Edmund Randolph of Virginia, trying to rescue the proposal, then made a motion that Franklin seconded: The Convention could have a sermon preached on the Fourth of July, and thereafter begin its sessions with a prayer. "After several unsuccessful attempts for silently post-poning the matter by adjournment," according to Madison's notes, "the adjournment at length carried, without any vote on the motion."

Though Madison spoke often in the Convention (it was a small group, after all), his only role in this matter, so far as we know, was to be a noncommittal amanuensis. Alexander Hamilton, about to give up on the Convention, appears in Madison's notes leading the opposition to Franklin's proposal. Another source—not Madison—yields the famous tale that Hamilton responded to Franklin's suggestion humorously, saying the delegates were competent to conduct their business "without the necessity of calling in foreign aid."

With or without such aid, the Constitution was written. In the strug-gle to get the states to ratify it—by the Convention's provision, rati-fication required only nine states, but actually making it work certainly would require the big ones, like Virginia and New York—Hamilton and Madison, with some small help from John Jay, produced the most influential of all American productions on government, *The Federalist*. Hamilton, it will be remembered, proposed the project—articles in New York newspapers defending the federal Constitution to the voters of that and other states—but Madison produced the numbers that have won the most enduring fame and constant quotation. It is this Madison, the writer of Federalist Ten, Fifty-one, and others, whom twentieth-century American political scientists love. (There may be some ques-tion whether he would love them back.)

The silence of *The Federalist* on religious matters is almost as striking as the silence of the Constitution. Nowhere in its eighty-five essays, covering the whole polity in defense of the Constitution, is there any discussion of religion as an element in the social order. Of course its focus was elsewhere, and as the Constitution it was defending was silent on that point, so is the defense. Among the few times that religion is even mentioned, in the most incidental way, in *The Federalist* are two brief references in the most famous of the essays, Federalist Ten and Fifty-one, both now attributed to Madison. These, of course, are the numbers that are considered to have developed, in two differing settings, the political stance that would now be called, perhaps misleadingly, "pluralist." They are also the primary location of that celebrated and much disputed subject, James Madison on human nature.

These two brief references, and the outlook to which they are attached, are, however, so important that we may draw back here and recapitulate the background in Madison's life that led up to them.

Even before he engaged in any battle, Madison had begun to believe that the uniting of political and religious power, as in Anglican Virginia and in much of Christian history since Constantine, was a mistake. Perhaps he had been encouraged to see that by the atmosphere of Princeton. In his youthful letters to Bradford up in Philadelphia, and to others, he had questioned whether uniting religious and political power was a good idea, had asked whether a civil state needs state-supported religion, and had taken a negative view of what would have happened if all the colonies had had an Anglican establishment. And he deplored Virginia's treatment of dissenters and found religious liberty a primary natural human right.

Then in his shaping political years, from age twenty-five to thirty-five, he was, as we have seen, the key figure in the legislative and political contest over the Virginia establishment, and in that actual and bitter contest had his ideas tested, confirmed, refined, and planted in his permanent convictions.

Out of these battles he added an important new dimension to his earlier bookish convictions. He had already believed that uniting religious and political power tended to produce oppression, and that each human being has a natural right to conscientious belief. Now he came to believe, in addition, that the actual existence of a multitude of "sects," with some division and opposition among them, was the realistic way to protect against religio-political tyranny and to secure religious rights. Madison's conscientious sobriety of tone had nothing of the acid humor of Voltaire, but Madison nevertheless picked up and liked to quote Voltaire's aphorism: "If one religion only were allowed in England, the Government would possibly become arbitrary; if there were two, they would be at each other's throats; but as there are such a multitude, they all live happy and in peace."

The protection of religious liberty, he now saw, was to be found not only in declarations of rights, in principles and convictions, or even in laws; it was to be found also in a power situation—a division and balance—in which the numbers of, and conflict among, religious groups made overbearing combinations unlikely. Both Madison and Jefferson would say that in a situation of multiple "sects," each would serve as a *censor morum* of the others.

Young Madison saw this nascent "pluralism" work itself out, as we have seen, in the long struggle of 1776–86 over the religious arrangements in Virginia, which ended in the passage of Jefferson's Virginia statute. The Baptists and the Presbyterians each had an essential role over against the Anglicans. The Methodists played an important role, too, by pulling away from the Anglicans at a crucial moment. The presence in the state of Quakers, Lutherans, and Moravians presumably helped, too, from Madison's point of view.

When, as the battle was reaching its climax, Madison sent a copy of his *Memorial and Remonstrance* to Jefferson in Paris, in the fall of 1785, he referred in this way to the politico-religious scene surrounding the tussle over Patrick Henry's General Assessment bill: "The Presbyterian clergy have at length espoused the side of the opposition, being moved either by fear of their laity or a jealousy of the Episcopalians."

When in 1784 the Assembly had provided, with Madison's strategic support, for the "incorporation" of the old Anglican Church as the new Episcopalian church, that action presumably gave rise to the "jealousy" to which he referred. Madison wrote further to Jefferson: "The mutual hatred of these sects has been much inflamed by the late Act incorporating the latter [i.e., the Episcopalians]. I am far from being sorry for it, as a coalition between them could alone endanger our religious rights, and a tendency to such an event has been suspected." Elsewhere Madison would write that divide and conquer, the strategy of tyrants, could on occasion be employed by the partisans of liberty.

At the Virginia convention considering the ratification of the federal Constitution, then, in June of 1788, Madison made explicit the realistic, or pluralist, point to which he had then come. To be sure, he was in that setting preoccupied with the Constitution as written, defending it against the demand by George Mason, Patrick Henry, and other Antifederalists for—among other things—a bill of rights *before* ratification, and against Baptist and sectarian wariness because it did not explicitly guarantee religious liberty. Nevertheless his remarks there in Richmond state a position that fits, in part, with much else he wrote and said.

He did suggest, rhetorically, that a bill of rights would be "a poor protection for liberty," a position, taken in the heat of battle, that he would later revise. But, he said, happily in the new nation the states "enjoy the utmost freedom of religion. This freedom arises from the multiplicity of sects, which pervades America, and which is the best and only security for religious liberty in any society." (The *only* security? Here again, Madison, in the midst of the fray, goes further than he would at other times, earlier and later.) "For where there is such variety of sects," he went on, "there cannot be a majority of any one sect to oppress and persecute the rest."

In discounting, for his immediate political purpose, mere "parchment barriers," in favor of real division and balances of power, Madison was discounting work he himself had done before, and later would do again, in behalf of such "barriers," written presumably on the equivalent of parchment, in the Virginia Declaration of Rights, including Article Sixteen, and later in the federal Bill of Rights. He would alter his position as ratification became secure, in part in order to make it so. In the long run he would see the necessity of both the written guarantee on parchment and the diversity of groups in the real world. Taking his career as a whole, one can see Madison's assortment of protections for liberty—in law and in declarations and in the mind of the people, and in a realistic balance of religious power—not over against one another as choices but as complementary.

Jefferson's statute had been enacted in January 1786. In September of that year Madison attended the Annapolis convention. In May a year later, the Philadelphia convention began. In the intervening period Madison made his famous study of ancient and modern constitutions, and drafted the elements of what has come to be called the Virginia plan, presented by Edmund Randolph to the Philadelphia convention. Immediately in the fall and winter after *that*, in 1787–88, he joined Hamilton to produce *The Federalist*. In other words, Madison's thinking about, and arguing for, the Constitution followed soon after the climax of the ten-year contest over religious freedom in Virginia.

At the heart of Madison's defense of the Constitution there was his notion of the realistic foundations of liberty: liberty defended not only by ingrained principle and constitutional fiat but also by (as we would call it today) "pluralism."

Madison was countering one of the strongest of the Antifederalist arguments: that, in general, "republican government" works only in small-scale units, and that, in particular, the powerful new central national government in the proposed Constitution would dominate, almost obliterate, the states, towns, and small units in which liberty, true democracy, could flourish. Madison not only countered this argument but turned it clear around, turned it (implicitly) against his opponents: It is exactly in an "extended Republic," a "compound Republic" under this federal Constitution, that liberty is protected, even while government is able to govern, because by extending and compounding, by joining together Virginia and Massachusetts and eleven others, with all of their diversities, the polity encompasses a sufficiently multiple and complex variety of "interests" to prevent any alone from dominating, to require combinations and compromise, and to allow alteration by new combinations.

In Madison's most famous contribution to *The Federalist* series, the well-worked-over Ten, when he develops his argument about the "latent causes of faction" sown in the "nature of man," he mentions, almost incidentally but first on the list, "a zeal for different opinions concerning religion." That is one item only, on the way through other causes of faction to the one that is planted most durably in the "various and unequal distribution of property." It is Madison's realistic presentation of the underpinnings of "republican government," and his linking of that realism to perennial conflicts of economic interests and classes, that have given Federalist Ten its fame. It is surely not a presumptuous inference to guess that one way Madison came to the underlying insight was from his experience with religious conflict in Virginia.

In the next most renowned of Madison's contributions to *The Federalist*, Fifty-one, he is applying his realism about human nature to the separation of powers in the federal government, and, more specifically, in the two houses of the legislative branch. He produces these often-quoted sentences:

> Ambition must be made to counteract ambition. It may be a reflection on human nature that such devices should be necessary to control the abuses of government. But what is government itself but the greatest of all reflections on human nature? If men were angels, no government would be necessary. If angels were to govern men, neither external nor internal controls on government would be necessary. In framing a government which is to be administered by men over men, the great difficulty lies in this: you must first enable the government to control the governed; and in the next place oblige it to control itself.

Madison argues that by dividing, separating, and limiting power the Constitution provides security of the rights of the people against their rulers. But that is not all that the nonangelic society of men requires: You must not only guard the society against the oppression of the rulers, but also "guard one part of the society against the other part." The best way to do that is "by comprehending in the society so many separate descriptions of citizens as will render an unjust combination of a majority of the whole very improbable, if not impracticable." That is what "the federal republic of the United States" proposes to do. "Whilst all authority in it will be derived from and dependent on the society, the society itself will be broken into so many parts, interests, and classes of citizens, that the rights of individuals, or of the minority, will be in little danger from interested combinations of the majority."

The analogy that Madison then chose came, we may guess, out of the events we have recounted. "In a free government," he wrote,

> the security for civil rights must be the same as that for religious rights. It consists in the one case in the multiplicity of interests, and in the other in the multiplicity of sects. The degrees of security in both cases will depend on the number of interests and sects. . . . In the extended republic of the United States, and among the great variety of interests, parties, and sects which it embraces, a coalition of a majority of the whole of society could seldom take place on any other principles than those of justice and the general good.

Thus the multiplicity of mutually balancing "sects" furnished Madison his sample and analogy for these larger claims about the realistic foundation of republican government in the nature of man and the balancing of ambitions and of interests, which is the contribution to political thinking for which he is best known, and which reverberates to this day.

One might, after two centuries of reverberation, ask a number of questions about this famous analysis, as it applies to religious groups: Does Madison really mean to say the more the merrier? Is there not, in religion, a strong impulse not only to express the diversities, but also the commonalities? Are religious groups really the exact political equivalent of the agricultural interest and the mercantile interest, the debtors and the creditors, the regions, classes, and economic units? May it not be, somewhat ironically, that Madison's realistic pluralism has a more clear-cut and unequivocal application to other kinds of "interest groups"—economic in particular—than to the religious groups from which he first derived it? To all of this Madison might have answered in part, as he does in effect in the rather attractive Federalist

Thirty-seven: Please do not examine these matters with "a disposition to find or magnify faults"; instead examine them in "a spirit of moderation" in the real world.

The Constitution *The Federalist* was recommending was ratified, but not easily. To those who, living after it was done, benefit from it, the ratification of the Constitution feels as though it must have been painless. It is one of those great historical accomplishments, the difficulty of which is hard to recapture imaginatively after it is done, and has been celebrated, and is taken for granted. In fact, it was a close thing. The Antifederalists, as they were called, who were chary about or opposed to the Constitution, had as one of their strongest arguments that it did not have a written declaration or guarantee, or "bill," of rights, as did all of the state constitutions. The Virginia Declaration of Rights of 1776, with its guarantee to all men equally of the "free exercise" of religion, was the most famous of these, and the model for many. The young Madison himself had been, as we have seen, the source of the important change in its Article Sixteen, from "toleration" to freedom of religion as a natural right held equally by all. But in 1787–88 Madison and other defenders of the Constitution had as their first priority getting the thing written and ratified, and putting a stronger Union in place. To have tried in Philadelphia to persuade the delegates from those thirteen, twelve, or nine separated and differing states to add a bill of rights would have been much more difficult than it had been in the more homogeneous colony of Virginia in 1776.

George Mason, the principal author of the Virginia Declaration, did try, toward the end of the Philadelphia Convention, to add such a bill, but the sentiment of the convention was against it. Mason, primarily for that reason, left the convention "in an exceeding ill humour" and declined to sign the Constitution. He was one of three still present in Philadelphia when the Convention was over who became an opponent.

Mason sent to Jefferson in Paris a copy of the Constitution, and a complaint about the absence of a bill of rights. Presumably that message from his older authority on bills of rights, a man whom Jefferson respected, influenced Jefferson's criticism of the proposed Constitution on the same score. Jefferson wrote letters from Paris, not only to Madison but to others, objecting to the Constitution on two grounds, the perpetual eligibility of the chief executive, which he thought would lead to monarchy, and the absence of a bill of rights, and he was quoted in the ratifying conventions of Virginia (by Patrick Henry!), North Carolina, and other states by the opponents of the Philadelphia Constitution. North Carolina, partly for that reason, at first declined to ratify.

The luxury of hindsight, on the part of Americans two hundred years later, is even greater than the luxury of distance provided to Jefferson at that time. With the long and important history of an efficacious federal Bill of Rights now behind us, there is an inclination on the part of some to fault Madison for not favoring such a written guarantee of rights from the start. But—as Jefferson himself recognized—being thus outside the prospective politics of the particular moment changes one's perspective. Madison had the luxury neither of distance nor of hindsight. He was fully engaged in the effort to secure the Union—a government "national" enough to satisfy folk like Hamilton and to get the job done, and "federal" enough to balance it and to pacify enough states' rights people. In *The Federalist* he descants on the partly national, partly federal character of the Constitution in a way that Patrick Henry was to mock at the Richmond ratifying convention.

The first priority in that situation was to get a viable republican government in place. The demand for a prior bill of rights became in some cases the instrument of those who were opposed to the Constitution and wanted to defeat it. The proposal by Mason and others that there be a *second* constitutional convention, to repair the work of the first by—among other changes—incorporating a bill of rights, was, to Madison and the proponents (it certainly seems rightly) an invitation to chaos. The problem was, and would continue to be, that the several states and factions and persons had many different objections to the Philadelphia Constitution. That Constitution, according to its defenders—with Madison one of the strongest—was as good as one could get; a second effort to write one would produce chaos and nothing.

The formula that solved the problem, in the ratifying conventions of Massachusetts, Virginia, and other states, was to ratify the Constitution as it stood, but with recommended amendments to be considered later. In another extraordinary story from the nation's beginnings, enough states did ratify to set the new government in motion—but with the promise, now, of the addition of a bill of rights.

THE FIRST AMENDMENT

James Madison was no longer the bookish and deferential novice sent to Williamsburg in May of 1776, asking Mr. Patrick Henry to introduce his amendment. Now, at forty, he was an experienced and intellectually self-confident politician who had beaten Patrick Henry in legislative battle, and was privately disdainful of the older hero's vanity and lazy vagueness. He had now opposed revered figures of an older generation like George Mason. He corresponded with Thomas Jefferson as an equal and a friend, and tactfully disagreed with him—or, at least, put the emphasis in a different place, as in their correspondence about the Constitution and a bill of rights. He had learned at first hand, day after day, issue after issue, as the most diligent of legislators in committees, councils, and congresses, in Williamsburg, Richmond, and Philadelphia, about the complex play of power and interest in the real work of governing (or, for four years in Philadelphia's Continental Congress, trying to govern). He was much younger than Henry, Mason, or Sam Adams; independence was for him not the climax but the beginning of a political career; he was somewhat younger than Jefferson and John Adams, so that independence was not for him personally even the first act. He was not yet on the stage. His role came thereafter, in building the government—the self-governing government—that would realize the Revolution's aims.

What Madison was concerned about first of all in 1787–91 was getting a functioning government of liberty drawn up, ratified, working, going. Perhaps as he wrote to Jefferson he had never really been opposed to a bill of rights, but only to an attempt to attain such a bill that would interfere with the delicate achievement of a working national constitution—with the writing of such a constitution, or with its ratification. He did to some extent share the view of his nationalist collaborator in the Philadelphia Convention of 1787, James Wilson of Pennsylvania, that "the rights in question" were already guaranteed by the *limitation* on the power granted, under the Constitution, to the federal government; since the proposed new government could do *only* what the Constitution permitted, it could not invade these liberties. Moreover, so the argument went, specifying some rights might leave the unspecified in doubt. But though Madison, under the pressure of getting a signable, ratifiable, workable constitution written and enacted, had for a time these substantive objections to a new federal written bill of rights, his main point was tactical: to get the Constitution in place without the distraction of a fight over a bill of rights (in particular the fight over a religious freedom plank) that would threaten to undercut it. But then as the ratification struggle developed, and Madison saw how strong was the desire for such a bill—on the part of Thomas Jefferson, George Mason, and others he admired, and large sections of the public—he shifted, again partly tactically, and promised the addition of such a bill after the Constitution was ratified. And after it was ratified introducing such a bill became a tactic, partly, to bind the disgruntled ex-Antifederalists to the new government.

One place Madison promised a bill of rights was the Virginia ratifying convention. After a long and very close fight he and the proponents of the new Constitution won, on a motion (by George Wythe) to ratify the proposed Constitution without amendments, and then *after* that, *separately*, to propose a list of amendments to be considered by the First Congress. That was more than acceptable to Madison, so long as the proposed bill of rights was not made a *condition* of ratification, interfering with the process. And having attained (barely) the vote he wanted for unconditional ratification, he set right to work debating the formulation of the proposed amendments. Other states had similar battles and similar results: a commitment to introduce a written bill of rights, like those in the most enlightened states—Virginia first among them—then loomed over the future, as a moral and political, though not a legal, requirement.

Madison and the others in the informal New York-based group that coordinated the efforts to secure ratification had already agreed that they would do what Virginia and other states voted: support a bill of rights, of course including freedom of religious conscience, to be added to the Constitution, by amendment, *after* its ratification. Indeed, Madison himself had promised such a result not only in the Virginia ratifying convention but also on his way to stand for election to it, in a meeting with the Virginia Baptist leader John Leland. Leland, who knew and respected Madison as a firm friend of religious liberty from their collaboration in the Virginia battles of 1784 and 1785, had been circulating a memorial attacking the proposed Constitution for, among other things, its omission of an explicit guarantee of religious freedom. Leland and Madison met, and their meeting assumed a certain legendary quality in some Baptist circles. It had two elements: Madison's agreement to support a written guarantee of religious freedom, and Leland's to support the unamended Constitution. Madison wanted to extract the latter and agreed to the former. He got Leland's support.

After the Constitution was ratified, then, Madison ran for election to the First House of Representatives. Patrick Henry—endlessly mischievous from the point of view of Madison and Jefferson—had prevented Madison's election (by the state legislature) to the Senate, and had seen to it that Madison's House district included Antifederalist counties, so that presumably he could not win. As part of what passed in those days for a campaign, Madison wrote a letter to another Baptist preacher to counter Antifederalist claims that he was so rigidly attached to every syllable of the Constitution as to oppose a bill of rights protecting religious freedom. His letter reiterated his promise to introduce such a bill in the First Congress. And, in an impressive display of political organization, Madison *did* win.

Though it does not have a place in public understanding remotely comparable to the earlier great events of the American founding, that First Congress was in fact almost another constitution-making body. The fledgling government of the United States at the time consisted—to simplify—of not much more than George Washington and a piece of paper. Everything had to be filled in, and Congressman Madison was a chief figure in doing the filling. In the midst of it all, he did announce that he would introduce a bill of rights, and then, on June 8, 1789, proceeded to do so.

His version began with theoretical natural-rights preliminaries, very similar to the Virginia Declaration, which preliminaries were dropped. He proposed interweaving the amendments into the body of the Constitution, instead of adding them at the end, which idea was not followed.

Among Madison's proposed amendments was the one on our present subject, his original clause on religion: "The civil rights of none shall be abridged on account of religious belief or worship, nor shall any national religion be established, nor shall the full and equal rights of conscience be in any manner, or on any pretext, infringed...."

Disputants in the twentieth century, especially after the series of U.S. Supreme Court decisions starting in 1947, have seized upon the second clause—any *national* religion—and have pointed out that Madison urged the use of the word twice again in the House debates, and have claimed therefore that the men, including Madison, who composed the First Amendment intended only to prevent a single national established church, and not to enact strict separation. Others respond that many of the participants used the word "national" in a broad way, and that among these was James Madison: When he opposed tax-supported congressional chaplains, he said they would represent the establishment of a national religion. Perhaps the point is not that he used the word *national* broadly but that he used the word *establishment* strictly. In any case, other congressmen did not like the word *national*, and it was dropped. In the setting of 1789–91, when both state identities and wariness about the fledgling general, federal, "national" government were strong, the word had a significance different from any that figure in twentieth-century disputes about church and state. Both states with separation, like Virginia, Rhode Island, and Pennsylvania, and states with an established church, like Connecticut, would be apprehensive about what this new overarching general government would do in the field of religion. It certainly does not follow that because a *state* still had an establishment of religion of some kind or degree that its representatives would favor the same thing at the national level; it might be just otherwise. These matters were much influenced by the Federalist debate, by the aftermath of the debate over ratification, in a way that has no meaning to partisans of twentieth-century argument over church and state. Eighteenth-century people had their own worries, and could not know how their words would be taken up by people with other worries in later centuries.

In some other respects Madison's proposal of 1789 did go beyond the First Amendment as eventually adopted. In the clause quoted above he sought to protect "the full and equal rights of conscience." If "conscience" should be taken, as we do today, to mean not only belief but also principled moral conviction, and not only religious but also nonreligious belief and conviction, then Madison's proposal would have been an "advance" (if you regard the direction as forward) over even what twentieth-century courts have come to hold.

Conscience is one of the many large and important words—*virtue, luxury, corruption,* and perhaps even *liberty* are others—that have undergone a considerable change in meaning across the centuries, and that had at the very least a different nuance in the ideological frame of eighteenth-century Americans from what they mean today. *Conscience* in that century and earlier—as in Roger Williams's attack on persecution for cause of conscience—meant belief or conviction about religious matters, including, to be sure, convictions that stood against this and that orthodoxy, but the word did not ordinarily move outside the realm of religion altogether, nor did it apply to any and all serious moral convictions. Many modern Americans may wish that Madison's phrase had been adopted. But the Constitution was not to be supplied with a Bill of Duties to correspond to its Bill of Rights, and the founding generation's awareness of the social whole and of the public goods (and public necessities) would diminish and diminish yet again as their nation's life would unfold, at the same time that the individualistic word *conscience* would broaden its meaning. If Madison's phrase had been placed in the supreme law of the land, and the word's meaning and the society's understanding had changed as they have done, then the twentieth-century result—to say no more about it—would certainly have been yet another bonanza for lawyers.

On a chief topic of conscience with which the modern courts have dealt, conscientious objection to war, Madison in 1789 made another proposal going well beyond the Constitution as we have it. He proposed that "no person religiously scrupulous of bearing arms shall be compelled to render military service in person." But that failed. Conscientious objection to war, on religious grounds, has been granted by the "legislative grace" of Congress—already by the Second Congress—but not as a constitutional right. Had this provision been included in the Bill of Rights, the Supreme Court's interpretation of the First Amendment's religion clauses would certainly have led to some curious litigation with respect to Madison's phrase "religiously scrupulous." Are C.O.'s who are not, in the ordinary sense, "religious" to be included? If not, is there an unconstitutional "establishment" of religion? But they have led to some curious litigation anyway.

Madison worked up his presentation to the First Congress not only from his own ideas but also from the bills of rights already existing in eight of the states, and the various proposals for a bill of rights submitted by the states. But he included one item that the states, for understandable reasons, did not submit: "No *state* [my italics] shall violate the rights of conscience, or the freedom of the press, or the trial by jury in criminal cases...." Had that proposal been adopted, almost the whole of the American arrangement as it has come to be, by court interpretation, after the Fourteenth Amendment and after the cases of the middle of the twentieth century, would have already been in place at the end of the eighteenth. In other words, there would not have been a long period—the nineteenth and early twentieth century—in which the First Amendment's restrictions ("Congress shall make no law...")

were not applied to the states, and to all the "creatures" of the states like school boards.

But this Madisonian proposal, with religion again encapsulated in the word *conscience*, presumably did not have to its author and his contemporaries the full meaning that was to be discovered in the eventual establishment clause of the First Amendment—that is, complete separation of church and state. If it had been understood to have contained all of that, there surely would not have been any hope the amendment would be ratified by the states, several of which still had in some degree or another religious establishments.

The Antifederalists were mainly states'-rights people, worried about oppression by the new *national* government. Indeed, some of them wanted amendments of a different sort from the personal-liberty ones, including some that struck at the functioning power of the national government—restricting its taxing powers, for example. That is one reason Madison was wary about bills of rights. When it came around to drawing up such a bill, he not only took the lead (forestalling the Antifederalists) and restricted the proposals to personal liberties, but also proposed the big step of protecting those liberties not only against the national government but also against the *state* governments. He felt—surely correctly—that the states were more likely than the national government to undertake illiberal actions. But although this proposal passed the House, it was rejected by the Senate. It is sometimes called the "lost amendment."

Let us return for a moment to the most controversial aspect of this story in the First Congress, although with no intention of trying to contribute anything to the settling of the argument. As a matter of fact, it will not settle.

The most important dispute centers on the meaning of the establishment clause, as it would come to be called, and whether that clause embodies the position inferred from—not quite explicit in—Jefferson's Virginia statute (and Madison's *Memorial and Remonstrance*), which is the meaning discovered in it by the U.S. Supreme Court in 1947 (or perhaps already in 1878 in a Mormon polygamy case). In other words, did the authors of the First Amendment intend it to mean the radical separation of church and state? Over that question hovers a great cloud of polemical literature and tendentious history, which it is hoped the present pages will not increase.

It is not so easy to identify even who those authors were. James

Madison was certainly one; he wrote and introduced those first proposals in the House, was member of the House's committee of eleven to consider them, and then was the head of the House delegation to the conference committee that negotiated with the delegation from the Senate to produce the eventual result—perhaps even, as his biographer Irving Brant at first claimed, wrote it. But a legislative enactment, especially a constitutional amendment, is a collective product—*very* collective. There were, first of all, the other members of the House, including especially the participants in the debate, and more especially those who offered alternative proposals to Madison's—"national" and all—which, it should be noted, did not pass. Among those who offered an alternative was Samuel Livermore, a judge and, as Anson Phelps Stokes puts it, an Episcopalian from New Hampshire whose proposal was the basis for the final result. (Canon Stokes lists the contributors to this history by denominational affiliation. His volumes reflect an amiable, unpolemical combination of clear-cut commitment to separation of church from state on the one side with a belief in a "friendly" and cooperative relationship between the state and religion, without sharpening the issue into a choice. He published his volumes in 1950, just as the modern debate was heating up; most of his work had been done in earlier years, before advocates and polemicists had stamped across every inch of the territory. With its many limitations, it is therefore not a bad guide; he insisted upon the importance of Livermore at this historical moment.) Livermore's proposal, specifically put forward as an improvement on Madison's, was that "Congress shall make no law touching religion, or infringing the right of conscience." The first half of this is certainly clearer than Madison's and—the important point—Madison withdrew his proposal and Livermore's passed the House, 34 to 20. That offers much comfort to separationists.

But then of course there was the Senate. In that body, amendments were offered to the House proposals specifically setting forth the position that the more thoroughgoing "accommodationists" (that is, those not happy with the Supreme Court's "absolute wall") would defend in the twentieth century—that all these Founders intended to do was to reject preference of one religious group over another, and not to make a separation. But those proposals were twice rejected. One may be allowed to infer that the majority in the Senate intended something more in the way of separation.

Then the conference committee between the two houses met, and from it came —perhaps from Madison's hand, but in committees, who knows?—the version that was to be ratified and then to weave itself into the life of the nation: "Congress shall make no law Respecting an Establishment of Religion, or prohibiting the free exercise thereof. . . . "

But there is more. The amendments (twelve were submitted by Congress; two, relatively minor, were dropped) had to be ratified by the state legislatures. Some modern extreme accommodationists make much of the fact that some Virginia senators were worried that the proposed federal amendment did not sufficiently protect the religious rights protected by the Virginia statute, and that as a result ratification by the Virginia legislature was delayed for two years. The point of this—these arguments from one century using the events of another become intricate—is that if there was such hostility to the amendment in the Virginia Senate then that amendment, contrary to the views of strict separationists, must not have incorporated the position of the Virginia statute and of Jefferson and Madison. But then the separationists respond that these Virginia senators were a minority, and the amendment *was* ratified by the Virginia legislature, so it may be that the senators' fears were mistaken and the amendment *did* correspond to the Virginia law and concept. So the argument goes on.

On December 15, 1791, Virginia did ratify the amendments, including of course the First, with its religion clauses, and became the eleventh state to ratify—eleven were required to make the necessary two-thirds, because Vermont had been added to the original thirteen—and on that day the Bill of Rights became the law of the land. Disputants can, of course, include in their materials for argument the ratification proceedings in the other ten state legislatures, and perhaps also the opinions of the citizens who elected them, and perhaps also the history, religious and otherwise, of the colonies out of which they came, and perhaps also the proceedings of Congress—and then of the ratifying state legislatures—after the Civil War, when the Fourteenth Amendment was added to the Constitution, so that the Supreme Courts much later could find that Fourteenth applying that First to the states . . . and so on.

A few abrupt but quite tentative remarks in conclusion. James Madison was the most important single figure in shaping the First Amendment, and much respected, but his were hardly the only views expressed on the subject, nor were they altogether determinative of what it "meant" then, let alone now. Virginia's law and experience was the most important of any state's on this question, by far, but it was not the only state or the only experience. There was a diversity of opinion then, as now, on these matters, though not so wide a spread as now. The larger group of the relevant figures, and the actual outcome at each point of decision, endorsed separation, and went further than the simple repudiation of *preference* for one religious group, but not necessarily as far as James Madison himself, or the strict or absolute separationists of the twentieth century. When extreme accommodationists appeal, as they certainly do, to the "religious" character of the American people as some kind of evidence for their side, they do not include the fact—should this count for anything?—that the late eighteenth century was a low point, a kind of religious depression, in American religious history, with sparse church membership and attendance. So in congresses and all those legislatures, there would not have been as many believers as at other times. More significantly, among them—this point does often get overlooked—there was a large body of sectarians and dissenters, Baptists in particular but also Quakers and continental sectarians, and also many Presbyterians and Methodists and others, who believed in complete separation of church and state not on nonreligious rational or political grounds but because of their religious conviction. Isaac Backus is perhaps the most outstanding representative of this position, but it characterized almost all Baptists, and many others as well. It tends to be ignored by twentieth-century religionists arguing against what they call "secularism," seeking greater governmental accommodation, and calling on all the religious folk in America's past as evidence for their modern argument. But a considerable part of the religious folk in America's past held, exactly on the grounds of their faith, almost the opposite of what these modern interpreters cite them to support.

At this stage of his career Madison's primary interest was to draw a bill of rights that, while perhaps adding a certain firmness to the ground of already established liberties, would also gather increased support for the new Constitution and the new government by meeting the dissatisfaction of the best of the Antifederalists, and of friends of his like Thomas Jefferson, and people he admired like George Mason. He was at this point a statesman of the Constitution and of the Union. The full expression of his view of religion in a republic was already in place in Virginia, and would require time to develop in some other states. In time, it would develop, but on grounds nearer to those of Isaac Backus than of Madison. Madison now wanted to put together the combination that would make a national government of liberty work.

When he presented the proposed set of rights, Madison's arguments in its behalf countered some of the positions he himself had been inclined to take in the Philadelphia Convention and shortly thereafter. Now he stated that a bill of rights could serve, though it be only a "parchment barrier," as a shaper of public understanding, and a basis for appeal by minorities against overweening majorities. After the water of much history has passed under the American bridge, and despite much disputing, that in fact is what it has come to be.

JAMES MADISON LATER, AND STILL LATER

James Madison went on to become an all-purpose longtime scholar-statesman serving in that bewildering assortment of offices and roles, and dealing with that wide spectrum of issues, possible for a person of his talent, brains, and diligence in the small and new country. The issue of religious liberty, more or less solved, receded into the background as his enormous career unfolded, and he became a legislative captain, an advisor to the first president, a factional party leader, a secretary of state, a president himself, an elder statesman. But though, as the country got rolling, the issue of religious liberty came to be outdistanced by many others—ratification of the Constitution; the money matters left over from the war; arguments over the French Revolution, the Jay treaty, the XYZ affair, and the beginning of parties; the Alien and Sedition Laws and the Virginia and Kentucky resolutions; the Louisiana Purchase; a national bank; the Embargo and the War of 1812; Nullification—nevertheless whenever in Madison's subsequent career this issue of religious liberty came round once again, he promptly responded with a veto message, a letter, or a statement that reaffirmed once again the position he had worked out and fought for in Virginia in his youth. Those modern interpreters who make of consistency the prime criterion for judging the positions of these giants from our past can give Madison (and Jefferson too) very high marks on this subject, as perhaps not on others.

A book by Leonard Levy, *Jefferson and Civil Liberties: The Darker Side*, puts together the episodes in Jefferson's actual performance—as governor, as president, in the Aaron Burr affair, in dealing with scurrilous journalists, and the like—in which Mr. Levy finds Mr. Jefferson's actual conduct falling short of the principles of civil liberty of which he was so eloquent a theoretical defender. But before getting down to his critical argument on other matters, Mr. Levy sets aside religious liberty and church-state separation. On those matters, he grants, or insists, Jefferson was consistent throughout, and therefore praiseworthy. If such a book were to be written about James Madison, it might be difficult for the writer to find such a fault in his career on the substance of civil liberties, though certainly one would find many changes in position on other subjects: for and against a federal bill of rights, as we have seen; in favor of a stronger, and then apparently a weaker, federal government, with respect to the states; and so on. But for him, too, religious liberty would have to be set aside. He, too, held to one position on religious liberty and church-state separation throughout his long career.

Madison has a posthumous career, like that of the other Founders, as an image and a symbol, and as an authority, in the developing culture of the American nation—though not of course approaching in visibility that of the Father of his Country, or of the Apostle of Liberty, or of the quintessentially American creator of Poor Richard, his Almanac and his "Way to Wealth," or even that of Alexander Hamilton or John Adams. Still, interest in him on the part of scholars and intellectuals, if not the broad public, has increased markedly since World War II; among other developments, recent scholarship has assigned to him numbers of *The Federalist* that had earlier been assigned to Hamilton or left in doubt. Quotations from Madison, usually from Federalist Ten and Fifty-one, abound.

Because the United States is so much conscious of itself as a nation brought into being by specific acts of specific persons at a specific time, and for other reasons as well—their individual and collective virtues— the Founders have become authorities to whom appeal continually is made by their countrymen. The story of the historical vicissitudes of the "image" of each one of them could be written, in the way that Merrill Peterson has done for Jefferson in *The Jefferson Image in the American Mind.* The book on Madison would be short.

But the chapter on Madison's image in the late twentieth century would be one of the longer ones, and the entries under the topic of church and state would be numerous. It is not clear that these two facets of the growing interest in Madison have as yet been put together by scholars: on the one hand, the study of Madison as part of the larger study of "republicanism" as an ideology in the Revolutionary and Founding periods—of which, more below; on the other hand, the continual references to Madison in the literature on church and state.

The authoritative provocation for much of the latter is to be found in decisions of the U.S. Supreme Court. In 1878, when the Court first dealt with the "free-exercise" clause, in a Mormon polygamy case, its decision summarized much of the Virginia history recounted here: the contest over the General Assessment; the *Memorial and Remonstrance* prepared by "Mr. Madison," the statute written by "Mr. Jefferson," and in particular the phrase in the statute's preamble "that it is time enough for the rightful purposes of civil government for its officers to interfere when principles break out into overt acts against peace and good order." This sentence was important to the Court because it was rejecting the claim that "celestial" or plural marriage as a part of the Mormon religion was protected by the free-exercise clause. By the First Amendment, as interpreted by these authoritative Virginians, Mr. Chief Justice Morrison Waite wrote, "Congress was deprived of all legislative power over mere opinion, but was left free to reach actions which were in violation of social duties or subversive of good order." Polygamy was such an action. The Court made a distinction between religious belief, which was absolutely free, and action based upon such belief, which could not be—a distinction still disputed.

On its way to that conclusion the Court opinion recounted also a brief history of the Bill of Rights. With Mr. Jefferson in France, Mr. Madison became the carrier who deposited the Virginia position in the First Amendment's religion clause. Then the 1878 Court made another historical reference: Thomas Jefferson's letter in 1801 to the Danbury Baptist Association, in which he floated upon the waters of American culture the figure of speech that has trailed the subject ever since. Mr. Jefferson wrote: "I contemplate with sovereign reverence that act of the whole American people which declared that their Legislature should..." and here Jefferson quoted the religion clauses of the First Amendment, and then continued, "thus building a wall of separation between Church and State." In the years since Jefferson wrote that sentence this subject has been accompanied by that figure of speech: by that wall, building it and resisting "breaches" in it and making it high and impregnable and finding cracks in it and making plays on words and poetical allusions about it and insisting it is no fine line easily overstepped and suggesting that a rule of law cannot be drawn from such a figure of speech and fearing that it will become as winding as the famous walls designed by Mr. Jefferson for the university he founded. In 1878, on first introducing it into judicial literature, Mr. Chief Justice Waite wrote of Jefferson's letter "coming as it does from an acknowledged leader of the advocates of the measure it may be accepted almost as an authoritative declaration of the scope and effect of the amendment thus secured." The "almost" is interesting.

Decades pass. In the 1947 New Jersey bus-fare case (Everson) to which we have already referred, the sharply divided (5–4) Court set forth, in the majority opinion by Justice Hugo Black, a thoroughly Jeffersonian and Madisonian position, and the strongest dissent, by Justice Wiley Rutledge, set forth an even more Jeffersonian and Madisonian position. Both opinions were drenched in quotations from, and references to, the two Virginians. Justice Black's was (explicitly) an absolute wall-of-separation opinion; Justice Rutledge's dissent was—one can say this, despite the logical impossibility—an even more absolute wall-of-separation opinion. The majority—Justice Black—though insisting, with a shower of references to Jefferson and Madison, that the First Amendment means no aid to religion, even nonpreferentially, and that it sets up an absolute, a "high and impregnable" wall, and that "we" (the Court) would not abide the slightest breach—nevertheless found reimbursement to parents for their children's bus rides to Catholic schools, by Ewing Township in New Jersey, to be constitutionally permissible. It was the contrast between the absoluteness of the opinion and the discriminate permissiveness of the decision that brought forth from Justice Jackson, in another dissenting opinion, a literary reference that is often quoted: that the most fitting precedent to the Court's performance was Byron's Julia, who "whispering 'I will ne'er consent'—consented." Justice Rutledge did not consent. He gave the subject the full Madisonian treatment, as understood by a twentieth-century individualistic Baptist, including another recounting of the Virginia history, many references to Jefferson and Madison, and the reprinting of the entire *Memorial and Remonstrance*, and the General Assessment bill as well, to insist, in effect, that James Madison would certainly not have allowed that reimbursement of those bus fares.

Then a year later, in the Champaign, Illinois, released-time case (McCollum), the Supreme Court for the first time applied the understanding of the Madisonian-Jeffersonian wall-of-separation First Amendment that had been announced in the New Jersey bus-fare case (it means no aid to religion, even nonpreferentially) in a way that had a bite to it: the Court struck down a "released-time" program of elective religious instruction, during school hours, in the school building, in the Champaign public schools, as constitutionally impermissible. This time Black and Rutledge were on the same side, along with the other dissenters in the New Jersey case—Jackson, Frankfurter, and Harold Burton. The decision was 8 to 1, with only Justice Stanley Reed dissenting. But out in the country there was a howl of protest—two howls, actually, when the two cases were put together. The modern argument about the Establishment clause was under way.

On the far edge of one side (roughly) were those strictest separationists who agreed with Justice Rutledge that the New Jersey bus-fare reimbursements were an unconstitutional breach in Mr. Jefferson's wall; they rejected the theory by which these payments were justified—that they were for the safety or benefit of the children, and of society, not directly of religion, and therefore allowable. A group with the perhaps revealing name, as it then was, "Protestants and Other Americans United for the Separation of Church and State," or POAU, came into being. A reading of its literature makes plain why it was necessary for the organization regularly to protest that it was not anti-Catholic. (It has since dropped the "P" [along with the "O"] from its name, and become much tamer.)

On the other side, roughly, were those who felt that the Court's high-wall interpretation of the First Amendment as meaning no aid at all to religion, was constitutionally mistaken; they would have found both the bus fares and the released-time program allowable. In 1952, with a New York dismissed-time case (Zorach), they acquired a name—accommodationists—and some valuable quotations from the Court, including their all-time favorite, from Justice Douglas in the majority opinion:

> We are a religious people whose institutions presuppose a Supreme Being.... when the state encourages religious instruction or cooperates with religious authorities by adjusting the schedule of public events to sectarian needs, it follows the best of our traditions. For it then respects the religious nature of our people and accommodates the public service to their spiritual needs.

The New York program under review was like the one in Champaign, except that the religious classes students were released to attend were held off school property, generally at churches and synagogues. The dissenters—Black, Jackson, and Frankfurter—were sharp to the point of bitterness; Jackson wrote that the distinctions found between the

Illinois and the New York programs were "trivial almost to the point of cynicism," and that "the wall which the Court was professing to erect between church and state has become even more warped and twisted than I expected." There were even those who were impolite enough to suggest that the large public outcry against the McCollum decision and the Everson-McCollum high-wall no-aid rule had something to do with the Zorach outcome. The day when the general run of Americans could comfortably believe more or less simultaneously in a wall of separation and in a friendly accommodation of the state to this (more or less!) religious people, without much strain or contradiction—that day seemed to have drawn to a close.

As time went on, the Court put aside references to walls; tried the concept of "neutrality" instead; stirred another angry public outcry with prayer and Bible reading cases in 1962 and 1963; chopped and split decisions about what the state could and could not properly do in indirect aid to parochial schools; risked an intellectual double hernia working out a complicated three-point rule to test constitutionality under the establishment clause, staying within both the Everson-McCollum rule and the Zorach rule. (The Zorach decision, despite its flavor and outcome, did not overturn the earlier one, but affirmed it, and it has since been reaffirmed.) References to Jefferson and to Madison faded somewhat from the Court's opinions, giving place to the Court's references to itself. But the two Virginians loom still in the background, the high principle they worked out in their nation-shaping moment, when high principle was appropriate, now called upon in the very different moment we live in, when something short of high principle— tact and wisdom, for example—might be more suitable.

The accommodationists have had to decide what to do about Jefferson and Madison. Justice Stanley Reed, in the sole dissent in the McCollum case, showed one tack they could take—to dispute the interpretation of the two Virginians' position. Jefferson and Madison did not believe *that*. Reed found that quotation from Madison about a "national" religion in the debates in the First Congress over what was to become the First Amendment, and interpreted it as signifying that Madison believed the Amendment was to do no more than prohibit a single established religion and compulsory worship. He wrote that a reading of the statements of these "eminent statesmen of former days" whom his colleagues had been referring to—he specifically mentioned the *Memorial and Remonstrance*—revealed that they had been dealing with a situation quite different from the facts in the Illinois case: with direct tax support of religion. When it came to religious education, they did permit it at the University of Virginia. Reed quoted a provision of Mr. Jefferson's university, based on Jefferson's own suggestions, and promulgated in 1824 while James Madison was a member of the Board of Visitors, that specified that if the "religious sects" of the state accepted the invitation to establish "within, or adjacent to, the precincts of the University" schools for instruction in the religion of their sect, that students would be "free, and expected to" attend religious worship at the place of their respective sects. Reed said that situation was more nearly analogous to the Champaign case than the General Assessment, and provided the more accurate reading of Jefferson and Madison in such a matter.

In the popular disputation that has developed since these Court cases, thoroughgoing accommodationists may quote a paragraph from Jefferson's Second Inaugural or refer to the edition of the gospels that Jefferson made late in his life (Julian Boyd's successor as editor of the Jefferson papers describes Jefferson as a "demythologized Christian," which seems reassuring to believers), or deistic references from the Declaration of Independence or even from Madison's *Memorial and Remonstrance*, as evidence intended to put some distance between the mind and belief of these Founders and that of the 1940s Supreme Court. (It is *very* hard to persuade the accommodationists out in the broad public that strict separation does not mean hostility to religion; therefore, evidence of belief in God on the part of these authority figures is taken to be relevant.)

But the other tack that may be taken by critics of the high "wall" is to do what the most formidable early champion of that position did and simply reject Madison's conception out of hand (and one would assume, Jefferson's, too). In 1949, after those two Supreme Court cases started the modern conflict, the distinguished American Catholic thinker John Courtney Murray, in Duke University's journal *Law and Contemporary Problems*, attacked with pungent force the *absoluteness* of the position the Court had proclaimed. At the start, Murray explained that although he knew Justice Holmes held the life of the law to be not logic but experience, still there could be no assurance that the Court was immune from "sudden attacks of logic." Therefore beware.

Murray held that if *absolute* separation were now found to be the meaning of the establishment clause of the First Amendment, then the Court would indeed have established a religion—James Madison's religion. Murray took over as accurate Justice Rutledge's interpretation of this Madisonian religion as holding religion to be a "wholly private matter." That conception—a conception, Murray insisted, in "the theological order"—was, he wrote dismissively, "an irredeemable piece of sectarian dogmatism." (Father Murray did not refer to Jefferson, but he did refer to the Virginia statute as representing "the Madisonian idea.")

Now, a reader of a different persuasion—a reader who, let us say, finds that, in a slight change from the familiar position of active politicians, he has enemies on both sides—may have difficulty joining Father Murray in putting James Madison (and Thomas Jefferson) so far off into the unacceptable fringes of the national life as he does. And such a reader may balk at Murray's phrase "a deistic version of fundamentalist protestantism" as a description of the position of Madison, or of the Court in the late forties, or of anybody else at any time anywhere. Father Murray, in the intensity of his powerful attack on the opinions of Black, Rutledge, Frankfurter, et al., may somewhat have distorted in his twentieth-century argument the eighteenth-century convictions of James Madison. Perhaps, on the other side, Rutledge did, too.

Murray did have the courtesy not to try to make James Madison over into someone who really would today have endorsed Murray's own position. But it does seem more than a little odd to find James Madison shoved clear over to an idiosyncratic periphery of American thought on religion and society.

Jemmy could not have guessed what would hit him over a century after his death: that Supreme Court justices would make him a rigid privatist, and then a distinguished Jesuit would accuse him of being a dogmatic fundamentalist, and outside the American tradition as well.

James Madison would become, in the twentieth century, a symbol for rather contrasting political convictions. One can imagine a young academic in the late twentieth century—a conservative Christian, let us say—stimulated by Murray's attack on Madison on the subject of church and state, but otherwise inclined to be sympathetic to Madison's political thought, who would construct an article for a scholarly journal, called "The Two Madisons." In such an article the premises and rhetoric of the pounding single-minded argument of the *Memorial and Remonstrance* would be contrasted to the complex prudential reasoning of Madison's contributions to *The Federalist*, and indeed, of Madison's work in general. As others examine the Adam Smith Problem, in which the puzzle is the relationship between the selfishness apparently endorsed by the Smith of the *Wealth of Nations* and the moral sense and humane possibilities envisioned by the Smith of *The Theory of Moral Sentiments*; or still others, the alleged conflict in Machiavelli between the familiar outlook of *The Prince*, especially the core chapters 18–25, and the more republican and less—well, less Machiavellian—flavor of his "Discourses on Livy" and other writings, so this budding scholar might formulate a James Madison problem: the conflict between the overarching prudence, caution, and balance-the-differences pluralism, and the realism and sense of historical continuity—greater than Jefferson's—which Madison displays in all other regards, and his uncompromising absolutism on the one subject of separation of church and state.

The chief of Madison's contributions in the domain of ideas, this article might say, was a political philosophy that shows that perennial human differences and conflicts, and a persistent human self-interest, can be made to serve not chaos or tyranny but "republican" government—serve liberty. Set ambition to check ambition; contrive institutions so faction balances faction. By implication his pluralism and realism recommend prudence and compromise and a toleration of diversity, and Madison as politician exhibited those qualities. But, this scholar might claim, Madison did not display the same characteristics on the subject of religion and the state. In that matter, it would be said, Madison's outlook or position or style was more characteristic of Henry David Thoreau and Tom Paine and William Lloyd Garrison on their topics than of Madison on his. The writer of this article—let us make him a male—might quote Ralph Ketcham's statement that the *Memorial and Remonstrance* is "worthy of Locke, Milton, or Mill" to ask, to the contrary, is it worthy of James Madison? Having encountered opening wedges and camels' noses in argument with modern strict separationists, he might cite in particular the parts of the *Memorial and Remonstrance* to which appeal in behalf of such arguments is most often made today. He would mention in particular the third of Madison's points: Do not let the question become "entangled in precedent," avoid the consequences by denying the principle; not three pence! But— the scholar might ask—do whole camels always follow their noses? Is not most of political life a matter of so far—and no farther? Was the analogy to the "late revolution" accurate? Was there indeed a *principle* at stake in the General Assessment—a principle, analogous to the great principles of the Revolution, that went so deep and was so exclusive as to make even the shadow of anticipation of its most extreme application as repugnant as the extreme itself?

Another of Madison's points would yield this scholar an illustration. In his stinging advocacy in the *Memorial*, he would say, Madison carried the projection of the dire consequences of a small "precedent," of a "three pence" tax for religion teachers as far as this: "Distant as it may be in its present form from the Inquisition, it differs from it only in degree."

Citing the Inquisition as the companion-in-principle to poor Patrick Henry's small General Assessment tax for Christian teachers in eighteenth-century Virginia might then be presented, by our putative young scholar, as a mite excessive—like the comparisons in the twentieth century of any local tyrant or objectionable regulation to Hitler and the Nazis. That excess, he might say, suggests that some passion has seeped into the mind and pushed it to leap over distinctions. Where Madison shows on other subjects a judicious, calibrated, distinction-making outlook, aware of the relativities, on this matter prudence and restraint are left behind. This article might cite as further evidence Madison's extreme position on other, later, occasions. Madison was to worry about a national census if it numbered the professions, because that would mean counting *clergymen*. He was opposed to government-paid chaplains in the armed services, and to chaplains in Congress. He objected to presidential proclamations of holidays. He vetoed a grant, by Congress, of land for a Baptist church in Mississippi. On this subject alone, this article might say, the statesman of artful accommodations shifted roles to become the single-principled absolutist. And it might conclude that what—instead—this issue needed then, and needs today, is Madisonian statesmanship.

The next issue of that scholarly quarterly would surely include a piece called "Only One Madison: A Rejoinder." This respondent might insist upon the difference in situation between James Madison in post-revolutionary Virginia and the disputants about quite particular church-state matters in the two-hundred-year-old already established and fully functioning United States. If Virginia in 1785 was a long way from the Spanish Inquisition, the United States in the late twentieth century is also a long way from Virginia in 1785. Madison was examining these issues not to decide whether there should be a crèche on the courthouse lawn, but to determine the essential shape of the new governments. It was one of those rare moments when they could be shaped, and when the most fundamental principles for doing so were in dispute. The nature of the "republican" governments now to be formed was still to be worked out; Madison was arguing about their very foundations. At that time there *was* a principle at stake. If Virginia then was not so close to the Inquisition, it was not so distant from ecclesiastical power in politics, and even from religious persecution. Madison was arguing strenuously to get a principle established in a setting in which that was appropriate. In any setting, even a politician who is not an absolutist but who follows the "ethic of responsibility"—here the responding young scholar would of course quote Max Weber's "Politics as a Vocation"—a mature politician who takes account of the average deficiencies of mankind, and the consequences of his action, and has a genuine vocation for politics, may nevertheless find himself in the situation in which he must invoke the clear finality of a principle: The making of a new government, although not the same as the moment one invokes Martin Luther's "here I stand, I can do no other," is not the same as the day-to-day shaping of policy in a functioning government, either. By its nature it requires recourse to first principles. And James Madison, like many others in his generation, had such recourse not only with reference to religious liberty but also to discover the other characteristics of the republican government they were now constructing. In other words, his thought on church and state was not different from, but continuous with, the reflective examination of the foundations of republican government that was his greatest work.

While citing points from the *Memorial and Remonstrance*, this respondent might refer again to point nine, which is the one that makes the reference to the Inquisition, but also argues in behalf of that "generous policy, which, offering an Asylum to the persecuted and oppressed of every Nation and Religion, promised a lustre to our country." He might allow himself the hint that Madison's principled position in Virginia, extended then to the United States, *did* offer such asylum, and did remove religion as an impediment to immigration, and did not only bring luster to our country but also the changed social composition of the nation from which now sometimes comes some of the objection to the principles of liberty Madison and his colleagues so powerfully defended. Moreover, this respondent might say, the founding period was not the only time, nor was religious liberty the only issue on which he sought, and argued for, a fundamental political principle. When in the 1790s the Alien and Sedition Laws put other rights at risk, Madison was, as author of the Virginia Resolutions, once again the pointed and fervent advocate of the fundamentals of liberty. His position on church and state, this respondent might conclude, was not contrary to, but part of, his statesmanship, and later generations should be grateful for it.

MADISON AS IRONICAL EXEMPLAR
OF REPUBLICAN VIRTUE

The historical understanding of the period of the American Revolution—now to leave behind imaginary articles and to draw upon real ones—has undergone since the Second World War a considerable alteration. At the center of this alteration is the ideological configuration called republicanism, and although that configuration is seen to have characterized all of the generation of giants, close to its center is James Madison.

The scholars who find this set of ideas at the heart of the Revolution and of the Founders alter sharply the earlier view, associated still in the minds of many with Charles Beard and the progressive historians, that saw in such events not political thought and moral argument but economic interest and historical force. To the contrary: Ideas mattered. In fact, as one reads the more recent historical accounts of late eighteenth-century America, one sees that ideas mattered supremely. And to find the Founders' republicanism to be an ideology is to see it extended beyond ideas about government to ideas about society, about human nature, about the moral requirements of citizenship.

The delineation now of the republicanism of the Founders means the comparative subordination, as a source and symbol of those ideas, of John Locke—compared, that is, to the day when Locke's intellectual role would be seen in such exaggerated terms as to describe him as the "Marx of the American Revolution," or the mind of the American nation as "John Locke writ large." Alongside Locke there now emerged a cluster of early eighteenth-century English radicals who continued, and revised, the ideas cast up in the great stirring of the English Civil War, and kept on developing those ideas after the Commonwealth was over, and after the ideas associated with it had lost out in England.

These Commonwealthmen, as they were called in one of the early books in this modern historical development, were not original political thinkers, but journalists, publicists, coffeehouse radicals—writers in early eighteenth-century England whose names are not much known to the general public but who transmitted the outlook of one better-known group (associated with the seventeenth-century English Civil War and Commonwealth: John Milton in his role as political-religious pamphleteer; Algernon Sydney; James Harrington; the Levelers) to another better-known group (the American Founders).

These transmitters, one learns, carried on the synthesizing begun in the Commonwealth, fitting together disparate ingredients to make something approaching what today would be called a "normative model" of a "republic." There were materials from the period of, and writers about, the republics of classical antiquity, Athens, Sparta, and particularly Rome; from Puritan and dissenting thought in England; from Whig versions of the history of English institutions; from Machiavelli and Renaissance thought about and experience of republican government; from Switzerland and Holland. These coffeehouse radical Whigs, looking back to the Commonwealth, had little influence in post-Restoration England, but—historians now tell us—their ideas reverberated in the colonies across the Atlantic, where they fit the situation, and where the colonists took them up into their own thinking and disputing and pamphleteering.

This historical material helps a reader to see that the Founders' now apparently eclectic references to classical sources and then to Biblical sources and afterward to Montesquieu or Harrington or Sydney, are not such a melange as they may seem, but a more coherent and focused, if vague, ideology: "republicanism."

Two of the most important books that have brought this out in recent decades deal with two eighteenth-century periods: the years leading up to independence, in Bernard Bailyn's *The Ideological Origins of the American Revolution*, published in 1967 after having been anticipated by the introduction to Bailyn's collection of the pamphlets of the American Revolution, and the years from independence to the federal Constitution in Gordon Wood's *The Creation of the American Republic 1776–1787*, published in 1969, in which Wood specifies a major indebtedness to Bailyn. J. G. A. Pocock's *The Machiavellian Moment*, published in 1976, casts a wider net, in which is found the American republic as the outcome of a long European history of republics, notably in the Renaissance.

One can see the American Revolution and Republic as a realization of the purposes of the Puritan Revolution and Commonwealth in England, aborted there but fulfilled, over a century later and an ocean away, in the colonies. So it is seen in the leading history of religion in America, *A Religious History of the American People*, by Sydney Ahlstrom. Or, without sharp contradiction, one can see these American events as a fulfillment of, and advance upon, the long Western tradition of thought about and experience of republican life and government, a stream that begins in Greece and Rome, trickles along underground to come up in Florence and Venice in the Renaissance and after the Reformation in Switzerland and Holland, and particularly then in seventeenth-century England. It is examined conceptually in and after and around the English Civil War—the Puritan Revolution, as it used to be called—and the Commonwealth. A deposit of ideas from that experience is put together by the radical Whigs—the Commonwealthmen—in early eighteenth-century England, and leaps across the Atlantic to the colonists. They apply, and revise, and realize the republican ideology, and apply it as was thought impossible, not in a small and homogeneous community but in a continent-sized state.

Meanwhile—exactly during the time the American colonies were puzzling out their political philosophy and their legal forms—there took place that intellectual flowering in Scotland known as the Scottish Enlightenment, which produced not only Adam Smith's *Wealth of Nations*, and John Witherspoon and other Presbyterian exports to the colonies, but also a ferment of moral and political thinking upon which the American Founders drew. The scholar/journalist Gary Wills, in recent books about America's beginnings, has placed special emphasis on this Scottish connection, and has linked Madison particularly with the political writings of one of the Scottish Enlightenment's greatest representatives, David Hume. In all this, Wills was developing the work of a Yale scholar of the World War II years, a man whose name crops up in all these books, Douglas Adair.

And here in the middle of all this new history is our friend James Madison. Prominent among the early articles arousing this outpouring were several about Madison, notably by Adair. Whereas the older interpretation by the progressive historians like Beard had seen in the Constitution-makers and in Madison particularly a defense of property and of economic interest, these more recent historians find the Founders moved, instead, by a moral and intellectual construct—republicanism—and no one more than Madison, who worked away during all those years thinking it through, reflecting on what it meant, and figuring out how to make it work.

But the republicanism of the Founders' generation is not identified, as the new scholarly examination develops, solely with the positions and the party of which Madison was later to be a leader. Varied, vague, and changing though historians find it to have been, it was something like the ideological ground music that can be heard in any political culture: Everybody hears it, all sides appeal to it, it is taken for granted. Patrick Henry would appeal to it as much when he supported, as James Madison when he opposed, the General Assessment; Henry and George Mason as much when they opposed, as Madison when he defended, the federal Constitution; Hamilton as much, or almost as much, with his high Federalism, as Madison and Jefferson with their "republican" party. One infers that it was a language and an angle on the world that was in the air, in something of the way that—let us reach for comparison— Romanticism was in the middle of the nineteenth century or existentialism in and around World War II. And it had come up out of the underground of an earlier time—as existentialism from nineteenth-century thinkers and themes not on the surface of culture in their own time, so with the Commonwealthmen obscure in theirs.

All cultural moments, of course, have such foci or themes or commonplaces or climates of opinion. The republicanism of the Americans in the last half of the eighteenth century, though, appears to have been a particularly potent brew because of its social and practical meaning, and the historical opportunity presented by the moment to make it real. It caught up James Madison and William Bradford and the others in the radical sense that they were bringing into being something distinct in human history: a real republic, correcting the deficiencies in those other republics, in the English "constitution," in the aborted English Commonwealth.

After the first utopian thrill of 1776, the now independent colonists worked out, in a piecemeal way, in the ricochet of responses among many experiences, and in the minds of many, but for all that at a highly accelerated, highly charged pace, a recognizably new political philosophy, breaking with the classical past: "diffusive and open-ended; not delineated in a single book . . . not political theory in the grand manner, but . . . political theory worthy of a prominent place in the history of Western thought." So it is described at the end of Wood's book.

Madison, as stated, was near the center of all this. Although John Adams wrote formidable speculative political treatises, as Madison did not, Adams's caustic honesty and vanity, and his absence, in England, from the new nation during the idea-filled rapidly changing eighties, left him, as Wood presents him, outside the mainstream of development of the American system of politics, not comprehending it. To be *present* is a great thing, as politicians know (also to be absent at the right time, but that is another matter). Thomas Jefferson certainly was not to be outside that mainstream of American republicanism in the longer run; he was to become its very apostle. But in the eighties, he, too, was overseas, as we know, enjoying himself in Paris, writing letters, to be sure, but not as important to its development in those decisive founding years as his younger friend. Hamilton was of course to be very important, the energetic organizer of *The Federalist* project and writer of the largest fraction of its numbers. He was closer perhaps to Madison in their collaborations in the eighties than a retrospective association of Madison with Jefferson, after the splits of the nineties, would see him to be. But still Hamilton's aristocratic inclination left him a little out of the center of the current. Others not well known, perhaps not sufficiently honored, played significant roles: James Wilson, second in importance only to Madison at the Philadelphia Convention and perhaps in interpreting it afterwards; George Mason; many others—a "diverse and scattered authorship," wrote Gordon Wood. But no one person was more important than James Madison, present all the time, acting all the time, revising his thought again and again, subordinating his ego to the objective task at hand (as Adams and perhaps others did not), on the winning side in the big decisions (politicians know the importance of that, too; perhaps everybody does) and giving the most influential statements of the constitutional and theoretical outcome.

The largest feature of this American theory when finally in place, as Bailyn and Wood present it, was a radical revision of the historic relation of power to liberty, of the rulers to the people. "In Europe," wrote Madison, in 1792, "charters of liberty have been granted by power. America has set the example and France has followed it, of charters of power granted by liberty." (This quotation appears as a headnote in Bailyn.) The radical Whigs had above all a suspicion of power—all power. James Madison would write that where power is, there is the threat to liberty: "Human nature" makes it so. One learns from a footnote in Bailyn's book that Madison's "realistic" view of human nature, especially in Federalist Ten and Fifty-one, the most discussed of all the topics in this domain, subject to multitudinous articles and references, is not distinctive to Madison but a common thread of Whig-republican literature.

After much arguing and writing and thinking, and many events, the theory develops: The people come to be seen as the fountain of *all* power, themselves their own rulers, making a government of mixtures which only in external form, and not in substance, resembles the "mixed" governments of the Western past. The several parts of the mixture do not represent separate parts of the body politic—this branch the monarch, this the aristocracy, this other the people; this the one, that the few, the other the many; one estate for this and another estate for that component of the social order. All, the federal government as well as the states, the executive and judicial branches as well as the legislature, the Senate as well as the House—all, in different degrees of mediation, are agencies to represent the single, whole, and undivided people. There are not *two* entities, ruler and ruled, who then make a compact, the ruler with the prior prerogative of power granting to the ruled their limited claims of liberty, as in the Magna Carta; there is only one entity, the people, at once the ruler and the ruled—self-government.

The people are the fountain of *all* power. The government is a complicated mixture not so that each part might represent a separate piece of the social order but so that the people might have several agents to represent them, the diversity of agents serving the several functions, and also checking and restraining one another.

Those sentences from Federalist Fifty-one, often quoted now, particularly but not exclusively by conservatives, about ambition checking ambition, about government being a reflection of human nature and men not being angels, appear in the treatment of the separated branches of the federal government. But the consideration of the balances in that domain—"giving to those who administer each department the necessary constitutional means and personal motives to resist encroachments of the others"—led Madison quickly out into the "whole system of human affairs, private as well as public," in all of which can be traced "this policy of supplying, by opposite and rival interests, the defect of better motives." In the further discussion of this "policy" Madison comes to the analogy between the protection of "religious rights" and of civil rights that has already been quoted: multiplicity of sects, multiplicity of interests.

In the eighteenth-century setting it still made sense to apply the "republican" suspicion of all power to "ecclesiastical power," as James Madison did from the days of his earliest reflections, and as a great many other of the colonists, the Americans, did, too. Bailyn shows the "contagion of liberty" spreading out from the powerful republican impetus of the Revolution to challenge dominion and authority across the social order: to the institution of human slavery, to all sorts of rank and privilege, to the establishment of religion. To some extent the story in Virginia and the parallel stories in other states are a phase of the spreading revolutionary republicanism, challenging churchly power, along with other power, to achieve or protect liberty.

It is not clear, however, that the historical scholarship we have been more or less describing has integrated into its new understanding the religious matters here-discussed—the *Memorial and Remonstrance*, the fight in Virginia, and the like. Wood's long book never touches the subject. Neither is it clear that the still larger, related subject—the relationship of the religious tradition of the West to this "republican" tradition and to the new American "republican" development—has been fitted together. Historians, like other people, can see only with their own eyes, and therefore selectively.

This new history-writing has supplanted Beard and the progressives, and their economic reductionism, with a heavy underscoring of the importance to the Founders of moral and political *ideas*. And with reference to ideas it has demoted John Locke, reducing him simply to one among a number of influences on American republic-making. The significance of this demotion is that demoted with Locke is the radical individualism of which he is taken to be (rightly or wrongly) the symbol. To us, looking back after the triumph of the capitalist ethos, and the earlier triumph of the individualism of evangelical Protestantism, it may appear a convincing notion that (as in Louis Hartz's presentation) a Lockean (i.e., individualist) absolutism dominated American culture from the start. But Madison and the other Founders did not, oddly enough, know what would be forthcoming in the centuries *after* their deaths, and for them—this new historical scholarship maintains or implies—humankind was meant to live together in society in a much more public and social, much more communally responsible, way than the later American ethos would accept: a way whose hallmarks were the public virtue, public liberty, public happiness of republicanism, the humane sociability of the Scottish Enlightenment.

But it is not yet clear how all of this may be connected with the prime teacher of mutual obligation and of the common good in the history of the West, the Christian tradition. Certainly there were in the days of our founding some togas and Latin names like Cato and Publius; but for all that, those Founders must have been closer to English Puritans and Scotch Presbyterians than they were to Romans.

Madison and the other defenders of the federal Constitution had by the end of the 1780s come to a striking trust not only in big-country pluralism but also in institutionalism—in arranging the machinery of government properly—as the true security of liberty and expression of republicanism. That meant a marked change in emphasis from the ideas of 1776, with respect not only to the size of a desirable state but also to the role of "virtue" in a republic. A decade earlier republicanism had regularly had in it a strong requirement of moral regeneration— the need for a new people with the habits required by, and in part brought into being by, republican institutions. In the ideological mixture there was an echo at least of Puritan sermons. But by the time of the making of the Constitution the somewhat disillusioning experience in the states led to the design of institutions to protect liberty even if such regeneration was not forthcoming.

One can trace this change in Bailyn's and Wood's books, and in Madison's life and work. In the radical Whigs and in the colonists' developing outlook before independence and in the period just afterward, the concept of public virtue had stood at or near the center of "republicanism," as indeed it had in much of Western history. A monarchy built on fear, an aristocracy on honor, a republic on virtue. By the end of the constitutional period, though virtue was of course still important, the defenders of the Constitution had come to the view that one should build republican institutions which could preserve liberty even in virtue's absence.

Virtue is a word that, like others in the republican lexicon, changes its connotation over time. Twentieth-century Americans who now refer nostalgically to this theme of virtue among the Founders may not always understand the word to mean *public* virtue, because the divisions in the mind since that time have relegated the language of morals almost entirely to the realm of individual conduct and "private" affairs. A twentieth-century American does not think of "virtue" characterizing a condition of public life. And this shriveled notion of "virtue" does not necessarily imply the collective frugality and even austerity, the simplicity of life and manners, the abjuring of "luxury" and avoiding of "corruption," that it meant or entailed for these earlier Americans.

In the heady utopian moment of 1776 and just afterward, the "Americans," newly independent, fighting the British, writing their state constitutions, forming new governments, thought that the republican governments they were bringing into being both required and would produce and sustain such virtue in the citizenry. Public virtue meant most particularly a general willingness to rise above, to set aside, to sacrifice if need be, private, personal, "selfish" interests in order to serve the *res publica*—the affairs that affect the good of the public, which would be at the center of any good republican's life. Of course a "republic" entails such public virtue, such general devotion to the public good almost by its definition, certainly by its needs: so it would seem. Patrick Henry defending the General Assessment bill and the petitions in its behalf and George Mason writing to Henry about the decline of virtue in 1784 reflected in their dismay at the post-Revolution condition of Virginia a version of this republican idea. By 1784 and 1785 the severe effects of the war had punctured the utopian enthusiasm of 1776, and led to real questions about whether the colonists, taken in bulk, could exhibit the attachment to the commonweal, the self-restraint, the simplicity of manners, the avoidance of self-aggrandizement and "luxury" and "corruption"—in short the virtue that it had been thought a republic had to rest upon.

Gradually during the 1780s, from the experience of the states and state governments, those Americans who were to make and to defend the federal Constitution came to see, with whatever sigh of regret, that the answer appeared to be no, that the requisite citizens' virtue would not be forthcoming. The James Madison who when young had advised his friend Bradford to stick to the high road of righteousness had come by the end of the eighties to see that not everybody was going to do that, and that one should not found a government on the expectation that they would. Madison did not expect much in the way of overt public service from religion, and not too much more from "morality." He wrote, for example: "If the impulse and the opportunity [to effect schemes of oppression] be suffered to coincide, we well know that neither moral nor religious motives can be relied on as an adequate control." So do not allow opportunity and impulse to coincide.

They—these moral and religious motives—are not found to be an adequate control "on the injustice and violence of individuals, and lose their efficacy in proportion to the number combined together, that is, in proportion as their efficacy becomes needful." The twentieth-century reader of Reinhold Niebuhr will say that that is the thesis of his book *Moral Man and Immoral Society*. It appears more than once in Madison.

And though the moral limitations of humankind are magnified in group life, they are not missing in individuals. "It is vain to say," wrote Madison, "that enlightened statesmen will be able to adjust these clashing interests and render them all subservient to the public good. Enlightened statesmen will not always be at the helm." So arrange institutions that will preserve liberty even without enlightened statesmen at the helm.

To simplify the complicated story Wood's book tells, and to sort out one thread of it: Madison and the Constitution-makers built institutions that could meet the test of a Republic (as Madison explains that test in Federalist Thirty-nine) and yet not require as virtuous a citizenry as had once been expected: "to supply by opposite and rival interests the defect of better motives."

George Orwell, in his essay on Dickens, wrote about Dickens's inclination to solve institutional problems by recommending a "change of heart":

> ...two viewpoints are always tenable. The one, how can you improve human nature until you have changed the system? The other, what is the use of changing the system before you have improved human nature? They appeal to different individuals, and they probably show a tendency to alternate in point of time. The moralist and the revolutionary are constantly undermining one another. Marx exploded a hundred tons of dynamite beneath the moralist position, and we are still living in the echo of that tremendous crash. But already, somewhere or other, the sappers are at work, and fresh dynamite is being stamped in place to blow Marx at the moon.

One may say, exaggerating a little, that back in this eighteenth-century context the first Americans went from (almost) one side of this division to (almost) the other.

But, "almost." The republican ideology before and during and just after the Revolution, though shot through with the importance of virtue, held institutions to be important too: republican institutions. Therefore the patriots eagerly set out upon all that making of new laws, as Jefferson did in Virginia, and wrote all those state constitutions— eight new ones in 1776 alone. And when the full federal constitutional theory had fallen into place, by the time of the federal Constitution and the Federalist papers, the reliance on institutions was not total: Virtue was not irrelevant, wholly unnecessary, or meaningless. In fact, in Gary Wills's interpretation (perhaps in Adair's), the argument of *The Federalist* is precisely that the big colonies-wide arrangements of the federal Constitution—covering multitudinous interests and balancing them through its complicated machinery, and siphoning them through the system of representation—would produce what the new nation needed: disinterested service of the public good, impartial public virtue.

Twentieth-century folk who seize with a happy eagerness on Madison, and particularly Federalist Ten and Fifty-one, to vindicate a modern outlook may move him too far out of his own world. Madison was still not the reductionist that some who follow in the procession of his ideas seem to be. His view of human nature—recognizing "ambition" and "self-interest" and the rest—was nevertheless not that of Hobbes, nor was the Constitution he defended remotely like the Leviathan. His understanding of the importance of economic interests, and even classes, was not the determinism discovered in Marx by the more rigid of his followers, nor was the government or the political party he helped to create anything like Marxist. His view of society was not that of social physics to which some modern behavioral scientists reduce it, nor was the theory he evolved with other republicans simply a "group interest" theory. His understanding of the public good did not find that good following automatically from the pursuit by all of private interest, as have done theorists of the market, nor was politics in his view some equivalent of the marketplace. The nearer analogy, to one reader at least, is to none of these but, as suggested, to the thought of Reinhold Niebuhr. In Madison's view of human nature—a much-discussed subject—it is difficult not to find some mixture like this: Human beings, especially in groups, are self-interested enough to require checks and balances and multiplied interests, but virtuous enough to make possible *republican* government, government by *representation* (a key to the new constitutional theory).

Madison and his fellows were presenting these facts about the political world as they had discovered them to be, in an argument in behalf of a moral purpose: liberty and republican government. In Federalist Ten Madison takes for granted that there is a "justice" that ought to "hold the balance" between contending interests, though no interested party can be trusted to see it completely, and on tax policy—for example—if there is an unchecked "predominant party," it will be strongly tempted to "trample on the rules of justice." But one may doubt that it would have occurred to him to hold that "justice" had no meaning. In Federalist Fifty-one he writes straightforwardly that "Justice is the end of government. It is the end of civil society. It ever has been and ever will be pursued until it be obtained." References to the "public good" and the good of the whole abound in Madison; presumably he regarded that as a meaningful term, to some degree discernible to human beings.

He certainly did think that the motive of the public good had marked his colleagues in the Philadelphia Convention, about whom he wrote in the highest terms in Federalist Thirty-nine and elsewhere. And though he would have been too modest to claim it, his own career ironically would serve as a vivid illustration of the possibilities of a citizen's virtue upon which he wisely came to see the society should not place too much reliance.

His modesty was such that one would not expect him to write a sentence with the dramatic self-importance a critic of Jefferson's might find in his famous oath: *"I have sworn upon the altar of God eternal hostility to every form..."* (italics added). That was not Madison's style. But he had his own steady commitments. If the word *religious* be broadened in the way that the U.S. Supreme Court in the twentieth century has been forced to broaden it, then one might even say that Madison, like the humanist conscientious objector Daniel Seeger, was more religious than he knew.

As with Thomas Jefferson and George Washington, Madison's personal finances, insufficiently attended to, were in bad shape when he died; his widow Dolley had to scrape; his home, Montpelier, like Washington's and Jefferson's, was lost to his family.

An American of this later century may be provoked to the intellectual equivalent of a double-take when he discovers the cultural anomaly that Montpelier came in the curious circling of time to be owned by Mrs. Randolph Scott. And then to another double-take when Mrs. Randolph Scott turns out to be a du Pont, with a clutch of fellow du Ponts disputing the will she wrote turning Madison's home over to the public. The western movie actor; the Delaware chemicals dynasty; Jemmy Madison. One may look at this cultural melange with the mental equivalent of Ben Turpin's eyes.

James Madison's career, in his simpler time, stretched from the decisive years just before the Declaration of Independence all the way to the settling in of the new nation in the Andrew Jackson period. He was a reflective statesman from the American Revolution until the Nullification crisis. He "served his country," as the sober phrase has it, from the time before there was a country until the first stages of the testing as to whether it would perish from the earth. He had no other focus of attention except government, this government, and its successful launching; he read, thought, and wrote about it continually; he held public office almost without a break from the time he joined the Orange County Committee of Public Safety, when he was twenty-three, until he retired from the Presidency in 1817, at the age of sixty-six. He continued to be consulted about, and occasionally to participate in, public life until he died, at eighty-five, in 1836. Witherspoon had taught these young men to make their lives count for something worthy, and James Madison did.

PART THREE

Roger Williams: The Root of the Matter

ANOTHER WALL

America's tradition of religious liberty is not the work of Jefferson, Madison, and the Enlightenment alone, nor is it simply the result of expediency and necessity. There is another body of principles with different underpinnings from those of Jefferson, and with a collection of supporters of rather a different stripe. They are represented in part by those Baptists and other dissenters who were the rather unlikely allies of Jefferson and Madison in the struggle in Virginia, and in a different way by Madison's teacher John Witherspoon and his cohorts. Before them there had been more than two centuries of protest, reform, dissent, and division within the Christian world; after them came many victories, many more schisms within the new nation, many camp meetings and revivals, and the permeation of the culture of the new nation by something like the dissenters' outlook. Religious liberty in America is not only the concoction of the Founders and the outcome of the realities they faced; it is also, sometimes in a backhanded and inadvertent way perhaps, the result of the radical wing of the Protestant Reformation and of Puritanism in England, and of the evangelical religious outlook it helped to bring into being in the New World. Indeed, without stretching very far, one could claim that this broad river of history—let us call it dissenting Protestantism—had more to do, over all, over time, pound for pound, head for head, with the shaping of the American tradition of religious liberty than did the rational Enlightenment.

There may not be one single figure conveniently provided by history to embody this tradition, or this congeries of traditions, as authoritatively as Jefferson and Madison do for the enlightened Founders. But the mythology of the American nation has found one anyway.

There would have been some candidates for that role from the era of the immediate colonial prelude, of the Revolution and of the Founding, associates at least indirectly of Madison and Jefferson—Isaac Backus in particular, and John Leland, and from somewhat earlier Samuel Davies, perhaps the redoubtable Witherspoon (opponent of "sacerdotal tyranny") himself—all of them dissenting clergymen who struck mighty blows in the battles for religious liberty at decisive moments in the eighteenth century, and some in the early nineteenth; all of them "patriots" who mingled religious liberty with the fight for liberty in general, and for independence, and helped make that mingling come to pass in the founding of the nation. But though these and others, many, were sent, none were chosen. These people are not known by today's American public—not even the book-reading public.

What happened, instead of the choice of any of these generals in the army of dissent at the time of the founding, was the elevation of a prophet from almost a century and a half before. When, in the elaboration of the culture of the new nation in the nineteenth century, the "Voluntary Way" in religion came to be solidly entrenched in American culture, the Baptists and the other free-church evangelical Protestants, and indeed many others, looked back to find an original American exemplar of their position—of the endorsement of religious liberty not on grounds of rationalism, indifference, or expediency, nor exclusively of republican government, but on grounds of affirmative religious belief—they discovered clear back at the very beginning of the American undertaking, before there was a United States, a figure to fulfill that symbolic role to the utmost, and maybe a little beyond. Roger Williams has become our national figure in that spot, because we need him. He has been placed up there on this particular Mount Rushmore of myth and memory, our first real hero of religious liberty. He deserves to be there, all right, but he does not fit very well on monuments as anybody's symbol or representative.

"In Geneva, Switzerland—within what was in the sixteenth century the mighty fortress of John Calvin—stands a massive monument to the memory of the Calvinistic wing of the Reformation." This quotation comes from the opening of Perry Miller's "essay in interpretation," which appears at the beginning of the seventh, and only new, volume in *The Collected Works of Roger Williams,* as published, or republished, in 1963. "In the center," Miller goes on, describing this "Reformation Wall," to which tourists visiting Geneva, that Rome or Mecca of Protestantism if Protestantism allowed for a Rome or Mecca, regularly are taken:

> In the center are the four most majestic figures: Calvin himself, Guillaume Farel, Theodore Beza, John Knox. Flanking them on

either side are the militant warriors of the many nations in which Calvinism fought, perished, or conquered. All but one are obvious choices, soldiers of the faith: Gustavus Adolphus for Sweden, William the Silent for Holland, Coligny for France, Oliver Cromwell for England, men who in the certainty of their calling and election waged bloody battles against the unregenerate. The exception is the space assigned to American Calvinism. In that portico there stands—to the never-ending bafflement of American tourists—not John Witherspoon, John Cotton, nor Cotton Mather; not even Jonathan Edwards, nor Lyman Beecher.... The stolid inaccurately costumed statue is of Roger Williams. Beside him, in letters of stone, are inscribed words from *The Bloudy Tenent of Persecution*. His "orthodox" contemporaries in New England have been heaving in their graves ever since that monument was erected.

This posthumous heaving by the Winthrops, Mathers, et al. Miller ascribes to their view of Williams as "the arch-radical of the age or of any age, a demon of discord and subversion," the opposite of one who should stand beside the great leaders and founders and makers of churches and shapers of doctrine and formulators of godly, sober, and righteous communities of the people of God and of the reformed faith. Roger Williams? How did he get there? He was known more for leaving churches than for founding them. An American of the reformed tradition—a Pittsburgh Presbyterian, say, or a Dutch Reformed tourist from Grand Rapids—may be baffled on more contemporary grounds. In sermons and Sunday school he will have learned that his great branch of the Christian religion has as its greatest leader Calvin himself, of course; that the greatest colonial leaders like John (as-a-city-on-a-hill) Winthrop, and John Cotton, stand in that heritage; that the greatest American "Calvinist" theologian was Jonathan Edwards; that the best-known early church leader in America was Witherspoon, for whom is named the Philadelphia building that is the headquarters of what was, before merger, the northern and largest Presbyterian body; that, perhaps because of the importance of the Scotch-Irish in America, the modern American Presbyterian presence in Geneva is a house named for John Knox, who carried the reformed faith to Scotland and helped to shape the Kirk of Scotland. But Roger Williams? Roger Williams was a *Baptist*. (So he functions in the symbolic assignments of American denominationalism; actually he was not a Baptist for very long, either.)

It was a bold and interesting choice made by the builders of that wall, and, one may presume to say, in the eyes of heaven perhaps it was right. Williams *was*, in straight doctrinal terms, a "Calvinist," a believer, like those others, in the main doctrines of the reformed tradition. And he was a symbol indeed of much that happened to the reformed faith in America. He does do service as a representative of the peculiar American concoction, the separation of church and state, supported not on secular but on religious grounds. Perry Miller wrote of him, in the introductory essay referred to above, "He is not a rationalist whose liberalism rests in part upon a cynical indifference to theological niceties. He did not demand freedom for all believers (or unbelievers) out of a deficiency of piety, but from an exuberance of it, from an extravagance of fervor."

But that exuberance makes him a little unreliable as a symbol. His support for church-state separation has twists in it that distinguish him not only from Jefferson but also from the nineteenth-century free-church devotees of the "Voluntary Way" who were to reach back and make them their hero. And as to his "Calvinism": One can say of him, standing there on that wall in uncomfortable proximity to those sturdy, energetic warriors in the cause of subduing all the nations of the world to the practical reign of Christ the Prophet, Priest, and King (to resort to some John Calvin language)—one can say that Roger Williams standing there unpersuaded represents the elusive possibility, the rare instance, in which the Christian religion, perhaps even its Puritan version, conceivably even Puritanism's parent version Calvinism, can find within itself the grace to overcome its own deficiencies, and give over any effort at the subduing of all the nations.

To extract what we want from Williams we need to go back a century and several decades before the period of Jefferson and Madison, the Revolution, the Constitution, and the new nation, and move north from Virginia to the colder, rockier world of New England and those legendary first settlers, with some side trips back to London.

Whereas in the civic celebrations of another day, young Americans were taught that these Puritan forefathers came to this continent for religious liberty, today's citizens learn, with less inspiration but more accuracy, that those forefathers came to institute religious liberty, at most, for *themselves* and were in their turn intolerant of others. (Actually, religious *liberty*, for whomever, was not the explicit point: worshipping and living as God and the Bible intended was the point.) We have accomplished that familiar debunking form of progress in which we censure the shortcoming of our forebears by the convenient standard of our own day, instead of recognizing their achievements by the standards of their own.

But today's revised and more accurate teaching may contain its own distortion. The Protestant Reformers, and particularly the English and colonial Puritans, for all their zealous narrowness and for all their participation in intolerant episodes, still promulgated principles that sometimes led by implication beyond their own behavior: Every man his own priest; justification by faith; the Bible as the sole authority; the gathered, congregational, nonhierarchical, internally democratic church. These religious ideas had unintended social and political consequences—unintended by and unwelcome to some, welcomed and explicitly affirmed by others.

The stream of liberty does not run straight from the Protestant Reformation, or from the main body of the Puritan movement in England, or from the largest group of Puritan settlers in America, in Massachusetts Bay. It does, however, run crookedly, as it were, from those sources, a tributary that grows. Religious liberty is a current set in motion, inadvertently, by that larger river of religious history, carried along beside it in turbulent interchange.

The most important early part of it happens in England, where a stream of dissent, nonconformity, even "separation," and something like democracy, came swirling out of the Puritan movement on its radical side.

It is not necessary to our purpose here to try to summarize the religious history of England leading up to the Puritan movement, but since Roger Williams himself often did so, polemically (almost everything he wrote was polemical) and succinctly (he was not by nature succinct, "prolixitie" being one of his admitted faults) we may let him do it for us. Here is Williams, exclaiming.

> Who knows in how few years the commonweal of England hath set up and pulled down? The fathers made the children heretics, and the children the fathers. How doth the Parliament in Henry VIII his days condemn the absolute Popery in Henry VII? How is in Edward VI his time the Parliament of Henry VIII condemned for their half-Popery, half-Protestantism? How soon doth Queen Mary's Parliament condemn Edward for his absolute Protestantism? And Elizabeth's Parliament as soon condemn Queen Mary's for their absolute Popery?

And what happened then? What happened then was the "Elizabethan settlement," a compromise arrangement combining Catholic or High

Church ingredients with Protestant ingredients to make the modern Church of England and to set it on its curious course through history. But many, influenced by those sturdy warriors on the Reformation wall and other Protestant leaders, and by their reading of the Bible, were not satisfied with the *via media*, that alloy, that Anglican mixture; they wanted to "purify" the English Church of the remaining "papist" (un-Biblical) elements, and began therefore to be called "Puritans." They multiplied in numbers, variety, and conflict with the churchly authorities. When Elizabeth died, she was succeeded by the first of the Stuarts, James, in whom, coming as he did from Presbyterian Scotland, the Puritans at first had hopes; he disappointed them severely when he crossed the border from Scotland into England by promptly changing from a Scottish Presbyterian into an Anglican.

And then, during the time of James's successor, Charles I, things got worse from a Puritan point of view, with a strong High Church party adding to the sequence of alternating persecutions. This was the time of the Star Chamber, and of attacks upon Puritans under Archbishop Laud. It was also the time, in 1630, that some Puritan clergy and merchants and others headed out in the *Arbella* and other ships across the Atlantic for Massachusetts Bay, with Roger Williams himself following soon thereafter, in 1631.

In England the conflict intensified, Parliament was dissolved, war came in 1640, Roundheads and Cromwell on the one side fought the Cavalier King-Church people on the other. The Long Parliament—Puritan-dominated—met and summoned the Westminster Assembly, a potent conclave of reformed divines, to straighten out the religious life of England. That assembly, much influenced by the major figures on that Reformation wall, produced among other things the Westminster Confession, recited around the world to this day where John Calvin and his fellow stalwarts have had an impact.

But the Assembly received a shock, on the then very important subject of church government, with all its ramifications in those days for national government. Five of the learned clergy, who became famous as the Five Dissenting Brethren, made known their view that the scriptural form of a true church was not *Presbyterian*, as in Scotland and Geneva, but *Independent* (in New England, more often *Congregationalist*).

It is happily not to our purpose here to try to discriminate the many and rapidly shifting distinctions among the Puritans, except to note two large ones, which have the weightiest bearing on Roger Williams, and for that matter on the United States of America. One is between the main body of Puritans, who were, up to the 1640s, more or less Presbyterian, and these Congregational or Independent Puritans, like the Five Dissenting Brethren at the Westminster Assembly. The other, even larger distinction, to be discussed in a moment, is between non-separatists and separatists.

One group of Puritans—at first the largest—was persuaded, or content to accept, that the form of church government discoverable in the New Testament was *Presbyterian*, like the church government John Knox had carried from Geneva to set up in Scotland. *Presbyterian*, to use the analogy of governments, meant a representative system instead of a local town meeting system. There were no archbishops, bishops, or priests, but there were "presbyteries" and "synods" and general assemblies—layers of church government above the local congregations that bound them into a web, supervised the local choice of pastors, and made creedal formulations like that Westminster Confession for them. It was in disillusionment with this development that John Milton wrote his best-known phrase on these matters, quoted in all the books since: "new Presbyter is but old priest writ large."

Milton, with whom Williams grew acquainted on his second trip to London, became what Williams already was: an Independent. The view of the Independents or Congregationalists was that each church—each individual congregation—is *particular*, independent of the others, self-governing within itself, composed of "visible saints." That conviction about the true, New Testament nature of the church stood against not only the hierarchical structure of state-linked bishops ("prelates" and "prelatry"), as all Puritans did, but also against any interconnection among, or supervision over, congregations. Thus Roger Williams, a thoroughgoing Independent, would ask whether the division of the whole land into "Nationall, Provinciall, Diocesan, Parochiall" churches and the centering and assembling of people into a parish church were "suitable to the true religion and Testament of Christ Jesus" or an "invention of Satan and anti-Christ." When Williams asked a question, you always knew what his answer was.

Thus these congregational Puritans cut the tie both between one congregation and another—no authority above the congregation itself—and between church and parish—an "inclusive" neighborhood unit carrying out governmental duties, defined by geography. They defined the true church instead by belief and experience, that is, by a religious test—it should be composed only of the "regenerate," or "visible saints." That set the stage for the later notion of a purely voluntary church, and it pitched the power onto each congregation and the people in it.

The "radicalism," if such it be, of John Winthrop, Thomas Hooker, John Cotton, and the main body of those who set forth for Massachusetts Bay extended to, but stopped at, that Congregational point. They were *nonseparating* congregational Puritans, who found in the New Testament the congregational form of church government and the requirement of a regenerate membership but no necessity to repudiate the Church of England—reform it, yes; reject it, no. Furthermore, they had a peculiarly favorable situation in which to develop their perhaps rather hairsplitting position: They could insist on their nonseparation from the Church of England while geography—the Atlantic Ocean—provided a convenient de facto separation.

In the early part of the English Civil War this Independency, or Congregationalism, itself was radical enough. However, there came a moment, following the warfare between king and Parliament, Cavalier-Anglican and Roundhead-Puritan, when it appeared that new battles might break out between the Presbyterian and the Independent varieties of Puritans.

It was exactly in the middle of all this religious-political turbulence in England just after the outbreak of the Civil War that an extraordinary figure arrived back in London for the first time since he had left in 1631 and—typically—plunged immediately into the rhetorical fray. Roger Williams had returned to England in 1643 to obtain a colonial charter for the grouping of settlements around Narragansett Bay, where he had founded Providence Plantation after being exiled from Massachusetts Bay, but while in England he poured out a flurry of publications presenting his views on the topics of the day. One of the early ones is called *Queries of Highest Consideration* and is addressed to the Five Dissenting Brethren of the Westminster Assembly. It has been quoted above; the quotation includes the pungent phrase "The fathers made the children heretics, and the children the fathers."

To the Dissenting Brethren, to Parliament, and to all who would read, Williams made his appeal. After all the religious twistings and turnings, the persecutions this way and persecutions that way, are you going to do the same thing yet again? Do not do it.

> And oh! since the commonweal cannot without a spiritual rape force the consciences of all to one worship, oh, that it may never commit that rape in forcing the consciences of all men to one worship which a stronger arm and sword may soon (as formerly) arise to alter.

The document from which this comes, Perry Miller wrote, would have seemed to almost all parties of disputing Puritans "a weird production, asserting that not only should Presbyterians and Independents refrain from cutting each other's throats, but that even Catholics should be tolerated." That was much too big a step for the embattled Roundheads, who were just then engaged in warfare because the Anglicans had not left Catholicism far enough behind. The main body of Puritans, whether Presbyterian or Independent, essentially *all* believed that there had to be one uniform national religious policy; they disagreed only about what it should be. For Williams to write that such uniformity could only be achieved by "spiritual rape" was a stunning proposition.

Roger Williams's next publication in this heated atmosphere was his most famous: his attack, nurtured for a long time in the Rhode Island wilderness, on *The Bloudy Tenent, of Persecution, for Cause of Conscience*. This remarkable production is a response to Williams's leading opponent in Massachusetts, John Cotton, the pastor of the Boston church. But though Williams's argument was presented as an answer to Cotton, it was actually produced in England and addressed to Parliament. (An American may not be fully aware how much of Williams's work was carried on in London. There were not many printing presses on Aquidneck Island in 1640, and the Boston authorities, whom his writings attacked, certainly were not going to print them.)

In *The Bloudy Tenent* (tenet) Williams referred once again to all those recent twistings and turnings in an appeal to Parliament to stop them:

> All former Parliaments have changed these yokes according to their consciences (Popish or Protestant). 'Tis now your Honor's turn at the helm, and as is your task so I hope is your resolution not to change (for that is but to turn the wheel which another Parliament, and the very next, may turn again) but to ease the subjects and yourselves from a yoke.... which neither you nor your fathers were ever able to bear.

Parliament and Oliver Cromwell were shortly thereafter to lift the "yoke" for some people for a short period, but the full realization of Williams's vision had to wait for history to roll over several more times.

We said there were two big radical branches in the world of Puritan ideas; one was that of the Independents (of many types) already described. The other could cut much deeper; it was that of the Separatists. The main body of Puritans—Presbyterians and Independents—saw themselves as a "church within a church," conscious of the need to reform the Church of England but staying within her, acknowledging the Biblical-historical authenticity of that church despite its corruptions. However, varieties of Separatism—a radical position that rejected the Church of England—began to appear in the late 1500s. Among them were the "Brownites," who would carry on the Reformation "without tarrying for any"—that is, without waiting for the church to catch up; one small early congregation of Separatists, from Scrooby in England, after a sojourn in tolerant Holland made their way across the Atlantic in 1620 to become our legendary Pilgrims at Plymouth.

In Massachusetts the Independent Puritans had, as noted, the advantage of geography; and after the Great Migration of 1630–40 they worked out a theory, the New England Way, which maintained that though they had the convenient intervention of the Atlantic Ocean between themselves and any actual Anglican churches, bishops, and archbishops, and could set up their own godly communities, they nevertheless were not spiritually separated from, and did not repudiate, the Church of England, "our deare Mother." They were Independents, Congregationalists—but not Separatists.

Indeed, they were careful to distinguish their belief from so radical an idea as separation. They needed to make that distinction not only because they read the New Testament that way but because they had to read the political situation that way: Separation was perceived to be a danger to the English state, and was illegal. As turbulence advanced in England to the Puritan Revolution, the killing of the king and the setting up of a Commonwealth, the spread of radical ideas—including those of varieties of Separatists and Levelers and Quakers and Baptists and Fifth Monarchy Men—the Massachusetts Puritans across the Atlantic, once moderate radicals, became a comparatively conservative group, shocked by what many of their hitherto companions in England were thinking and doing. But one colonial Puritan was not shocked: Roger Williams. Indeed, he had been forced into exile from Massachusetts Bay in 1636 because of his radical ideas, among them the most thoroughgoing repudiation of the Church of England as no church of Christ's.

Roger Williams had proved more radical not only than the Independents of Massachusetts Bay but also than the Plymouth settlers from the *Mayflower*. Those Pilgrim fathers, landing on their rock and getting through their hard winters and celebrating their Thanksgiving, gradually came round, ten years after their fabled landing, to affiliating themselves with the much larger group of non-Separating Puritans who had settled to the north in Massachusetts Bay. Roger Williams held to ideas that got him thrown out.

Although not much is known about his early development, he appears to have been a Congregational Puritan already at Cambridge University and a Separatist soon thereafter. He was thus a kind of radical. But he was not a radical from the street or village, a common man without much education, like those who would predominate among our Pilgrims and also among the Levelers, the Anabaptists, etc.—the sects that spilled out of the boiling passions of Civil War. Neither was he a radical in theology, splitting off from the mainline of ideas about God, Christ, and the Bible that came over from the Continent and mingled with indigenous English developments to form the Puritan mixture, the Calvinist ingredient strong in it still. He did not hold with any Quaker Inner Light, or any watering down of the severities of Geneva. Indeed, so far as the main propositions of Christianity are concerned, he believed the same Reformed Protestant doctrines his principal opponents believed. But he applied them with a boldness and moral imagination that carried their application to the actual world of institutions quite beyond the point to which his fellow Puritans were willing to go, and with practical results for political life that were almost the opposite of those most often derived from them by the mainline Calvinists and Puritans.

Williams was born in London, of a middle-class family, as we would put it now, and educated—as were most of the Puritan intellectuals—at Cambridge University. When he was young he had the great figure of the law Sir Edward Coke as his patron, and he served as chaplain in the house of a noble family. He shared the learning and position of the Puritan leaders—of Winthrop, Cotton, Hooker.

When he came to Massachusetts Bay in 1631, not long after the *Arbella* folk, he was promptly offered, presumably because of his reputation for learning and piety, one of the ministerial posts in the Boston church that was later to be filled by his great antagonist John Cotton. He as promptly declined it, not because the members were not "regenerate" but because, nevertheless, some of them, on returning to England, still attended Anglican churches, and thus by proxy or infection stained the purity of the home church in Boston. (Perry Miller speculates that this was one of the several causes of the intensity of the opposition that Cotton was soon to exhibit toward Williams: "Cotton now occupied the throne in Boston which could have been Williams' had Williams not refused it out of a scruple of conscience; where Cotton now lorded it, Williams could have strutted had he been able to swallow the casuistry of nonseparation.") Williams went instead to Salem, and then to Plymouth, where he found the avowedly separatist Pilgrims not separatist enough for him. Following his return to Salem the conflict with the Massachusetts leadership inherent in his position developed inevitably; five years after he crossed the Atlantic, the General Court exiled him, and he took off into the wilderness of Aquidneck Island with the Narragansetts. The rest, as they say, is history.

Or became so when he published in London the arguments that he developed there in the wilderness. The publications of Williams's first trip to London, in 1643–44, made him famous, or perhaps notorious; it appears that the Licensing Act of the Puritan Long Parliament, against which Milton's *Areopagitica* is an eloquent protest, was directed not only at Milton's own writings but also at these startling productions of the colonial Puritan Roger Williams. It may be that the first printing of *The Bloudy Tenent* was burned. In any case it stung. John Cotton wrote an answer to it entitled *The Bloody Tenent, Washed, And Made White in the blood of the Lambe.*

And Williams, of course, eventually produced a reply to this reply, with, of course, a still longer title, perhaps a record-setting title: *The Bloody Tenent Yet More Bloody by Mr. Cotton's endevour to wash it white in the Blood of the Lambe; of whose precious Blood, spilt in the Blood of his Servants; and of the blood of Millions spilt in former and later Wars for Conscience sake, that Most Bloody Tenent of Persecution for cause of Conscience, upon a second Tryal, is found now more apparently and more notoriously guilty.* This was published during his second trip to England, in 1651–54, again on Rhode Island business, again pouring out stored-up publications that had been scratched out in canoes and Indian huts. Once again he included among his arguments a picture of the terrible turning wheel of persecution in recent English history.

> Hath not the God of Heaven, *the Father of Lights*, written it with the beams of the noon-day-sun, that (notwithstanding *pretences*) the truth is, That the *Parliament of England*, and the *Religion of England* [were] all Popish in *Henry* the seventh's days? But in his son's, *Henry* the eighth, the *Parliament* and *Religion* divided, and turned half *Popish*, half *Protestant*. In *Henry* the eighth his three children's days, what *turns*, what *wonders*? Was not the *parliament* and the *Religion* all *Protes-*

tant, in that most hopeful *Edward's* spring, &c. and as altogether *Popish*, when the Sword fell into the hands of that bloody *Mary*? And when *Gods providence* and *vengeance* wrung the *Sword* from the paw of the *Lioness*, and teacht it to the hands of that tender *Lamb Elizabeth*, how that the *Parliament* and the *Religion* of *England* (since her time) carried the *face*, and hung out the *flag* of all Protestants? &c.

In all these twistings, religion has followed not truth and conscience but the sword.

Meanwhile, there had been another chapter or two. The conflict had led not only to the shoving aside of the Presbyterians by the Independents but to the beheading of the king and the instituting of a Puritan Commonwealth, for which Williams had some hopes:

> In these late Earthquakes and Combustions (which the late King begun, by imposing upon the consciences of the Scotch Presbyters, in favour of his Prelates) how dreadfully hath a naked Arm from Heaven snatcht away the Sword from both, and fixt it in a hand more merciful (I hope) to the souls of all men, Jews and Gentiles!

He wanted soul freedom and mercy even for Jews.

And what is the lesson of all these tergiversations of religion-politics? The plain lesson is, End all this persecution on all sides.

> Who sees not this to be the designe and the decree of Heaven, To bring into the light, and to break to pieces the more than iron Yokes and Chains upon the souls and consciences of men? Who sees not, with holy fear and wonder, that this his Decree hath begun to break the arms and necks of all both Popish and Protestant persecutors?

Williams did not succeed. To paraphrase T. S. Eliot, not then, and not in England.

The first point about Roger Williams is that he was a Puritan even more intensely devoted to the purity of the church than his fellow Puritans. The second point is that he was an Independent, more sharply devoted to congregational independence from all polluting unregenerate hierarchies and authorities than his fellow Independents. The third point is that he was so much a Separatist that eventually he separated even from his fellow Separatists.

He pushed the effort to purify the Church of England clear outside the Church of England, as did the other Separatists; then he pushed the purifying impulse outside even a Separatist church like the one in Plymouth. Indeed, he pushed separation—New Testament purity—to the point that he eventually separated himself from every actual church, and (perhaps—so Winthrop reports) even to the point that he believed a man should not have communion with his own wife and children if the wife and children were not "regenerate." Edmund Morgan dryly observes that "Williams had clearly pushed the principle of separation to the point where the church was threatened with extinction for lack of suitable members."

He carried the effort to achieve a separated purity so far as to arrive at a paradoxical acceptance of unseparated and "impure" inclusiveness that becomes one source, though not the only one, of his condemnation of religious persecution. Since no actual church on earth is pure enough, then give up the effort to exclude anybody in the false churches that actually exist on this earth. One might say his intense exclusiveness turned around on itself: Having pushed separation and purity so far as to remove the true church from the existing institutions of the real world, he settled in that world for a most humane and inclusive civil relationship with everyone. Surely no man ever arrived at straight thinking by a more circuitous route.

═══════

THE STUDY OF WILLIAMS

═══════

The scholarly interpretation of Roger Williams has been a bit circuitous, too. The biographies of the nineteenth and earlier twentieth century often presented Roger Williams as an heroic forefather of "religious liberty" as it would be understood in modern American liberal democracy, which is also pretty much the terms of the popular (and Baptist) legend. One biography bore the title *Irrepressible Democrat*; another, earlier one had the subtitle *A Hero of Religious Liberty*. Still another, *New England Firebrand*. But by all odds the most influential presentation of Williams as a figure whose thought-world and values were thoroughly congenial to the progressive strand in modern thought—as an irrepressible democrat, indeed—was that of Vernon Louis Parrington, in his three-volume voyage on the *Main Currents of American Thought*. Parrington's work, produced in the 1920s, was still widely read in the 1940s—is still available today—and was one of those large omnipresent books so influential in one generation of college life as to receive, in the contrapuntal way that scholarly and intellectual life often works, a thorough "revision" or even demolition in the next. His presentation of Roger Williams was so attractive, and so well pruned to fit a twentieth-century democratic mind, as to bring many, reading him when young—reading him, let us say, as a midwestern college sophomore—enthusiastically to attribute to Roger Williams all their own opinions.

Parrington, a western progressive, tended to have villains and heroes, and looking around in those dim early days of "crabbed theology" for *someone*, some proto-Jefferson, he could be wholeheartedly enthusiastic about, he seized on Williams and gave him the full progressive treatment. When the present writer looked at Parrington's chapter on Williams again after forty years, he laughed out loud, which must be one of the few times that has ever happened to anyone reading Vernon Louis Parrington. The laughter did not reflect disdain but a kind of reminiscent affection for Parrington's Williams, for Parrington, for young American progressives from the hinterland who vibrated in tune with that chapter. Parrington made Williams almost the first democrat, the first American progressive. Williams, said Parrington, was "a child of light," "a humane and liberal spirit," "a democrat," "a Leveler"; was "convinced that society with its caste institutions dealt unjustly with the common man"; "spent his life freely in the cause of humanity." And so on. Moreover, Parrington's Williams was, in the religious field (insofar as Parrington allowed him to be in it), a "Seeker." To many who saw the world as Parrington did, if one is going to have any relation to religion at all, it is certainly better to be a "Seeker" than a "Finder."

Parrington, and many of those who went before him, thus emphasized the more congenial political and social, rather than the forbidding Biblical and theological, elements in Roger Williams. The way to arrive at the truth of the matter, it seemed, in those vanished days of crabbed Puritan theology and antique hairsplitting theological quarrels, was to turn one's attention not to ancient, stupefyingly boring, and now passé religious matters but to their underlying political and social meaning. By that means, by looking at what the religious material meant in the realities of power and politics and class (as between Williams and John

Cotton, say, or Williams and Governor Winthrop), one would then comprehend what it really was all about. Parrington said explicitly that this was the line to take.

It is, of course, a quite familiar twentieth-century line, deriving from the great unmasking figures of the nineteenth and twentieth centuries and from a whole *zeitgeist*, now popular as well as (or even more than) scholarly and intellectual: Behind, beside, underneath the presented surface of what is said or thought there is some deeper reality, the true explanation for this merely surface material. Parrington went so far as to assert that Roger Williams "was primarily a political philosopher rather than a theologian."

In the generation of World War II, when serious religious scholarship and even theology became again a visible and respected part of the intellectual world, that was not going to pass. The modernizing and liberalizing views—the dereligionizing views—of Roger Williams were blasted out of the scholarly water by the appearance in 1953 of a book by that formidable Harvard figure Perry Miller: *Roger Williams: His Contribution to the American Tradition.* As to His Contribution, Miller came perilously close to saying Williams did not make any, but he certainly disposed of the view that Williams was a modern progressive democrat more interested in politics than in religion. Laboring indefatigably in antique graveyards, exhuming the orthodoxy of Massachusetts and the thought of the Puritans and embalming it imaginatively for the edification of modern scholars of American culture, he performed this service now for Roger Williams. He reprinted long pieces from Williams's books and pamphlets, extracting from the repetitious, argumentative, difficult crab claws of Williams's productions a good deal of digestible meat. And he surrounded these extracts from Williams with his own prose, making clear that Williams was a figure very much rooted in the seventeenth century, not in the nineteenth or twentieth. He was an intense Puritan, a Calvinist, and not a democrat who shed the theological dogmas Parrington did not like. Most emphatically, Williams was almost the reverse of what Parrington (and others before him) had seen Williams to be: He was an extremely earnest religious thinker, and not at all primarily a political philosopher. Williams's social and political ideas, Miller explained, were the fallout of an intensely religious mind, more intense even than that of his fellows in that God-soaked, Bible-soaked environment.

Miller made Williams interesting in a new way, freeing him from stereotype and platitude. One result was the publication in 1963 of a new edition of *The Complete Writings of Roger Williams*, in several volumes, by Russell and Russell. The publisher explained, in a foreword to volume seven, that "the warm reception accorded by the reading public in 1953 to Perry Miller's book...has encouraged the Publishers to set the present edition before the academic world." Six of the volumes simply reproduced a Narragansett Club edition of 1887, crawling with all Williams's italics and et ceteras and further decorated with the old "f" in place of "s," yielding sometimes a comic effect to an irreverent reader, as when Williams complained, as he often did, about his *fevere fuffering*. The seventh volume included new findings, or pieces inexplicably omitted before, and the "essay in interpretation" by Perry Miller quoted above.

The Yale historian Edmund Morgan, quoted before in these pages, had produced in 1958 a little book about John Winthrop called *The Puritan Dilemma*—a book that is, in paperback, ubiquitously available and widely used in college classes to this day. It was fundamentally sympathetic to Winthrop, perhaps somewhat against the grain of what had become the picture of the Massachusetts Puritans, showing the dilemma of governing a living human society with its share of human conflict and orneriness while holding to righteous Puritan intentions. In it there briefly appeared, as a kind of extreme and perfectionist screwball with whom a responsible Puritan governor must contend, Roger Williams.

After the new edition of Williams's writings in 1963, however, Professor Morgan took a new look at Williams and produced another book, *Roger Williams: The Church and the State*, which is rather different in its emphases not only from Perry Miller's work but also from Morgan's own earlier book on Winthrop. Williams had appeared there as a minor character, a bit of a nuisance in the drama of John Winthrop. But Morgan's view of him had changed. "This is a book I had not intended to write," Morgan said, in his foreword. "When the complete publications of Roger Williams were reissued a few years ago, I took the opportunity to read them consecutively and systematically. As I read and reread, I gradually recognized that I had formerly misunderstood and misjudged the man, and I thought many other historians had done so too."

Unfortunately, this book of Morgan's—the best there is on Williams—is rather difficult to obtain, and by no means as widely available as either Miller's book or Morgan's own earlier Winthrop book (thus the accidents, mechanics, and economics of publishing also impede our effort to understand the past and its people).

Morgan did not in his book directly join issue with Miller (he did elsewhere appraise "Miller's Williams," in a scholarly article) but gently changed the emphasis. Morgan writes:

> The cast of Williams' mind, Perry Miller has reminded us, was theological, rather than social or political. And theological it certainly was, if we take the statement to mean that Williams' every thought took its rise from religion. But in his writings, from which alone we can know his mind, Williams was more often concerned with ecclesiastical and political institutions than with theology. Except in two or three treatises, he was moved to write only when he found Church or State engaged in activities he disapproved. Moreover, his own thinking seems to have been orthodox except where it touched institutions. He quarreled with the Puritans of Massachusetts not because he disliked their theology—he defended it against the Quakers— but because he disliked their institutions.

(One discovers on delving into these issues something that one knows in a general way, but has brought home on exposure: The meaning of these ancient, important, instructive people—James Madison, Roger Williams—is much altered by the intermediary interpreters, now this way, now that. One is interpreting American culture not only by looking at Roger Williams, but by looking at Vernon Parrington and Perry Miller and Edmund Morgan looking at Roger Williams.)

Of course Williams was not a modern liberal democrat, not a defender of religious liberty in the terms of Jefferson and Madison, let alone of Justice Hugo Black. So scholars since the middle of the twentieth century, led by Perry Miller, have corrected the tendency to strip away Roger Williams's religion to make him simply a hero of liberal democratic ideas: a defender of religious liberty and freedom of conscience in the manner of a modern member of the American Civil Liberties Union. It does not take much of an exposure to Williams's own writing to disabuse one of that idea. One teacher of these matters (quoted by David Little of the University of Virginia) wrote that "students have been known to open one of Roger Williams' pamphlets under the impression that they are going to meet a familiar figure, only to shut it hastily again with the feeling that there has been some mistake."

Everything Williams wrote is drenched with the evidence that he was a most earnest Christian believer, a Calvinist, a Puritan, a Biblicist. But in his time the religious atmosphere was not—as it is today—a separated compartment, rather special and even peculiar, divorced from the great issues of politics, government, and the shaping of institutions. On the contrary. In that world of Puritan disputation, of a heady new-born Reformed Christianity, with the Bible itself available now to every reader, these realms were not separated; indeed, religion provided the all-embracing terms in which the great issues were debated. And the issues Williams chose to debate, as Morgan says, certainly were those having to do with *institutions*: with the church, and very much—more than you might think—with the civil state. Though Williams certainly was an intensely religious man and a serious Biblical and Christian thinker, nevertheless what caught his attention, took up his intellectual energy, and came out in his writing, was a distinct subsection of religious thought dealing with what the church is and should be, and what the state is and should do, and, in particular, how the "conscience" of human beings should be treated.

THE MAIN POINT
IN ROGER WILLIAMS

The dominant theme in Roger Williams's work is certainly not difficult to discern. However complicated the subordinate themes, however arcane the argument on ancillary subjects, however roundabout the method of presentation, however distinct the method of Biblical interpretation by which he supported it or the millennial piety by which he came to it, there is no doubt at all about the main point of his main productions. It is blazoned in his titles and reiterated again and again and again, with passion, color, logic, rhetoric—one might almost say with love and squalor—and certainly with blood. As Perry Miller wryly remarks, "Williams had the sort of mind which, once convinced, finds truth improves with repetition." The point so unremittingly insisted upon is, of course, the pernicious evil of persecuting anybody, of coercing anybody, "for cause of conscience."

There is no mistaking how appalled Williams was that people were killed and tortured and imprisoned and made to bear all sorts of civil disabilities because of their religious belief—appalled by the "blood" spilled in religious persecutions. Indeed, an article examining the use of the word "blood" and its derivatives in Williams's work—starting of course with the titles of his two most important texts, *The Bloudy Tenent, of Persecution, for Cause of Conscience* and *The Bloody Tenent yet More Bloody: By Mr Cottons endevour to wash it white in the Blood of the Lambe* (for short)—would make quite a sizable and sanguinary monograph. So would a compilation of his references to the forms and devices by which the blood is spilled, and the persecutions carried on in the "bloody, irreligious, inhumane, oppressions under the mask or veil of the name of Christ"; in the "wrong and preposterous way of suppressing, preventing, and extinguishing such doctrines or practices [false and "idolatrous" ones] by weapons of wrath and blood— whips, stock, imprisonment, banishment, death, etc." Lists like that, piled up as was his style, often with an "etc." at the end, appear again and again, along with figures of speech like "spiritual rape," "soul yokes," "soul oppression," and words like murder, slaughter, torments, and references to the "bleeding heart of this affected nation" (England) and to the "spilling of the blood of thousands and of the civil peace of the world" and to "rivers of civil blood" and to "the blood of so many hundred thousands of slaughtered men, women, and children, by such uncivil and unchristian wars and combustions about Christian faith and religion." There is no mistaking the fact that, however we now interpret his reasons for being so, Roger Williams was a very strong and persistent opponent of the ancient and persistent evil of killing and persecuting people for reasons of religion. He was so at a time when very few others were. His opposition to such persecution was more thoroughgoing than others' not only in his own time, but later. And he made that position the foundation of an actual society, the settlement he founded on Narragansett Bay that became Rhode Island: "...no person in this colony shall be molested or questioned for the matters of his conscience to God, so he be loyal and keep the civil peace. Sir, we must part with lands and lives before we part with such a jewel."

How did Williams arrive at this strong central conviction—this "jewel"? If one looks at his hyper-Puritan, hyper-Separatist view of the Church (or his attempt even to find the Church), or at his way of reading the Bible, or at his interpretation of the millennium and the prophecies in the book of Revelation, or at his effort to understand the ministry (he had to give it up), one finds not only a complicated answer but also one that makes him remote and inaccessible to almost all (perhaps all) modern readers. The scholarship of the last half of the twentieth century, beginning perhaps with an article by an Italian scholar in 1954, represented most visibly and powerfully by Perry Miller and Edmund Morgan, and including now *The Millenarian Piety of Roger Williams* by W. Clark Gilpin, 1979, and many other contributions, has done the honorable and necessary work of restoring the complexity and remoteness of an intense seventeenth-century Puritan, to everyone's benefit. One can nevertheless find, without any stretching, streams of argument in Williams that do not depend so heavily on his peculiar version of the distinctive seventeenth-century Puritan outlook. One is an appeal to reason and to a common humanity. Another (not separate) is an appeal beyond doctrine to the central moral impulse of the Christian religion at its best.

Williams was like those other "Calvinists" on the Geneva wall in doctrine, except that he gave that doctrine a moral twist and an application to church, state, and conscience—and to human beings outside the fold—so different as almost to shift that high-speed Calvinist movement from overdrive all the way back to reverse. The "Reformed faith" in the hands of other stalwarts of the Reformation Wall provided the impetus for righteous crusades; in the hands of Roger Williams it provided the insight to challenge righteous crusades. He made it critical and, in effect, self-critical, and added a dimension of sympathetic world-embracing moral imagination that caused its function to be quite different from what it was for others. It became, to use modern words, and to risk sounding a little like Parrington, self-critically humane.

In *The Bloudy Tenent* the arguments against persecution for cause of conscience in the conference between "Truth" and "Peace" are said to be written in milk ("in milke, soft, meek, peaceable, and gentle, tending both to the peace of States and kingdom") while the arguments for such persecution are written in (the reader may have guessed) blood. Williams appealed to the spirit of the "Lord Jesus Christ," whom he calls in one place "the greatest and wisest politician that ever was," in a way that the Reformed tradition—indeed, orthodox Christianity in general—does not always remember to do, despite its credentials. One can read pretty far in Calvin's *Institutes* without finding the Jesus of the Gospels, of the Sermon on the Mount. Williams, on the other hand, wrote repeatedly—he was a bit of a Johnny-One-Note—that persecuting people is "opposite to the very nature of the Christian church, the only holy nation and Israel of God. Opposite to the very tender bowels of humanity (how much more of Christianity?), abhoring to pour out the blood of men merely for their soul's belief and worship." He certainly perceived that it was a little paradoxical to chop people's heads off in the name of the religion of love. "How canst thou say thou followest the lamb of God who so abhorred that practice?" (As himself a serious Puritan Christian arguing with other serious Puritan Christians, he appeals often thus to the "Lamb of God," the spirit of Christ Jesus, and to that "love" the Christian religion represents from time to time when it remembers what it is supposed to be about.)

But many of the arguments this argumentative man (sweet, warm, and peaceful, but argumentative) gives against persecution are not by any means derived exclusively from the Bible or from Christian doctrine, let alone any particular way of interpreting the Bible, or of understanding the "millennium." He says at the start of *The Bloudy Tenent* that he will present to their Honors, the members of Parliament to whom the tract is addressed, "arguments from religion, *reason*, and *experience*" (this time the emphasis is not Williams's).

One premise in reason from which he argues, at least implicitly, but very often explicitly, too, is that of our common humanity—the humanity we share across lines of difference...the differences, to start with, among varieties of Puritans. And then among Christians generally, even including the Anglicans, against whom the Puritans were doing spiritual, and then literal, battle—from whom they had fled. And then further, even including "papists." (This, as noted, was a shocking point when Williams put it forth—in London in 1643, to the newly triumphant Puritans, who had just beaten the Cavalier defenders of an Anglican/monarchical state/church, fighting against them precisely because they had not cleaned out the remnants of "popery" in their reign and rule and mind.) Still further, all those varieties of Christians share a common humanity with the Jews, Turks, Mohammedans, and Pagans who appear in Williams's pages, and with the Narragansett Indians, whom Williams treated with respect. Of course, none of his opponents denied that all these other folk were fellow human beings; but they did not draw from that obvious and admitted fact the conclusions that Williams did: Therefore do not whip, imprison, banish, or burn them— do not do any of those bloody things you do to them because of their *belief*, because of their *conscience*. Do not do those things even against those whose consciences are false, heretical, idolatrous, pagan, heathen, or even anti-Christian, as Williams certainly believed most consciences to be. Williams's appeal to this common humanity had in it a breadth of moral imagination, and a transcendent, self-critical turning, that are rare.

One example of Williams's implicit reliance on, and critical application of, a perception of our common humanity is his repeated reference, of the sort already quoted, to the twistings and turnings of English religious-political history. That picture of the religious somersaults, from king to king to queen to king, appears very often in Williams. It is easy enough for someone spared those views of the world and born conveniently in another time and place, to look at those sequences—Protestant persecuting Catholic, Catholic persecuting Protestant, High Church Anglican doing the same to Puritans, Puritans returning the favor, beheading Archbishop Laud and even the king, Massachusetts Bay nonseparating Puritans banishing Separatist Williams, even Presbyterians and Independent Puritans eyeing each other edgily—it is easy enough for someone with no stake in any of that, living in an atmosphere of "toleration" and "liberty" so far as those ancient disputes are concerned, to say: Cut it out. It is ridiculous; everybody stop killing, jailing, persecuting one another.

But Williams was *not* outside the battle of the time. He was an intense partisan, in a time when such partisanship led to such persecution. He held the whole battery of orthodox Puritan Christian beliefs that Winthrop, Cotton, and the others held. He was as quick to call the Catholic church the "Anti-Christ" and the "Whore of Babylon" as the next Puritan. And he was even quicker than the next Puritan to condemn the Church of England and all its political-religious minglings and "popery." He felt strongly about the defects of many sorts—most or all sorts—of his fellow Puritans. Nevertheless, surrounded by all this Error and False Doctrine and even the Anti-Christ, he nevertheless insisted that *all* persons should have—in a good phrase of his—soul freedom. That crackerbarrel modern folk unwisdom that claims that one should not believe in any truth (not "too strongly") because if one does, one will "impose" it on others, is refuted in the rare case of Williams. (It is also brought into question, in our day, by that not-so-rare case of those who though they confess all the requisite tentativity and uncertainty are nevertheless intolerant.)

Not every serious partisan in the grip of Truth would interpret that turning wheel of changing religious regimes in England—or its equivalent—in the way that Williams does. The more common response of human beings, Puritan or otherwise, then or now, would be—would it not?—along these lines: Now it's our turn. Seize the moment to plant our truth. Squeeze out their Error. And do to them what they did to us. To the differing conceptions of the truth then are added reciprocal resentments.

To reach Williams's conclusions, if one is a partisan and not a distant uninvolved observer, requires a purchase on a larger vision—the common humanity running through all the turnings—that either transcends one's own piece of the "truth" or is caught up in it, or pointed to by it.

Another variation of the same fundamental point—an imaginative and self-critical universalism—appears in Williams's way of presenting not the revolving door sequence of regimes in the past but the spread of contenders in the present: "If Paul, if Jesus Christ were present here at London and the question were proposed what religion they would approve of—the Papists? Prelatist? Presbyterians? Independents?—would each say, 'of mine, of mine'?"

Most partisans would indeed respond "of mine." But Williams, a partisan himself, nevertheless presents this deflationary picture of the whole group. (When Williams thus punctures the pretensions of all these scrambling claimants to a final truth by dramatically setting them against what all of them, and he, too, regarded as its source, the modern reader is tempted to hear in him a kind of relativism. It is important to remember that he identified with the last of those claimants, at least more than he did the others, which he fiercely rejected.)

In still another variation he presented to his reader's moral imagination the whole world... usually in "queries" to the Puritan Parliament. So suppose the whole world were in England, and under your sway. What would you do with the Turks, Mohammedans, Chinese, Indians, Pagans, heathens, and false religions of all sorts that populate most of the globe?

Many of Williams's points were made by such questions and "queries" (of "highest consideration"). These all can be seen as entailing underneath their concreteness the abstraction that modern moral philosophers call the "generalization test": Can the rule of the action be generalized to everybody "so situated," as the lawyers put it, or is the "moral agent" making an exception of himself? Kant's first formulation of the categorical imperative is the central location of this point in the philosophical history of the West. Something close to it appears in many other forms, popular and formal. The "Golden Rule" is one.

Closely related to this test by making the "maxim" of one's act universal or general, a rule for all, for others as well as oneself, is the test by the reversal of roles with a particular other. . . . What if the shoe were on the other foot? Put yourself in the other's place. Williams very often uses such a shoe-on-the-other-foot argument against his chief opponent, John Cotton: "I doubt not to affirm that Mr. Cotton himself would have counted it a mercy if he might have practiced in Old England what now he doeth in the New, with the enjoyment of the civil peace, safety, and protection of the State." Sometimes he uses it with reference to his own situation: "I conceive Mr. Cotton himself; were he seated in all England again, would not count it a mercy to be banished from the Civil State."

Here is Williams turning the abstract universal—do not persecute—against a rather vulnerable target in Cotton:

> *Peace.* He [Cotton] ends this passage with approbation of Queen Elizabeth for persecuting the Papists, and a reproof to King James for his persecuting the Puritans.
>
> *Truth.* I answer, if Queen Elizabeth, according to the Answerer's tenent and conscience, did well to persecute according to her conscience, King James did not ill in persecuting according to his.

And here he links the reversal to what we called above the turning wheel:

> When Mr. Cotton and others have formerly been under hatches, what sad and true complaints have they abundantly poured forth against persecution? ... But coming to the helm (as he speaks of the Papists), how, both by preaching, writing, printing, practice, do they themselves (I hope in their persons lambs) unnaturally and partially express toward others the cruel nature of such lions and leopards?
>
> O, that the God of heaven might please to tell them how abominable in His eyes are a weight and a weight, a stone and a stone, in the bag of weights! One weight for themselves when they are under hatches, and another for others when they come to helm.

Implied recommendation: Do to others when you come to the helm what you would have had them do to you when you were "under hatches."

But these moral rules found in the rational makeup of humankind do not come down neatly out of pure reason to an unequivocal particular application. An analytic philosopher, or anybody else for that matter, can find many difficulties in their abstract formulation: Which elements of the particular situation does one select to generalize? How abstract or detailed a description enters the "maxim" of one's present action? Which shoes of which others does one walk for a mile in? An element of concrete moral insight, not found in reason alone, must do some filling in and selecting. Reason alone does not decide these matters. And human beings do not need to be trained moral theologians or philosophers to give twists this way and that to the abstractions of morality, Christian or otherwise. This way or that—but mostly this way: mostly to serve the defenses of the self, and the aggressions of the self—so that the interpreter comes off well and others (his "enemies") do not come off well, in the picturing of good and evil, right and wrong. No moral system, neither Biblical nor Christian nor other religious system, nor any nonreligious one either ("rational" or otherwise) is of itself proof against the human inclination to twist the interpretations it yields so as to favor oneself, and disfavor preselected others: to use it defensively and aggressively, in other words.

The Christian religion has its way of describing and understanding this inclination (sin and pride and so on) and sometimes even partially correcting it; the Reformed tradition and Puritanism were not without their considerable resources in that regard. Roger Williams, for all his distinctiveness, did not after all come out of nowhere. Other moral understandings have their ways of doing it, too. James Madison, an Enlightenment thought-world away from these bleak New England Biblicists, noted in his argument in Federalist Ten the inclination of self-love to distort reason in hot matters of public dispute. But noting that sort of thing does appear to be something of a Christian, and perhaps Protestant Christian, specialty.

Noting it, and avoiding it, are two different matters. The noting of it may itself be used defensively, perhaps at a subtler level; as Pascal said, discourses on humility may be a source of pride to the proud. All thinking and writing, including this, on such matters is subject to a similar twisting. Reformed Christianity certainly had resources for self-criticism, and perhaps (although less clearly) for the humane enlargement of vision and generosity and human sympathy that may follow from it, but that does not appear to be its main historical effect. Perhaps in the nature of the moral complexity of the most difficult points, they cannot be sustained in a larger public and over time: They are fragile and rare.

And they cannot be made into abstract rules to be transported here and there to many destinations; whatever they are, they will be turned by the pulling of human "self-love" to do its service. So this kind of thing—moral understanding—is not akin to engineering, but to literary criticism: It requires particular insight.

Now back to the case in hand, Cotton and Williams disputing with each other in 1642–52, a considerable moment in American history even before there was an America.

John Cotton could have formulated his defense of the Bloody Tenent so that it could be rationally universalized, or so that he would have been willing to have it applied to himself under the Golden Rule. He argued in *The Bloody Tenent, Washed*, and elsewhere, not only that the correction of heretics, blasphemers, idolaters, and the like was necessary to protect what we would today call the common good, and innocent others, against the influences of evil ideas and the disturbance of the church and civil peace, but also—the more interesting point—against *themselves*. Cotton explained that he did not favor persecuting a person for his conscience but only for *sinning against his own conscience*...for a "blind and erroneous conscience": "The Word of God is so clear in fundamental and weighty points that such a person cannot but sin against his conscience, and so being condemned of himself—that is, his conscience—he may be persecuted for sinning against his own conscience."

Cotton's last point, in its setting presumably not congenial, perhaps ludicrous and incomprehensible to most twentieth-century Americans, nevertheless is not without its parallels in other orthodoxies and aggressive creeds. The phrases "forced to be free" and "false consciousness" may come to mind.

Presumably Cotton would have been willing to have a rule drawn from his position made universal, and applied to himself: Let all, everyone, including me, be instructed so as not to sin thus against our own consciences. Williams's response was blunt and often had quite a modern flavor. In effect he said: All persecutors fool themselves thus. His imagination leaped to long lists of folk, in the Bible and elsewhere, who made self-deceptive claims of the sort Cotton did, and persecuted Christ Jesus. (Let us spare the reader any more of his lists.) Leading people astray indeed is very bad, he admitted to Cotton, but can only be combatted "spiritually." The errors and truth (Christ Jesus) are so mixed in the wilderness of the present world that you may otherwise be persecuting the latter. "Evil is always evil, yet permission of it may be good."

> If Master Cotton granteth this freedom to other consciences beside his own, why preacheth he persecution against such a liberty which other consciences beside his own believe they justly challenge? If to no other conscience than his own, it is

not his ten thousand times that his conscience is true and others false, nor any other distinction in the world, can clear him from most unrighteous and unchristian partiality.

The blessed followers of the true Lord Jesus Christ "are so far from smiting, killing, and wounding the opposites of their profession and worship that they resolve themselves patiently to bear and carry the cross and gallows of their Lord and Master, and patiently to suffer with Him."

Williams attacked Cotton's self-deception and partiality and saw him identical in principle with the persecutors of all stripes—and all of them contrary to ("opposite" to, he would say) the spirit of Jesus, the "Lambe," which is love. To return, then, to the starting point: Williams fills in or orients what he draws from reason with what he draws from— where? His Christian belief perhaps. He is repelled by all that blood, "opposite" to Jesus' love. And Christianity can use against error, and wrong conscience, only *spiritual* weapons—argument, "perswasion"— not persecution.

Cotton had said that erring consciences lead to a breach of peace. Williams responded:

> Breach of the civil peace may arise when false and idolatrous practices are held forth, and yet no breach of civil peace from the doctrine or practice or the manner of holding forth, but from that wrong and preposterous way of suppressing, preventing, and extinguishing such doctrines or practices by weapons of wrath and blood-whips, stocks, imprisonment, banishment, death, & co.—by which men commonly are persuaded to convert heretics and to cast out unclean spirits, which only the finger of God can do, that is, the mighty power of the Spirit in the Word.

The "breach of civil peace" does *not* necessarily arise from "false and idolatrous practices" (Williams certainly *does* believe some religions are "false") but rather from the efforts (perhaps by believers in the "true" religion) to suppress that falsity by all those weapons and bloody whips and so on. That is an extremely hard doctrine for the Governor Winthrops of this world, then and now, to comprehend.

Williams answered with an intellectually tedious but morally impressive passion all the arguments of John Cotton, and therefore the others, who believed in enforcing religious conformity. He answered them with scripture, fully. He used a method of interpreting the Bible, called "typology," which Perry Miller made the key to his whole outlook. "Typology" meant that Old Testament stories were seen to be "types"—metaphors or symbolic representations—of the events in the New Testament. Thus Jonah and his whale and Joseph and his brothers and Noah getting drunk and Jacob and his concubines and the peculiar story of Lot were not literal historical events—at least not primarily— and were *not* to be taken as guides or instructions for a new Israel of Christians in England or in Boston (that is the point that had a bite to it). Rather they were made clear in the New Testament. This method of interpreting the Bible was not new with Williams; it had an ancient lineage and tended to attract people of an imaginative temper who enjoyed allegory, mystery, hidden meanings. Scholars since Perry Miller have demonstrated that Miller exaggerated—as it seems Miller had a tendency to do—the remoteness, the mysterious and peculiar idiosyncrasy, of Williams's typological method, and also the centrality of the peculiarity to his thought as a whole. Williams was not distinct on *that* score. So one asks rather, what use did he make of it?

The most pungent effect of interpreting the Bible in this way, when Williams did it, was to cut the tie between the Israel of the Christian's Old Testament and any modern, indeed any actual earthly existing, entity: England was not a new Israel, nor was the Puritan Commonwealth, nor was Massachusetts Bay. This of course was the kind of point that made Williams, attractive though he was personally, a genuine difficulty to Governor Winthrop, John Cotton, and the others. To cut the tie between Massachusetts Bay and Israel, to say there was no successor nation to Israel with any special role to be played in God's purposes, struck at the foundations of the "city on a hill." As did Williams's claim that, not being God's chosen Israel, but one civil state among others, Massachusetts should not attempt any state-enforced religious belief.

One is impressed to discover how regularly Williams, on reading the Bible, with however arcane a method, came to generous and humane conclusions. That does not happen, needless to say, with all Bible readers. Here is an example from his use of "typology": In the Pequot war of 1637 (in which, incidentally, Williams, then in Providence, was of service to Massachusetts despite his recent banishment in 1636), John Winthrop, governor of Massachusetts, had won victories and was apparently expecting either to capture or perhaps even to slaughter the Pequots in satisfying numbers, on the model drawn from what Israel in the Old Testament had sometimes done with *its* enemies. Williams wrote to Winthrop explaining that because "the scripture is full of mystery and the Old Testament of types," Israel was *different* from all other states, including Massachusetts; therefore Winthrop did not have that Biblical justification, and should instead be *merciful* to the captives.

Williams may not have been exactly a hero of self-criticism, but he was a hero of the generosity that is allied to it. He did have some profound conception of the "conscience," of the "soul" of *all* human beings—profound in a way that the leaving people alone and indifference of later ages does not approach. Further examples will appear in the "more particular" illustration with respect to four groups later in these pages.

STATE AND CHURCH:
NO GARDEN FOR NOW,
JUST WILDERNESS

Williams resembled mainline Calvinistic Puritans not only in doctrine but also, as may not be so well comprehended, in his understanding of the moral role of the state. He agreed with them on all except a couple of decisive matters, and on those his views resembled those of many left-wing sectarians, who also condemned state-enforced religion and religious persecution (partly presumably because they had suffered from it). But he differed from them, too. He did not hold, as they did, that the Christian should withdraw from or denigrate the state and other human institutions. That point is somewhat obscured by the interpretations old and new, although it is brought out clearly by Edmund Morgan. Roger Williams, the sometime beneficiary of Sir Edward Coke, believed fully in the role of law and of civil government. The joining of that belief with his opposition to all religious persecution makes him distinct.

It is often said in twentieth-century discussions of the separation of church and state, in a kind of snappy formula, that Jefferson believed in separation to protect the state from the church, but Roger Williams believed in it to protect the church from the state. That has a nice and memorable neatness about it, but it does have this fault: It is mistaken. It is mistaken in the case of Williams, at least, if the church that the state is to be separated from is any one of the actual, visible churches. (It may not be quite true in the case of Jefferson either.)

Williams was at least as critical of the pretensions and dangers of the ecclesiastical power of these visible churches as was Jefferson—more so, probably. Even more passionately. And he was as committed to a civil state that fulfilled its proper functions without regard to the religious belief of its citizens. He too did not want an intermingling of churchly claims with the state and civil affairs; for the purposes of a civil state, we should appeal to the moral foundations we share in consequence of our being human.

What of the church? Let us devise a snappy formula of our own. In Anglican Virginia it was difficult to get *out* of the church. In Massachusetts Bay it was difficult to get *into* the church. In Roger Williams's case it was difficult to *find* the church. As to Jefferson: For him, one might say, after the worldly power of state churches was broken, it was difficult to take the church—the many "sects"—seriously. Williams took the true church very seriously indeed—and found all, or almost all, the actually existing religious assemblies in all, or almost all, regards—false. And then concluded that, until the time when Christ should come again, and all that were saved were transplanted into the garden of the church, we should live together in the wilderness of the world as civil human creatures.

The two chief movements that would shape the American arrangement of church and state—roughly speaking the Jeffersonians and the Baptists or dissenters—were both inclined to individualism and a withdrawal from—and a negative picture of—the state and, at least in the Baptist case, other large social institutions, indeed, the links and claims of the social order itself. That impulse to withdrawal and inclination to individualism, and that hostility to the state, contributed some of the sting to the doctrine of radical church-state separation. But Williams, the retrospective hero of at least one of these traditions, was not like that.

He was a thorough believer in the civil state doing its legitimate work, and in law, and in punishment of offenders against the *civil* peace. He was a believer, moreover, in a natural moral order, which human reason could discern sufficiently to carry on a civil life across many religious persuasions.

Williams attacked, with honorable, memorable, and inspiriting thoroughness, the "bloudy tenent" of persecution for cause of conscience—but only religious conscience, and that only in what today would seem (it did not seem so then) the rather restricted domain of "spirituals," of belief and worship. Along with other Puritans, he believed that the commonwealth must enforce, for the common good and order and safety, the "second table"—that is, the latter five of the Ten Commandments that deal with morality, with obligations to one's neighbor. And the civil government must carry out its legitimate civil role, protecting the lives and goods and safety of all, even requiring actions objected to on grounds of conscience, including religious conscience.

Williams did not accept appeals to one's "conscience" as a basis for exemption from a shared social duty. When as "president" of Rhode Island, he attempted to organize a militia, and Quakers and some Baptists who were what we would call conscientious objectors to war objected, he penned what is perhaps the most quoted of all his writings, the letter about the mixed religious company on a ship. This letter can do service, as it has often been used to do, as an epitome of Williams's views in general, but a reader should note the context, and note, too, the duty Williams would have the state require, as well as the liberty he would insist the state should grant.

The letter was written to the town of Providence in January 1655, at a time of real turmoil in the turbulent life of the colonials, when Williams feared with some reason that the community might be left without defenders. It presents a picture of a ship at sea—a metaphorical ship sails often into Williams's discourse—on which many hundreds of souls share the ups and downs of the waves of the journey. The first lines are responding to the claims of the Aquidneck conscientious objectors that by his principles of liberty of conscience he ought to exempt them. "That ever I should speak or write a tittle that tends to such an infinite liberty of conscience is a mistake, and which I have ever disclaimed and abhorred." Then comes his ship.

> It hath fallen out sometimes that both Papists and protestants, jews and turks, may be embarked in one ship; upon which supposal I affirm all the liberty of conscience that ever I pleaded for turns upon these two hinges; that none of the papists, protestants, jews, or turks be forced to come to the ship's prayers or worship, nor compelled from their own particular prayers or worship, if they practice any.

That is one side of the outlook of Williams. But the letter goes on:

I further add that I never denied that, notwithstanding this liberty, the commander of this ship ought to command the ship's course, yea, and also command that justice, peace, and sobriety be kept and practiced, both among the seamen and all the passengers.

He goes on to say that all the seamen of whatever religious or non-religious affiliation ought to do their duty by the ship's needs, to perform their services, to pay their freight, to obey the common laws and orders of the ship for their common peace or preservation, and that they should be punished alike for infractions of the rules of the ship.

He furthermore says,

If any should preach or write that there ought to be no commanders or officers because all are equal in Christ, therefore no masters or officers, laws or orders, corrections or punishments—I say, I never deny but in such cases, whatever is intended, the commander or commanders may judge, resist, compel, and punish such transgressors according to their deserts and merits.

Roger Williams was not an anarchist; he was not really—despite Parrington—a Leveler; like other Puritans, he believed that the civil state should restrain those who took action detrimental to the public order and safety, even though such actions should be conscientious, and even though the conscience in question should be (it was a little hard in those days to imagine how it would not be) religious. To reach forward a century, the sentence in the Virginia statute upon which the Supreme Court still another century later would ground its distinction between religious *belief*, which the First Amendment makes absolutely free, and *action* based upon such belief, which cannot be—the Jeffersonian statement that it is time enough for the rightful purposes of civil government for its officers to interfere when principles break out into overt acts—would certainly be Roger Williams's position. Jefferson included in that clause the allowance for governmental restraint on overt acts as a concession to strengthen his true point, that belief itself should be free; the Supreme Court, in the nineteenth century, picks up on the concession; and one may presume Roger Williams, had he had the statute available in the seventeenth, would have, too.

Moreover, Williams's conception of the overt acts that are injurious to order and peace and general welfare and that the state might (or must) therefore properly restrain was a large one. Though libertarians of conscience in all times and places—including Jefferson and twentieth-century Americans—face at *some* point the claims of order and peace and justice to others against overt acts by free exercisers of religious conscience, Roger Williams called upon those claims much earlier than would most citizens today. Most twentieth-century Americans—conceivably, not quite all—would dissent from Williams's apparent view that the state should make sure that citizens have their hair cut properly (this against some Quaker men, conscientiously shaggy). Williams would have the state prohibit activities like those that appear in the footnotes and texts of twentieth-century court cases as examples of activities from other lands that, even though practiced for religious reasons, the state should not permit: human sacrifice, temple prostitution. He approved of the censorship of "wanton," "immodest," and "unclean" books, and of expressions of contempt for the authorities. Perhaps enough has been said to make clear that he was not a premature candidate for membership in the American Civil Liberties Union. That ship of Williams's was going to be a tight ship.

If we say that Williams was not a "libertarian," but rather what we might call a high communitarian, that may make clearer, and perhaps the more impressive, his defense of unqualified liberty in that domain in which he did defend it, the domain of the "spirituals"—soul freedom. Later centuries would be inclined to fold the several liberties into an interconnected whole. Sometimes when one talks to some people in the twentieth century, it almost seems that if there is freedom of speech and freedom of thought and freedom of association, a distinct freedom of *religion* would be a superfluous, perhaps even a problematic, addition to the list. Not for Roger Williams. For him it was distinct and profound. (It should be said lest in overcompensation he be made too uncongenial to modern convictions, that the government of Rhode Island he founded was "Democratical"; and that Williams saw the people as the source of all power; and that he certainly believed in argument.)

He affirmed the work of the civil state, and of our common duties to each other and our shared life as human beings, independent of religious conviction. He took the work of the civil state seriously. In his own life he had to do a lot of politicking and governing, being for a time the "president" of Rhode Island, a difficult job given the motley collection of folk who gathered in Providence Plantation, and had to negotiate the charter in London for the colony, and carry out negotiations with the Indians, and deal with the New England neighbors. He believed in the civil law and civil order, in its own right and on its own bottom.

If Roger Williams had a high communitarian view of the state and of shared human institutions here in the wilderness of the world, he had an extremely exacting set of criteria for what the garden of the church truly is, or should be—so exacting, as we have said, that it may be that no actually existing church fulfills them. Williams, reading the Bible and disputing, left Boston for Salem, Salem for Plymouth, Plymouth for Salem again, and Salem for the Aquidneck wilderness, all within the five years of 1631–36, almost entirely because of his extremely exacting views of the true church of Christ.

In Rhode Island, then, his further reading and disputing led him briefly to become a Baptist, then to leave the Baptists to become a "seeker" outside all existing churches.

He had a severe test of the ministry. On his second trip to London he published *The Hireling Ministry None of Christs*, which along with his familiar attacks upon *national* and *parishional* churches and the "yoake" of persecution and unfreedom, asserts that the "Hireling Ministrie" enforced upon the nation is not only an "oppressing yoake" but "none of the ministrie of Christ Jesus." If one is paid by the state, one is not a Christian minister.

> ...as to the Labourer worthy of his Reward, I answer, we find no other patterne in the Testament of Christ Jesus, but that both the Converting (or Apostolicall Ministry) and the Feeding (or Pastorall Ministry) did freely serve as minister, and yet were freely supported by the Saints and Churches, and that not in stinted Wages, Tithes, Stipends, Sallaries, &c. but with larger or less supplies, as the Hand of the Lord was more or lesse extended in his weekly blessings on them.

If the tangible blessings were not forthcoming, then the true minister would make do.

> ...when either through poverty or neglect, support and maintenance failed, yet still they eyed (as Sea men and Souldiers say) the God of the Voyage, and the Battel (the common Cause of the Lord Jesus) and their owne hands day and night, supplied their owne and others Necessities. And this was and will be the onely way of the Labourers of the Son of God.

Obviously that was *not* an idea whose time had come, or was likely to come. It was not received well by anybody, outside the most radical sects. "Hireling" was an offensive word, already used in the same way by the Quaker George Fox. It was to turn up again a century and a quarter later in the Virginia quarrels, already referred to; those Anglican clergymen supported by tax funds were, in the eyes of the New Lights, "hirelings." Dolley Madison's Quaker relatives objected to her being married outside the meeting and by a "hireling priest."

But the Quakers and other radical Puritans and sectarians rejected, or had reservations about, other institutions in addition to the Church and the Priest: Many were pacifists; many wondered whether a Christian could be a magistrate; many rejected secular learning; some rejected conventional manners and dress. None of this applied to Williams.

For one example, Williams, the well-educated Cambridge graduate, rejected the universities that train a hireling ministry: "The *Universities* of the *Nation* as subordinate and subservient to such *ministries* and [national] *Churches*, are none of the Institutions of Christ Jesus." But he did not therefore attack and reject the universities, as such. He differed markedly not only from some sectarians of his own time but also from the evangelists of later times who would attack such institutions, root and branch, as "Godless," "secular," "humanistic," and so on. He wrote, for just one example, "I heartily acknowledge that among all the *outward Gifts* of God, humane learning and the *Knowledge* of *Languages* and good *Arts*, are excellent and excell other outward *gifts*, as far as *light* excels *darkness*, and therefore that *Schools* of *humane Learning*, ought to be maintained . . . and cherished."

But for all that, they are "none of Christs," and not the proper source of a true "ministrie."

Perhaps we would not be too far wrong to summarize this way: He had almost a conservative churchman's view of the institutions of human society—secular institutions—but he had more than a radical sectarian's view of the church, the ministry, "Christian" institutions.

One enormously important consequence of the view thus inadequately encapsuled is Williams's understanding of, as we should put it today, religion and the nation, religion and the general culture, religion and political institutions. He had an extremely exacting criterion for what the Christian religion is.

One of the publications given to the printer on his first trip to London was *Christenings Make Not Christians*. In it Williams in effect made the same point as Kierkegaard's attack in the nineteenth century on

"Christendom": "Where everybody is a Christian, nobody is." Williams was writing in the context of a discussion of the conversion of Indians, explaining why he did not make the great mass conversions he could well have made, and discoursing also on the word *heathen*, which appears in his subtitle. As one reads his discussion of that word, one gradually comes to a startling realization. Of course he sees the Narragansetts to be "heathen"—but so is Massachusetts Bay! So is England. So is all of "Christendom," a word, or rather a concept, that particularly offended him. "Heathen" just means all nations and peoples except the People of God. Who are the people of God? None of the above.

In the nation formed a hundred years after his death, there has continually been, and still is, an effort to picture the United States as a "Christian Nation." Roger Williams certainly did not expect, or in one sense even want, a "Christian" Rhode Island. He did not see God saving whole peoples in bulk—in nation-sized lots, or in whole civilizations at a time.

A Christian believer, according to Williams, should not necessarily want or prefer Christians in places of command—"Christian" statesmen or leaders—or exclude people of other beliefs. There is for him no necessary link between what it takes to be a "visible saint" and what it takes to be a good magistrate, governor, or public official. If one makes some kind of religious test, one is shutting out people who might be good at public office, and putting in people who may not. In fact Williams suggests it will be relatively rare that there will be Christians, of the very pure sort that may be gathered into the garden, who will be good at being officials of the civil state. Most of the original believers were poor, and despised, fishermen and carpenters; and Williams expected it to continue to be more or less like that, the claims upon the faithful witness to Christ Jesus being what they are.

Though the stages of grace in Williams are like those in Puritan writings generally, in John Bunyan and the Puritan theologians—Williams wrote a little devotional manual for his wife, one of the few items he produced not dealing with church, state, and conscience—there is a thread of sharp and practical moral criticism running through him: Poverty and labor are the appropriate life for all true Christians, not worship of God-Belly, God-Wealth, God-Honour, God-Pleasure.

As we have seen, Williams, with his Biblical interpretation, denied the identification of the Israel of the Old Testament with any existing state. Neither Massachusetts Bay nor England nor Rhode Island nor any other actually existing nation—by extension, not the United States of America—is the equivalent or approximation of Israel as God's people, God's nation. Israel was a one-time-only arrangement, a "nonesuch." No subsequent nation is chosen, or covenanted with God, or favored by a special providence as a particular people.

It is a matter "of the highest consideration" that the understanding that won out, as the United States developed and grew, was not that of Roger Williams but of John Winthrop, perhaps of John Cotton—a mainline Puritan view. Massachusetts Bay had picked up and carried on the disposition of Englishmen to identify England with Israel, as chosen and favored of God, selected and cared for by a special providence; and that view had entered into the bloodstream of America, and appeared even in the deists of the founding period, and continues to add an element of self-righteousness to American self-interpretation to this day.

Perhaps it was inevitable that so exacting and difficult a view as Williams's should not prevail across whole nations or over stretches of time. In a sense, for the same reasons he did not expect whole nations to be "Christian," one should not expect whole nations even to comprehend, much less to follow, an exacting conviction like his.

When more than a century later the Baptist leader Isaac Backus defended religious liberty and separation of church and state throughout the revolutionary and founding period, he did draw heavily on Roger Williams—but not on his view of "Christendom" and the wilderness of all present nations. Backus, admirer of Williams, nevertheless wanted a "Christian America."

MORE PARTICULAR:
WILLIAMS AND FOUR
SEGMENTS OF HUMANKIND

Let us now examine Roger Williams's attitudes toward four groups—Quakers, Jews, Catholics, Indians—to illustrate his thought. Williams had a querulous argument with Quakers in Rhode Island toward the end of his life, and published a pamphlet that came out of it, argumentative, tedious, polemical. Many of his later admirers who find appealing the central core of Williams's teaching as they understand it—religious liberty in our modern terms—also have a considerable affection for the Quakers as a peace-loving, humanitarian, and undoctrinaire religious group, whose practices should be affirmed, not refuted. Therefore they have seen this episode as a blemish, in his old age, on the otherwise exemplary career of Roger Williams, that generous and tolerant man. In regarding it so, they interpret him, again, by their own standards. He was not supposed to argue or disagree? Argument and disagreement were his métier. He thought the Quakers were doctrinally *wrong*. There may have been something else that gave bite to the controversy: On some matters—such as institutions—he was not so far from the Quakers, who were, like him, a product of the radical wing of the Puritan movement. Not so far, and yet very far.

He was seventy-two when this three-day debate took place, and—as all the books tell us—he rowed alone all day from Providence to Newport to take part in it, to straighten those fellows out. Three days there, and then another performance back in Providence. He wrote the story of the encounter in a publication with a dreadful, heavyhanded pun for a title, *George Fox Digg'd Out of His Burrows;* Fox was the great Quaker leader Williams thought he was going to Newport to debate, but who had left before he got there; Burroughs was a disciple, and—but it is not worth explaining further. This relentless report appeared in 1676, the last of Williams's work to be published during his lifetime—this time in Boston itself, where, Perry Miller remarks, "in the strange revolutions of time, a work of Roger Williams was enthusiastically welcomed."

These early Quakers were not always like those of a later era. Some insisted on wearing long hair, a few on wearing no clothes in public. They could be rude. They were disinclined to be orderly and respectful. Their "radicalism" in behavior and conduct made them somewhat more like the New Left or the youth culture of the late 1960s than like the peaceable middle-class Quakers we know today. Williams did object, as a believer in the civil peace, to the way they behaved. He objected to the way, in the debate, the most obstreperous of the three Quakers kept interrupting him and not letting him finish his side of the argument. He objected to their falling down in prayer in the middle of the point he was trying to make to them. (Williams could indeed be lengthy and tedious in making his point, but that was surely a disconcerting way of responding.) He objected to their incivility; he did, as noted, believe in civic order.

But the Quakers' behavior was, of course, not the issue; their doctrine was. Williams, though an imaginative interpreter of the Bible, in whose interpretations we can today find the self-critically humane elements noted above, believed in the authority of the Bible, and, we can say, in an objective moral order accessible to all men's reason. Therefore he did not believe in an "Inner Light" that set the spiritual promptings of each person free from these objective authorities. He was, and remained, as noted, in such matters of doctrine pretty much aligned with his companions on the Reformation Wall.

But now comes the point that vindicates his outlook: He never for a moment suggested any expulsion or persecution. The Quakers, after all, had been welcomed in his Rhode Island as they were not elsewhere. In 1659–61 Mary Dyer and three others had been hanged, for being Quakers, on the Boston Common. Nothing like that had taken place in Rhode Island. To the contrary: Rhode Island was the first base and haven in the colonies, before Pennsylvania was founded, for this new radical Puritan group. They had tried in 1656 to settle in Boston, but, being rebuffed, had tried again and landed in Newport, Rhode Island. When the aroused New England authorities asked Rhode Island to prevent the settlement, they received a blunt rejection from Rhode Island's governor: Rhode Island does not meddle with matters of conscience. Moreover—exactly one of Williams's arguments—these Quaker radicals are less dangerous than what you New England authorities are doing to send them away. Subsequently, the Quakers came to be an important force in Rhode Island; Mary Dyer herself was the wife of a Quaker official in Rhode Island. In 1672, Williams, disagreeing with, and disliking, the Quakers, nevertheless did not at all suggest any civil penalty against them. All he did was to argue—try to argue—his opposing doctrinal case.

His argument with the Quakers, far from being a slip or dereliction on Williams's part, a falling away from his significance taken as a whole, is another indication of it. In Massachusetts they had been hanged. In Rhode Island they were welcome, helped run the colony, used it as a base for their expanding presence in the New World—and had to put up with Williams's arguments.

Roger Williams's defense of soul freedom, being complete, surely extended to Jews (or, as he sometimes wrote, his spelling in general having the spontaneity of his time, "Jewes"). That extension is of course a central test, particularly for Christians, whose historical record is so atrocious. The emerging seventeenth–eighteenth-century toleration in England and America by no means distinguished itself on that point. Disabilities for and limitations on Jews, in many states and places, extended much later into America's allegedly tolerant (or libertarian) history than most citizens today realize.

The treatment of Jews is a test in particular for a person who held intensely to the truth of the Christian revelation, as Williams did, at the time and among the folk with whom he lived, when religious beliefs were taken as seriously as some economic, political, and scientific beliefs are taken now. It is all too easy for us, for folk in a radically different setting, for whom religious liberty is a platitude, to dismiss these intolerant wrongheaded ancients en masse. It was not easy in Williams's world, or in Williams's world-view. In one of his short papers, published on his second trip to London, he wrote: "I judge it here only seasonable to say, that no opinion in the world is comparably so bloody, or blasphemous as that of punishing, and not permitting, in a civil way of Cohabitation, the consciences and worships, both of Jewes and Gentiles." From another paper on the same trip: "I humbly conceive it to be the Duty of the Civil Magistrate to break down that superstitious wall of separation (as to Civil things) between us Gentiles and the Jews, and freely (without their asking) to make way for their free and peaceable Habitation amongst us." His presentation included, to this Christian-Biblical audience, arguments of a special Biblical sort, much like those fundamentalists today make with respect to Israel:

1.   The holy Scripture saith, that they are a Beloved people, and beloved (as we sometimes love unworthy children) for their Fathers sake.

2.   They are a people above all the peoples and nations in the World, under most gracious and express Promises.

But in addition he argued—to make the point again, now with this specific example—on grounds of the humane meaning of Christianity:

As other Nations, so this especially, and the kings thereof, have had just cause to fear, the unchristian oppressions, incivilities, and inhumanities of this Nation against the Jews, have cried to Heaven against this Nation and the Kings and Princes of it.

What horrible oppressions and horrible slaughters have the Jews suffered from the Kings and peoples of this Nation, in the Reigns of Henry 2. K. John, Richard I. and Edward I. Concerning which not only we, but the Jews themselves keep Chronicles?

For the removing of which guilt, and the pacifying of the wrath of the most High against the Nation, and for the furthering of that great end of propagating the Gospel of Christ Jesus; It is humbly conceived to be a great and weighty Duty which lies upon this State, to provide (on the Jews account) some gracious Expedients for such holy and truly Christian Ends.

Propagating the Gospel, to him, includes gracious expedients to undo and overcome the horrible oppressions, the guilt, of "Christian" England against the Jews. That was not the usual idea of what was required to "propagate the gospel."

Arguing that the spirit of persecution is "opposite" to the "very tender bowels of humanity," "opposite" to the essentials and fundamentals of the nature of a civil magistry, and so on, he added "opposite to the Jews conversion to Christ, by not permitting them civil life or being."

Rhode Island under Williams became a haven for the Jews. Newport came to include after 1658 one of the earliest sizable Jewish settlements in colonial America. The colony became the first center for other religious groups, too. The historian Sydney Ahlstrom, in his *A Religious History of the American People*, grants to Rhode Island the palm (it gets handed around a lot, and scrambled for, in these books on religious freedom) as "the first commonwealth in modern history to make religious liberty (not simply a degree of toleration) a cardinal principle of its corporate existence and to maintain the separation of church and state on these grounds." Apparently feeling the heat from the competition, Ahlstrom adds, "This honor cannot be withheld." Among all the Christian commonwealths in all the history of Western "Christendom," the prime test would be, how was it for the Jews? In Roger Williams's Rhode Island, it was soul freedom.

The case of Catholics is perhaps the most difficult for people like Williams. For a modern mind to comprehend its significance one has to think oneself back into the world of seventeenth-century Puritans, to whom, interpreting the book of Revelation, the Catholic church was the Anti-Christ. It was the whore of Babylon, the concentrate and epitome of all that had intervened between the true Christian religion of the New Testament and the polluted world of bishops, popes, earthly powers that had evolved since Constantine made Christianity the official religion of Rome. The reason for a need to purify or pull away from the Church of England was the remnant in it of "popery," of the Church of Rome. Getting rid of all that Rome represented in the conduct and governance of Christian churches was a core belief. And Williams certainly shared it. To add to examples already given of his antichurchly sensitivity: He had great doubts about how he could be a minister because the succession of apostles had been broken by the intervening centuries of the reign of the (Roman Catholic) Anti-Christ. He therefore quit the ministry, as he quit all churches. None measured up—and Catholicism was the furthest from the truth, worse than that, a Satanic perversion. So he was by no means indifferent about, or cordial to, Catholicism as a religion. In addition, there were then powerful political reasons for Englishmen (Williams was an Englishman) to fear the Catholic powers. But—nevertheless—he defends the right of the "papists' " conscience.

Compare two of his famous acquaintances in the Puritan world of mid-seventeenth-century England, both of them heroes, too, in some measure, in the struggle for toleration: John Milton and Oliver Cromwell.

Milton, the greatest literary figure in the Puritan movement, interrupted his literary pursuits to join in the polemics of many of the controversies in which Williams participated. He is, of course, regarded as one of the most eloquent and important spokesmen for liberty. And yet there is a limit to the reach of John Milton's libertarianism. Toward the end of the *Aereopagitica* Milton explained:

I mean not tolerated popery and open superstition, which as it extirpates all religions and civil supremacies, so itself should be extirpated. . . . That also which is impious or evil absolutely, either against faith or manners, no law can permit that intends not to unlaw itself: but those whose neighboring differences, or rather indifferences, are what I speak of, whether in some point of doctrine or discipline.

Williams did not stop at "neighboring differences." He asked "why even the papists themselves and their conscience may not be permitted in the world?"

Religious bigotry and persecution in Ireland do not require much of a reminder down to the present hour. One of the worst of many persecutions in that sorry history was carried out by Williams's acquaintance or friend Oliver Cromwell, whom he came to know on his first trip to London in 1643, and whom he tried to influence in the direction of full religious liberty, even including "Papists." But whatever gain for religious liberty Cromwell did contribute—he figures, somewhat halfheartedly, in Canon Stokes's list of such contributors—stopped abruptly when he crossed the water and faced the Irish Catholics. As part of his conquest of Ireland in 1649, Cromwell led the sack and massacre of Drogheda and Wexford, Irish cities that refused to surrender under siege, and were therefore treated to the systematic murder of civilians and quite specifically the priests. Cromwell did put up with the Roman Catholics in England. But not in Ireland. "I meddle not with any man's conscience," he wrote, about Ireland, "but if by liberty of conscience you mean liberty to exercise the mass, I judge it best to use plain dealing, and let you know, where the Parliament of England have power, that will not be allowed of."

A curious little echo of the different memories on these ancient matters in our many-religions country turned up in the 1952 presidential election. General Dwight Eisenhower, the Kansas sectarian and novice politician with the predilection for the metaphor of a "crusade" for righteousness, referred spontaneously in his earliest days in his new role as political leader to the model of Oliver Cromwell, leading his righteous army to victory. More experienced advisers, who no doubt would have blanched at that illustration in any year, were particularly aware in this one that this Republican nominee had prospects for deep inroads into the normally Democratic Irish-American vote. They promptly squelched all references to Oliver Cromwell, and the Eisenhower "crusade" thereafter proceeded to victory without any specified historical antecedent.

Now hear Roger Williams exactly three hundred years before Mr. Eisenhower's gaffe.

> Ireland hath been an Akeldama, a field of blood; probable it is, that the guilt of all that blood, Protestant and Papist, will fall upon this Bloody tenant, of which both Papist and Protestant are guilty; to wit, of not permitting the Hereticks, the Blasphemers, &c. as the Sword falls either into the hand of a Popish or a Protestant Victor....
>
> From Henry the second his time, when Englands first yoke was clapt on poore Irelands neck, I say from Henry the second his time, unto Henry the eight, while their consciences had freedom under Popish Kings of England, how little bloud was spilt, English or Irish, compared with the showers and rivers both of one and the other spilt in the few years of our Protestant Princes, while the consciences of the Catholics have been restrained by the civil Sword and Penalties?

Once Williams used that imaginative leap to the whole world mentioned above: "For otherwise if England's government were the government of the whole world, not only they [the "papists"] but a world of idolators of all sorts, yea, the whole world, must be driven out of the world." Williams had a precocious awareness that there was a great world full of many different kinds of religion with which one had to do something in one's theory of church and state and religious liberty.

Moreover, he asked, "Whether the common body of protestants, impertinent and unregenerate, be not further off salvation, and lie not under a greater guilt, than does the body of ignorant papists?" And he followed with a further reversal, another application to ourselves of what we are applying to others, as suggested above.

> We humbly desire it may be deeply pondered what should be the kindling of jealousy of God, to pour forth the blood of so many thousands of protestants at the bloody hands of the papists (Since most just He is and righteous in all His judgment); whether or not the laws enacted in violence offered even to the consciences of the papists themselves have not kindled these devouring flames?

We Puritans did *our* part in starting these fires. Defining "conscience" in a letter about the persecution of three Baptists in Boston, Williams wrote:

> I speak of conscience, a persuasion fixed in the mind and heart of man, which enforceth him to judge (as Paul said of himself a persecutor) and to do so and so with respect to God, His worship.
>
> This conscience is found in all mankind, more or less: in Jews, Turks, Papists, Protestants, pagans.

Then he gives a startling example:

> And to this purpose let me freely without offense remember you (as I did Mr. Clarke newly come up from his sufferings amongst you)—I say, remember you of the same story I did him: 'twas that of William Hartley, in Queen Elizabeth her days, who receiving the sentence of hanging and drawing spake confidently (as afterwards he suffered), "What tell you me of hanging? If I had ten thousand millions of lives, I would spend them all for the Faith of Rome."

This was a Puritan Protestant writing to other Puritan Protestants, using as an example a Catholic martyr, paralleling him then with a Protestant, a "Holy English woman," linking the two as fellow victims of the Bloody Tenent.

Finally, as to the Indians. One of the most attractive features of Williams's life to many modern readers is his respectful treatment of what we today have come to call (Williams would certainly agree) the "native Americans." The first of the four offenses for which he was "enlarged" out of Massachusetts by its general court was his assertion that the land belonged to the Indians and that they should have been paid for it. Williams purchased his land from the Indians and also befriended the Narragansett sachem. "It was not price nor money that could have purchased Rhode Island," he said. "Rhode Island was purchased by love."

His first published work is a *Key to the Language of America*—that is, of the Indians of Narragansett Bay—written on shipboard on his way to London on his first trip (lest it be lost, before he forgot it). And it is a careful, respectful transcribing of their language, said by anthropologists today to be largely accurate. It does not include any derogation of the "heathen" Indian, although it is not sentimental about them either. He lived among the Indians, came to know them, treated them with respect, and befriended them. He was able therefore to do great service to Massachusetts as well as Rhode Island, and to all of New England, in clashes and dealings with the Indians.

And although he had apparently earlier intended to be a missionary to the Indians, he does not in fact when he gets there among them work very hard at converting them. His reasons for coming to know them and respecting them were not solely the instrumental ones, either of his own time or ours, of pure anthropological scientific curiosity or missionary strategy.

There was, to be sure, an element of practical necessity, in that he had been exiled from Massachusetts and had to live surrounded by the Narragansetts in the wilderness of the island. That, too, however, involved a choice. The elders of Massachusetts Bay were planning to send him back to England, where his writings had made him a notable figure. A friend of Milton and Cromwell, he could have stayed and been honored for a time, warmer and better fed. Nevertheless he went to the wilderness, stayed there, and returned both times from London. Most white men going among the Indians on this continent have behaved toward them in a way very different from Roger Williams's.

As noted, he did not try hard to convert them. Massachusetts Bay had as part of the justification of its Royal Charter that these Christian Englishmen would go to the New World to convert the heathen natives. Some critics of Massachusetts Bay back in England commented sardonically on their failure to accomplish very much in that line—except for Roger Williams. But the exception was a mistake: Williams certainly had a relationship with the Indians different from that of the main body of colonial Puritans, but partly for reasons of his own sharp religious sensibility, it did not include explicitly doing what Mark Twain, two centuries and many thought-worlds away, would call "missionaryin' around."

In Williams's own judgment he could have converted many:

> I can speak it confidently, I know it to have been easy for myself, long ere this, to have brought many thousands of these natives, yea, the whole country to a far greater anti-Christian conversion than was ever heard of in America. I could have brought the whole country and observed one day in seven: I add, to receive Baptism, come to a stated Church meeting, to have maintained Priests and forms of prayer.

He could have done all that, and they would have taken on the outward form of conversion, out of respect for him, in great numbers. But he did not, for reasons suggested above. He does not call it conversion to God, "which is indeed subversion of souls of millions and christened them, from one false worship to another." Because he did not believe that the bulk of actual unreformed Christianity was itself what the true church was supposed to be, because it (almost?) did not exist on this earth, he did not seek to bring about a subtler version of what would be called, in a much later context, "rice Christians."

In one winning passage of the *Key*, he tells of a conversation he overheard while, after a long discourse with Narragansetts, he lay in bed waiting to sleep. One Indian, marveling at the white man's teaching about the soul going up to Heaven or down in the other direction, said: "Our fathers have told that our souls go to the Southwest."

The sachem answered: "How do you know yourself that your souls go to the Southwest: do you ever see a soul go thither?"

"When did *he* [Williams] see a soul go to Heaven or Hell?"

The sachem: "He hath books and writings, and one which God himself made, concerning men's souls, and therefore may well know more than we that take all upon trust from our forefathers."

They went on talking about the way of Christian worship that Williams had described to them, and they were open to persuasion to his superior book-grounded wisdom. But he did not do it.

Williams's treatment of the Indians was respectful, courteous, and charitable throughout his *Key to the Language of America*; his comments in the *Key* emphasize a common humanity: "Nature knows no difference between Europe and Americans in blood, birth, bodies, God having of one blood made all mankind (Acts 17) and all by nature being children of wrath (Ephesians 2)."

Sometimes this insistence on the shared characteristics of all children of wrath takes an amusing, or a startlingly modern, turn:

> They are impatient (as all men and God Himself is) when their speech is not attended and listened to.
> The Whole race of mankind is generally infected with an itching desire of hearing news.

A solid perception of the all-of-one-bloodness of humankind provides the factual underpinning for that moral test by generalizing which one can discover throughout Williams. One can also discover the further step, to perceive that others different from one's own kind in some lesser regard than the unifying blood are *better*. Of course it was then, and is now, a conventional point in Christian preaching, often tinged with sentimentality or patronage, to note that assorted "heathens" can be in some regard superior to "Christians." In Williams that point is filled out, solidly grounded, purged of sentimentality and patronage by his solid knowledge of the particular "heathens" he lived with. "It is a strange truth that a man shall generally find more free entertainment and refreshing amongst these barbarians than amongst thousands that call themselves Christians." Some of the most engaging of these contrasts occur in the little poems that appear as the "more particular" expression of points he has made (these are quoted not from *The Collected Works* but from Perry Miller's book, in which Miller cleaned up the typography).

> The courteous pagan shall condemn
>   Uncourteous Englishmen,
> Who live like foxes, bears and wolves,
>   Or lion in his den.
>
> If nature's sons both wild and tame
>   Humane and courteous be,
> How ill becomes it sons of God
>   To want humanity?
>
> I have known them leave their house and mat
>   To lodge a friend or stranger,
> When Jews and Christians oft have sent
>   Christ Jesus to the manger.

In another of his poems, he wrote, " 'Fore day they invocate their Gods, though many, false, and new." But as he does not refer to the newness and manyness of their Gods with the indifference of Jefferson, so also he does not refer to their falseness with the condemnatory personal superiority of a considerable part of the Christian world, and in particular of the followers of those warriors on Geneva's wall. In that poem, as a matter of fact, he is noting that they "invocate" these gods " 'Fore day," and by implication asking then how early the worshippers of the God who is "but one and true" are willing to arise.

Williams believed the Narragansetts' worship, however early in the morning, of their new and many gods to be false and idolatrous. He believed the God that Christians worship, almost always in the wrong way, to be "one and true." He was very far from being a relativist or indifferent about religious truth. For Parrington and others to call him a "seeker," after he has, at the end of his life, for his reasons, left the ministry and all churches, may lead to a considerable mistake. He was definitely not a seeker in the way that a twentieth-century person would use the word: one who climbs various Asian mountains and visits various Southern California retreats in an unending, open-minded search for truth. Roger Williams had found truth in the Bible, and in Christian revelation, and stayed with it all his life. He wrote, in fact, in one of the sentences Perry Miller liked best: "Having bought truth dear, let us not sell it cheap." Williams was a "seeker" only after the proper institutional expression, in the wilderness of the world, of the truth he had already found.

Parrington, comparing Williams to William Ellery Channing and other nineteenth-century Unitarians, uses about him the phrase "open-minded": surely an anachronism. Williams was not one of those whose mind is open so that when the winds of doctrine whistle through it they meet no impediment. The argumentative, disputing, Puritan, Biblical, "Calvinist" Williams, firm in the orthodoxy he shared with Puritan Christians and firm in his quite heterodox interpretation of it, was humane not because he believed no truth but because humaneness was the essence of the truth he did believe.

The dearly bought truth is that the "Lamb of God" means love. So do not persecute *anybody* for cause of conscience because of that truth—or you already contradict it. "I plead for impartiality and equal freedom, peace, and safety to other Consciences and Assemblies, unto which the people may as freely goe, and this according to each conscience, what conscience soever this conscience be."

A NOTE ON THE IDEA
OF RELIGIOUS LIBERTY
AMONG BELIEVERS

By this interpretation Roger Williams becomes such a good symbol of the Christian contribution to America's freedom of conscience that, paradoxically, he transcends it—in something of the way that Abraham Lincoln at once symbolizes and transcends the essence of Americanism, and for something of the same reason. A believer's religious humility and a patriot's national humility are necessarily fragile, not easily spread or transmitted to other believers or patriots, given the limitations of average human nature. What these two men are taken to symbolize they represent as better than in general, it was, or is; they express it at its ideal best—which in the real world it rarely attained, and often contradicted. They penetrated to the essence of a moral ideal that by its nature is difficult, subtle, and rare, and therefore is usually flattened, changed, made into something else; it is not to be discovered in large numbers, or over an extended time.

So we might move forward again from the seventeenth to the eighteenth century, and descend briefly to one of those other, and perhaps more ordinary, candidates for this representative role—that is, to stand for Protestant dissent among the causes or sources of the achievement of religious liberty in America.

But before we do that let it be noted that among those sources there were not only ideas, Enlightenment and dissenting Protestant, but also practical necessities, that among the latter were the rise of commercial (nonreligious) interests; the large numbers of the "unchurched," particularly in the West, in the late eighteenth century; the exigencies of Revolutionary War, which required the embattled colonies to collaborate across religious differences and avoid alienating fellow patriots; and, by far the most important, the pragmatic fact of the differences within and across state boundaries. There were states with established churches still, which themselves came in two kinds: The Anglicans, whose church was the established church in southern colonies, were themselves somewhat curiously cast as "dissenters" in Congregational Massachusetts and Connecticut. There were other states, Pennsylvania and Rhode Island, that never had an established church, and still others, Virginia and New York, that had had one but disestablished it in the revolutionary period. The complex of patterns of nonestablishment in the "middle colonies" was a particularly important practical fact for the new nation. One of these middlers, Maryland, was the one colony that had had a considerable Catholic population in the seventeenth century, because the proprietary family, converts to Roman Catholicism, wanted to provide a haven for their coreligionists. In order to do that, and in order to make a commercial success in an overwhelmingly Protestant setting, they extended "toleration" to both Catholics and Protestants. Members of both religious groups began to settle the colony in 1634. The Maryland Act of Toleration of 1649, though very restrictive by later standards—it extended only to "trinitarian christians," with some severe exclusions and restrictions for others—was nevertheless a considerable advance at a time when a great deal of that "blood" to which Williams referred was spilled by Catholics and Protestants.

But by all odds the most important of the middle colonies, from one point of view the most important of all, was Pennsylvania. And to mention Pennsylvania is to dramatize how inextricably the practical necessities that required religious liberty were mingled with convictions, beliefs, and ideas. (There was not so long ago a mode of interpretation—hard-headed, realistic, no-nonsense, in keeping with a reductionist cast of mind—that dismissed the ideological sources of the American arrangement, and found those causes entirely in the sheer realities that the newly independent colonies faced. What else could they do? But—one responds—a set of convictions, beliefs, and ideas did much to create those realities—as in Pennsylvania. As in Virginia and Rhode Island, too, for that matter, and elsewhere. As in the ideas of the Enlightenment—John Locke's in England, leading to the Act of Toleration of 1689, which then had effects in the colonies; Madison's and Jefferson's and George Mason's ideas, as we have seen. And—our present point—the ideas and beliefs of dissenting or radical Protestantism. These beliefs and convictions then created many of the conditions, the realities, the necessities to which, it may be, practice had to yield.)

Unlike Maryland's, but like that of Roger Williams's Rhode Island,

Pennsylvania's liberality was grounded not only in necessity and opportunity but also in such moral and religious convictions; unlike both of those other colonies, Pennsylvania retained that original liberality and, almost a century after the colony's founding, it was still there to furnish a model for the new nation.

After 1656, Quakers, based in Rhode Island, spread to other colonies, including a sprinkling in Virginia at the time of the events recounted in Parts One and Two, above. In 1681, out of the Quaker movement in England came the founding of what was to be their most important contribution. That extraordinary figure William Penn created the "holy experiment" of Pennsylvania as a sanctuary for the oppressed of Europe—the religiously oppressed in particular—with toleration for all who believed in God. Pennsylvania was a refuge for Quakers, who rather quickly turned into something very different from the extremists in conduct to which Roger Williams and others objected, becoming sober and often wealthy pillars of the community. But Pennsylvania was also a haven for a wide variety of sectarian and pietist groups from the Continent: Mennonites, Moravians, Dunkers, Amish, and other German sects, for example. And it was important to many other groups as well: It welcomed Roman Catholics in a way that Puritan New England did not; Lutherans and Baptists would find a welcome in Pennsylvania. It offered a point of immigration for the Scotch-Irish, whose role we have noted in the discussion of events in Virginia. Many of the groups that came into Pennsylvania had a history of opposition to an establishment and memories of persecution, which they imported then into the other colonies. Pennsylvania became almost a model for the nation as a whole, presenting to the young James Madison that example of Liberty of which he expressed Virginian envy when he was writing his letters to "Billey" Bradford up in Pennsylvania.

So there was a diversity among the colonies. Even more important was the diversity among the kinds of Protestants, especially the newer kinds, which diversity helped to create the diversity of colonies and both the practical necessity of at least some kind of "toleration," and, among certain of these Protestants, the positive endorsement, on Christian grounds, of religious liberty and separation of church and state—but in the main with emphases in that endorsement that differ both from Jefferson and Madison and, by the interpretation above, from Roger Williams.

THE DISSIDENTS OF DISSENT

Let us draw back for a summary and a running start, because there are threads of complication that run through the whole story, and that will lead, eventually, into what America became. The colonial political-cultural terrain—and America itself—has been molded by an interconnected series of unusually strong movements of protest, reform, and dissent within the Christian religion, each of them at once a renewal and a partial rejection of what had gone before. There was the Protestant Reformation itself, especially as represented by the stalwarts on the Reformation Wall: every man his own priest; scripture alone. There was the Puritan movement in England, at first a minority but then for a time in the seventeenth century permeating England, leading to a Civil War and the great dream, and not so great actuality, of a Christian Commonwealth. There was, within that movement, Congregational Puritanism, objecting to the insufficient break with the hierarchical past on the part of Presbyterian Puritans, depositing its enormously important representatives on Massachusetts Bay. There was Separatism, objecting to the retention of any tie whatever to a national church, even on the part of Congregational Puritans like the proponents of the New England Way in Massachusetts, of which Separatism Roger Williams was a distinctively separated example. There were a congeries of groups still more radical than, so to speak, the ordinary Separatist: Quakers from within the English ferment, Baptists (with some separate Continental and English antecedents) from within the American, and Moravians and Mennonites from the Continent, heading for Pennsylvania, and other sectarians who in various ways moved outside even the forms that other Separatists maintained—dismissing the preacher, qualifying the decisive authority of the Bible by reference to an Inner Light, rejecting the baptism of children, rejecting war, the magistrate, the churchly legitimation of the state's use of power. This potent Protestant sequence created a diversity that may have *required* liberty; it also created in many a conviction that *insisted* on it. There is a widely used quotation from Edmund Burke about those American colonials on the brink of their revolt, that they represented "the dissidence of dissent and the protestantism of the Protestant religion." If one asks today where the radical individualism shot through American culture comes from, this is an important place to look for it. A pietist-Protestant form of religious liberty—*Christian* liberty, gospel liberty—was not just its corollary but its essence.

THE RIGHTEOUS NATION

But along with this widening stream there was another that flowed into it, from the same headwaters, that may now seem contradictory to many observers but did not, for a long time at least, seem so to the main body of American Protestant Christians.

To go back to those headwaters: If one divides the manifold complexity of the Protestant Reformation into four large groupings—Lutheran, Anglican, Calvinist/Reformed, and sectarian—then the last two are overwhelmingly the most important in the shaping of American political culture, and American culture generally. After immigrations from Germany and Scandinavia, the Lutheran heritage would become important in the developed nation. The Anglican background of all the English colonies, and the Anglican establishments in the southern colonies, and in particular in Virginia, had no doubt considerable importance; those colonists, those forefathers, were English, and carried within themselves the culture of the English church. Robert Handy, the historian of the present point, describing in his book *A Christian America* the "long spell of Christendom" hanging on into the America that had declared liberty and separation, ascribes it in part to the memory, habit, and expectation of the common heritage in England, and the Church of England—which in turn of course transmitted the longer heritage of the Christian West. But the forming power of the new nation at the decisive moments came not from the Anglican or Lutheran heritage but from those sturdy warriors on the Reformation Wall in Geneva, and their agents and successors and followers, and from the sectarian impulse on the Continent and in England.

These last two movements—Calvinist and sectarian—mingled in England to make the Puritan movement, the importance of which for the forming of American culture no one now is likely to miss, "Puritanism" having become a major category, with whatever degree of accurate meaning, in the assessment and explanation of America.

Perry Miller, who had much to do with the modern intellectual recovery of the Puritans not so much perhaps from neglect as from stereotype, wrote that one cannot understand American culture, for good or ill, without understanding the Puritans. Sydney Ahlstrom's *A Religious History of the American People*, the leading book on its subject, treats that history, for all its enormous complexity, sprouting ever new branches continually in all directions—a complexity Ahlstrom handles with tact and skill—nevertheless as centrally the story of the continual unfolding of the Puritan movement.

Our present point about this particular stream of religious history is its strong and active impulse to make over nations and cultures in the image of righteousness. Or to try to. That high Puritan impulse had in it a purpose to build and to dominate a culture—"Calvinist," if you will—that went well beyond what Catholic and Anglican Christianity had intended, because it wanted to "order all under God" *directly*, without gradation, relative autonomies, or intermediaries linking the regenerate soul with the Christian Commonwealth. The full impact of that drive was felt, for a time, in seventeenth-century New England, and the further impact, diminished perhaps and much altered in method certainly—altered by the events described in this book—has been felt bumping and banging through American culture down to the present time. It continues right alongside the dissent and protest, the liberty and individualism, melded eventually with it in a unique way.

The Calvinists, whether supporters or opponents of a state church, whether supporters or opponents of religious liberty, were purpose-filled followers of a purpose-filled God in a purpose-filled society in a purpose-filled universe. God specifically orders the fall of every raindrop (not just letting it happen under a general principle of rainfall, as in Aristotle and all who follow him—Calvin was contemptuous of Aristotle's First Cause), and how much more therefore does He act upon, perform, direct, order by His Providence the life and destiny of human souls—and human communities and human history.

This Calvinist or "Reformed" strain was reinforced by other parties to the making of the New World: especially the Scotch-Irish, whose comparatively early arrival and numbers and Presbyterian intensity made them a potent influence (as we have seen), and also the Dutch Reformed in New Jersey and New York, and other Reformed groups. Sydney Ahlstrom wrote: "Puritanism provided the moral and religious background of full seventy-five percent of the people who declared their independence in 1776." He added in a footnote: "[I]f one were to compute such a percentage on the basis of all the German, Swiss, French, Dutch, and Scottish people whose forebears bore the 'stamp of Geneva' in some broader sense, eighty-five or ninety percent would not be an extravagant estimate." If there once were those (Louis Hartz for one) who saw America as John Locke writ large, an interpreter with a different focus might see it as John Calvin writ large—as yet another culture much affected by those other people on the Reformation Wall—except, ironically, Roger Williams.

But English Puritanism was more than Calvinism. It was English. Americans may not realize how much in the transatlantic Puritan antecedents to the founding of America there was a very high view of *England's* role in carrying out the purposes of God upon this planet. One can find it, for example, in a kind of "I have a dream" speech at the end of Milton's *Areopagitica*: "Lords and Commons of England, consider what nation it is whereof ye are, and whereof ye are governors. ...God is decreeing to begin some new and great period in his church, even to the reforming of reformation itself. What does he then but reveal himself to his servants, and as his manner is, first to his Englishmen...the mansion house of liberty." For English Puritans the Reformation had begun not with Luther and Germans or Calvin and Swiss or Hus and Czechs but with Wyclif and God's England. This sense of a nation's dramatic particularity in God's reforming purposes, a *special* Providence, a covenant nation, was transmitted in concentrate to the New World, and entered into that sense of a particular relationship to God and his purposes, especially his reforming purposes, that certainly has become a part of American culture. (It was another of Roger Williams's peculiarities that he did not share it, as we have seen.)

On the one side the Puritans revived the inward personal intensity of the Christian religion: a particular sharply etched conversion, with continual introspection and self-examination, and the visibility of saints. On the other side they reached out toward the righteous remaking of the entire social life, with a particular nation in a distinct relation to Divine Providence and to righteousness.

Something of Puritanism's world-remaking moral intensity was picked up by the evangelical Protestantism that was to follow. But the context of that moral intensity was changed: The *explicit* state-religion corporate expression of it was left behind, and a pious and moralistic individualism took its place. That did not mean, however, that the corporate aspect vanished; it took a new form.

THE STRANDS COME TOGETHER IN THE AWAKENING

After the Puritan impulse sloped off into halfway covenants and compromises with the unpurified world, there came the first of the long sequence, that explosion of the 1730s and 1740s in the colonies to which we have already referred, the Great Awakening. This prairie fire of revivals started with several local flames in the brush—notably among the Dutch Reformed and Presbyterians in northern New Jersey, and in the Connecticut Valley under the greatest of American theologian-preachers, Jonathan Edwards—and then was turned into a conflagration through all the colonies by the extraordinary English traveling evangelist George Whitefield. (Whitefield, twenty-four years old when he first came across the Atlantic, is the powerful orator-preacher about whom it was said, in a story whose familiarity has surpassed the name of the man to whom it was attached, that he could bring tears to your eyes just by the emotional power he could pour into pronouncing the word *Mesopotamia*.)

Whitefield preached not only in any pulpit to which he was invited (already startling) but also, since he would say as John Wesley did, "The *world* is my parish" (Tom Paine four decades later: The world is my country), in the "open air" without any formal pulpit or parish structure whatever, directly, to all who would come, pulling loose from institutional form, parish-geographical location, communal-traditional continuities. And although the revivals of this first awakening were orthodox in their creedal base and sedate by the measure of what would happen in later ones, still, an appeal to the emotions was an essential part.

When Jonathan Edwards encountered the "surprising Work of God in the Conversion of Many Hundred Souls in Northampton in 1733," and George Whitefield preached his way from Philadelphia to New York and then all the way to Georgia and then sailed to Newport, Rhode Island, and preached his way around New England in 1740—the central core of the religious culture of the nation that was to come into being after the last of Whitefield's four evangelistic tours (in 1770) started to change. Indeed, the Awakening left a permanent stamp upon the whole culture. The twin phenomena of conversion and revival were planted at the foundation of American culture, where they have remained, to some degree, ever since. But the sharp individualism of the Awakening on the one side did not erase the corporate-national aspect on the other. Speaking from within the communities of both nationality and belief, H. Richard Niebuhr called that Great Awakening "our national conversion."

It was a national conversion that produced the New Side Presbyterians, who founded the College of New Jersey in time for Madison to study there; Samuel Davies, the founder of the Hanover Presbytery, who became the best-known dissenting preacher in Virginia; the Presbyterian, Baptist, and Methodist New Lights, who furnished the petition-power that enabled Madison to steer Jefferson's statute through the Virginia Assembly; similar New Lights throughout all the colonies; and some important influence—scholars debate how much—on the coming of the American Revolution and on the ideas that created the American Republic.

One important group it produced, of course, was the Baptists, especially a particular variety called Separate Baptists. Their most important leader in the period of the Revolution was Isaac Backus, whom we mentioned above before departing for the seventeenth century and Roger Williams. He really *was* a Baptist. We may say a word about Backus both as he mediates, represents, and continues, and as he may not mediate or continue, Roger Williams—and as he anticipates what is to come in the formative period of the new nation.

Born, baptized as an infant, and raised within the established "standing order" of Congregationalism in New England as a member of a prominent family of Norwich, Connecticut, Backus was converted by the preaching of George Whitefield in the Great Awakening, and suddenly found himself by his new convictions outside that establishment. He became an extraordinary Separatist Congregationalist and then Separate Baptist clergyman who agitated, wrote, spoke, and preached full whistle, mostly in Massachusetts, for complete religious liberty and separation of church and state (a particular *kind* of liberty and separation) for forty years right through the whole revolutionary era and beyond. He was sent ("unanimously") by the "Antipaedobaptist churches of New England" ("the reverend and beloved Mr. Isaac Backus as our agent") to the Continental Congress in Philadelphia in 1774, just as the decisive events of revolution and independence were breaking, to present the case for religious liberty, and did so especially to the Massachusetts delegates in a famous meeting in Carpenter's Hall. The Massachusetts delegation seems to have patronized him a bit, and wondered why he (and his Antipaedobaptist sponsors) were so bothered by a little tax for Massachusetts churches that was really nothing much at all anymore; maybe they were "enthusiasts" who had something of a taste for persecution. The Massachusetts delegates—Sam and John Adams among them—had much bigger fish to fry: the portentous matter of actual independence from England, revolution, and war. The delegates may have been given momentary pause when Backus said it was a matter of *conscience*, and of natural and human *right*, God-given right—terms some of these delegates were getting ready themselves to use against Parliament and even George III—but still John Adams explained to Backus that we might as well expect a change in the solar system as expect Massachusetts to give up its establishment. In the end, the response of the Massachusetts delegation to Backus and his Baptist colleagues was the 1774 equivalent of "Don't call us, we'll call you."

Backus made his arguments, especially against taxing Baptists to support Congregational churches, on many occasions to many assemblies within Massachusetts. He published, his biographer, William G. McLoughlin, tells us, 37 tracts, mostly on religious liberty. (Much of what is recounted here is taken from McLoughlin's *Isaac Backus and the American Pietist Tradition*, and from Canon Stokes.) Although some of the patriots were worried that these obstreperous Separate Baptists might have a Tory strain in them, Backus proved in the event to be a passionate supporter of the Revolution, especially because he saw full religious liberty bound up in its purpose. What others call the American Revolution, Backus and his Separate Baptist colleagues called the "new reformation": Providence overthrowing the established churches against which they had fought. For them, political liberty and religious liberty were the conjoined objectives of the revolution and political tyranny and ecclesiastical tyranny were the intertwined opponents.

But in the complex forming of the new constitution for the state of Massachusetts he and the Baptists lost out. This was the Massachusetts constitution of 1780 already mentioned in Part One of this book, in the composition of which John Adams played an important role. That constitution *did* make an important change in the state's religious setup, one that Adams, and almost everybody else, understandably regarded as a major step forward for liberty. Adams, in helping to compose it, was even said to have been influenced in the liberal direction by his friend Jefferson's bill (not yet, of course, passed in Virginia). The old constitution provided by law for the Standing Order—the established Congregational Church of Massachusetts, reaching through the vicissitudes of colonial history all the way back to John Winthrop and his companions on the *Arbella*. All citizens were taxed to support that church *except* those citizens who could get themselves specifically exempted as bona-fide Anglicans, Quakers, or Baptists (an exemption for which, failing the better, Backus had fought).

The Massachusetts constitution of 1780 technically ended that most formidable of American establishments—quite a moment, if one dramatized it that way. But it was no bang of an ending, as perhaps one can say Virginia's was. It instituted in its much-debated Article Three the interesting local variety of "establishment" already briefly mentioned in Part One: Each town was to provide its own "public Protestant teachers of piety, religion, and morality," with its own tax money. Theoretically these "teachers" (preachers) could be Baptists or Anglicans; the Congregational Standing Order was therefore, in that sense, disestablished, and most citizens of Massachusetts at the time regarded the new arrangement as a major step forward toward religious equality. But

Isaac Backus had no such opinion—because Article Three had in it still the unscriptural evil of compulsory taxation for the support of religion. (And, incidentally, its apparent equality would make it harder for Baptists to claim exemption.)

In effect Article Three was almost what the Patrick Henry bill in Virginia would be four years later: a general assessment for religion, distributed to the several denominations by the believers' choices. And the arguments in its favor were exactly the same: "Good morals are necessary to promote the peace, safety and happiness of the community; religious impressions have a natural tendency to produce good morals." Therefore: "whatever then tends to promote religious impressions is for the civil good of society." (Most twentieth-century Americans are probably inclined to expect defenders of established churches—or of tax support for religion, as in Massachusetts' Article Three—to be the "conservatives," religiously and politically, and their opponents to be found in the other direction. But that is not so in all times and places. The most vigorous defenders of the Article—one learns from McLoughlin— were two Standing Order ministers who were liberal or Unitarian in doctrine. In Witherspoon's struggles against the established Kirk in Scotland, many defenders, and beneficiaries, of that Establishment were distinguished representatives of the Scottish Enlightenment, who had been given by the state church a sort of tenured position for their erudite studies. Pastors chosen by congregations—as Witherspoon fought for them to be—would have been generally more "conservative" in doctrine. Populistic conservatism, especially in religious matters, is not new.)

Backus fought vigorously and continually against the obnoxious aspect of Article Three (significantly, he did *not* oppose its commitment of the state to religion, and to the religious foundation for morality; he opposed *only* its provision of tax support for religion). He fought in the votes in the towns on whether to accept the Constitution, and in the legislature, and in the courts. But the outcome of his long battle was the opposite of that of the ten-year struggle by James Madison and the equivalent of Backus's forces in Virginia. Backus and his fellow Massachusetts Baptists lost. A system of tax support for religion prevailed. Backus died in 1806, before its final downfall, the last such system in the nation.

Meanwhile, Backus had supported ratification of the Federal Constitution. He was chosen as a delegate to the Massachusetts ratifying convention, and although many of his fellow Baptists opposed the Constitution because it did not seem to them to go far enough to protect religious freedom, Backus voted for ratification because of the "exclusion of any hereditary, lordly power, and of any religious test." It was but one more episode in Backus's lifelong battle for religious liberty and republican government—based explicitly and fully on pietist Christian-Biblical grounds—in a setting in which these social goods were (as they are not today) in dispute, at the founding of this country.

But now it is necessary to come to the important point. One of Backus's tracts, *An Appeal to the Public for Religious Liberty Against the Oppression of the Present Day* (1773), McLoughlin writes, was "central to the whole movement for separation of Church and State in America . . . the best exposition of the eighteenth century pietistic concept of separation . . . pietistic America's declaration of spiritual independence." It attacked the Puritan establishment for reasons like these:

—because the right to tax was a claim to the right to govern in Christ's kingdom, which is not of this world;
—because "bringing in an earthly power between Christ and his people has been the grand source of anti-Christian abominations."

Backus's (and the Baptists') grounds for supporting separation of church and state were markedly different from those of Jefferson and Madison—his "becauses" differ from Madison's—and in that difference lies the seed of the American future.

Another of Backus's thirty-seven tracts is titled *Truth Is Great and Will Prevail*. But, writes McLoughlin, "by 'Truth' he meant the revealed doctrines of grace." That is scarcely what Jefferson meant. McLoughlin: "Basic to the Baptist position was the belief that all direct connections between the state and institutionalized religion must be broken in order that America might become a truly Christian country." The skeptical modern reader, as no doubt the Jeffersonian skeptic or rationalist in Backus's own time, may jump in surprise at the second part of that sentence and find it to be a contradiction to the point and meaning of separation and state. It was directly otherwise for Backus and the pietists. The title of yet another of Backus's tracts puts the parallel point succinctly: *A Door Opened for Equal Christian Liberty and No Man Can Shut It*. The door of equal liberty was to be irrevocably opened, but it was still *Christian* liberty.

Somewhat in the manner of Roger Williams, if you will, Backus became first a "Separate" (one of those New Light enthusiasts who pulled out of the Standing Order Congregational Church because of its compromises with the world and its lack of saving fire) and then took the still more radical step of becoming a Baptist. For Backus, as not for Williams, that was the last stop, and the definition of his lifelong role. He came to be a Baptist despite the opprobrium in which Baptists were held because he came to be persuaded that there was no scriptural ground for infant baptism.

Rejecting infant baptism was a threat to the continuities of the Congregational Standing Order, and radically individualistic in implication (*your* own *adult* conversion, not your parents' decision while you are a baby). So were the other two New Light counts (the same as the complaints, as we have seen, of their Virginia counterparts) in Backus's indictment of the Standing Order: that they required "academical" degrees for ministers, and compulsory tax support of churches.

The most widely held early American idea of the separation of church and state flows from such *religious* ideas—from pietism, not from rationalism. How is it compatible with the drive for a Christian America, even a Baptist America? It is compatible (more than compatible, in its own view) because the two ideas—separation of church and state, and a Christian America—have a shared evangelical center... a common center in revivalism and conversion, in a faith that each believer personally *experiences*, and that is preached and spread. It has to be *voluntary* in order to be real, and personal. Churches established by law and supported by taxes, tied to the earthly power of the state, cold, formal, and usually soon decadent, are unscriptural in their foundation, and block the New Light energy of individually experienced religion that will convert a nation.

Both Jefferson and Backus believed in religious liberty. But the meaning of "liberty" depends upon what you are being freed from and freed for. Both believed the New World needed to be liberated from state churches—but Jefferson, so that the casting off of superstitions and shackles on the mind will free men for enlightenment, and Backus, so that casting off unscriptural, unfervent, corrupted churches will free men for the preaching and accepting of the freely given grace of God.

Backus read, borrowed from, and praised Roger Williams, took arguments against religious persecution from him, and devoted the first volume of his four-volume history of the American Baptists to him. He is a chief mediator of the name and work of Roger Williams to the American Revolutionary generation and to the Baptist world. Moreover, Backus was similar to Williams in many ways: He, too, was an orthodox Calvinist in theology; his conflicts and discoveries, too, had to do not with theology but with the nature of the church, and its government, and the state, and, though they came more than a century later in a quite different community—in the much more settled world of the late Puritan halfway covenant Standing Order Congregationalism of Connecticut and Massachusetts, in the late eighteenth century—still Backus's positions had certain apparent similarities to those of Williams. Both sought the true meaning of scripture, in particular with respect to the nature of the church. But Backus lacked the unusual moral imagination and critical universalism one can find in Williams.

Backus was a pietistic product of the Great Awakening, whose conflicts with the Standing Order in Connecticut, where he grew up, and in Massachusetts, where he spent his long ministry, were the same as those of the New Lights in Virginia with the Anglican Establishment there: itineracy, tax support for the established church, licenses to preach and worship, a "cold" educated ministry against preaching in the spirit, enthusiasm versus decorum. As in Virginia, so in Massachusetts and Connecticut: These New Lights, and in particular the Separate Baptists, represented a threat not just to a rival church but to the whole social order—to the corporate Christian commonwealth. Backus represents, in his northern setting, with a slightly different opponent, exactly those forces that fought to victory alongside Madison (and Jefferson) in Virginia. But Backus had no Madison and Jefferson to join with, no Founder or Enlightenment allies—John Adams was on the other side—and no complex denominational politics to aid in the fight. In his lifetime, he lost.

After his death, however, not only was the Standing Order in Connecticut overthrown in 1818, and the Article Three tax for teachers of piety, etc., overthrown in Massachusetts in 1833, but there came into being a social-religious America (of which more below, in Part Four) that had in it much less of the sacral communitarianism of Virginia Anglicans or the stiff old Congregationalist Puritanism of Timothy Dwight and the Standing Orders, less (alas) of the humane, imaginative, and critical Christianity of Roger Williams, even somewhat less perhaps (and also alas) of the Republicanism of Madison and Jefferson, than it had of the pietism of Isaac Backus.

ON ROGER WILLIAMS, LATER

In conclusion, to return to our original subject: Did Roger Williams himself have an influence on all of these subsequent American events? That is, in the nature of such things, difficult to know. Perry Miller almost answered: No, he did not. Miller wrote that "although Williams is celebrated as the prophet of religious freedom, he actually exerted little or no influence on institutional developments in America; only after the conception of liberty for all denominations had triumphed on wholly other grounds did Americans look back on Williams and invest him with his ill-fitting halo." Others have followed Miller's magisterial lead. David Little of the University of Virginia, on the other hand, contradicting Miller and others, finds Williams linked to developments in eighteenth-century colonial America through two intermediaries: John Locke and Isaac Backus. With Locke, the case is made by inference from the many and striking parallels to arguments made by Williams in Locke's *Letter Concerning Toleration*. In the case of Backus, though, the debt is explicit and large.

Roger Williams became in retrospect a hero to Baptists, later to progressives. Then scholarship restored him to his Puritan setting. Roger Williams is one of those figures, sufficiently attractive, and sufficiently prestigious in a nation's past, to draw many efforts at interpretation, and sufficiently complicated to yield quite a variety . . . a tendency, perhaps not altogether avoided in these pages, to appropriate him.

In the late 1950s, the Fund for the Republic, described as a "wholly disowned subsidiary of the Ford Foundation," in the witticism of its leader, Robert Hutchins, brought together a sufficiently disparate crew— the present writer among them—to carry on a continuing series of discussions on "Religion and the Free Society," to issue pamphlets and presumably to "make a contribution to the dialogue," in its publications and conferences (perhaps the group had something to do with the subsequent ubiquity of the word "dialogue" in what were once called "interfaith" circles). Two of the participants in that enterprise were to make their own contribution to the "dialogue" about Roger Williams, whose name had cropped up around the discussion table.

The first of these, who has already appeared in this book with his commentary on James Madison, was the formidable John Courtney Murray, the most important American Catholic thinker of the twentieth century. He would sit, tall and imperious in the clerical garb priests always wore then, at the table in a big room in a midtown Manhattan building reached by tunnels from Grand Central Station, or, more impressively still, looming dark against the sunlight coming through the bank of windows, with the Pacific Ocean behind him, in Santa Barbara, and he would bring to bear upon these little questions of here and today the full force of Jesuit learning in the longest continuous intellectual tradition of the West. "Ah, yes, there's Roger," he said one day, as Williams was mentioned again, as a sample of a certain kind of American support for religious liberty. In one of the articles he published in the years of those meetings (1957–61), put together in his book *We Hold These Truths*, Murray dealt with, as he called him once in the article, "Master Roger." The New World's intellectual terrain is flat enough, especially with respect to religion, so that the encounter of these two across three centuries had in it something of the drama of a conversation between giants, although it was not altogether clear that Father Murray regarded Williams as a giant.

Murray insisted that the First Amendment's clauses incorporated no "theology," but represented only "Articles of Peace." "They are not true dogma but only good law"—good, that is, because they serve the common good under conditions of fundamental disagreement: a way to get along. "These clauses were the twin children of social necessity, the necessity of creating a social environment, protected by law, in which men of differing religious faiths might live together in peace." Strictly articles of peace. Father Murray gave a full list of those practical necessities—the ones listed above, about the "unchurched," the rising commercial interest, the sheer multiplicity of denominations—as the complete explanation of the First Amendment, of religious liberty and separation of church and state, in the way that used to be done by people he would call "secularists," of the thoroughgoing variety. The reason for insisting upon the entire sufficiency of those more or less "material" causes was to dismiss the possibility of any ideological, substantive, "theological" content in, or cause of, the American arrangement on these matters: on the part of others—reductionistic "secularists"—because they would not want to grant that *any* "ideas" (particularly religious ideas, particularly principled ideas) had effects in history; on Father Murray's part, on the other hand, because the ideas in this case, if granted any room, would be wrong ones. (Civic argument makes strange bedfellows.) So here "Master Roger" came in.

> Theologians of the First Amendment [Father Murray used this terminology for any substantive interpreter], whether Protestant or secularist, are accustomed to appeal to history. They stress the importance of ideological factors in the genesis of the American concept of freedom of religion and separation of church and state. However, these essays in theological history are never convincing. In the end it is always Roger Williams to whom appeal is made.

Then Murray dismissed Williams on the basis of Perry Miller's book, which had been published not long before: Williams not only was "no child of Enlightenment" but also (Murray cites the quotation from Miller given above) had no "genetic" influence on the First Amendment. In addition, just to squeeze out the last drop of any possibility of a Williams-related intellectual substance in this "American proposition" (the First Amendment) Murray holds that Williams himself was a powerful spokesman for exactly the position he (Murray) is defending (which he said is both the Catholic position and "the only view that a citizen with both historical sense and common sense can take"): Religious liberty and separation of church and state are articles (simply and only) of *peace*, under conditions of *social necessity*. He proceeded to quote a number of favorable statements by Williams about "Sweet Peace," which, "stands at the center of his [Williams's] doctrine." (Here, Truth must query Peace: At the *center*?)

"Roger Williams was no partisan of the view that all religions ought to be equally free because, for all anybody knows, they may all be equally true or false. He reckons with truth and falsity in honest fashion." (Here Truth concedes to Peace: That is certainly sound.) Murray wrote, further, that Williams was "a seventeenth-century Calvinist who somehow had got hold of certain remarkably un-Calvinist ideas on the nature of the political order in its distinction from the church." (Here Truth is pleased to find Peace, with his magisterial authority, making such an interesting and perhaps congenial formulation.)

In this encounter—really rather "piquant," to use a word Father Murray will employ below—between the superior twentieth-century American Catholic mind and the unusual seventeenth-century proto-

American Protestant mind, Murray then, having already linked Williams to Pope Pius XII through their mutual use of the parable of the tares, elaborates the following rather distinctively Catholic connection:

> Roger Williams had many a quarrel with the Roman papacy; in fact, he wanted it abolished utterly. It is therefore piquant in itself, and also a testimony to the strength of the hold that the central Christian tradition had upon him, to read this basic principle of Catholic teaching in the *Bloudy Tenent*: "It must be remembered that it is one thing to command, to conceal, to approve evil; and another thing to permit and suffer evil with protestation against it or dislike of it, at least without approbation of it. This sufferance or permission of evil is not for its own sake but for the sake of the good, which puts a respect of goodness upon such permission."

Father Murray goes on: "In substance Pius XII says the same thing. ...In fact the Pope goes much further when he flatly states that 'in certain circumstances God does not give men any mandate...'" (Here Truth, guessing what is coming, must interrupt: For Williams, would it not be rather, "in *no* circumstances does God give men any mandate"?) "...does not impose any duty, and does not even communicate the right to impede or to repress what is erroneous and false."

Father Murray, so very critical of finding any "theology" in the American proposition, then on his own part made the following observation: "The First Amendment is simply the legal enunciation of this papal statement."

(Here Truth, distressed, must say to Peace: But whatever the exact proportion of its sources—how much expediency, how much ideas and principles; how much Enlightenment, how much dissenting Protestant—surely the First Amendment had in it none whatever of that telling papal reservation: "in certain circumstances." It was not a guarantee of freedom from social necessity only—to be removed, perhaps, when necessity changed, when the "certain circumstances" altered—but a genuine and lasting *all*-circumstances principled guarantee. And as to Master Roger: Was there not in him a strong, repeated affirmation of the claim of the freedom of *every* human soul, *not* for peace only but as a condition of faith itself? As a consequence of faith itself? As part of the meaning and application of the Christian faith itself?)

We have thus managed to create a passage that in its complicated argumentativeness and parenthetical screwiness resembles some of the pages of Williams himself.

It remains to be said, with respectful memory, of John Courtney Murray: These encounters, in person with the American religious bouillabaise in Santa Barbara, and on the page with Roger Williams, took place before—just before—Vatican II, at which he was a most influential figure, specifically on the statement on Religious Liberty, opening windows.

The other relevant participant in the Fund for the Republic's dialoguing did not dialogue very much, but listened, smiling, to the rat-tat-tat-tat of theologians and philosophers, and to the references to Roger Williams, commented amiably at the lunch breaks, then resigned when the enterprise skipped to California, and gave lectures, published in 1965, to which Roger Williams lent a title and a point—again, a point he does not, by the reading here, quite represent. This discussant was Mark De Wolfe Howe, the distinguished Harvard constitutional lawyer. His little book was called *The Garden and the Wilderness*, with an epigraph from Williams in which, in addition to the metaphor in those words, there appeared also, presumably for the first time in American history and long before Jefferson, the further metaphor of a wall of separation:

> When they have opened a gap in the hedge or wall of separation between the garden of the church and the wilderness of the world, God hath ever broke down the wall itself, removed the candlestick, and made His garden a wilderness, as at this day.

There are a great many books about "church and state" in the United States, but few as subtle and original as this slim volume of Howe's. He gently chastised the inclination of the modern Supreme Court, when dealing with religion, to make over history and ignore the "evangelical" principle of church-state separation, present there in the actual life of the American past alongside the Jeffersonian or rationalistic principle— which "evangelical" principle has deposited in the nation a cluster of institutions and customs that can be called a de facto establishment. The Court, wrote Howe, gently, by refusing to acknowledge the totality of the American past and the existence of the historical-cultural "establishment" that it created, has had to use "acrobatics of logic" to keep from overturning it altogether.

We will examine these acrobatics and the large matter of the de facto Protestant establishment in Part Four. Our present point about this good book is perhaps a small one: Howe used Roger Williams as a symbol of the "evangelical" foundations of the First Amendment and America's de facto establishment and as the source of his governing metaphor (that garden and wilderness). But Backus, or Lyman Beecher, would have served better... a host of evangelists would.

Was Williams "evangelical"? Yes and no. Would he have fought for the features of a de facto "establishment," as the late eighteenth- and nineteenth-century evangelicals did? It is anachronistic to ask, but one may doubt it. Williams's "wall" separated from the wilderness of the world the garden of the true church of Christ that is (almost) invisible and is not identical with any actually existing institutions—not the churches, and presumably not the laws protecting Sunday either. That garden was separated not just from "the state" but from a wilderness that included most, or all, existing earthly "Christian" institutions.

One other modern reference to Williams, of a very different sort. In the 1970s and 1980s, as is known, there came a resurgence of evangelical and fundamentalist Protestantism, a segment of which became very active politically. There were television shows, political associations, rallies, revivals, magazines, clubs, Christian rock music, paperback books—all a separate domain from the wilderness of mainline culture, although perhaps not necessarily a garden. A large part of the constituency of this movement was, in one branch or another, Baptist—in which denominational territory there was once no post-Biblical name held higher than that of Roger Williams. And so in looking through a boxful of the books of this movement, one is startled to discover starkly negative pictures of Williams. For example, *The Light and the Glory*, by Peter Marshall and David Manuel (a book that asks on its cover: "Did God have a plan for America?" and certainly answers in the affirmative), has a chapter called "The Pruning of the Lord's Vineyard" in which it turns out that the writers, the modern Christian reader, and God's Plan for America are identified completely with John Winthrop and John Cotton and their program in Massachusetts Bay—and one of the aberrant shoots that was producing wild grapes (Isaiah 5:1–2) and therefore had to be pruned is Roger Williams.

> Roger Williams desperately needed to come into reality and see his sin—how arrogant and judgmental and self-righteous he was. If only he had humbled himself, he had the potential to be a great general in Christ's army, who could have led the troops smashing through the very gates of hell.

That metaphor—about the great general and the troops and smashing hell's gates and so on—and the mode of thought it conveys runs throughout the book, and shows how much its authors identify with the sorts of people who did the persecuting against which Williams protested. God is using Williams's troubles in Rhode Island to teach him a lesson: "In Providence, God began to deal with Roger Williams in earnest."

The authors quote with disapproval, as evidence of Williams's self-pity and despair, a memorable passage of Williams's that Perry Miller found particularly moving: "As to myself, in endeavoring after . . . temporal and spiritual peace, I humbly desire to say, if I perish, I perish. It is but a shadow vanished, a bubble broke, a dream finished. Eternity will pay for all."

And what about the key subject, religious liberty? The writers explain that Williams could not share Winthrop's vision of a "covenanted kingdom" because that vision stood in opposition to "the principle that Williams held dearest of all: *liberty of conscience*," a principle to which they are clearly not as firmly committed as was Williams. This is their own disapproving explanation of its meaning to Williams: "Nobody is going to tell me what I should do or believe."

The authors then remark:

> Liberty of conscience is indeed a vital part of Christianity—as long as it is in balance with all the other parts. But taken out of balance and pursued to its extremes (which is where Williams, ever the purist, invariably pursued everything), it becomes a license to disregard all authority with which we do not happen to agree at the time.

Roger Williams's faults in this view were intellectual pride and purism, which led him to refuse cooperation in God's plan to make a Christian America by way of Massachusetts. God was pruning his Massachusetts vineyard, and Rhode Island became a dump for the defective vines that yield the wild grapes of too much liberty of conscience.

Reading further in this chapter, one discovers a truly chilling passage. It seems that Anne Hutchinson, who was also banished to Rhode Island by the Massachusetts authorities, and Mary Dyer, her follower (the Quaker subsequently hanged on Boston Common), both gave birth to deformed children. These authors, who have been commenting unfavorably on Hutchinson's heresies, and describing her troubles with a certain grim relish, quote a gruesome account by Winthrop of the birth of Dyer's deformed child, and testify that Winthrop was "too mature a witness to [be suspected] of distortion or exaggeration . . . if anything, his presentation would be conservative." They then conclude as follows: "And perhaps the Puritans, who somberly regarded it as a sign of Satan's authorship of Mrs. Dyer's and Mrs. Hutchinson's teachings, were not that far wrong."

One should say in fairness that some further perusing of the books in the box discloses nothing else as bad as that, and along with what seems to the reader much nuttiness some worthy and earnest materials. Still, the book here quoted must have its audience. The modern Christians who wrote it both have Yale degrees.

Well, Eternity will pay for all. To return with renewed sympathy to Roger Williams, and what he fought for, let us note in closing the climactic sentences with which the best modern scholars examining Williams have ended their studies. Edmund Morgan puts at the end of his book this comment: "We may praise him . . . for his defense of religious liberty and the separation of church and state. He deserves the tribute . . . but it falls short of the man. His greatness was simpler. He dared to think."

Perry Miller wrote near the end of his book that "out of the exercise of his imagination he [Williams] perceived that no man can be so sure of any formulation of eternal truth as to have a right to impose on the mind and spirit of other men." He added, "Roger Williams was a profound Christian who, like Pascal, refused to identify the Christian vision with worldly appearance, with either any political order or even the words of the Bible itself. He knew that the meaning of life lies not on the surface, but somewhere underneath, and that it must be perpetually sought." And that: "In the end, it may be that he is most valuable to us because he incarnates the fighter for ends who keeps always present to his consciousness a sense of his own fallibility, of his own insignificance, without ever for that reason giving over, without ever relaxing, the effort."

And in a later generation of the Puritans themselves, Cotton Mather, looking back, said—a quotation that appears in all the books about Roger Williams—that "juditious persons" have "judged him to have the root of the matter in him."

PART FOUR

Reflections After
Two Centuries

MODERN TIMES

When in the fullness of time a great commonwealth, much grander than Rhode Island, was brought into being in the New World, it was surely something quite different from anything the millennial perfectionist Roger Williams would have expected God to send. More surprising, that commonwealth soon became something rather different, at least with respect to religion, from the republic Thomas Jefferson and James Madison, who helped to design it, might have expected a rational humankind to carry on. And yet it became so in some part because of the institutions they had helped to design, and the theories for which they had argued.

Between Roger Williams his time in Providence Plantation and Andrew Jackson his time in Washington, D.C.—as Williams would have put it—the "new world" worked out a fresh solution, quite unusual in the history of the human race, to the ancient tangled matter of religion and the state.

The story of the strictly formal and strictly national developments of that solution—that is, of the American constitutional law about church and state and religious liberty—then takes an enormous leap from those first days of the nation to our own time. It jumps from the framing of the Constitution and the First Amendment, and the ending of the last establishments in the states, and lands in the lap of the Supreme Court in the time of World War II. In between there were vast changes, of course, in the religious composition of the nation, as in everything else, and an immense expansion of the role of governments, so that by the middle of the twentieth century the "state" and "church" that were to be separated were both very different from anything Madison and Jefferson, let alone Williams, would have imagined. In the intervening time there had been a sufficient supply of litigation at the *state* level, including for example cases in which puzzled judges in the *civil* courts—in a peculiar new situation, now, with no ecclesiastical courts, and no "committee on religion" in the legislature—had forced upon them decisions about what to do when factions in a church, disagreeing about doctrine, or polity, or the Christian position on human slavery, contended with each other over who possessed the church building (church and state might be separated, but they still occupied the same worldly space, and somebody had to decide who got the property). But in the *federal* law—in the interpretation of the meaning of the majestic U.S. Constitution, as its Supreme power rolled out over the Alleghenies, up through the Northwest Territory, across the wide Missouri, down the Mississippi Valley, around all the Louisiana Purchase down to the Rio Grande, and finally out to the far Pacific—in federal constitutional law in all those years there had not been much more than a lonely Mormon polygamy case or two.

But then in the 1940s, in the very different America of the mid-twentieth century, for technical legal reasons to be explained below, all of that changed. Rather suddenly the two little First Amendment phrases that had been worked out by James Madison and his fellow members of a conference committee of the House and the Senate in 1789 were to be subjected to an enormous outbreak of litigation, and public uproar over litigation, and commentary and argument and dispute, and even some political fireworks.

There will follow eventually below some remarks about this tradition as we find it now in our time, to some degree centering around the Supreme Court. And yet the first thing to say, looking back after two centuries, is that the Supreme Court's recent work, and the controversial religio-political matters of recent times, are a very small part of the meaning or the continuing effects of the original arrangements, the story of which—part of the story of which—we have been telling.

The most significant effects are not to be found among the items talked about in conferences and editorials, fought over in legislatures, and, in particular, placed on the dockets of courts under the heading "church and state." Neither are they to be discovered in those recurrent episodes—a particularly spectacular cluster at the time of this writing—in which a religious affiliation, practice, or belief, or a moral position put forward with particular visibility by a religious community, erupts into civic life, usually to the astonishment and consternation of the political professionals. It is of course of great importance that the public school classroom would come to be ringed with partisan parents and partisan citizens, often angry, contesting issues in one way or another connected with religion. And it is of great importance, too, that there would come into being the remarkable system of parochial schools, unique in the world, that the Roman Catholic Church built as Catholics came in numbers to this country—originally built, in considerable part, in reaction not against the "secular" but against the Protestant coloration of the public schools. Controversy through the centuries would touch a string of other places and practices, some of them important, that Thomas Jefferson and James Madison—not to mention Roger Williams—either would not have recognized, or would not have thought to be a likely location of disputes about the mighty issue of religious freedom: school buses, airport waiting rooms, and motion picture palaces; Sunday mail deliveries, Saturday night saloons, and Wednesday afternoon religion classes; the high school gym classes of Wisconsin, the plural-marriage farmhouses of Utah, discount houses of northern New Jersey and the official state highway maps of North Carolina; the public park, the courthouse lawn, the street corner, and the front porch; the Internal Revenue Service, the unemployment compensation office, the census bureau, the marriage license office, the adoption center, and in particular, at this writing, the abortion clinic. And of course, again and again, the courtroom. (When a list like this—it could be much longer—was cited to a political reporter, he picked out Sunday mail deliveries, and observed: "Well, they certainly won *that* one.")

But even when one takes into account issues larger and less definitely resolved than Sunday mail delivery (not such a small issue, symbolically, in its time), it is still true that all of these later controversies took place within boundaries that were essentially settled. The tradition of religious liberty, in its essentials, is securely embedded in the nation's institutions, despite the uproar. Moreover, these original institutions and principles had a meaning and effect reaching far beyond the rather narrow arena of later church-state controversies. The effects of the original American tradition of religious liberty reach to every issue. Looked at with "scope"—as Samuel Goldwyn used to say—religious liberty is to be seen as a part of the essence of the nation.

Although the United States, in its social life, was certainly not to be free from the mistreatment of people because of their religion—there has been more of that than most Americans realize—and although there was even to be a little persecution by *law* (a heresy trial in Massachusetts as late as 1838), nevertheless the official commitment of the nation rejected the premise from which in other societies such persecution proceeded. That is not unimportant. The most terrible old issues of official state-sponsored religious persecution were really not to be issues any longer here, though from some shrill statements one might think they were.

And religious liberty was more central to the nation's original moral self-definition than is comprehended by a modern generation's routine inclusion of (for example) "freedom to go to the church of your choice" on the list (rather far down on the list) of basic freedoms "enjoyed" by Americans. It had a depth and centrality not comprehended by—for example—the modern journalist for whom the phrase "the First Amendment" simply means an absolute grant to the press. For Madison and Jefferson and the "republicans" on the one hand, and for the enthusiasts, dissenters, and sectarians on the other hand, the First Amendment, and the Bills of Rights in the states, contained something more basic. Liberty of "conscience," meaning freedom of religious belief and conviction and activity, was near the center, or at the center, of the whole revolutionary American project.

It is of some importance to assert the larger dimension of the fundamental accomplishment, despite the loud noises of current battles, because it is of the nature of this topic to obscure it. In these lesser battles of today, the partisans borrow the passions and the principles of the large battles of yesterday, heightening animosities, distracting the public, distorting public discourse. When the local fundamentalist minister gets the notion of putting John 3:16 on the public water fountain at the municipal softball field in order to combat juvenile delinquency, fight communism, and maintain Godly softball—this example, so far as is known, is imaginary—the local Unitarian minister, the local chapter of the American Civil Liberties Union, and the liberal columnist up on the state's metropolitan newspaper attack this plan, citing the First Amendment, the founding fathers, and the principles that have made this country great, and perhaps also referring to the bodies burned in the Spanish Inquisition. The fundamentalist minister and his now much-augmented support counterattack, and in their turn refer also to the founding fathers and to their firm belief in God, and also to the principles that have made this country great—its institutions presupposing a Supreme Being—and mention angrily the dangerous inroads of secular humanism. The mayor, after having it explained to him that it would not do to have a Menorah on the other side of the water fountain, maintains total silence. Some judges, with a slight headache, then puzzle it out: Are *taxes* used to pay for the fountain? Does any *state employee* turn on the water?

To be sure, there are issues in the church-state field of greater moment than the facetious exercise indulged in above. But it does suggest the inflation that affects them all. The field is afflicted with a premature or anachronistic invocation of principle and of historical analogy, a too quick leap to absolutes, and an overinvestment in inadequate symbols. Many of today's conflicts are, of course, by-products exactly of that "pluralism" that the American tradition itself has brought. But the instant absolutism surely is not necessary.

It appears, too, that the role of the Constitution and of the particular interpretations of the Supreme Court in this field have heightened the absolutism. Controversies, however minor in substance, that involve religious belief are notorious for heightening emotion and for pushing disputants toward intransigence. And in the modern United States something of the tendency toward fanaticism that is rightly discovered in the religious temper is matched by what we might call constitutional moralism. Often where tact and wisdom are called for, there is an instant resort instead to law and principle and passion, and probably epithet, too. And of course the founding fathers.

Whatever else they did and believed, one thing those fathers did do was to establish the framework of principle that can properly be called religious liberty, and the framework of independence of religious and civic institutions each from the other, a framework now formed not only in constitutional law but also, despite polls and headlines, in the mind of the now rather complicated public—that is, in the ethos. Furthermore, it is reinforced by the groundwork of a reciprocally balancing diversity—a diversity that the tradition itself helped to create and that gives the principled framework, at its outer margins, a realistic foundation in the actual bodies of commitment and opinion in the population.

One can say, then, looking back across two hundred years, that in the rough way that history, or human society, works, with respect to religious liberty in the narrow sense, James Madison was right.

He appears to have been roughly right, that is, if we put together the emphases of the different stages of his career. The United States has the written constitutional protections—Bills of Rights in particular—that are certainly not now to be dismissed as mere "parchment barriers." It has also an ethos developed by the many persuasive and celebratory appeals to the moral underpinnings of the nation and by all the appeals by evangelical Protestants for religious liberty too. But in addition to these securities and accomplishments in law and in the ethos there came to be the realistic reinforcement of an actual multiplicity of faiths and convictions, cultures and publics, limiting each other—that fundamental protection at least against the worst extremes by the mutual balancing and reciprocal rivalry of what Madison called "sects." In our time it has come to be a much wider and more complicated spread of diverse bodies of opinion than Madison knew.

Some may have a certain reluctance to admit the force of this "pluralist" or balance-of-power point as it applies in general to religion, or to one's own community of belief, or to ideas. But though from inside a community of belief may appear to be virtue, from outside it more often appears to be power. And although neither Madison nor Jefferson sufficiently appreciated that virtue-supplying possibility, or the complexities—their view of the multitudinous "sects" was essentially external and a tad patronizing, and did not plumb the potential civic significance of religious belief, let alone the still larger significance of such belief—Madison did nevertheless nail the "outside" view into the intellectual history of the West. That is, he saw the religious groups as power units, and saw liberty preserved by having multiplicity, rivalry, reciprocating balance, among them. Whatever "more" they may be, beyond power units and interest groups, and however much saying so goes against the grain of the religious groups' understanding of themselves as bearers of transcendent and universal truths and teachers of virtue, they are also power units and self-aggrandizing collectivities. Therefore it is best, for the preservation of liberty and other reasons, to have a certain healthy balance among them. (Perhaps it should be added here that most, at least, of the perils to be discovered in religious groups appear also among nonbelievers, when they have cultural domination.)

Madison's theory has shown its rough truth, and given to the ideal of equal liberty a rough bulwark in reality. The diverse bodies of belief—different religions, and believers and nonbelievers—provide a realistic underpinning to liberty by counteracting by sheer presence one another's power and insularity.

This was not so true, however, in the early days of the Republic. "Religious Liberty" in that mostly Protestant America had the limitation, perhaps the distortion, that such a general social ideal will have when interpreted by one dominant group, and especially when the group finds the ideal coinciding neatly with its own nature. A large part of the American denominational Protestantism of the nineteenth century evidently saw no contradiction to the religious freedom, the Voluntary Way in religion, the separation of church and state that it overwhelmingly and explicitly and even proudly endorsed—regarding itself as a chief bearer and embodiment of that ideal—in the legal requirement that the Sabbath be observed by everybody on Sunday, that all children in the public schools be required to hear Protestant versions of the Lord's Prayer and be read to out of the King James Bible, and much more.

Although the Protestant denominations often developed fierce rivalries in limited ways—the Methodists against the Baptists on the frontier, for example—the more important fact about these mainline Protestant groups was not their disagreement and reciprocal balancing but their agreement and shared cultural penetration. They did not fulfill very well the Madisonian desideratum of securing liberty by a realistic balance of diverse religious groups, because although there certainly came to be plenty of them and although they certainly were in some ways diverse and rivals and *censor mora* to each other, on the larger issues of the culture they formed powerful pan-Protestant alliances.

In their cultural penetration they did perpetrate infringements of religious liberty. But the moral universals of equality and liberty carried the potential for rescue and extension within themselves: By opening the gates of religious liberty, Puritan-Protestant America inadvertently gave itself a vast enrichment program. Into the (Protestant) Christian America there came, by immigration, other kinds of Protestants who were not from the British Isles and were not part of John Calvin's troops. There came, perhaps most important of all, in very large numbers, members of that Church of Rome against which Protestants had protested and against the remaining traces of which the Puritans had sought to purify the Church of England. There came to be in time a sufficiently large presence of Judaism, the mother religion of Christianity, against which across the ages of its domination, before the founding of this liberal "Christian" country, Christianity had repeatedly shown its un-Christian illiberality. And there developed a congenial atmosphere for a distinctive form of nonreligion: not dogmatic atheism or aggressive "free thought" on the European model but soft indifference—practical preoccupations, amiable inclusiveness, the social idealism of "democracy."

This unfolding diversity played its part, along with law and principle, in securing at least the minimum requirements of religious liberty. But it accentuated the other, larger matter that had always accompanied the dispute about religious liberty: how to form a culture. In the newly built republican governments of the New World the matter of providing the moral underpinnings of a social order took on a new shape, perhaps a new urgency. Who is responsible for shaping "Virtue" in the citizenry? How is it done? With what institutions? Supporting what ultimate convictions? History keeps moving. The solving of one problem gives rise to conditions in which there are new ones. Let us oversimplify: The problem of religious liberty was solved; the problem of the forming of a culture was intensified by the historical working out of our solution to the problem of liberty.

The formal definitions of religious liberty, as philosophers refine it, is one subject, and an important one; alongside it is the informal historical reality within which such definitions arise. The "juridical" arrangements between church and state are one subject, as constitutional lawyers discuss them, and an important one; surrounding it there are the real churches and the real state in whose particular history those juridical definitions work themselves out. The domain of churches, sects, religious groups, as theologians and churchmen and prophets and specialists in religion deal with them, is one realm, and it is, or was, important, too; surrounding it, penetrating it and being penetrated by it, there is the culture. In sum, the American achievements of religious liberty and the separation of church and state did not take place in a vacuum, but in a particular time and place, with specific historical and cultural antecedents and with specific historical and cultural results.

THE SELECTIVE APPROPRIATION
OF THE FOUNDING FATHERS

As the United States settled into the grooves of nationhood, it took a somewhat different shape, religiously speaking, from what the founding deists (we may suppose) would have expected. Presumably it was somewhat different from what in their secret heart they wanted, too. Religion certainly did not fade away under the continual unfolding of scientific evidence, and it did not become either as peripheral or as rational as Thomas Jefferson and James Madison might have preferred—as peripheral, that is, to public life. On the one hand, that severe separation of church and state for which they fought in Virginia achieved a complete victory, not only in the nation's institutions but also in the nation's mind. On the other hand, as part of that achievement, the religion of "enthusiasm" flourished, and soaked the nation's culture in its characteristic themes.

That nineteenth-century saturation then produced rather a different moral foundation—rather a different kind of nurturing for the citizens of the new republic—than, again we may presume, Jefferson and Madison and most of their colleagues had pictured. It was not the rationalism of the Enlightenment—of those French books Jefferson sent across the Atlantic to Madison—that carried the day, important though it was. Neither was it the classical exposition of "civic virtue." Out among the common people the evangelist's Bible was even more important. And partly as a result of the ideas and institutions that Jefferson and Madison and their colleagues had set in motion, the common people came to count for more than they had in colonial Virginia, or colonial Massachusetts, or much of anywhere else in centuries past.

In the eighteenth century, as we have seen in Virginia, the "enthusiasts" from the dissenting sects had joined with the rationalists like Jefferson and Madison in the alliance for a common political objective—religious liberty and separation of church and state—against the common opponent, the traditional orthodoxy of the established churches. Once that objective was accomplished, as often happens, the erstwhile allies fell apart.

These developments are pithily described in *The Lively Experiment*, published in 1963, by the University of Chicago historian Sidney Mead. Mead wrote that "pietism" and rationalism had had a common seventeenth-century beginning. They were "in origin but obverse sides of a single movement which gathered momentum during the eighteenth century to sweep in religious freedom and separation of church and state over the opposition of traditional orthodoxy in the churches." But after this momentous achievement, pietism discovered its latent incompatibility with rationalism and rejoined traditional orthodoxy. (Both parties, of course, had changed—and changed each other.) American denominational Protestantism is the outcome of this reunion, under the conditions of religious freedom achieved during the earlier alliance.

Pietism parted from rationalism, and joined or rejoined traditional orthodoxy, Mead makes clear, when the issue of religious liberty, and church and state, subsided and the religious-theological issue came to the fore. The primary early stimulus for that realignment was the French Revolution, and the opposition to the Christian religion of which it was perceived to be the international agent. A fear of spreading sympathy with French "infidelity" had been a motive already among the proponents of the General Assessment in Virginia, including Patrick Henry, in 1784–85, and came to be a major theme in the 1790s and the early part of the nineteenth century, especially potent, of course, as an object lesson in the horrors of infidelity after the Terror and the advent of Napoleon.

The situation of the major Founders became a bit of an anomaly, did it not? Here was a nation that, when it got itself formed, was shot through with evangelical Christianity—that is, a particularly energetic expression of "revealed" religion—which nevertheless came to celebrate a remarkable original group of founding heroes, all of whom stood outside that religious persuasion. Or, to put it the other way around, there came into being a new nation whose chief builders were representatives of the Age of Reason, which nation, once launched, sailed off promptly into what some of them might privately have seen as a particularly murky section of the swamp of unreason.

This is to exaggerate somewhat, to be sure. Still, the most important of these Founders intellectually speaking, Thomas Jefferson, who shaped the phrases and formed the ideas that gave the nation its soul, looked upon the old religions of mysteries, creeds, and emotion-charged symbols, the "shackles" on the human mind of "revealed" religion, as an impediment—perhaps the most important impediment—to the truths on which rested his new nation with all its hope for the world. The most important Founder institutionally speaking, James Madison, who did the most to give the nation its constitutional form and justifications for it in political philosophy, was perhaps in his quieter way as much a man of the Enlightenment as his great Virginia friend. As we have seen, religious liberty, with a certain cool distance from all those "sects," stood at the foundation of his political life. The most important Founder, symbolically and culturally speaking, the elder statesman who became the very epitome of the American ethos, Benjamin Franklin, wrote, early in that most American of books, his *Autobiography*: "I soon became a thorough Deist." The most important Founder, practically speaking, the Father of his Country, without whom none of it could have happened, George Washington, was, underneath his circumspection and intellectually unadventurous prudence, really a deist, too, despite the pious picture that later generations would paint of him at Valley Forge and elsewhere. (Washington, though a conventional Anglican by observance, is described as a deist by his biographer James Flexner.) The most important pamphleteer, if we may add this lesser figure to the list, who in 1776 provided the essential ringing phrases that reached the broad populace and gave the cause of independence its fire, Thomas Paine, not only was a deist but was polemical and aggressive about it, in a way that his aristocratic deist colleagues did not think particularly wise. Even so sober and conservative a Founder as John Adams, a son of Massachusetts Puritanism in many other ways, and a strong proponent, for the civic good, of "religion," turned out, in the correspondence of their old age, to hold doctrinal views not much different from Jefferson's. His Quincy church became Unitarian. About one of the expressions of that startling rise of evangelical Protestantism in the new nation, a missionary appeal in 1816, Adams asked: "Would it not be better, to apply these pious subscriptions, to purify Christendom from the corruptions of Christianity, rather than to propagate these corruptions in Europe, Asia, Africa, and America!" And yet before long these men were all, or almost all, heroes; certainly they were heroes as a group. These founding deists and rationalists came to be honored, indeed, but their skepticism and rationalism in religious matters were not—were, in fact, obscured.

To be sure, in the most important case, that of Thomas Jefferson, the elevation to unequivocal Foundership took some time, and his views on religion (real or alleged) were an important impediment to his elevation. His expectation that the new nation—his new nation— would soon become Unitarian was not to be fulfilled. It was yet another way in which "reason" did not quite gain its triumph, in a not quite so reasonable world. In the non-Unitarian country, he was to be attacked, and attacked fiercely, by Federalist opponents and orthodox clergymen, for his "infidelity" and sympathy with the antireligious ideas of the French Revolution. The story of Jefferson's actual or alleged religious views as an important thread in the vicissitudes of his reputation throughout American history is told in Merrill Peterson's *The Jefferson Image in the American Mind.* Jefferson was, at various stages in American history, called not only an "infidel"—that was the prevailing word in the early nineteenth century—but also "anti-Christian," a "Virginia Voltaire," and much else along the same line. But then the years went by, and at last he would come to rest on Mount Rushmore and the Tidal Basin, on the shortest short list of finalists among American heroes, heroes to conservative American Christians as well as to everyone else. (His memorial was dedicated in 1943.) But in order for him to achieve that eminence, his views on religion would be at the least muted. One might say that eventually popular American attitudes did to Thomas Jefferson something like what Jefferson did to Jesus: they granted him very high honor indeed, but at the same time were highly selective in what was to be taken from his teaching, and in what he was to be interpreted as having stood for. And if there is so much muting for Jefferson, the erstwhile "infidel," there certainly is plenty of it for the others and for the founding fathers as a group.

With the permeation of much of the popular culture of the new nation by evangelical Protestantism, especially in the second quarter of the nineteenth century, there began an appropriation of the nation's Founders to the purposes of more or less orthodox Christianity—at least of the mainline of the Christian religion as it came to be understood in the United States—that has continued until the present day. The conservative popular religious culture of the new nation, once it had developed, wanted to believe both in the Biblical revelation on the one hand, and in the founding geniuses and heroes, who rejected it, on the other, and so gradually the edges of the original opposition between these two beliefs were softened, and then softened some more, until finally they were all folded into one great package of "American" religion, the God of the Bible and the Founders of America now joined together by the believers in both.

This was not unduly difficult. The deism of the eighteenth-century Enlightenment, even in Europe, was something of a middle way between traditional theism and "atheism" or thoroughgoing skepticism. That is the way Carl Becker presented it in his graceful little book of a generation ago, *The Heavenly City of the Eighteenth Century Philosophers*:

> In spite of their nationalism and their humane sympathies, in spite of their aversion to hocus-pocus and enthusiasm and dim perspectives, in spite of their eager skepticism, their engaging cynicism, their brave youthful blasphemies and talk of hanging the last king in the entrails of the last priest—in spite of all of it, there is more of Christian philosophy in the writings of the *Philosophes* than has yet been dreamt of in our histories.

And there was more of it still in the American representatives of the Enlightenment. They did not even talk about hanging the last king in the entrails of the last priest. Their pious countrymen of later generations could find in them what they wanted, including many references to Providence, the Creator, and the Supreme Being, all material for later quotation. And they insisted on the importance of morality, as would also the evangelical Protestants of the next generation—as would Americans of almost every generation.

One may take as an exemplar of this convenient ambiguity of the American Founders' deism not Jefferson, with his sharp skeptical edges, or Madison with his silence, or John Adams, with his substitution of a more general "religion" for Puritan orthodoxy, or Washington with his practical man's avoidance of troublesome intellectual issues, but the genial all-American figure Benjamin Franklin. It is true that he did not subscribe to the specific doctrines of orthodox Christianity: "I had been religiously educated as a Presbyterian, and...some of the dogmas of that persuasion such as the eternal decrees of God, election, reprobation, etc. appeared to me unintelligible, others doubtful, and I early absented myself from the public assemblies of the sect, Sunday being my studying day...." It is true that he did not believe more central doctrines: "Revelation had indeed no weight with me as such." It is pretty clear that he did not believe the most fundamental of Christian doctrines, looked at in an orthodox way. Asked in old age about the "divinity of Christ" he answered, in a letter that is often quoted, "I have...some Doubts about his Divinity." It is true, as he explains in his *Autobiography*, that he could not stomach it when he tried going to the one Presbyterian church then in Philadelphia ("once for five Sundays successively," as he plaintively explains) only to find "polemic arguments" and "explications of the peculiar doctrines of our sect" with "not a single moral principle inculcated." He wrote that the aim of those sermons seemed to be "rather to make us good Presbyterians than good citizens." And he "went no more."

But, though he went no more, and he rejected central doctrines, he separated himself from orthodox Christianity in a way that later generations of American Christians could scarcely notice, and rarely object to...indeed, would often match. His manner was irenic, amiable, humorous...in a way that Jefferson's was not. (There is not much humor in the other founding fathers, by the way, not counting of course the later figure Abraham Lincoln.) This last quotation, for example, from the letter answering the question about the divinity of Christ (which Franklin wrote just a month before he died) goes on to say: "...it is a question I do not dogmatize upon, having never studied it, and think it needless to busy myself with it now, when I expect soon an Opportunity of knowing the Truth with less Trouble." An orthodox Christian who objected to so deft and genial a side step as that would have his hands full persuading any American audience to grow indignant at the insufficient orthodoxy of so amiable a man.

Moreover, Franklin, like the others, affirmed much that American Protestants would affirm, after a time, with more practical fervor than the formulations of the creeds. Franklin goes on to explain—in the passages in his *Autobiography* about religious upbringing and beliefs and nonbeliefs, and about his futile efforts to get the blood of moral instruction from the turnip of Philadelphia Presbyterian preaching—that despite it all he "never was without some religious principles." He goes on to tell which ones, and his list would serve for most of the other Enlightenment pillars of America's founding: "I never doubted, for instance, the existence of the Deity, that he made the world and governed it by his providence, that the most acceptable service of God was the doing good to man, that our souls are immortal, and that all crime will be punished and virtue rewarded either here or hereafter." He adds—and this would certainly be the view of all of the deists—"these I esteemed the essentials of every religion." He goes on to say that these essentials "being to be found in all the religions we had in our country, I respected them all, though with different degrees of respect as I found them more or less mixed with other articles which without any tendency to inspire, promote, or confirm morality, served principally to divide us and make us unfriendly to one another."

If one reads through that set of Franklin's beliefs, one will find everything that the "pluralist" America, the "religious" people, the "civil religion," would later affirm—and also deny (gently deny). Belief in God, in the first place, but very often put, as the deists do, in those other terms, softening God's apodictic particularity: The Supreme Being, Providence, the Almighty—these terms abound in George Washington and Benjamin Franklin and also in Jefferson and even Madison, especially in an official or public context. For all of them, as we have said, morality was the real test and point and meaning. For John Adams, a generalized "religion" was its necessary source. For Jefferson, morality could as well replace religion. For none of them did creeds matter very much. Sharply pointed doctrines not only were unnecessary but were an impediment to this morality.

Not right away, and not everywhere, but in the long term and in general the flow of the pietistically flavored multifaith practical American Christianity would be toward exactly those points, and Benjamin Franklin would be, not an opponent, not a man affirmed on other grounds in *spite* of his views on religion, but the representative American figure, on those subjects as others, and for American Christians as for others. There would come a day when, out in the American West, there would be Presbyterians much, much closer to Benjamin Franklin than to that Philadelphia Presbyterian preacher—not to mention John Calvin.

There is one other central point: that however creedally vague Americans may become about "Providence," they do know that He, She, or It cares particularly about America. We have already described the event at the Constitutional Convention in Philadelphia, when Franklin, noting the absence of opening prayers, connected the activity of a governing Providence specifically with the American undertaking. The whole scene, from the point of view of a subsequent American piety, is perfect: the eighty-one-year-old patriarch; the reminder of how that Great Friend had answered prayers in the dark days of the Revolution; the perfect sentence for quotation forever after: "I have lived, Sir, a long time, and the longer I live, the more convincing proofs I see of this truth—that God governs in the affairs of men." What American could object just because such a man has difficulties with the doctrine of the Trinity?

Franklin's ideas on "morality" are perfect, too, poised to make the transition to another era and a more individualistic meaning. In his *Autobiography*—that worldwide American best seller—Benjamin Franklin goes on from the paragraphs about his religious outlook to describe a rather ambitious effort: "I conceived the bold and arduous project of arriving at moral perfection." Hundreds upon hundreds of thousands of Americans must have read those pages with a straight face. Franklin lists, originally, twelve virtues he is going to acquire, and since it is too much to attain them all at once he proposes to take them one at a time, seriatim. He made a chart for each week with the days of the week across the top and a symbol for each virtue down the side (T for Temperance, S for Silence, O for Order and so on through R, F, I, all the way to H). In the first week "my great guard was to avoid even the least offense against temperance, leaving the other virtues to their ordinary chance, only marking every evening the faults of the day." He put checkmarks in columns for each violation of each virtue—a sample page of his chart is reproduced in the *Autobiography*. Perhaps that is enough about Ben Franklin's scheme to attain moral perfection. One can imagine some ancestor of it—different of course and not as amusing, shot through with theological and Biblical worries that Franklin has thrown overboard—in one of the introspective self-examining, self-improving manuals of devotion or journals of the Puritans. And after a time one can certainly find the progeny of Franklin's amusingly mechanical program for self-improvement— point one, point two, point three—on every bookshelf, in every magazine, in every domain of American life. And the spirit of it, the application of such "practical" checklists and "techniques" to *moral* self-improvement, as to other aspects of life, would be completely compatible with the mainstream of American Protestant Christianity as it would later develop.

Franklin's scheme, with its cheerful analytic moral mechanism, stands at a far remove from the profound struggles of Saint Paul, and many others in the Christian tradition, with the dark problems of the will— For the good that I would I do not: but evil which I would not, that I do—or from Martin Luther's discovery, hard as he tried, that he could not confess all of his "sins," and must hope for salvation by grace alone, or from the explication by many Christian writers of the subtle pervasiveness of pride. Franklin stands a long way from any of that, but, then, so will the American Protestantism that comes after him.

At the end of his discussion of his scheme for moral perfection, Franklin makes some remarks on the subject of pride. They are in a curious way an echo of a sentence of Pascal, and of others. But in what a different tone! Franklin's is honest, amiable, really unconcerned: "For even if I could conceive that I had completely overcome it [pride], I should probably be proud of my humility."

In Franklin one can feel the purview of "morality" changing. Although he certainly was a "patriot," and rendered many and indispensable services to the new nation, at home and in London and Paris, there were among his many personae two or three that were more congenial to the coming culture than the unequivocal civic vocation of, say, Madison. Americans have known whom God helps (them that help themselves) and what early to bed and early to rise will make a man, and what happened for want of a nail, better perhaps than they have known precepts or reflections from any other of the Founders. The "moral" precepts Poor Richard teaches are ways to do good, but also to make good. Franklin himself had been the poor boy coming into Philadelphia who made good. And he explained how other poor boys could make good, too. And kept on explaining it. Poor Richard became a teacher of a kind of practical personal advancement, while the civic virtue of the Founders faded from the nation's consciousness. When Max Weber would write his influential treatment of *The Protestant Ethic and the Spirit of Capitalism*, his illustration would be drawn from the United States, from Benjamin Franklin, and the spirit and explicit teaching of Poor Richard and the *Autobiography*: Time is money. Franklin was happy to instruct a broad readership of Almanacs about practical morality—very practical indeed, the "way to wealth." For his religious views, on the other hand, he did not seek proselytes.

There were Americans who in the great stirrings of the Revolution at home and the Enlightenment abroad sought aggressively to promulgate, perhaps even to institutionalize, a "republican religion": Ethan Allen, the hero of Ticonderoga; Joel Barlow, the "Connecticut Wit"; Elihu Palmer, organizer of a deistical society, publisher of a journal called *The Temple of Reason*; and, most important, Tom Paine. But in the long view these efforts came to little, except perhaps to add stimulus to Timothy Dwight and the other leaders of the Second Awakening, who attacked the threat of "Infidelity" that this rational religion was taken to represent. The major political leaders who were part of the Enlightenment in America, whose views did have a considerable resemblance to those of the aggressive deists—Ben Franklin, Thomas Jefferson, even John Adams, who had given over a ministerial vocation after hearing a rationalist speaker—did not seek to disenchant the public, and disapproved of attempts to do so.

Thomas Paine was to violate their implicit rule by carrying the argument against "revealed religion" aggressively and polemically out into the public forum, frightening the conventionally religious in a way his more responsibly placed fellow deists did not think wise. Paine's *Age of Reason* took the issue against the orthodox Christians with the same bold ringing insistent and unsubtle clarity that he had argued for independence in *Common Sense*. Against the trinitarians he said, "I believe in one God *and no more*"; about the resurrection of the body, he remarked, I'd like a better one; about revelation, he said it may be binding on the one revealed to, but to anybody else it is hearsay, and comes to be "mental lying," much of which goes on among priests. The *true* revelation—the *universal* revelation—is "the Creation we behold!" Of Saint Paul he said: a manufacturer of quibbles. Of the Bible he wrote: It has many morally cruel stories in it, and I detest it, as I detest anything cruel. The three frauds of the Churches, he said, are mystery, miracle, prophecy. Of that then standard epithet of the orthodox, "Infidelity," Paine wrote, "Infidelity does not consist in believing or disbelieving; it consists in professing to believe what one does not believe." Of Jesus's resurrection he said, "Thomas did not believe it, so neither will I."

There was perhaps not much in this that differed from what Jefferson and Franklin believed, and disbelieved; they, too, were products of the Age of Reason and believers in what Paine called the "chastity of the mind." But they did not think it wise or strategic, and perhaps also in some sense did not think it right—not a service to the public good— to join the issue with the orthodox believers in this explicit, resolute, aggressive way. Jefferson had the most severely restrictive ideas about how "private" opinions about religion should be. And although Franklin did not keep his ideas altogether private, he did not approve of Paine's undertaking. Sidney Mead quotes a revealing letter that is thought to be from Franklin to Tom Paine:

> [T]hink how great a portion of mankind consists of weak men and women, and of inexperienced, inconsiderate youth of both sexes, who have need of the motives of religion to restrain them from vice, to support their virtue, and retain them in the practice of it till it becomes *habitual*, which is the great point for its security.

Something of that point, muted, may be discerned in that famous product of the Founders, the composition in part of Alexander Hamilton, a document written with an eye toward public effect in the nation then taking form, the "Farewell Address," as it has come to be called, of the most respected of all the Founders, the first president. George Washington, if he may be called a deist in belief, was, it seems, rather a conventional Virginia Anglican, observant to a point in practice, but not at all doctrinaire, and not any sort of enthusiast. In his presidential role he strove to be—in his own words—"a faithful and impartial patron of genuine, vital religion." The word "impartial" is important. Washington, enjoining the citizens of the new nation to a spirit of concord and unity, remarked in a passage about national unity that "with slight shades of difference, you have the same religion." That impulse to assert some unity, some sameness of religion—in contrast to Madison's emphasis on the multitude of sects—keeps on appearing, for all the nation's religious diversity, throughout its history.

Later in the Farewell Address, Washington included a passage, very often quoted, that reverberates through all the public gestures toward religion in the country of which he was to be called the "Father":

> Of all the dispositions and habits which lead to political prosperity, religion and morality are indispensable supports. In vain would that man claim the tribute of patriotism who should labor to subvert these great pillars of human happiness—these firmest props of the duties of men and citizens....

It certainly was an unabashedly instrumental view of religion's role. Next he made the application of the point that John Locke had made, and Timothy Dwight would make, in their differing contexts, and thousands of others as well: "... where is the security for property, for reputation, for life, if the sense of religious obligation *desert* the oaths which are the instruments of investigation in the courts of justice?"

Then comes the familiar insistence that "morality," at least in the large, requires religion:

> And let us with caution indulge the supposition that morality can be maintained without religion. What ever may be conceded to the influence of refined education on minds of peculiar structure, reason and experience both forbid us to expect that national morality can prevail in exclusion of religious principle.

Note that the effect of "refined education" on a few minds "of peculiar structure" (Thomas Jefferson? Tom Paine?) is conceded. But for large public purposes, for the nation en masse, that point can be set aside. The "political prosperity" and fabric of obligation of the nation require "morality" as its foundation; and that morality, in the large, unrefined, unpeculiarly minded public, requires, as its support, religion. That is a theme that, unlike the civic dimension of virtue and the public aspect of liberty, never goes away.

Patrick Henry, arguing for the General Assessment in 1785, and Timothy Dwight, the president of Yale and "Connecticut pope," defending his state's establishment in the early nineteenth century, would add to those two points yet a third: that religion, the support of the morality on which the republic depends, therefore deserves and requires public (tax) support. The battles at the time focused upon that last point: on state support, taxes, establishment. To a considerable extent that same issue has been the focus of attention in retrospect, as Americans in the very different world of the twentieth century invoke history when they carry on their battles over church and state. The other points, which are cultural or philosophical, not legal, become a part of the ethos, and not only are conceded but are underlined, perhaps exaggerated, in a kind of rhetorical compensation in the course of the struggles over disestablishment.

The pietists, the enthusiasts, the dissenters, who vigorously rejected establishments and tax support for religion, who opposed Henry in Virginia and Dwight in Connecticut, made sure that they would not be outdone in claims on behalf of the importance of religion as the support of morality, and morality as the support of republican government. One may presume, to be sure, that they *believed* those points; their successors in nineteenth-century America, after all the disestablishment battles were won, certainly did (a certain kind of religion supporting—almost becoming identical with—a certain kind of moral-ity). But at the same time the rhetorical situation for opponents of religious establishments and state aid to religion has consistently re-quired that they make very clear that they are *not* opposed to religion as such, and not opposed to "morality." The enthusiasts in the eight-eenth century insisted that they were as committed as their opponents from the once established churches—soon to be religious allies—to the nation's need for religion in order to support morality, and to the importance of morality to the social order. (The pietists in Virginia were quite sure they were *more* committed both to "religion" and to "morality" than the Anglicans, whom they saw to be lax.) The enthu-siasts were not only willing but insistent that state power be used to enforce certain moral tenets, and certain props to religion like the protection of the Sabbath.

And their rationalist allies in the eighteenth-century fight would in general agree, either with solid private convictions (as apparently John Adams) or simply strategically, not to join in the Enlightenment's cen-tral worldwide project to show that religion was not indispensable to morality. And in their turn, perhaps partly also in rhetorical compen-sation, they were as vigorous in defense of "morality" as their opponents.

All of this surely encouraged, and helped to define, the powerful moralism that was to become one of the most familiar of all the char-acteristic attitudes of the new American nation. That moralism could with a certain plausibility adduce the Founders—as in the quotation above from Washington. But as other cultural forces rolled to a cultural victory, the meaning of that "morality" was to shrink and change. It was to be "public" virtue no longer, but a pious and moralistic privatism that would be quite compatible with the competitive individualism that would take public virtue's place. The other Founders would have their monuments and their memorials. Poor Richard would live on.

"A CHRISTIAN AMERICA":

THE PROTESTANTS FORM A CULTURE

A great flood of religious history thus flowed over and around the American Founders, leaving much of their attachment to the Enlightenment on the river bottom. Neither Jefferson nor Madison nor the other Founders expressed the whole mind of the developing American nation, important though they were in the making of a part of it. There were other influential themes, overlapping but different, among their allies in the struggle for separation of church and state—the sectarians, the Baptists, the pietists, the revivalists—who eventually rejoined or merged with the momentarily defeated High Puritan and old churchly parties. That new or renewed combination, with the "enthusiasts" setting the tone, and the disestablishment furnishing the opportunity, shaped the new nation.

Protestantism, in the American colonies, in the United States, was in an unusual position. H. Richard Niebuhr described America as the land of "constructive Protestantism." Here, almost uniquely, the Protestant movement was not in protest against an immediately present Catholicism, in a culture that the Catholic past had shaped, but instead had a culture to build, afresh, of its own.

In his *The Liberal Tradition in America*, Louis Hartz expanded to the length of a book Tocqueville's observation that America was born free or born equal (really born "liberal") and did not have to become so. That suggests the related fact that America was born Protestant, and did not have to become so. America was already Protestant at birth, and had to endure no Reformation, Counterreformation, or religious wars. As there was little feudalism in the American past, and hence little leftover aristocracy, little remnant of feudal classes, traditions, unities, and servilities, so there also was little Catholicism in the primary American background, and hence no leftover national church, no remnant of nation-embracing Catholic authority, little sacramental sense, no hierarchy of higher and lower ways.

There was also little memory-ridden clericalism or anticlericalism, which is a cardinal point in understanding American society, including its politics. One of the many benefits of the American tradition of religious liberty and independence of church from state is that it pushed even further out to sea, outside the politics and culture of the new nation, the anticlericalism and clericalism that divided every French village, threaded through every stage of Italian history, marked the politics of Europe and of South America. Jefferson as a loyal member of the international Enlightenment tried to work up a certain amount of anticlericalism, and it certainly was understandable that he felt strongly resistant to the New England Federalist clergy and other clergy, who called him various unpleasant names. Some of them— such as Timothy Dwight—did indeed represent something like that combination of churchly authority, orthodox theology, and political power against which a proper Enlightenment anticlerical should direct his Voltairean barbs. But it would have been anomalous to have done that against John Leland, enthusiastically rousing his congregation to present to Jefferson the gift of a monster cheese. Partly for reasons of the religious culture already in place, partly for reasons of the accomplishment Jefferson himself did much to bring about, anticlericalism and clericalism in America were not going to have much to work with.

The negative institutional accomplishment that was brought about in the events recounted above—the ending of established churches—is associated with a cluster of other, related facts that distinguish the religious situation in America even from the tradition it is closest to, the English. The English tradition took over more directly from a Catholic past, retained something of its geographical parish system and its connection with the state and the national culture, and had something of its communal social thought and ethic; the American is (let us exaggerate) a traditionless tradition that, not having had these, starts fresh with Protestant principles.

There is a familiar passage in Henry James's biography of Nathaniel Hawthorne that describes the cultural barrenness an American novelist has to try to work with if he deals with his own country. It is notable how often ecclesiastical items occur in James's list of "absent things in American life," and one may infer how much their absence unravels the threads of the culture:

No State, in the European sense of the word, and indeed barely a specific national name. No sovereign, no court, no personal loyalty, no aristocracy, no church, no clergy, no army, no diplomatic service, no country gentlemen, no palaces, no castles, nor manors, nor old country houses, nor parsonages, nor thatched cottages, nor ivied ruins; no cathedrals, nor abbeys, nor little Norman churches; no great universities, nor public schools— no Oxford, nor Eton, nor Harrow; no literature, no novels, no museums, no pictures, no political society, no sporting class— no Epsom nor Ascot!

At the core of the Protestant principles that (spiritually speaking) leveled all those ivied cathedrals, there was a powerful purposiveness: purpose-filled followers, we may say, of a purpose-filled God. They did not need, or want, quaint abbeys and parsonages and robed and mitred clergy; they had the Bible, and they found therein not Aristotle's first cause or Jefferson's "Nature's God," which, having played their part retire from the stage, but the God of Calvin, active, intervening, specifically ordering the destiny of every person and nation. Many elements of this religious culture faded away with the passage of the decades and successive stages of thought and life, and the Calvinist God himself became dimmer, but the purposiveness survived.

How does this purposive activist "constructive" Protestantism construct a social order? That comes to be the problem, the religious form of the general American problem: How do the liberating, dynamic, antitraditional, individualistic movements that inform this society develop constructive communal standards, goals, and structures?

The answer, in the religious case, is "voluntarily," by permeation, by cultural domination through revival, conversion, voluntary association; by the extension to the whole nation of the method and outlook of the Awakening.

The period of the Revolution and its aftermath was a time of comparative religious decline. The fires of the Awakening, still flaring up now and again in the backcountry, generally smoldered or went out. Scholars cite quite small percentages of the population—perhaps fifteen percent, perhaps fewer—who were church members at the time of the Revolution, although there are difficulties about how one counts, and how one knows. The "unchurched"—curious word—were especially numerous out in the growing settlements of what was then the West. As the Daniel Boones made their way over the mountains into Kentucky, the then existing churches had not yet found an effective way to follow or to reach them, an important contrast to what was to come afterward, in the next chapter of American religious history. The disruption of the Revolutionary War, and the letdown after it, played a large role in causing this "unchurching"—as we have seen in Virginia, where Tory clergy fled, patriot clergy joined the army, churches were destroyed or abandoned, the population moved, fought, was distracted. Those were the postwar conditions that George Mason and many editorial writers and petitioners deplored, thereby encouraging Patrick Henry, and others, to support the General Assessment. The republican ideology of the revolutionary period—before, during, after—did derive to some extent from older sources of "dissent," and did draw support from the "black regiment" of patriot clergy; still, it was also to some extent a competing enthusiasm if not a competing point of view: the revolutionary era did give a boost to the Enlightenment's ideology, including skepticism about religion; the American Republic was conceived in liberty and dedicated to the proposition that all men are created equal at one of the lowest points in the influence of religion in its history.

But just at the end of the eighteenth century the situation began to change, and in the early years of the nineteenth—as it happened, exactly while the two Virginians who have been principal figures in these pages were presidents of the United States—it changed drastically. There came a new religious movement, or a series of movements, that markedly altered the spiritual essence of the new nation that these two had done much to construct. The institutions they had devised played a significant implicit role in encouraging this new development; it is not at all likely, however, that it represented what they wanted their nation to be.

The name that has been given to the religious revivals of the first half of the nineteenth century is the Second Great Awakening, but that borrowing and numbering may obscure the differences in its nature and context from the "First." For one, the First Awakening, in the 1730s and '40s, took place in the separated colonies, colonies sufficiently diverse that the Awakening is sometimes said to have been the first bond among them, and Whitefield the first "American" figure, known throughout the colonies. The Second Awakening took place after the nation was formed.

But the nation's self-understanding was still in the process of formation; its institutions and its national ethos were settling into place. The Evangelical Protestant resurgence helped define them. One of these institutions was the new relationship of church to state. The resurgence was much helped by that unique new arrangement, and in its turn helped to fasten the acceptance of it into the mind of the American public. Significantly, Tocqueville was to discover no American who rejected the voluntary way in religion.

The First Awakening had taken place among Englishmen in English colonies, most of which colonies had some kind of establishment— Anglican in the South, Puritan-Congregationalist in the North—and all of which colonies had, in their background—whether they followed it, rejected it, qualified it, or wanted to purify it—the shaping experience of the Church of England. That is, they had, or their parents or grandparents had, been accustomed to a church that had form, and authority, with bishops in the line of the apostolic succession, and with sacraments and thirty-nine articles and the Book of Common Prayer, and an institutional link to the *whole people,* to the *nation,* to the society. Whitefield himself was an Anglican clergyman, although a friend of John Wesley and inclined to the Methodist persuasion. Jonathan Edwards encountered in Northampton the wonderful working of God's grace while preaching in an "established" church of Massachusetts Congregationalism. To go back—even our legendary Pilgrims, though "Separatists" so far as the Church of England was concerned, were not separatists with respect to the community they *themselves* formed: The Mayflower Compact was a religiopolitical document, forming a church-state combination in Plymouth. The expectation and atmosphere, and largely the practice, of the colonists, was that there be a backbone ecclesiastical institution in society, and a shared and unifying religious understanding in the community.

But by the time of the Second Awakening, the scissors of Revolution and the sharp knife of ideological transformation had cut through a great many threads to the past. There was now in place this stunning and unique new arrangement by which the state and the churches were mutually independent of each other. The churches had been cut loose from the new federal government, and soon would be from the last of the states. They were thrown out into the water of the developing society to sink or swim. The enthusiasts were better able to swim.

By enacting the First Amendment and ending established churches in the states, the early American leaders, to change the metaphor, deregulated the religion market. The resulting "free" market, as is usually the case in the real world with free markets, was not neutral among the competitors; it favored those in a position to take advantage of its particular conditions. These well-positioned entrepreneurs were the evangelicals, the revivalists, the "pietists," the "free churches," the "churches of the common man."

Some groups were well positioned to take advantage of the new "market" because the "voluntary way," to which the nation was now committed, was their métier; because the method most of them used— the emotion-loaded revival, their marketing tool, as it were—fit the situation, especially the opening of the vast territory to the west; because the comparative lack of emphasis upon an educated ministry made it easier to open new franchises, so to speak, more quickly; because their creedal requirements came after a time not to be particularly exacting. ("Is your heart as my heart?" asked John Wesley. "Then give me your hand.")

The somewhat aristocratic deism of Thomas Jefferson and Benjamin Franklin was not going to send circuit riders out West to hold enthusiastic jumping-up-and-down camp meetings to convert people by the thousands—disapproved of that, in fact—and neither were the staid old orthodox churches, with their formal creeds and rituals and their educated ministry. Revivalistic evangelical Protestantism did do those things, and did them at a time when the West was being settled and the nation was taking form.

The earliest phase of the Second Awakening was not in the West, however, but in New England, within settled congregations in the still established churches, and it generally avoided the emotional excesses of the Western and later phases. Indeed, it had as a chief leader no less a figure than Jefferson's great critic, the Federalist Congregationalist Timothy Dwight of Yale, Jonathan Edwards's grandson. It did, however, entail two other features that marked the whole decades-long and nationwide phenomenon: the beginning of the adaptation of the severities of reformed theology to the realities and needs of popular revivalism, and the beginning of that remarkable product of the religious-political situations the new arrangement brought forth: the voluntary association.

Some of these cooperative pan-Protestant voluntary associations promoted missions abroad and at home (that is, in the West), and distributed Bibles and tracts, and spread that new institution, the Sunday school ("Jesus loves me, this I know; for the Bible tells me so"). Others sought the reform of "morals," as they would come now to be defined: They opposed demon rum or dancing or lotteries or theatergoing or profanity. One early association at Yale, according to Canon Stokes, was "versus vice." There were also humanitarian associations: for aiding the poor, the deaf and dumb, the mentally ill, and, above all, for the ending of slavery. The "interfering spirit of righteousness" had already been present in Puritanism, but in the New England Protestantism of the first half of the nineteenth century it took this new form, wider-gauged, "voluntary," particularistic, implicitly optimistic whatever the theology. It has left an indelible stamp on American culture, and shaped the political style of religion in America—the crusade, the specific moral sortie out into society—to this day.

This New England revival took place, at first, within still-established churches, but during its heyday the state establishments were ended: in New Hampshire in 1817, in Connecticut in 1818, in Massachusetts— if you call its arrangement an "establishment"—in 1833. By then there was no formal establishment of any kind in the United States. But by then conditions of the voluntary way had created, by carrying that volunteering beyond anything Jefferson or Madison would have dreamed of, a de facto establishment, a "voluntary" establishment, a penetration of the culture (in a new way) that few of the formally established churches of the past could have matched.

Lyman Beecher was a great power in, and great defender of, the Congregational "Standing Order" of Connecticut and, like his mentor Dwight, fought hard against its disestablishment. When, however, he and his fellow battlers were defeated, he changed his mind. The "free trade in religion" provided a "moral coercion which makes men work." The churches were "roused from their lethargy, compelled to assume responsibility both for their own institutional life and for the moral and spiritual life of their society, and were able to exert by voluntary efforts, societies, missions, and revivals, a deeper influence than ever before." Canon Stokes quotes a passage from Henry Ward Beecher, editing the autobiography of his father, Lyman, who discovered that disestablishment was not a disaster but "the best thing that ever happened in the State of Connecticut."

> It cut the churches loose from state support. It threw them wholly on their own resources and on God. They say that ministers have lost their influence; the fact is, they have gained. By voluntary efforts, societies, missions, and revivals, they exert a deeper influence than ever they could by queues and shoe buckles, and cocked hats and gold-headed canes.

The enormously important phase of the Second Awakening out in the raw and newly settled West, where those "unchurched" folk were available to be "churched," or at least "saved," would feed back into

New England and affect it by its energy and outlook and theological tendency and especially its method, the camp meeting revival. This was a new technique, often days—and nights—long, social as well as religious, undeterred by the decorum of the New England revival ("Walk together, children, and don't be weary; there's a great camp meeting in the promised land"). The most famous revival took place in Cane Ridge, Kentucky, in August 1801, and quoting descriptions of its leaping and squeaking is hard to resist, and no doubt distorting; one does not resist passing on the comment of a critic—presumably a critic—who said there were more souls begot than saved.

There was yet a later phase of the Awakening, beginning in upstate New York, which featured the lawyer-turned-revivalist Charles Grandison Finney, whose statue still stands there on the Oberlin College campus, where he ended his career. These Finney revivals, in particular, spilled over into abolitionism, women's rights (the Seneca Falls declaration, now rescued by a later women's movement), and a host of other humanitarian, "moral," and religious undertakings like those begun in New England. When a mid-twentieth-century scholar (Gilbert Barnes) regarded *The Anti-Slavery Impulse* of the 1830s and after, he drew back in a kind of surprise that so much of it came out of the revivals and the churches.

Perhaps general American history in the twentieth century has somewhat neglected the shaping penetration of the new American nation in the first half of the nineteenth century by this "voluntary," "evangelical," "free" Protestant Christianity. Intellectual history travels down from Puritanism not to Cane Ridge but to Concord. Religious historians perforce treat these matters in a compartment for religious history only, and there does not yet appear to be an equivalent, for this phenomenon, of Perry Miller and his followers for Puritanism. Perhaps there are reasons why there will not be. It is unprepossessing to modern scholars who are outside its thought-world. It lacks the literary and intellectual interest, the founding priority, and the convenient remoteness of Puritanism. But this nineteenth-century evangelical Protestantism, which is not the old Calvinism or Puritanism extended but another movement, another sorting, took place after the nation was formed, while religion still had cultural punch, and it definitely left its scar upon the American earth.

The Baptists and Methodists, the dynamic new firms of the deregulated religion market, rose past the staid old companies to become, by the time of the Civil War, the largest American Protestant denominations. In colonial America the largest religious groups had been those that came out of seventeenth-century England: the Anglicans, and the two big branches of the Puritan effort to remake—to purify—Anglicanism, the Presbyterians and the Congregationalists. At the time of the Revolution these three English-rooted groups were still, in numbers and in power, the leading religious bodies in the colonies. The Baptists, although growing rapidly in numbers after the Great Awakening, were still a relatively smaller and very much a powerless collection of sectarians. The Methodists were an even smaller group, just pulling out of the Anglican/Episcopal church in 1784. And yet by the time of the Civil War, these two had passed, by a very wide margin, the older "denominations." The Baptists and Methodists remain to this day the largest Protestant groupings in the nation. Each of these denominations, and their largest rival on the frontier, the largest indigenous American denomination, the Disciples of Christ, may be taken to suggest features of the unintentional fallout from religion that left a deposit in American culture.

The defining practice of the denominational group that played the most prominent role in achieving separation of church and state, the Baptists, is present in their name: adult baptism. The Antipaedobaptists, who sent Isaac Backus to those conventions, were, as one sees when one sorts out the word, opposed to the baptism of children. Adult baptism—baptism at the age of discretion, when the converted one is old enough to have made his or her own decision—very much heightens, of course, the distinct and separate place of each individual, and correspondingly diminishes the place of the continuities of institutional life. The immediate decision of the individual will is brought to the fore, as revivalism does, as American evangelical Protestantism in general does. A christening or the baptism of a baby (or a bar mitzvah) heightens the emphasis upon a family, and the family's past, and the relation of the child to a continuous tradition and institution; an adult baptism heightens the born-again believer's independent decision. The continuities and institutions fade. The Baptists, pitching all that overboard, requiring no educated ministry, adaptable, anarchic, various, popular, responsive, each congregation its own boss, each Baptist his own boss, flourished in an American West and in an American populace that wanted to be *its* own boss and had pitched all that old European stuff overboard, too.

Or almost all that old stuff. After the sectional division in the denominations wrought by the controversies over secession, slavery, and Civil War, one segment of the vast Baptist world—the largest single organized (insofar as it is organized) Protestant unit, the Southern Baptists—would come to represent in fullest measure the near paradox that in lesser degree would characterize the evangelical Protestantism of that early national era out of which the whole configuration came: that is, a religious body with the individualist mentality of a sect, but the collective role of a church; with the explicit commitment to a Voluntary Way that pretended not to notice the reality of power, but with the implicit capacity to exercise a great deal of it.

During Holy Week of 1964—to skip to more recent times—the president of the United States, Lyndon Baines Johnson, no stranger to the patterns and uses of power, made an extraordinary appeal to a visiting group of Southern Baptist preachers that combined rather homey references to the "grace that I learned at my Baptist mother's knee" with an analysis of the political role of their churches of a kind not often found in discourses beginning with that maternal joint. "Your people are part of the power structure in many communities," Johnson told the white Southern Baptists. "The leaders of states and cities and towns are in your congregations and they sit there on your board. Their attitudes are confirmed or changed by the sermons you preach and by the lessons you write and by the examples that you set. Help us to pass this Civil Rights Bill" (the bill, in process when President Kennedy was shot, which was to become the Civil Rights Act of 1964). It was the kind of explicit reminder of their political responsibility in the civic order that Southern Baptists had not heard very often.

The rise of the chief rivals to the Baptists on the frontier, the Methodists, is one of the more striking episodes in American religious history at least, perhaps American history in general. They did not even exist as a separate religious body until 1784, right in the middle of those events in Virginia; by 1844 they were the largest religious group in the country. They were a perfect fit for the new country's nature, condition, and needs.

The Methodists had the advantages but not the disadvantages of the hierarchical or connectional church government that they took over from their parent, the Anglicans. On the one hand they had bishops—as it happened, extraordinary bishops, in particular Francis Asbury—and they had the overall connected churchly organization that enabled them to plan. And plan they did, methodically, thoroughly, aggressively, mapping out districts, the circuits for circuit riders to ride across the opening West, almost before there were any people to ride to to be converted or "churched."

But though they had the *form* to which all sorts of Protestants had objected for two centuries—bishops and an autocratic connected church organization—they did not give it the content, or use it for the purpose, that the Church of England, and all the hierarchical churches of Christendom, had done. They put the aristocratic efficiency of bishops and overarching church government at the service of a democratic sectarian outlook. They were not connected to the social elite; to the contrary, they came from and appealed to the common people. They did not insist on an educated ministry, a formal liturgical service, or an exacting creed. Sydney Ahlstrom quotes the circuit rider Peter Cartwright:

> I have seen so many educated preachers who forcibly reminded me of lettuce growing under the shade of a peachtree, or like a gosling that had got the straddles by wading in the dew, that I turn away sick and faint.... The Presbyterians, and other Calvinist branches of the Protestant Church, used to contend for an educated ministry, for pews, for instrumental music, for a congregational or stated salaried ministry. The Methodists universally opposed these ideas; and the illiterate Methodist preachers actually set the world on fire (the American world at least) while they [the others] were lighting their matches.

The Methodists had a doctrinal advantage as well. They had none of the problems concerning the theological mysteries that split and constrained the Presbyterians, the Congregationalists, the declining Calvinistic wing of the Baptists, or others of the orthodoxy of the Reformation. In the long term the most severe doctrines of the Calvinist heroes of the Geneva Wall, or of Augustine, were not going to go over well in a new, open, revivalistic, "republican," "modern" country of the common man: that is, doctrines that deny the human will a role in one's own salvation. It is not just Ben Franklin who will have trouble with an idea like that. The logic of the revivals, even the logic of "this new man, this American," was against it.

The Methodists had inherited from Anglicanism an "Arminian" tendency—a doctrinal inclination that gave a place to human will—and John Wesley with his perfectionism had given it a shot of enthusiasm. But Wesley, though "perfectionist," was more orthodox than his many American followers, whose outlook would be said to be "Arminianism set on fire." Some took the "voluntary principle" all the way up into the central transaction of the Christian religion itself. An American Methodist revivalist put the troublesome doctrine of the "Elect" and

Election in the following distinctly un-Calvinist way: God has one vote, the devil has one vote—and *you* have one vote.

The Disciples of Christ, gathering together several impulses to return to "primitive Christianity," did not plan to be a new denomination at all. Typical of an impulse much wider than its own eventual constituency, it intended to cut across them all, to gather together in a simplifying, unifying *movement* all Christians on the basis of the elementary essentials of the New Testament, with no creedal elaboration. It gained many members, then settled down and became a denomination, too, alongside the others—a group that had not even existed at the time of the nation's founding, a wholly indigenous non-English, non-European development that not only came into existence on the American frontier but rose in this atmosphere to become one of the biggest Protestant groups—larger than the Congregationalists of John Winthrop and Timothy Dwight or Virginia's Anglican/Episcopalians.

In their outlook and abrupt rise the Disciples may be taken to symbolize this characteristic of the American denominations: They tended to jump all the way from New Testament times to nineteenth-century America, and to regard everything in between as more or less a mistake. The religious sense of connection that expresses itself in the idea of the apostolic succession, of an authentic handing down from this one to that one back to the very source, is gone. A church historian's observation that on every day for almost 2,000 years somewhere the Mass has been celebrated—that sort of thing rings no bells, except perhaps of alarm, in the American nineteenth-century free-church Protestant mind. The history that is forgotten, ignored, or repudiated is that of Europe, the civilization the United States derives from. The American Protestant fascination with the Holy Land, which set in motion that trip Mark Twain described in *The Innocents Abroad*, is matched by the uneasy ambivalence toward the accumulated centuries of European Christendom that that book also records. There is the one Holy Land around the Jordan River, and the other around the Missouri-Mississippi Valley, and in between, geographically and historically, the European mistake.

And even the groups that did not begin just yesterday—the older branchings of the Protestant stream—have either forgotten or explicitly rejected the long centuries of Christian history. Jefferson and the rationalist Founders would join in that. They and the revivalists might disagree about the depravity of man, but they would agree about the depravity of Europe; they might disagree about Jesus as the Messiah but agree about America as the Messiah. It is clear, in the newsstand books of the popular religious right of the 1980s, that, for all the other language, the true revelation and savior is America.

Under the conditions of deregulation and "free trade," the "denominations" competed, sometimes fiercely, particularly on the frontier. They disputed with one another a good deal about what Peter Berger— who in the best of books on the sociology of religion, *The Sacred Canopy*, uses the analogy of the market to its utmost—is willing to call "product differentiation." The Presbyterians took the heat in disputes about predestination and free will, and Methodists and Baptists went at each other about infant baptism and immersion, and many offshoots and varieties and splits and additions from immigration com-, peted with each other. But at the same time they cooperated in a wide variety of common enterprises, among them those voluntary associations, alluded to above, that Tocqueville admired. At the level of the national culture, one might say, these Protestant competitors were an oligopoly engaged in price fixing.

They cooperated in an attempt to make a "Christian America." Despite their doctrinal and practical and territorial competings, and their competition for church members, they did not compete for the nation or the world. They joined together. They did not seek a Methodist America, or a Baptist America, or a Presbyterian America; they sought, together, a "Christian" America. (By "Christian" they always meant Protestant; they took that meaning for granted quite without consciousness of irony. As late as the 1980s Frances Fitzgerald, reporting for *The New Yorker* on Jerry Falwell's domain in Lynchburg, Virginia, heard an athletic person at Liberty Baptist College say that he hoped one day to develop a *Christian* football team good enough to beat Notre Dame.)

The American nation's version of this strain developed out of popular "voluntary" religion. Dramatizing a little, one might say that though Madison and Jefferson erected one "wall" (between church and state) they inadvertently helped to knock down another one—the institutional and intellectual barrier of definition between the religious and the national ethos. The one ethos and the other combined in the enthusiasms of the common man. America in its formative days developed out of those enthusiasms a kind of a seminationalist religion and a semireligious nationalism with some of the results of which we are living still, with which the world is coping still.

Two collaborative activities of the nineteenth-century American Protestant denominations—the defense of the Sabbath, and the defense and promotion and penetration of the public schools—may suggest, in quite different ways, some anomalies in the way they applied their fervently professed support for religious liberty. Each, as it happens, would store up piquant puzzles for the U.S. Supreme Court in the twentieth century.

The American Protestants strenuously defended not simply the observance of the Sabbath by the devout but the legal requirement that everybody observe it on Sunday. They fought hard against the shocking "Jeffersonian" idea that the Sabbath might be desecrated so that unbelievers could get their mail. In supporting blue laws and Sunday closings they were not, of course, proposing anything new, but defending laws and practices that had a long history, stretching back through the Christian ages—or rather, through Puritan Protestant ages. Here, as we have seen elsewhere, "Christian" is simply taken for granted to mean Protestant. And despite a quite earnest endorsement of religious freedom—that feeling that they, the free-church American Protestants, were in some distinct and unusual way the representatives and defenders of religious freedom, and of the separation of church and state— they nevertheless felt no compunction about insisting that the *state* through *its laws* defend the Sabbath observance. For them, religious liberty and church-state separation did not at all mean that this was not to be a Christian nation, and, at important points like this one, by legal action imposed on all. The opponents of establishments joined as enthusiastically in "The Lord's Day Alliance" as did the former state churches.

The same Virginia Assembly that passed Jefferson's statute also enacted a statute protecting the Sabbath. That was one of the issues that would bring together the two religious factions that had been on opposite sides of the struggle over establishment. Robert Handy, whose book *A Christian America* tells the story of this Protestant penetration of the earlier American society, wrote,

> On the Sabbath issue, Protestants whose background had been in state churches readily teamed up with those who had opposed all religious establishments.... Protestant forces across a wide sweep of denominational and theological opinion persistently struggled for the Sabbath as a day apart—a day that would characterize American civilization as Christian. For them, this was a distinctive symbol of the kind of Protestant culture they were laboring to maintain and extend.

They succeeded in planting laws in the codes of the states, many of which persist to this day. According to Henry Abraham, in his *Freedom and the Court*, in 1980 there were still Sunday laws—blue laws—in half of the states. Mr. Abraham raised some doubt about the logic of

> such intriguing provisions as those that—under the very same state laws—ban the sale of hosiery in hosiery shops on Sundays yet do not forbid it in drugstores; or those that permit the sale of "antiques," but not "reproductions"; or those that require candy stores to be closed but permit roadside candy counters to be open; or those that allow clam-digging but forbid oyster-dredging!

Supporting the public schools was a much bigger matter, of course, and indicated the uncritical at-home-ness of Protestant Americans in quite a different way. There would be those who would wonder about the combination of a strong devotion to church-state separation on the one hand with a strong support for Sunday observation by law, as a symbol of Christian civilization, on the other. But another sort of question might be posed by the remarkable nineteenth-century pan-Protestant support for the new system of universal free public schools. Robert Handy, who cites the most extraordinary quotations from Protestant leaders endorsing and defending the public schools, quotes also a modern scholar who asks why those churches did not recognize the "Erastian" implications of that support—support for turning over to "the state" the central culture-forming, commitment-making activity of the education of the young, which through all the centuries of Christendom had been in the hands of the church. ("Erastian," misnamed for a Swiss theologian, means a pattern in which the "state" dominates, uses, orders around the "church"; Nazi Germany and the Soviet Union, and some older and less frightening cases, are sometimes cited as examples.) Father Murray remarked in a moment of exasperation in Santa Barbara, "If those Protestants just hadn't been so *dumb...* " So dumb, he meant in context, and from an aggressive Christian point of view, as to yield those keys to culture to "the state."

But of course to mainstream nineteenth-century American Protestants, as one reads about them in Handy's book, or Sydney Ahlstrom's or Timothy L. Smith's *Revivalism and Social Reform*, or in the older histories like those of William Warren Sweet, that kind of a problem or question, that way of *posing* a question, did not exist. That little red schoolhouse was not representative of a "state" that stood over against the "church" in some sharply defined institutional separation and potential hostility; still less was that schoolhouse a potentially dangerous agent of "secularism." It was the agent of "civilization," and civilization and Christianity were virtually identical, and both were represented at their highest achievement by America, and the expansive American Protestants embraced and supported church and school, and filled the latter of course with "Christian" (i.e., Protestant) references, teachings, and practices. Along with the right number of "Rs" the school was especially to teach *morality*, which, again, is almost the same as civilization, which is almost the same as . . . and so on. The lines were not then sharply drawn, to put it mildly. The mainline American Protestants, by *voluntary* means, as they would insist, "established" themselves as the dominant cultural force and rather took for granted that they would remain so.

At the core of this whole pan-Protestant enterprise was the "voluntary way in Religion" well, favorably, and sympathetically described in *The Great Tradition of the American Churches*, by an historian of religion in America, Winthrop Hudson. The voluntary principle or way has more in it than meets the eye, if the eye should be watching religion only. Taken in the round, the voluntary principle stands at the center of the effect of a particular kind of Christianity on the civic culture of the United States.

The voluntary principle may at first be thought to signify nothing more than the outcome of the events described in the early chapters of this book: that church and state were separated, and that the sort of religious liberty sought by Jefferson and Madison and Isaac Backus and John Leland had been instituted. There was to be no church "by law established." There was to be no tax support for religion. Citizens were to be free to believe or not believe, to join or not to join, to support or not to support whatever religion they chose, or did not choose— voluntarily. When a European asks an American about the "juridical" status of the "church" in the United States, the American may fumble for an answer. The "church" is not singular, and does not seem to *have* a "juridical" status as such. It is, or rather each one of the religious bodies is, what John Locke, and, following him, Jefferson and Madison, said it was or should be: a voluntary association.

But the voluntary principle accompanies, implies, or carries with it strong tendencies or affinities in other regards, beyond the institutional or "juridical" arrangements and beyond even religious institutions. In one aspect it grew in part out of, and had to do with, the innards of the churches and their government: congregational, egalitarian, "gathered," "democratic." Of course since virtually every European religious group came to the United States in one immigration or another, every form of church "polity" is represented here; nevertheless the voluntary-congregational form set the tone, and had its effect even upon the nominally hierarchical religious groups.

How did the believers—troops of new ones in the 1800s—come into these churches? Voluntarily, of course. But as every private knows there are different kinds of volunteering. In the early high-Puritan days, churches, though perhaps "gathered" in a sense, were put together by collecting only the visible saints. In John Cotton's church in Boston, one had to establish one's religious credentials as regenerate in order to be admitted. But the impulse of revivalism, even in the First Awakening, was to go out and persuade.

Eventually the barriers to entry were lowered, and members were sought—as many souls as possible were to be saved, by the evangelistic reaching out of itinerants and the revivals and the missions. Sought—one by one, by the *choice* of the individual, by his or her *will*, or "heart" changing. Think of the social philosophy, and the picture of human nature, implicit in the idea of the revivalistic form of conversion, with its appeals, its pressures, its torment of the sinners on the mourner's bench, its altar calls, its sawdust trail, its decision all in one dramatic moment to alter all of one's life.

In ancient and in Reformed Christianity—in Calvinism in particular—that decisive happening was a gift of God, the grace of God, something you prayed and hoped for, like the rain in a drought, but which you could not cause to happen. And so the preachers of the First Awakening, for the most part, saw it to be. But the strong tendency of evangelical American Christianity is to give that event a boost—to *make* it happen, by human effort. Already in the 1740s awakening, Jonathan Edwards, whose Calvinist theology was certainly buttoned down firmly and who wrote classic and sophisticated refutations of John Locke and others who exaggerated, or believed at all in, the free will of human beings, nevertheless had to face critics of the *means*—emotional preaching—that encouraged the conversions to come about. And by the nineteenth-century revivals like those of Cane Ridge, and Finney's efforts, the emotional means were unabashed and strongly defended against the critics. The direct emotional appeal by the individual revivalist to the "heart" of the individual believer, in the setting of hundreds, thousands, of others, produced *results*: These unconverted frontiersmen are going to decide *freely* to have their souls saved, and if they do not, by God, we are going to *make* them freely decide. Finney defended the "anxious seat," and the pressure on the individual convert-to-be to stand in the crowd and be exhorted by name. There is a reason for putting "voluntary" in quotation marks.

To sum up: Implicit in conversion and revival, in gathered churches, adult baptisms, congregational polities, and homiletical services was the image of the powerful role of the free decision of the individual, and that image carried over into society at large. There is in the resulting American social outlook little Jacobin voluntarism of a collective kind, which sees one great entity, a people or folk, imposing a single will on history; neither is there much of the Nietzschean voluntarism of a superior few, imposing their strong will on the passive many. Instead, the American emphasis on human "will" is liberal, democratic, individualist, seeing many separate and more or less equal individuals exercising diverse initiatives, pursuing many careers, "cooperating" maybe in "teamwork," but fundamentally separate.

These separate individuals, by force of will, can have a great influence on their own destiny; they can also, joined together, have a great influence on the society. One can alter society by changing individuals, first, from within, and one can make that change by persuasive appeals to the will.

The "voluntary" theme is plainly connected to the familiar American individualism, and "moralism." All three are tied to the very high place given to "individual freedom" in the American scale of values—the highest place, actually. Americans of almost all persuasions come to think of some original condition—some (Lockean?) mythic state of nature—consisting of a collection of discrete individuals, before there was society. And the assumed individualism-as-an-original-fact is thought to be essential to freedom as a goal. In order to hold to a high view of the "dignity" and "worth" of the individual, it is felt, one must also hold to a large view of his importance in making himself, mastering nature, and determining history. The American resists much emphasis on social conditioning, on the limits of human freedom, on the power of historical forces, on the place of the communal forms of life; he sees in each hint of determinism a threat to individual responsibility.

These themes reinforce each other. An enlarged picture of the scope of what an "individual" *can* do implies culpability, praise and blame, moral judgment. He was *free*. Therefore he is subject to moral appraisal. Each of us in relationship to others—to our children, our adversaries, our friends, even ourselves—insists on the expanded view of free choice when we have reason to blame or praise, a contracted view when we have reason to exculpate: *You* can do otherwise; *I* could not help it. American culture sees a large place for human freedom, and hence for moral judgment; a wide range of moral judgment and therefore of freedom.

Critics of the performance of the actual institutions of American Protestantism in the social and political arena may remark that it is not the voluntarism that worries them, but the legalism: the resort to *law*, in a manner often attributed to the Puritans, to enact "morality" in matters of personal behavior, and thereby to "impose" it on others. That inclination, such critics might say, seems contradictory to a devotion to a "voluntary" way. But it is not contradictory to the configuration of an individualistic moralism of which the "voluntary" outlook on society is a part. The typical representative of the religious formation here sketched is no anarchist, or live-and-let-live permissive person, but is fully supplied with the "interfering spirit of righteousness." Neither Backus nor Beecher nor their colleagues and heirs were reluctant to press others, and society as a whole, into a righteous, a "Christian" mold.

On many matters they were, and are, willing to use the instrument of law—blue laws, prohibition, and a variety of laws "versus vice." All of us, of course, Protestant moralists or secular rationalists, except for anarchists, do want to use law for moral ends; we use the word "impose" about those laws with which we have a moral disagreement. But—perhaps not alone—the Protestant Christianizers of America did not have a social and political philosophy that admitted, or criticized, what they were doing.

This voluntary-coercive way of looking at society, or not looking at it, comes not only from religion in America but from almost every other aspect of America's history and culture as well. It has been helped along by the country's relative peace, wealth, and isolation; by the winning of wars, overcoming of depressions, and living long years in the great spaces and resources of a separate continent. America's popular social philosophy is so lopsided because the forces bearing upon it have turned in the same direction. After the Civil War the capitalist engine picked up the individualistic outlook and hardened it into an insistent creed.

The ideas about society that spring from religion in America have a close tie to some of the best attributes of the American nation, at the same time that they lead to some of her political faults. One praiseworthy aspect of American life that can be connected to these ideas is a large supply of ordinary human friendliness, of charitable feeling, and charitable action. At least it used to be true. The Swedish social scientist and observer Gunnar Myrdal wrote in the 1940s *An American Dilemma*:

> Competent and sympathetic foreign observers have always noted the generosity and helpfulness of Americans. . . . I cannot help feeling that the Christian neighborliness of the common American reflects . . . an influence from the churches. . . . it shows up in the American's readiness to make financial sacrifices for charitable purposes. No country has so many cheerful givers as America.

The contributions go beyond the obvious merits of charitable giving and friendly face-to-face relationships to the tradition of humanitarian social reform. Americans, their own rather conservative "revolution" accomplished, have not provided much support, despite some sentences in their Declaration of Independence and the outlook of its author, for the revolutionary overturn of political and economic systems, and particularly not for efforts in that direction in their own country. But they have had a marked penchant for particular reforms. The older religious tradition, with its inclination to elevate the nation's significance to the highest plane and to amalgamate Christian and national symbols on the one side, and its interfering spirit of righteousness, its voluntary-moralizing impulse on the other, is surely one source of both of these features of the national life: the absence of systematic revolutionary attitudes; the recurrence of ad hoc reforms. The "social idealism" this heritage helped to produce, looked at positively, is the chief defense against the oft-heard charge that the country is simply a materialistic technocracy. If the reader were to list the humane American social reforms that have his or her endorsement, from the abolition of slavery to whatever it may more recently be, he or she would find those reforms had strong support, and probably initiative, from this old Protestant American heritage.

The merits of this heritage appear where there is a clear, humanitarian issue; the faults appear more prominently where issues are embedded in the collective historical setting. The characteristic contribution of American religion to American civic understanding therefore has been not perspective, wisdom, depth of insight, but the rousing of the sentiments and energies for particular acts of charity, generosity, and social reform. The characteristic vices have been those of a vulnerably over-simple implicit social conception: a radical pietistic individualism of the change of heart, which knows too readily what is "moral" and expects too easily to persuade people to do it—and topples into cynicism when that does not happen. If one were to try to build a giant modern experiment in civic republicanism, one might conclude that this particular moral nurture, valuable though it is in certain ways, would not alone suffice. There should be also some link to the practice of statecraft and the tradition of reason and the heritage of the common good that these American Protestants had left behind in Europe.

THAT GENEROUS POLICY

Even as the Protestant "crusade" was rolling out across the new nation, the nation's institutions were making possible the growth of other sources of moral and social understanding. There were taking place, likewise in considerable part as a result of the founding arrangements about religious liberty, an extraordinary series of events that would upstage the mainstream free-church Protestant America which thought (to some extent, correctly) it had invented those arrangements. The new nation, by the time of Madison's death in 1836, came to have a bewildering assortment of religious groups, far beyond anything required to fulfill Madison's principles of balance. That assortment of newness would slice, crowd, dissipate, and eventually, after many, many decades, disestablish the de facto or voluntary Protestant establishment those same arrangements had helped to put in place.

Often the first thing that strikes observers from countries with more orderly religious configurations is the sheer bewildering multiplicity of sects, cults, churches, movements, and indescribable spiritual entities that seem to make up the American scene. Often that is the first thing in the mind of a superficial American observer, too.

When in the late twentieth century, one mentions the more than 250 different "religious bodies" listed in the annual *Yearbook of American Churches*, a Southern California student of these matters, who counts the cults and religious exotica from the rather special perspective of that region, responds that he and his colleagues had noted more than

1,500 such bodies and were still counting. At each meeting he explains the origins and beliefs and practices of a new religious body one has never heard of, and perhaps never wanted to hear of.

Before we say something about this religious variety, however, it is important to say something about its limits. The religious composition of the United States is not as kaleidoscopic and as inclusive of every possibility in this world and all possible and some impossible other worlds as it may appear to be in the sunny fecundity of Southern California. The sheer multiplicity that often strikes foreign visitors and contemporary observers as the dominant fact is not quite as far-flung, or as significant, as it seems superficially.

In the first place, there is an important concentration. If we are looking simply at "religious bodies"—the organized units of denominations, churches, sects, measured by numbers of adherents—the large and lasting changes are those that came out of the first Protestant enthusiasm in the first three-quarters of a century of the nation's life, to which we have already referred, with some additions, especially Roman Catholicism, from immigration. A pattern emerged by the time of the Civil War that has remained fairly stable ever since. In sheer numbers, the Roman Catholics already had joined or surpassed the large Protestant groups; the Baptists and Methodists had risen past the older Presbyterians, Congregationalists, and Anglicans, who nevertheless remained important, numerically and otherwise; the new group from the frontier that we mentioned—the Disciples of Christ—and one of the Protestant groups from the immigrations—the varieties of Lutherans—joined the top group in size. Despite the further immigrations and spiritual stirrings and splits and everything else that has happened since, those rankings have not changed very much in a hundred years. The Mormons, geographically concentrated, alone among the extra-Biblical new groups, have become large enough to join these others.

The dozen largest "religious bodies"—the ones that have been named here—would have, since the Civil War, continuously included far over 90 percent of the membership of religious groups in the nation. The more than 200 lesser groups that cover the pages of yearbooks, though they include many that have an importance measured otherwise, by this sheer numerical measure are of minor importance. If one shifted to a more substantive measure—cultural power and effect—one could say by such measure, too, there is a concentration. If it be said that the organizational units—the denominations—have often been less important in American religion than movements that cut across them—as in the crusadings and the many pan-Protestant movements of the

1830s and after, as in liberal theology, social gospel, fundamentalism, as in the division in the 1970s and 1980s between the rising new Evangelical Right and the declining "mainline" Protestantism—if that be said, truly enough, the point still stands, that the picture of religion in America has a form, a history, a tradition, and is not a totally random scatter of individual "preferences," a pluralism of the more the merrier. The United States came out of the religious history of Europe, in particular of England, and has been adding its own chapters.

But the fecund New World certainly did enlarge the world's roster of religious groups by addition, multiplication, division, and spontaneous combustion. There came, especially in that first half of the nineteenth century, many homegrown American parts, branches, and offshoots, and a proliferation of cults, sects, communes, utopias, and what Mark Twain somewhat disrespectfully called wildcat religions. There were divisions about doctrine, creating Unitarianism and Universalism, and about practice, creating the branch of the Disciples who would not use the organ in church, and about "Biblical Holiness," creating the Nazarenes out of the Methodists, and about which day was the Sabbath, creating the Adventists. There were new bodies, including two important "third-scripture" religions—Mormons and Christian Scientists. Many of these nineteenth-century developments lasted and grew and stored up problems for the twentieth-century Supreme Court—such divisions coming from "the world" as, for example, the splits of the major denominations over slavery. One can presume that the causes of this nineteenth-century American spiritual excitement and sectarian proliferation prominently include the new openness of the state and society to free religious preaching, decision, organization—religious liberty, no priority to any group, no restrictions—and also the voluntary Protestant atmosphere it helped to create.

But all of these internal American sources of religious diversity are still not as important as the other, the external, source: immigration. Both H. Richard Niebuhr and Sydney Ahlstrom make the following observation, conceivably even a little testily for such untesty people; Niebuhr, for example, in *The Social Sources of Denominationalism*, says: "When European critics point a scornful finger at the multitudinous sects of the New World and ascribe their presence to 'the typically American' spirit of individualism, they ignore the rather patent contribution which the 'typically European' spirit of nationalism has made to this variety of religious experience and organization." Writing in 1929 Niebuhr lists religious groups from every nation in Europe that had preserved their identity in the American scene and added thereby to the lengthening roster of "American" denominations: German Seventh-Day Baptists, German Baptist Dunkards, Scandinavian Independent Baptists; Albanian, Bulgarian, Greek, Rumanian, Russian, Serbian, and Syrian Orthodox churches; the Armenian Apostolic and the Assyrian Jacobite churches; the Reformed Church of Soviet Russia, and the Polish National Catholic Church; the Norwegian Lutheran, the United Danish Evangelical Lutheran, the Danish Evangelical Lutheran, the Finnish Evangelical Lutheran Nation, and the Swedish Evangelical Free churches; the Eielsen, Icelandic, Suomi, Slavak, and Norwegional Lutheran synods; the Swedish Evangelical Mission Covenant, the Norwegian-Danish Evangelical Free Church Association, the Moravian Church, and Evangelical Union of Bohemian and Moravian Brethren. That was just for a start. He went on to give another list, of groups that did not include a national reference in their denominational *name* but were nevertheless derived from a European national identity: Lithuanian, Polish, German, Swedish, Norwegian, Finnish—the point is made.

The point of those lists, again, was to show how the *nationalism* of continental Europe contributed to the variety of religion in America. The religious composition of the American nation was derived, in its colonial and formative underpinnings, primarily from England—from all the religious aspects of the British Isles—and then, after the nation with its policy of religious liberty was instituted, took into itself all the religions of continental Europe. One might say that was the most important of all the results of the "generous policy" of American religious liberty, adding "lustre to our country."

Of course the epic of the immigrations from Europe to the United States in the nineteenth and early twentieth centuries is not to be explained simply by religious persecution in an old country and religious liberty in the new. But the many reasons for those great migrations—the material motive certainly prominent among them—would have been warped and impeded had the "liberty" of the New World not included religious liberty. No doubt to the tired, the hungry, and the poor of the world, the huddled masses yearning to breathe free, the golden door of America represented economic possibilities and material rewards unavailable in the Old World. But had there not been also freedom of religion, then that motive would have been qualified and impeded, and the broader "Liberty," which was another motive, would have been incomplete... and presumably the flow of immigration would have been altered. As the Maryland Act of Toleration of 1649 (quite limited by later standards) and the policy of Lord Baltimore came about partly for reasons of economic needs and possibilities—in order that his fellow Catholics would have a refuge but the more numerous English Protestants would come, too, to boost the economy—so it was in the subsequent history of the nation as a whole. A free-thinking German socialist on his way to St. Louis or Milwaukee, a Norwegian Lutheran farmer who wants to make a better life in Minnesota and maybe later becomes a Methodist, a Neapolitan who reads the fliers advertising for workers at the Winchester plant in New Haven, where the streets are paved with gold, these and a thousand other sorts are not inhibited by religious scruples from immigration to the New World. The touching picture of "America" in the mind of much of Europe in the nineteenth and early twentieth centuries, like the picture of "Pennsylvania" in the minds of the sectarians of Central Europe in the seventeenth and eighteenth (and of the eighteenth-century philosophes, too) would have featured economic opportunity and political and civil liberty in different mixtures. For some it must have featured religious liberty, too. And the absence or legal diminution of religious liberty inhibited the first and qualified the second of those other appeals. Religious liberty must have been at least implicit in the attraction of America for the millions who made their way across the Atlantic.

And for many it was explicit, and religious persecution a specific reason for the journey. There has been, and still is, a good deal of pushing against the opening of that golden door—in the 1920s it was almost shut—and the record of the empire of liberty is as checkered and sporadic and intermittent, as much resisted and qualified and forgotten, on this as on other facets of the moral undertaking that is America. But still and all, the New World has had a sufficient portion of that "generous policy" not only to add to itself a "lustre" but also by its own original decision to allow itself in time to be made over into something it had not been.

The immigrations brought into this hitherto sectarian-Calvinist or Puritan Protestant or evangelical Protestant nation—"Christian" America in a special sense—not only that wide variety of other sorts of Protestants from the Continent but also all of the other historic religious communities of Europe (more Eastern Orthodox than most Americans might guess), and eventually, to a smaller extent, from the rest of the world as well. But in particular Catholics and Jews. At first these groups, in the nature of the sociology of such immigration, would remain more or less in a separate domain, with comparatively little effect on the main currents of culture except to make a segment of it apprehensive. But over time, with the passage of generations, that of course would change. One might say that the full effects of those changes are being felt just at the time of the present writing, during the many bicentennials.

These immigrant groups would be at first much affected by the dominant culture—not only "American" but also "Protestant." Will Herberg, whose book *Protestant-Catholic-Jew* caught the features of the religious scene in the 1950s, including the effects of the succession of generations of immigrants, agreed in conversation after one of the Fund for the Republic's gatherings that the others of those "three faiths" that had now become according to his book variant "ways of being American" had all nevertheless been—neither he nor his interlocutor liked the word—"Protestantized." But of course. A particular kind of Protestantism saturated the American nation in its early days; peculiarly vulnerable in part for the same reasons that it permeated the culture, as years wore on and institutions and points of view multiplied, it was permeated in return, creating the underlying American amalgam. If you read the descriptions of the characteristically "American" in the accounts of nineteenth-century European observers or twentieth-century social scientists, and then read descriptions (theirs or others') of the characteristics of mainline American Protestantism, you will find they are identical: individualistic, voluntaristic, "moralistic," ahistorical, self-reliant, proving worth by upward career, optimistic, philanthropically but not "politically" generous; a phrase like "practical idealism" bridges the two, if indeed they are distinct. And all of this could not help but affect the Lutherans, Catholics, Jews, and others who came into the nation in the period from the 1840s to the 1920s. It is of course often said that the immigrants became hyper-American, not only in the flag-waving but also in the cultural sense. This, too, had its religious dimension.

Nevertheless, even in early times the action was not all one way, and by the late twentieth century it has become another story. Among these immigrant religious communities there are most importantly the two to which Protestant Christianity is linked in what this nation in particular would learn to call the "Judeo-Christian tradition." And they have in common, although in utterly different ways, sharp contrasts to the prevailing American Protestant culture as it developed on two salient points: They are both communal-traditional-historical (and in the Catholic case institutional as well), as against the opposites of all those among the righteous dissidents of dissent in the New World, and they both have a high and serious intellectual tradition, which American Protestantism as it became pietistic and revivalist dropped over-board. The slightly utopian hope is that these historic religious communities can now do more affecting of the culture in *their* way, correcting what many would see to be limitations and faults—partic-ularly when it comes to what a "Republic" needs—in American Protestantism.

Judaism, of course, comprises such a comparatively small group in numbers as perhaps to make such a hope utopian indeed: about five and a half million American Jews, fewer than each of a number of Protestant denominational units, about the same as the number of Mormons, not a tenth of the number of Catholics, a smaller fraction still of the total number of Protestants. But Judaism has an importance to the American religiopolitical drama out of all proportion to its nu-merical membership—a distinct, complex, and essential relation to the central American tradition of religious liberty, and potentially to the American problem of the cultural-moral underpinnings of republican government as well. It is to be hoped that the emphasis on the latter will increase.

Jews have very strong reasons for a particular attachment to the separation of church and state. Judaism is a minority; it is a minority throughout the diaspora; it is a minority with a close kinship to the dominant religion, Christianity, which grew out of it and took over the Hebrew Bible as its Old Testament. It is a close-kin minority within Christendom which has experienced continuing waves and patterns of persecution, fed by the backdrop of Christian beliefs, and often at the hands of Christian authorities: the yellow badge, the ghetto, the po-grom, the Inquisition. Although there has been much anti-Semitism in popular Christian folk belief—"Jews and unbelievers"; in medieval myths Jews as poisoners of wells; an epithet carrying into modern times, "Christ-killer"—such belief was encouraged, and made into something worse, by the union of Christianity with the power of the state. In the Constantinian triumph of the church and combination with the Roman Empire, and in the emergence of medieval Christendom, the religious disagreement reflected in the partly shared, partly not shared scrip-tures—in which Jews who believed Jesus was the messiah and became Christians are arguing with Jews who did not—came to be established in patterns of social discrimination. In the high Middle Ages, in the period of Christianity's fullest triumph in the Western world, the Chris-tian discrimination against the Jews was institutionalized: The Fourth Lateran Council, under the greatest of the medieval popes, Innocent III, at the height of the power of the Christian Church, instituted the requirements that Jews must wear a special distinguishing yellow badge and live in a special separate section of the community, a ghetto.

After the Reformation the situation was not necessarily a great deal better; the pattern of national states in which the religion of the ruler was the religion of the nation continued legal discrimination—the religion of the ruler, in Europe, was always of course some form of Christianity—and the new Christian zeal and energy and scriptural authority the Reformation released were sometimes expressed in anti-Semitism. Martin Luther himself turned in his later days against the Jews, when they did not join the new church, and wrote a pamphlet against them that anti-Semitic organizations still reprint and use.

But the sociopolitical story of the life of Jews in Christendom is not only that of a *religious* minority. Jews were also what today we call an "ethnic" group, a separated minority. Although in the amiable popular American politeness that would develop in the twentieth century—in brotherhood gatherings of the sort that flourished after World War II—it would be implied that the three great religious communities that have come into portentous juxtaposition in this country are really at bottom similar, simply parallel versions of the same thing, in fact they are not. Reform Judaism in nineteenth-century Germany presented itself as just another choice in belief, like Methodism, without a necessary tie to a people. But historic Judaism differs from Christianity exactly in not being like that—not doctrinal and evangelical; it finds its expression not in creed or conversion but in the continuing communal and ritual life of a particular people. Judaism then suffered the compound of discriminations because of ethnicity with those based on religion: the need for a scapegoat, the nasty but persistent human inclination to hate the "stranger," the "out-group." It may be tied to economic conditions: When the crop was plentiful we ate, and gave to strangers; when the crop was poor, we ate, but did not give to the strangers; when the crop failed, we ate the strangers. A major multi-volume study published in the anguished aftermath of World War II—undertaken, with a kind of symbolism, by European refugees sponsored by the American Jewish Committee—found the kernel of anti-Semitism in the rigidity of mind and psyche, the inability to tolerate ambiguity and difference, that furnished the title of the study, *The Authoritarian Personality.*

The compound of ingredients that have made the anti-Semitism of Christendom, then, in the twentieth century helped to bring about the Holocaust, an event so horrific that the collective psyche of the Western world has still not absorbed it, if it ever can.

Although the Nazi madness was fired by an anti-Christian—"pagan"—ideology, the backdrop for the Holocaust, for making Jews the primary, although not the sole, victims of the mass killings, was a culture saturated with Christian teaching. A rabbi tells of the S.S. guards, at their party on Christmas Eve, singing, with tears in their eyes, "Silent Night, Holy Night . . . Round yon virgin mother and child," within the hearing of the Jews packed into railroad cars headed for death camps.

To return to an earlier time, and to the United States: Jews had sufficient reason, long before the twentieth century, to yearn for a land free of both religious and ethnic persecutions, discriminations, prejudices. It would be saying far too much to claim that the United States became that land. But it came closer than others.

In some parts of the left wing of the Protestant movement, as we have seen, there were ideas of religious toleration—the attitude of Cromwell and the Puritan Commonwealth toward Jews stands in contrast to most Christian states—and in the Enlightenment the reign of Reason was supposed to obliterate the prejudices and inhumanities of the past. These movements had the opportunity in the seventeenth and eighteenth centuries to build out of the materials of Europe a new world, and eventually to include at its foundation, religious liberty. And the separation of church from state.

There were only handfuls of Jews in the American colonies: a first settlement in New Amsterdam, in 1654, of Jews fleeing from Brazil; fifteen families coming to Newport in Roger Williams's Rhode Island in 1658; small groups in Charleston, Richmond, Savannah, and Philadelphia. Sydney Ahlstrom writes: "On the eve of the Revolution there was not a single rabbi in the American colonies. As late as 1800 all of American Jewry probably did not exceed two or three thousand."

But then after the nation's institutions were formed—including its institutions of religious liberty—there came to this most "Christian" of modern nations, especially in the decades beginning about a century after its founding, the largest Jewish population of any nation in Christendom. America became a haven for Jews from all over the world fleeing from pogroms and discrimination, seeking liberty: German Reform Jews in the 1840s, Orthodox Jews from Eastern Europe between the 1880s and the 1920s, coming to a new world—"asylum" indeed.

In the colonies and the early years of the nation the dominant prejudice associated with religion was not anti-Semitism but anti-Catholicism, and that of a more theological—idea-based and theoretical—type than came later, after the immigrations stirred nativism. America, with the "church" at last separated from the state, and with the Enlightenment's rationalism as part of its background, became a beacon for the Jews of Europe. The ugliest thread of religious discrimination in Christendom was broken in the formal structure of the United States. The fact is the more remarkable because a popular Christianity thrived here and a militant Christianity, with many official and unofficial discriminations against Jews, informed the most energetic colonies. But when the nation was formed, Judaism had no legal or formal disabilities; anti-Semitism has no support from the fundamental law of the nation. Furthermore there has been an ethos of freedom, encouraged by the constitutional arrangements, that has helped to limit popular prejudice. It is often said that Jews have felt more fully at home here than anywhere in the modern world until modern Israel came into being. (Israel represents many things, among them a great hope and idealism, though when American Jews go there they are sometimes disillusioned, finding human life as elsewhere. But Israel also may represent to American, and world, Jewry after the Holocaust a kind of grim realism. Let us say it is a practical principle that can be extracted from James Madison, extended to the scale of the *world*: Avoid depending entirely on the structure of conscience, goodwill, even law; secure a realistic basis for your own protection, too.)

It is by no means the case that anti-Semitism has been absent from the popular and social and political life of the United States. As American anti-Catholicism increased and changed character after the big Irish immigrations in the 1840s, so anti-Semitism, comparatively absent earlier, increased with the immigrations of Eastern European Jews of 1880–1920. Moreover, immigration added some Catholic—Polish for example—varieties of anti-Semitism to the native Protestant variety. But although there have been and continue to be many ugly episodes and backslidings—the Anti-Defamation League charts the annual ups and downs—and considerable anti-Semitism in American social life—polite in WASP clubs, quotas, and gentlemen's agreements, impolite and raw in backcountry stereotypes—and although the nation did not perform well with respect to the enormous test of the Holocaust (it failed, for example, to adapt an immigration policy to grant asylum, and its diplomats and leaders and non-Jewish citizens were late and shallow in responding; even forty years later this enormous human evil is often treated as though it were just a special concern of Jews as an interest group, like the price supports for milk for dairy farmers) it is nevertheless true, and significant, that this ugliest thread in all of Christendom at last was broken in the legal structure of the United

States, and the time may be coming when it is broken in society as well.

Jews have reasons, then, deep in their historical experience in Christendom, for unequivocal devotion not only to religious toleration and religious liberty but also to the separation of church and state—to a secular, or a nonreligious, civic order. And "Christian" history has instilled that devotion to the most thoroughgoing separation of church and state not only among secular but also among religious Jews in America. (Judaism worldwide, as an historic religious entity, has at the same time the contrary impulse, reflected to some degree in the present-day state of Israel.)

The strong endorsement of separation of church and state in America by religious Jews is sometimes hard for conservative Christians to understand. Some of the latter associate thoroughgoing church-state separation with aggressive, "unbelieving" secularism. But religious Jews have their reasons that are not "secular" at all.

An illustration: In the 1950s the New York Board of Regents, which guides public school policy for the state public school system, put forward (along with the "Regents' prayer" that was to become the occasion for the first U.S. Supreme Court prayer-in-the-schools case, in 1962) a "guiding statement," explaining how God, and a religious outlook, could be taught or at least "recognized," throughout the public school curriculum, from mathematics to manual training. This Regents' statement was like many others issued by school authorities, but it brought a distinctively revealing response in New York City, where the proportions of Catholics and Jews (fifty and thirty percent of the population respectively) at that time were such as to display with dramatic clarity the differences among the "three faiths of America": The Catholic Archdiocese promptly supported the statement; the Protestant Council of the City of New York, representing a constituency that ranged from strong supporters to strong opponents, debated awhile and finally made some comments that were partly appreciative but mostly critical; the New York Board of Rabbis solidly opposed it, issued a negative analysis of it, and organized concerted preaching against it in the city's temples and synagogues. The Jewish opposition was unanimous. Orthodox, Conservative, and Reform Jews stood side by side, and rabbis of quite widely differing positions in other matters joined together, five hundred strong, to preach against the statement throughout the city. A bemused Catholic priest remarked: "And they say *we* are monolithic!"

One reason for that unanimous clarity, of course, is the long history of persecution and present fact of minority status: For a child in a minority—especially *this* minority in Christendom—religion in a public setting can be an uncomfortable matter or worse. A non-Jew need only do a reversal and look at the situation from under hatches.

And in addition there is the particular nature of Judaism. In this episode in New York, as often elsewhere, the universal and doctrinal character of Christianity, especially Catholicism, bumped squarely against the communal and ritualistic character—the "peoplehood"—of Judaism. A Catholic, with his commitment to a fully worked-out, intellectually formulated truth for all men, may try to get as much of that truth as possible taught wherever he can—as for example, to every child in the schools: "Because we are convinced that moral and spiritual values have their ultimate source in God and are meaningless without God," said the Archdiocesan statement, "we are anxious to see God given due recognition in our public schools." (There are some historical ironies in this: The ways the dominant Protestants wanted to "recognize God" in the nineteenth century were one reason the Catholics started their own school system.) For a Jew, on the other hand, the formulations of "theology" do not have the same authority, and religious words are not so easily separated from the context of the ritual and history of the group. The Jew's faith resides instead in a whole fabric of historic observances of a particular law by a particular community. "We deny," said the rabbis, "that a non-Jewish teacher, however deeply devoted he may be to his own faith, can conscientiously and properly teach Jewish children the fundamentals of their faith."

So, for reasons that may be quite different from Jefferson's optimistic and universalistic rationalism, religious Jews in America became, retroactively as it were, far better allies of Jefferson in support of the statute than in the long run the Baptists proved to be.

Judaism is communal, traditional, historical, filled with memory, filled with social duty, as the Baptists and the Disciples are not. But from the fall of the Temple to the birth of modern Israel, through the centuries of dispersal, minority status, ghettoes, and persecution, Jewish communities have not, to put it mildly, been in a position to direct the destinies of great nations. Christians—and particularly the sorts of Biblical Protestant Christians who shaped the United States—have regularly turned to the Hebrew Bible when they wanted to be political: the Puritan leaders of the Commonwealth in England and John Winthrop in Massachusetts making their analogies to Israel in the Bible; in a very different way the American social gospel activists citing the prophets Amos and Micah and Hosea to ground the claims of justice in society and care for the oppressed. But although the contribution of persons who are at least ethnically Jewish—as humane social thinkers, responsible philanthropists, social reformers—to social and political understanding in the twentieth century has been very large, such contribution has not characteristically been connected with religious belief in the way it has been for American Christians.

Minority status has a lot to do with these matters—that is, how and whether a religious group takes into itself, in a fundamental way, as a religion, a sense of overarching social and political responsibility, and nurtures its adherents in that responsibility as part of religious belief itself. Obviously if you are too small a group to have any such responsibility you are not likely to develop the thought and feeling for it. Part of the American story after the Founding is that groups with the history and mentality of "sects" (in the narrow, proper sense, groups outside the structures of power and responsibility, withdrawing from "the world") come to occupy the position of a "church" (the ecclesiastical institution tied to and embracing the powers-that-be). For all their faults, those Virginia Anglicans did nurture those Virginian gentlemen in some sense of connection between the way one dealt with the ultimate mysteries and one's obligations to the social order. But the Baptists, once a small, despised collection of lower orders, looked down upon by the Anglican gentry, have come to be the biggest and most powerful church in (for example) Dallas, without acquiring in that transition a larger social and political understanding. Though now in the position of responsibility they carry still the leave-us-alone outlook developed in a situation of opposition, individualism, and rebellion.

The Jewish community, with respect to this matter, is quite another story, with interesting possibilities for this remarkable nation. Though certainly outsiders and a minority in the Christian world, Jews provided the scriptures with which Christianity developed its foundation of political understanding, insofar as that understanding is Biblical—as in the varieties of Protestantism that shaped America, it very much was "ethical monotheism," as it used to be put, one God of all peoples whose significance for human life has centrally to do with that justice that is to run down as waters, and righteousness as a mighty stream. Moreover, Judaism has of course an immense heritage of social responsibility...often expressed, however, by the "spent Jew" who has left religious connections behind. The time may be coming when a religious Judaism can be a more vocal part of the American conversation, helping to shape not only the Jewish community but non-Jewish America as well, and not only on a standard set of issues, but as part of the cultural perspective from which all "issues" are seen. This country can represent in fact, and not just in a slogan, the Judeo-Christian tradition.

In perhaps the most remarkable of all the remarkable developments of this New World's system of religious liberty, the Roman Catholic Christianity against which its founding movements were rebelling has come, after two centuries, to be its single most important religious presence. It is becoming one of the most significant sources of political understanding as well.

The warring Protestant and Catholic branches of Christianity (the religion of love, fighting its bloody way through Western history) have come at the very least to a peaceful coexistence. At several levels of life it already is a good deal more than that. The eighteenth-century Enlightenment rationalism in which the nation was born finds itself now in conversation with an older tradition of reason, carried by a Catholic church from whose mystery, miracle, and authority it once thought itself to be liberating humankind.

With respect to this ancient opponent the "generous policy" of the New World was not always so generous, at least in social practice. The conjoined movements in seventeenth-century England that were to form the mind of the new nation across the seas, the Enlightenment and the Puritans, each had as its ultimate enemy the Church of Rome, which was also, not incidentally for Englishmen, the Church of Spain and of France. The Puritans who settled the most energetic colonies and put their stamp everlastingly on America of course wanted to "purify" the Church of England by stripping it of the vestiges of "popery." We have noted that the eminent acquaintances Roger Williams made on his trips to London in the days of the Civil War and Commonwealth, Oliver Cromwell and John Milton, though tolerant up to a point, did not share Williams's willingness to extend toleration all the way to "papists." In Milton's great invocation of the power of truth against all the winds of doctrine, the *Areopagitica*, as we noted above when contrasting him to Roger Williams, Milton turns out not to mean exactly *all* the winds of doctrine: "But as for popery and idolatry...Their religion the more considered, the less can be acknowledged a religion, but a Roman principality rather...who know it not to be evidently against all scripture, both of the Old and the New Testament." One of Milton's last pamphlets was subtitled "What means may be used against the growth of Popery." If that was true of Milton, who became one of the more tolerant Puritans, how much more was it true of his generally less tolerant brethren who crossed the Atlantic to set up their Godly City on a hill. The "republican" ideology out of which came the American Revolution and the American Constitution was thus nurtured in an environment of nonconforming, dissenting Protestantism, of sectarianism, of puritanism, of a Whig outlook, and of the Enlightenment, too—all of which had Rome and "popery" and authority of the church and the Catholic powers of Europe as opponents in the realm of ideas, and often also as enemies in the realm of power.

In fact one of those events that led to the final break of the colonies from England had in it a considerable component of anti-Catholicism. This was the colonials' response to a stunning act of Parliament— stunning to the English colonies—the Quebec Act of 1774, a somewhat quizzical episode in the mighty history of liberty in America.

In the Quebec Act, Parliament not only recognized French Canadian sovereignty down through the Northwest territory to the Ohio River but freed French Catholics from the traditional oath of loyalty to the Crown and granted them full freedom of religion. Looked at from the English side—not to mention the French Canadian side—this action may be seen as yet another step in the great march of religious liberty. No doubt our American forefathers should have seen it that way, too. But they did not; they saw it as a threat to *their* liberty, and yet another in the series of unconscionable acts—one of the five "Intolerable Acts"— of the English authorities. One can even find in the very Declaration of Independence itself—the new nation's reigning statement of its moral meaning to the world—a veiled reference to this Quebec Act as a serious threat on the part of the king to the liberty of Englishmen. "He has combined with others"—that means Parliament, which Jefferson and the Continental Congress of course did not recognize—"giving his Assent to their Acts of pretended [*sic!*] Legislation . . . For abolishing the free System of English Laws in a neighbouring Province, establishing therein an Arbitrary government, and enlarging its Boundaries so as to render it at once an example and fit instrument for introducing the same absolute rule into these Colonies [*states*]."

Of course there was in this apprehension of the colonists a heavy political element, but it was ideological at the same time, and prominent in the ideology was a rejection of Catholicism as an enemy of liberty.

Canon Stokes includes in his amiable and celebratory account of the American accomplishment a nicely ambiguous section on the Quebec Act: "the most significant official declaration involving religious toleration covering a large area of the continent prior to American independence." But it was of course an official declaration not by the Americans-to-be, but by their *opponents* of the time, the English Parliament, and very much against the "American" grain. Stokes lists and quotes founding fathers—Hamilton, Samuel Adams, John Adams—and popular colonial opinion attacking the act. "Much more is to be dreaded from the growth of Popery in America," said Sam Adams, "than from Stamp Acts or *any other* Acts destructive of men's *civil* rights." An American versifier wrote:

> If Gallic Papists have a right
> To worship their own way
> Then farewell to the Liberties,
> Of poor America.

And the Pennsylvania *Packet* warned: "We may live to see our churches converted into mass houses and our lands plundered by tythes for the support of the Popish clergy...and the city of Philadelphia may yet experience the carnage of St. Bartholemew's day."

In summary Canon Stokes wrote: "The Quebec Act is considered to have been on the whole a wise and farsighted one on the part of a dominantly Protestant nation dealing with the large Roman Catholic population of an important province." Moreover, he continued, the Act, despite the colonists' apprehensions in 1774, was in the longer run to become one of the sources of the liberal policy regarding religion that would mark the Northwest Ordinance of 1787. It was a contribution to the American heritage, though it was not exactly the work of the "Americans" themselves.

It may be argued that the American Revolution, religious liberty, and the radical new arrangements between church and state had a more abrupt and far-reaching significance for Roman Catholicism than for any other group.

In the English colonies Catholics had been a very small minority— perhaps 25,000 by 1790—mostly in Maryland and Pennsylvania, an insignificant cultural drop in a vast sea of English, Scotch Irish, Dutch, German—but mostly English—Protestant Christianity and English Whig republicanism. Then came the Revolution, the Constitution, the First Amendment, the new nation. Already by 1850 there were perhaps 1,600,000 Roman Catholics, constituting the largest single religious institution in the nation.

Let us recapitulate and dramatize these changes in numbers after the founding and the radical new religious policy. The Methodist movement, a minority movement that came into independent existence just in 1784, spread so rapidly as to be the largest religious group in the new nation by 1844. The Baptists, the scattered collection of sectarian outsiders in the late eighteenth century, would also explode in numbers in the new nation, passing the Methodists, becoming the largest Protestant grouping, as they remain today. The Disciples of Christ, altogether nonexistent at the nation's founding, put together on the American frontier out of several impulses to return to "primitive Christianity," would spread rapidly enough to pass the old English groups—the Congregationalists and the Episcopalians—and almost the Presbyterians. And then the Roman Catholics made a dramatic rise like that, too, and in roughly the same period—in the ferment of the first half of the nineteenth century. In the 1830s and 1840s the Catholics passed all of those old colonial denominations—and then they passed all the popular new denominations, too.

But the story for Catholicism had a different source, and a different cultural setting. The popular Protestant denominations, powered by revivals, rose on the wave of a spreading democratic spirit in the expanding West in the Jacksonian era, building, as they saw it, a Christian America out across the continent. The Catholics, on the other hand, coming into a new land, by boat rather than by conversion, usually from Ireland, escaping the terrible hunger in the potato famine, ran up against barriers, not least from the Christianizers of America.

In the Second Great Awakening and the settlement of the West "infidelity" was one enemy, but "popery" was the other. Saving the West from "Romanism" and "popery" were quite explicit objectives of many of the leaders of the revivals of the first half of the nineteenth century—of Lyman Beecher, for example, heading out for Cincinnati to become the leader of the Lane Seminary. Opposition to Catholicism was one of the bases upon which the competing Protestant denominations could unite. As happens on other issues in other times, the heightened and inflammatory language of some of the Protestant leaders led to acts of violence by some of their followers, notably the burning of an Ursuline convent in the Boston area in 1834.

A segment of American Evangelical Protestantism greeted the members of the Roman Catholic Church from Ireland in the 1840s with "No Irish Need Apply" signs, with nativism, the Know-Nothing Party, and best-selling novels about sensational doings in convents. Few Americans today, non-Catholics anyway, appreciate how widespread anti-Catholic feeling was in nineteenth-century America. Interpretations of the First Amendment itself often turned out to have an anti-Catholic flavor; sometimes one can detect a trace of that even today. The term "religious liberty," in some sectarian groups, has overtones, as the explication and illustrations indicate, of categorical anti-Catholic animus.

There was enough anti-Catholic prejudice remaining almost to dominate the presidential election of 1928, and to distort the election of 1960. Not all of it came from the Protestants of the West and South, although the election returns indicate that much of it did. (There was also—almost forgotten now—a good deal of opposition to Kennedy, with anti-Catholic overtones, among the urban intelligentsia, in the period 1956–60, before his nomination. Theodore Sorensen, the Unitarian from Nebraska who was the earliest active exponent of a Kennedy presidency, said thoughtfully one day in the late 1950s that he now saw what was meant by the old European epigram, "Anti-Catholicism is the anti-Semitism of the intellectuals.")

One strongly suspects that "church-and-state" was not John F. Kennedy's favorite subject. He has, nevertheless, a kind of inadvertent importance in the American history of that matter. He has such importance not only because he was the first Roman Catholic to be president and perhaps, in his truncated term, a successful president, and certainly an attractive one, but also because of the two-pronged directness with which he dealt with church-and-state.

Kennedy used to its maximum effectiveness, against the lingering anti-Catholic animus in American society, that rhetorical device in which the speaker first makes a statement with which his bearers are known wholchcartedly to agrcc—and follows with another, entailing the same principle, which they must then (perhaps reluctantly) concede. First of all, he gave the bluntest reassurances about church-state separation. An ambassador to the Vatican? "Flatly opposed." Funds for parochial schools? "I'm opposed to the federal government's extending support." Direct aid to religious schools is "clearly unconstitutional." Birth control issues? The "public interest" would determine them. Church and state? "Strict separation.... The first amendment is ... infinitely wise." This continued throughout his candidacy and his presidency—blunt, flat, direct, explicit, repeated, absolute.

Moreover, during the West Virginia primary in 1960 (which he had to enter because he needed to show he could win in a heavily Protestant and—may we be pardoned for putting it this way—rather unvarnished Protestant state) he invited a Protestant academic with a West Virginia background onto his campaign plane, and got a dose of a rather special meaning of "religious liberty": Explain that the pope will not "tell you what to do." He then went out of his way to insist on his freedom from any churchly "dictate," and in the following September, in his notable Houston speech to Texas Baptist and other preachers, he gave a pledge to *resign* should there be any conflict between his religious "conscience" and his oath to uphold the Constitution.

That sentence had a history. In *Look* magazine, in March 1959, just as his candidacy was blossoming, and he was venturing out into these rough waters of religious controversy, Mr. Kennedy had said, "For the officeholder, nothing takes precedence over this oath to uphold the Constitution." This way of formulating his point brought severe lectures from the religious press on the primacy of conscience, on the priority of loyalty to God over loyalty to the state, and even on the way totalitarianism follows from unqualified allegiance to the nation. But of course Kennedy was caught between the unvarnished evangelical Protestant stereotypes of the Roman Catholic church on the one side, and the varnished conceptions of sophisticated theologians on the other. If you are running for office, you must pay somewhat more attention to the former. Kennedy obviously was not exploring the ranking of ultimate loyalties; he was just reassuring those who needed the reassurance that if and when he took the oath to uphold the Constitution he would mean just what he said. After the first loud negative reactions to Kennedy's statement, there came more careful and favorable ones— among them, three columns by John Cogley in *Commonweal* and a letter by Arthur Schlesinger, Jr., in *Christianity and Crisis.* Talking about the incident later, Kennedy cited Cogley's columns with some satisfaction. The West Virginia primary, the Houston speech, Kennedy's presidency in general, represented an interesting, if perhaps somewhat distressing moment in American history, a confrontation of two variant meanings of "religious liberty." In a certain kind of older Protestant stereotype, a Roman Catholic cannot believe in or represent true "religious liberty"—Isaac Backus's religious liberty, let us say—because he (this devout Catholic) is *told* what to do and believe by the pope or the hierarchy or the church or his priest, and his "conscience" is therefore not "free." Kennedy in 1959–60 had to have a crash course in that outlook, the State of Massachusetts not being a particularly good school in the matter.

Kennedy did not respond with resentment, dismissal, or argument; he did not say, as did Catholic journals: "This kind of cross-examination, directed as it is solely at Catholics, as Catholics, is discriminatory, insulting" or that "such groveling is not required of Baptists" or that the stereotype was a ridiculous misconception of Catholic life. Instead, he replied with direct, repeated, explicit denial and reassurance. By the time of the Houston speech he had changed the form of his remarks about the oath to that dramatic pledge to resign: "If the time should ever come—and I do not concede any conflict to be remotely possible—when my office would require me either to violate my conscience, or violate the national interest, then I would resign the office." And he made a significant addition: "I hope any other conscientious public servant would do likewise." Thus he hinted to anti-Catholic critics that any person of conscience, certainly any serious religious person, might appropriately be asked all the questions about conflicts between personal moral conviction and state policy that were so insistently asked of him.

The joke was that he turned out, in effect, to be our first Southern Baptist President—one, that is, who defended a thoroughgoing separation more characteristic of that group than of his own church. "The American people," one journal observed, "... elected a Catholic president whose interpretation of the proper relation of church and state would have driven Orestes Brownson and Leo XIII into a suicide pact." This was, of course, a political necessity in that time and that situation, like Jackie Robinson keeping his temper. It did have consequences for Kennedy's presidency. Sorensen observed in the midst of it, on the then conflicted effort to pass federal aid to education, that a compromise could be worked out with the roadblock over aid to parochial schools— but not by the nation's first Catholic president. (Such a compromise *was* effected by his successor, a sufficiently unvarnished Disciples-of-Christ Texan.)

But all of that flat reassurance about absolute separation of church and state (religious liberty in that sense) on Kennedy's part was tied to another meaning of religious liberty that his hearers could scarcely deny: *equal* treatment for *all* creeds. "Do you mean that forty million Americans lost the chance to be president when they were baptized?" Kennedy used that line in the Houston speech and many other times. Repeatedly he made reassuring statements of the one kind and then followed with companion implications of the other: Yes, we would not violate the Constitution's absolute separation of church and state— *and* we would not violate, even by implication, the Constitution's prohibition of a religious test. The Houston speech is a case study in the rhetorical device described above.

In the West Virginia primary he had underlined the service of Catholics, like the Kennedys, in war; he did so again in his Houston speech, and he also noted that men with Irish and Spanish names fell at the Alamo and "no one knows whether they were Catholics or not" (no one did, including the Kennedy staff; they had not found out in time for the speech).

Kennedy's presidency happened by fortunate historical accident to occur at exactly the time of great events within his own church. John XXIII was named pope in 1958. John's call for an opening of windows and a modernizing within the Roman Catholic Church, and his convening of the Second Vatican Council, were of the greatest historical significance. They were more important within the religious world than anything having to do with President Kennedy. In the domain of public affairs, however, the two figures and regimes complemented and reinforced each other. The first three sessions of the Vatican Council came in the three years that Kennedy was president. The two world figures, Roman Catholics named John, died in the same year, 1963. The extraordinary changes in the atmosphere set in motion in their short overlapping regimes have continued to the present day. In 1984 a national political figure from the West, the Republican party chairman Senator Paul Laxalt, speaking at his party's national convention, would indict a leading spokesman for the other party, a Catholic, Governor Mario Cuomo of New York, not for following his bishop but for *not* following his bishop (who advocated the outlawing of abortion). And, a quarter of a century after Kennedy, it is possible for the substance of Catholic thought to enter into the whole nation's conversation as perhaps not in his day—not by his agency because as it happened he did not represent it.

The first member of the ancient Church of Rome, the intellectual bastion of the perennial philosophy of Natural Law and the major institutional opponent of the skeptical, reductionist, relativist, and pragmatic philosophies of modernity—of the Enlightenment, of "liberalism," even at one point of "Americanism"—turned out to be the first man of a thoroughly modern "pragmatic" temper to occupy the White House. Kennedy's own outlook was not that of the perennial philosophy rooted in Aristotle and Aquinas, the tradition of Reason with a capital letter, of objective Truth and of received Dogma; it was instead markedly empirical, skeptical, unideological, thoroughly in tune with that "technical reason" that the best of Catholic thinkers find a limitation of the age.

The old anti-Catholicism, and the barriers to mutual influence, have not vanished entirely, but the window openings by Pope John XXIII, and Vatican II, and the presidency of John Kennedy, and the maturing of both the Protestant and Catholic populations under the tutelage of the American system of liberty, have brought about at least a more harmonious, and perhaps soon a more substantive, relationship than the history of these antagonists and of this country's founding might have led one to expect.

If Catholic Christianity was perceived to be a kind of ultimate opponent by the movements most immediately associated with the forming of the United States—that is, Puritan and sectarian Protestantism and the Enlightenment—it may 200 years later prove to be a chief source of correction to the exaggerated effect of their limitations.

Of those limitations, at least with respect to American Protestantism, perhaps enough, or too much, has already been unkindly said. The immense, historic, worldwide "Catholic" institution has within it resources that American Protestantism has lacked, and that the sort of government and society which was the original American project—let us call it again a Republic—requires. As we have seen, Jefferson's negative or "liberating" proposals—most notably the Virginia Statute—were enacted, but his constructive proposals, for nurture in civic republicanism in the schools, were not. And as we have said, the dissidence of dissent of American Protestantism had at its center "liberation" from past communal constraints, not the construction of a new social order. So then, into the nation shaped by these forces would come their ancient primary enemy—now to do its communal, constructive work on cultural ground that they had cultivated.

"The common good," the central term—the res publica—is a theme running down through the Catholic ages. Catholicism, like Judaism in a different way, may bring to this excessively individualistic American Protestant culture that sense of life being bound up with life, of "solidarity," as say not just the Polish but other trade unionists and French Catholic thinkers, and many others—the awareness, as part of the fundamental religious insights and commitment, of the interweaving of human beings in community. All of that—a personalistic communitarianism, let us call it, may be distinguished both from the collectivisms of our much-denounced world adversaries and from the all too individualistic libertarianism created by the forces—very much including our sort of Protestantism—that have combined to build a prevalent form of American culture. Something like such a personalistic communitarianism is the necessary base for a true republic in the interdependent world of the third century of this nation's existence. And the Roman Catholic community is the most likely single source of it—

the largest and intellectually and spiritually most potent institution that is the bearer of such ideas.

Also of intellect in political morality—of the tradition of reason as applied to complex matters of collective life. The shock of nuclear weapons, and then the shock of Vietnam, sent many non-Catholics hitherto disdainful of such moral reasoning back to the ancient Catholic tradition of reflection on the question of just wars.

After the triumph of pietism the intellect was not American Protestantism's strong point; Sidney Mead saw the negative side to the development of religion in America in its loss of intellectual structure; Richard Hofstadter found it to be a source of American anti-intellectualism. Mead quoted Henry Steele Commager: "It is scarcely an exaggeration to say that during the nineteenth century and well into the twentieth, religion flourished while theology slowly went bankrupt. From Edwards to Royce, America did not produce a first-rate religious philosopher."

The strong intellectual component of Puritanism, of the Reformed tradition, and of other structured Protestant traditions was washed away in nineteenth-century America by the wave of revivals, and the growth of the churches of the common man, the triumph of pietism, and of a Romantic Christianity. In American religious culture the heart would win out over the head, one might say (if it were not anatomically confusing) hands down.

And of course the effect is not simply the evaporation of distinguished theology and religious philosophy, but of respect for the intellect in other lines of work as well, and not for intellectual workers only but for one's own intellectual powers. And in particular with respect to "moral" matters. About "moral" matters one is supposed to know, or feel, what is "right"—right away, and with certainty, from a text in the Bible, or the "heart," or the conscience. The American Protestant ethos—therefore the American ethos—resisted the concept, and even the word, *casuistry*, revealingly turning it into a pejorative. *Talmudic* may have suffered almost the same fate. But these were, and are, honorable words for honorable traditions, reflecting something very much needed, perhaps especially in a complicated modern republic in a complicated modern world. Where moral issues are complicated, one needs casuistry, not instant certainty. Where there is disagreement, one needs reason, argument, and conversation. One also needs something like "natural law," which term non-Catholics have taught themselves to be frightened of by their stereotypes of, and sometimes perhaps their experiences with, Catholicism. One needs something of authority—an ambiguous but necessary contribution to the radically anti-authoritarian American libertarian-Protestant culture. And then one needs being open to other pieces of truth's body, on which point, for all its limitations, America and American Protestantism may be better than the historic Catholic world. The latter, with its claims to finality in central matters of faith and morals, sometimes exhibits an inclination to creeping infallibility out from the center.

Suppose then, one says Catholicism needs to be itself affected and modified by its experience in American "Protestant" democracy, a democracy that, with all its faults, has in it social goods that it does seem unlikely an originally Catholic culture would have produced. Suppose one adds that that classically liberal, once Protestant, culture now needs what a Catholic community can supply. So would one come out with a result in social philosophy better than either at the beginning; so would American pluralism work at its best, by a positive internal dynamic very much different from the more external watch-out-for-each-other balancing that our friend Madison had in mind.

Father Murray sometimes startled his non-Catholic colleagues, as together they explored "Religion and the Free Society," by his view of religious liberty. Once he offered the famous distinction, best known in the presentation by Isaiah Berlin, between *negative* liberty, meaning the "mere" absence of restraint (you are "free" to fly to the moon; nobody's stopping you) and *positive* liberty, meaning the providing of the means, or ability—in Father Murray's word, *empowerment* (here's a space ship to make your moon-reaching freedom effective). And he said that the American proposition supported a *positive* religious liberty—empowerment. Many colleagues around the table stirred uneasily at that idea. And stirred still more when the religion whose liberty was to be empowered turned out to mean exclusively the traditional religious groups of the West—agnostics and atheists and oddballs could get their liberty (negative only, presumably) under some other provision—free speech perhaps.

But then the American Catholic thinker who caused this uneasy stirring in the American setting, became in Rome, in the world Catholic setting of the Second Vatican Council, a chief author of the window-opening statement on religious liberty which revised the older Catholic position that "error has no rights." Without presuming to claim that Father Murray himself needed to be influenced by any lesser beings, one may nevertheless use this sequence as a symbol: So might the American environment, even the Protestant American environment, have a desirable effect on a world church that is now so powerful a presence in its midst, and American Catholicism in turn an effect upon the whole church. But meanwhile, back in America in the late twentieth century, now is the moment for Catholicism to have its desirable effect upon the America within which at last it is coming to be at home.

That there can be negative effects of American religious pluralism is obvious; it almost inevitably has a trivializing effect, a relativizing effect, upon popular religion. And there certainly can be a negative dynamic as well: the groups bringing out the worst in each other, contributing their worst to each other. The contending popular movements in the late twentieth century dealing with the deep and serious and complicated moral issue of abortion with absolutistic simplicism are examples; there are problems about the so-called pro-choice movement, too, but it is a disappointment to see a considerable segment of the American Catholic world displaying in the 1970s and 1980s, on the issue of abortion, the absolutistic moral-political method that has marked too much of the social and political role of American Protestantism: the isolated, sharply defined crusade, focused on one issue, with its "moral" dimension made final, without compromise or listening; a crusade, rousing the troops, without much recourse to the tradition of reason. This method is deeply flawed, whether it be employed on an issue large or small, whether the adherent be inclined to the right or to the left. It characterized the meat-ax approach of Wayne Wheeler of the Anti-Saloon League (better to drink wet and vote dry than the other way round), a pan-Protestant pressure group for Prohibition. It also characterized the more extreme of the abolitionists. It is much to be deplored that the dispute over abortion, with all its human quandary, has been heightened, simplified, and vulgarized as it has. One wishes that in the debate, in which religious groups have been so much involved, had been displayed more depth, wisdom, and generosity.

In the longer term, however, one pictures and hopes for something else: a reciprocating deep pluralism in which the several communities affect each other for the better, not just by overt actions on the issues, but in the much more important indirect way, by their seepage into that true melting pot, this unique culture of which they are all a part.

THE ESTABLISHMENT CLAUSE
COMES TO SOUTH MESA BLUFFS

We set aside at the beginning of these concluding reflections the narrower issues—the modern issues—of church and state as they arise
under the federal Constitution, and as they have come in the last four
decades to cause public excitement. We provided, by way of reminder,
although perhaps no reader needed it, a little list of the loci in which
such issues have arisen. As we remarked then, to see these matters in
perspective is to see that the significance of the great shaping decision
of the late eighteenth century on religious liberty and church and state
reaches far beyond the issues that create certain public churning in the
middle of the twentieth. These disputes about the constitutional law
on church and state arose, really rather recently, after the long mainline
Protestant cultural hegemony had weakened, and perhaps even as a
sign of its weakening. They arose—these modern church-state cases,
and the disputes that have followed in their wake—as a stronger modern
post-ghetto Catholic presence was beginning to be felt nationwide (it
had of course long been felt in certain cities and states); it would surely
not be mistaken to ascribe some of the heat surrounding these disputes
to anti-Catholic and Catholic feeling. And these cases began their course
at a time, or just following a time, when the—what is the term one
should use?—intelligentsia (perhaps including law school students who
become judges) had been furthest from any commitment to, interest
in, or understanding of, religious matters. It was as though the religion
clauses of the First Amendment had been held in escrow for a century
and a half while the social and religious implications of the arrangement
they symbolized and all the forces of the modern world had worked
themselves out in American history in the ways we have been suggesting, and then when the dynamics of pluralism had created a sufficiently complicated cultural scene, those clauses were brought out of

the vault and given pointed and, as they say in the papers, "controversial," applications. And segments of the public gave also their "controversial" responses.

So in these altered conditions of the middle of the twentieth century—let us say—that imaginary situation we conjured up earlier about the fundamentalist minister inscribing John 3:16 on the water fountain at the city softball park becomes an imaginary case. Let us call it *Murchison* v. *Municipal Softball League*. Let us say that it will wind its way through the intricate court system that James Madison helped to work out in the First Congress, all the way up to the United States Supreme Court. It will come to that highest court, the magisterial interpreter of the supreme law of the land, even though the specific issue at hand might seem to be rather a small matter in the scheme of events in the nuclear age. It will be agreed by all the multiplying lawyers and advocacy groups and friends of the court on both sides— the one thing they agree on—that there are great principles at stake.

The case will be decided by the Supreme Court (5–4, with two concurring opinions, one concurring only in part, and two separate dissents), thus promulgating more or less great principles, all across this great land, even though the city council of South Mesa Bluffs, with some encouragement from the Reverend Billy Bob Smathers and his Moral Christian American Athletes for God, will have passed an ordinance specifically granting the softball league permission to place the Biblical inscription on the water fountain at the softball park.

How is it possible that the otherwise legitimate decision of this democratically elected legislative body, supported by a clear majority of the citizens of the town, could be overthrown by a distant court? By—as the Reverend Mr. Smathers would say, in his own syntax—"a bunch of lousy brainless, black-robed atheists sitting in Washington that nobody elected"? It is possible because of the Constitution—the Constitution and judicial review—and some important decisions the Court had made, and was to make, about the Constitution's meaning.

The United States has that written Constitution that James Madison and his fellow workers in Philadelphia constructed in the summer of 1787. It has the first ten amendments, added by Madison and others in 1789–91, with the First Amendment's provisions for religious liberty and nonestablishment. This Constitution (as so amended) is the Supreme Law of the Land, superseding the actions of all the other engines of government, even though chosen by majority votes, where those actions contravene the Constitution. The Constitution represents a one-time superior ground-rules-defining action by the whole people putting limits upon itself—upon all subsequent particular actions of its governmental instruments.

And who shall determine when such actions conflict with the Constitution? The courts. This last is the remarkable institution of judicial review put forward already by "Publius" in *The Federalist*, in number Seventy-eight, it is usually said, and perhaps elsewhere as well: "Whenever a particular statute contravenes the Constitution, it will be the duty of the judicial tribunals to adhere to the latter and disregard the former." The doctrine of judicial review was then secured into the American constitutional system by the decisions of the Virginia colleague (and mostly opponent) of Jefferson and Madison, Chief Justice John Marshall, especially, it will be remembered, in the case called *Marbury* v. *Madison*.

THE FOURTEENTH AMENDMENT BRINGS IN THE STATES

But despite all this the First Amendment, and the rest of the Bill of Rights, could be applied only to the federal government. Although James Madison had tried, as we have seen, to secure a federal constitutional protection against *state* infringements of liberty in the First Congress, he failed, and the federal Bill of Rights applied only to the *national* government (Justice Marshall was to reaffirm that in a case in 1833). The First Amendment, as it came out of that conference committee in 1789, said only that "*Congress* shall make no law..." How then did that mighty federal restriction come to be applied to so humble and remote an engine of human government, very far from Congress, as the South Mesa Bluffs Municipal Softball League? The answer, of course, is complicated.

It came so to be applied because eventually there was added to the Constitution, after the Civil War, the Fourteenth Amendment, which provided, in the course of its protections for the newly freed ex-slaves, that *no state* shall deprive any person of life, *liberty*, or property without *due process* of law. (These last words are borrowed directly, of course, from the *Fifth* Amendment—the point is now specifically to apply that part of the Bill of Rights to the states.) Each of those highlighted words was to have a meaning important to this story. "No state" would mean, though it might not seem to, no lesser level of government. No deprivation of "liberty" without "due process" would come to mean, though it might not seem to, no government aid for religion.

In other words, to hold that no *state* can deprive any person of liberty means that no "creature" of a state like a county, a school board, or a city government can do so either. It means that the federal Constitution's protections of liberty will apply not only to Congress and therefore to all of the other parts of the federal government for which Congress is the lawmaking arm, but also to the actions of the states of West Virginia, Pennsylvania, Ohio, Connecticut, South Dakota, Oregon (et cetera) and therefore to all the lesser levels of government for which *they* are the ultimate lawmaking arm—to the actions, for example, of the city councils of Opelika, Alabama; Struthers, Ohio; Jeannette, Oregon; Dallas, Texas; Havre de Grace, Maryland; and (with an odd little historical echo because Roger Williams once owned it) to Pawtucket, Rhode Island; and therefore to all the parts and levels of local government for which *they* are the lawmaking arm, including a city board of recreation that has official softball in its province, and a city park department that causes official drinking water to flow at its command.

And it applies also—very important—to the actions of school boards (for example in real cases in Ewing Township in New Jersey and Champaign, Illinois; all of the states and towns listed above appear in real church-state cases, too). And to the Tax Commission of the City of New York. To *all* of the pieces and parts of the many-layered American governmental system, because none of these lower entities—counties, cities, school boards—has any *constitutional* existence; they are, rather, "creatures" of the states. Even New York City and Chicago have no constitutional existence; legally speaking, they are created by their respective states, and sometimes they are made to feel it. That is why there are those contests in state capitals over degrees of "home rule"— why New Haven and Bridgeport must go more or less humbly, though grinding their collective teeth, to Hartford, to be permitted to do this or that; why one can sit in the state capital in Raleigh and hear Carolina legislators debating the names of particular streets in particular North Carolina towns. The Fourteenth Amendment, by restricting states, restricts thereby *every* part and level, however lowly, of the entire American governmental system. And thus it is that there is that link between our fictitious South Mesa Bluffs Municipal Softball League and the nation's highest judicial tribunal two thousand miles away.

THE NATIONALIZATION OF THE FIRST AMENDMENT

But then what do "liberty" and "due process" in the Fourteenth Amendment include? What is it that the states are forbidden to infringe? In 1925 the Supreme Court discovered that the Fourteenth Amendment "incorporated" some of the protections of liberty in the First Amendment. It later (in 1934, 1940, and 1947) found that the Fourteenth Amendment "incorporated" or "absorbed" others—perhaps even all—of the protections in the federal Bill of Rights ... and thereby now applied them to the states. (There was, and still is, lawyerly dispute over the different terms—"incorporation," "absorption," "carry-over"—for the way the Fourteenth Amendment soaked into its being parts of the first ten amendments.)

So that is the explanation for the long hiatus in federal church-state cases before 1940, and the outbreak of cases since. Before those decisions, church-state matters arising in the states—which meant almost all cases—were not subject to review by the federal courts, and therefore did not fall under U.S. Supreme Court adjudication. The only church-state cases that came under federal jurisdiction in the nineteenth and early twentieth centuries arose in unusual circumstances: because some dispute crossed state lines, or, as in the Mormon polygamy cases of the late nineteenth century, because Utah and Idaho were still federal territories at the time.

In 1934 and 1940 the Supreme Court decided that among the liberties the Fourteenth incorporated, and which now applied to the states, was the First Amendment provision protecting the "free exercise" of religion. That was not, perhaps, so surprising; "free exercise" is a fundamental *liberty*, after all. But then there came another decision that was by no means so easily digested. In that 1947 New Jersey bus-fare case that the reader may remember from Part Two—the case that thrust Mr. Jefferson and his wall, and James Madison and his *Memorial*, back into the center of twentieth-century argument about these matters—the Court managed to find that the Fourteenth Amendment "incorporated" the "establishment clause" of the First Amendment, too. So now—as not formerly—no *state* could violate whatever it is the First Amendment prohibits not only by its provisions about liberty but also by its phrase "no law respecting an establishment of religion." To put it another way, whatever meaning the U.S. Supreme Court gave to the establishment clause was now nationalized, to be applied *everywhere*.

This finding by the Court, about the Fourteenth Amendment "incorporating"—nationalizing—not just some, but all of the First Amendment, has more than a technical significance, although in its particulars, as the reader may have discerned, it is one of the more complicatedly technical matters in the dusty reaches of American constitutional law. (Henry Abraham, in his extremely useful book *Freedom and the Court*, gives a lucid, fact-filled, chart-accompanied account.) By applying these federal guarantees to the *states* the Court in effect shuts off (for good or ill) state and local diversity on the matters to which it is found to apply. After these interpretations by the U.S. Supreme Court all of the cases that for a century and more were decided at the state level now rose to the federal level, and therefore potentially came to the Supreme Court. Now, in effect, *all* church-state disputes potentially fall under the jurisdiction of the federal courts.

So, however the lawmaking bodies and the majority of the citizens of South Mesa Bluffs may feel about it, and whatever the *state* constitution and lawmaking bodies would allow, all of these lower entities now potentially may be overruled by the federal courts, and the lower federal courts by the U.S. Supreme Court, applying to them their construction of the phrase in the First Amendment, "no law respecting an establishment of religion."

STATE AND NATION: LETTING A HUNDRED FLOWERS BLOOM, BUT NOT THE WEEDS

Let us pause a minute on this matter of the Fourteenth and the First, the federal government and the states, although we are eager to get back to South Mesa Bluffs and its fountain. At stake in this apparently recondite matter of constitutional law there is a fairly straightforward issue of American political philosophy (there was a long period in the middle of the twentieth century when there did not seem to *be* any active American political philosophy, except as squeezed into the law— and there did not often seem to be any there, either). The issue is, as they say in the textbooks, federalism, or federal government and state government, or national power and local power, national principles and local diversity.

Madison and his co-workers in Philadelphia devised a feature that many had hitherto thought impossible: each citizen fully subject not to *one* but to *two* governments, the federal and the state (and all the state entails). The new federal government acted (alongside the state) directly upon the individual citizen, as the central government under the Articles of Confederation had not. (Most of the laws we abide by are state laws, or city ordinances that rest upon state power; if we work at it, though, we can abide by some federal laws, too—certainly the laws regarding the federal income tax.)

And of course from this unusual multigovernmental situation come complex and interesting features of American "federalism," of states' rights, and the national government's role. It is to be remembered that American citizens are subject to *state* constitutions, including state "bills of rights," all of which during the nineteenth century came to include protections for religious liberty. What that "incorporating" of the First by the Fourteenth (as the lawyers say) does, then, is to *add* the federal Bill of Rights (or whatever part of it) to whatever is already there in the state provisions—add to, and supervene over, what the state would allow and protect.

Where one thinks a matter should be left to the states, this "nationalizing" may appear to be objectionable; where one thinks a matter (e.g., the most fundamental liberties) should *not* be left to the states, then one may hold this "nationalizing" to be desirable. There were many decades of the nation's history, of course, including a sizable number after the Fourteenth Amendment was ratified, before the Court nationalized the federal Bill of Rights. And there are those who regard that entire project—"incorporating" any part of the federal Bill of Rights against the states—as mistaken "constitutionally" or in political wisdom and policy (perhaps it is impossible to distinguish).

Some of these prudentially minded folk suggest that the Court's decisions unfortunately have done what the Prohibition amendment did: converted what "should have been state and local issues, such as abortion and school prayer, into national ones." ("Should have been?") Some go on to say there should now be "local option" on religious-moral matters, as there is local option in drink: an adaptation of law to the enormous variety of the nation. Instead of a national moral logjam, this argument proceeds, allow many jurisdictional tributaries to separate the differences. *Use* the federal system, with its layers and levels of government, to accommodate the variety of local opinion on intensely felt issues connected with "morality" and religion, and thereby take some of the nation-rending fury out of them.

But then the other side responds that the argument is very much like the "popular sovereignty" that Stephen Douglas defended in the debates with Lincoln, to let majorities in each territory decide whether to be slave or free. Was slavery not a moral issue so fundamental, as Lincoln said, as to require a national resolution? Is not in our time legal segregation by race, struck down by the Court, such an issue also? Are there not matters on which the deepest of human rights, the soul and identity of the nation, are at stake? Are there not in the First Amendment matters of that fundamental kind? Are not claims of freedom of speech and press and assembly—freedom of religion—matters that cannot, or should not, be decided by majority votes, either nationally or locally, or left to the states? The South Mesa Bluffs City Council should not be able to shut down *The Weekly Coyote*, however much it might like to, even in the unlikely event the state courts would allow it. Such matters stand beyond the reach of majorities and beyond the powers of the states, in the moral foundations of our whole national society, as individual rights of the human person transcending the claims of any social order, and as moral requirements of our entire common life as a nation.

But now comes the question: Is the establishment clause of that fundamental weight? There are those who answer yes—the majorities on the Supreme Court through its many vicissitudes for almost forty years, for an important example. The Court even said in 1963, in the public school Bible reading cases, that contentions that the establishment clause is not applicable to the states (or that it prohibits only governmental preference of one religion over another) "are of value as academic exercises only." But there are others who continue to carry on such academic exercises, and believe that the Court, as an important participant in our intellectual history, might carry on some, too.

Meanwhile it is the establishment clause of the federal First Amendment that points its finger down through all this complexity squarely at our fountain in South Mesa Bluffs.

THE GEOMETRY OF TWO CLAUSES

As we already know now, the composers of what came to be the First Amendment in the First Congress—James Madison and others—thoughtfully provided, although surely without knowing what it would one day come to, in the case of religion, *two* clauses, so that the lawyers and the courts subsequently could play out not only all the possibilities of each, but also all the possibilities of the relationship between the two.

For the other items in the First Amendment—freedom of speech, freedom of the press, freedom of assembly—there is only one straightforward clause, and to that degree the constitutional situation is simple (not of course in other respects). But the religion provision was complicated already at the foundation by the fact that the conferees between House and Senate in the summer of 1789, working with the proposal of Samuel Livermore, or of Madison, or perhaps of others, devised what was almost surely a compromise between differing emphases: *Congress shall make no law respecting an establishment of religion*—the first clause, which came to be called the establishment clause (meaning of course the *no* establishment clause)—*or prohibiting the free exercise thereof*—the second clause, which employs the phrase "free exercise" that James Madison had used back in Williamsburg in the spring of 1776.

The question of the two clauses and their relationship to each other becomes yet another complicated and disputed matter. There are those who say there are not really two clauses, that they should be, as the lawyers phrase it, "read as one." One may take the entire provision in one gulp and make from it just one constitutional restriction. But those who say that the provision should be read as one may put one or the other of the two clauses in the superior or governing position, and that of course makes a radical difference.

Some of these interpreters who say that the two should be "read as one" then find the combination essentially defined by absolute separation—by the first clause as they understand it. In other words any violation of the strict separation of church from state is identical with a violation of religious liberty, which is *defined* as an absolute split between the state and religion. An example of this view is the dissenting opinion of Wiley Rutledge in the New Jersey bus case, to which we made reference in the section of this book on James Madison. That position has been ably defended across the decades by Leo Pfeffer, perhaps the leader among all the specialists in this field. Pfeffer wrote *Church, State, and Freedom*, an essential book, and many other books, and revised Canon Stokes's three volumes down to a more manageable and up-to-date one volume.

Others—former Solicitor-General (and Harvard law professor) Erwin Griswold and Professor Wilbur Katz of the University of Chicago, for example—read the two clauses "as one"—to the opposite result: Church-state separation is justifiable because it is and (this is the cutting point) *only insofar as it is* a servant of the fundamental principle, religious liberty, which is the only and governing principle.

These two positions represent almost opposing poles (although the situation is too complicated to admit of simple polarization). Those who do not hold to either—the Court does not—then have the problem of relating the two clauses. Some find that making one or the other absolute—or carrying one or the other "too far"—would infringe the other. So there may be a pushing and pulling between them, a tension, or a "paradox of the First Amendment" (of its two religion clauses), as Justice Brennan said at length in a concurring opinion in the prayer and Bible-reading case of 1963: "Free exercise" that gives religious majorities their head, freely to exercise, may in effect establish their religion, as it may be claimed more or less happened with evangelical Protestantism in the nineteenth century; Justice Frankfurter, in important opinions to be examined below, held that exempting this "sect" and that "sect" from otherwise legitimate governmental requirements would mean the "establishment" of all the "sects"; Justice Douglas suggested that exempting the Amish from Wisconsin's compulsory school laws above the eighth grade (in a case to be explained further below) *might* have in it just a touch of "establishing" the Amish. On the other hand no aid, no establishment carried to extreme separation, may be seen to interfere with the believer's freedom—as of children trying to pray somewhere in school, as of a devout soldier drafted to serve his country, sent to a far outpost, left with no pastor because absolute separation of church and state has chopped off the chaplains corps. Defenders of aid to parochial schools often claim that absolute separation (the establishment clause) violates their free exercise (to educate their children in a religious school without penalty).

So the complexities multiply. Simplicity at least would have been better served if the First Congress had confined itself to one clause. And need it now be added that it is the establishment clause that has provided the more spectacular fireworks in the constitutional law of church and state?

NO ESTABLISHMENT MEANS NO AID TO RELIGION—AND LESS

There is more—another step. A big one. At the same time that that First Amendment phrase about establishment was "applied to the states" (et cetera) through the Fourteenth Amendment, it was also tightened in meaning. The court in that New Jersey bus case in 1947 not only found the establishment clause "incorporated" in the Fourteenth Amendment but also found, in perhaps the most "controversial" item in the series, that it meant that there should be no government aid of any kind to religion, even without preference and in general: "The First Amendment has erected a wall between church and state. We could not approve the slightest breach."

But that case was decided, it will be remembered, by a 5–4 vote. One pictures Hugo Black, Wiley Rutledge, Felix Frankfurter, William Douglas, and the others using that case—with the many references to Madison and Jefferson—to plant the flag of absolute separation all the way through the American polity: not the slightest breach! But—it will also be remembered—they did not quite agree among themselves. Black, for the majority, despite the language from him quoted above, nevertheless would *allow* the reimbursements for the bus rides, as aids to the child or benefits to society: "New Jersey has not breached it here." Wiley

Rutledge, on the other hand, dissented, and his dissent, as we have said, is a statement of the most thoroughgoing separation, absolute indeed, with which three of his colleagues, including Felix Frankfurter, joined. This was the opinion that first reprinted the entire text of Madison's *Memorial and Remonstrance*. Rutledge wrote: "We have staked the very existence of our country on the faith that complete separation between state and religion is best for the state and best for religion." The *very* existence! *Complete* separation! Not everybody would agree that the very existence of the United States itself rests on that "faith," especially not with the modifier "complete." Neither would some others say that part of the "stake" is that such complete separation is "best for religion." There are those who would hold that the U.S. constitutional law, unlike the enactments of the pre-Jefferson Virginia Assembly, should not consider as the basis of policy, one way or the other, what is "best for religion." Certainly there would be those who would find a little paradoxical such a premise for the position taken in this opinion.

The key idea in Rutledge's opinion was this: "Legislatures are free to make, and courts to sustain, appropriations only when it can be found that in fact they do not aid, promote, encourage, or sustain religious teaching or observances, be the amount large or small." A legislature presumably would have to look over each enactment, and an official every act, to be sure that no religious teaching or observance would be in any way helped by it, before it could constitutionally be permissible. No bus rides, no textbooks, no city dental assistants looking at the parochial school child's teeth, no overflow of governmental actions that happen to "aid" religion.

Another sentence from Rutledge said: "Like St. Paul's freedom, religious liberty with a great price must be bought." Would the Court be willing to see great prices charged for exercise of other fundamental liberties?

That most thoroughgoing position did not prevail. Although Black's majority opinion insisted on its Absoluteness—not the slightest breach!—it nevertheless distinguished the doctrine of "indirect aid" or "child benefit" or public welfare, in which—as in the bus fares—the "aid" was not to the religion, and was therefore no "breach." Much of the lawmaking about possible aids to religious schools, for almost forty years now—all of those "parochaid" bills and cases and controversies—has maneuvered between those two pronouncements (as later modified and extended, but not overturned).

But wait. That 1947 decision with Black and Rutledge contending about how absolute absolute was going to be, was close—5–4—as we said. One of the five—one of the majority, joining his frequent colleague Hugo Black—was William O. Douglas, whose career through these church-state cases was to resemble the homeward journey of a New Year's Eve reveler. In 1962, in the New York prayer case, he went out of his way to take back what he had voted in 1947—to say that he now rejected the majority opinion (allowing "indirect" aid), in which he had joined. In effect he now went over to the side of Rutledge and Frankfurter—the then dissenting four—making, except for the irreversibility of time, a kind of shadowy retroactive majority for Rutledge's most absolute opinion.

But of course the moving finger of law had by then already writ, and Douglas' repudiation fifteen years later could not wash out a word of it. And time in its inexorable movement had seen much water go under the bridge of constitutional law, an important part of it carrying some still other words of Justice Douglas himself.

ACCOMMODATION, TOO, MAYBE

It will be remembered that the 1947 New Jersey bus case (Everson), which caused a double-barreled furor (attacked both by those who rejected the height of the wall, and by those who opposed benefiting religion even indirectly) was followed in 1948 by the Champaign released-time case (McCollum), in which the public outcry—a loud one— was all on one side (against this first clear-cut application of all these establishment-clause points we have been assembling actually to strike down a local practice). And now in the post-outcry mood of the early 1950s there came another interesting development.

Albert O. Hirschman, the distinguished economist, social scientist, and historian of ideas, tells in his book *The Passions and the Interests* about a finance minister in Colombia who issued decrees rather impulsively and who explained to Hirschman, when the latter counseled prudence,

> that he did not have the funds needed to employ a large research staff: "If this decree really hurts some groups," so he would say, "they will do my research for me after the decree is out, and if they convince me I will issue another decree!"

One may sometimes suspect the Supreme Court of using something like that Colombian method, especially in the terrain, not altogether familiar to judges and lawyers, of religion and society.

However that may be, as we noted in Part Two, the Court in 1952 made a decision that many believed contrasted sharply with what it had decided, to a great outcry, in 1948. They concluded in the New York dismissed-time case—Zorach, for short—that a program of religious instruction resembling the constitutionally impermissible program in Champaign, Illinois, now was constitutionally permissible. The opinions in that case have a remarkable heat, passion, and sarcasm—Black, Frankfurter, and Jackson each writing a dissent more indignant than the last. But by a vote of 6–3 the Court upheld the New York program that the three dissenters believed indistinguishable from the one in Illinois. The majority opinion, with its passage beginning, "We are a religious people whose institutions presuppose a Supreme Being"—by far the most quoted of all productions of the Court, by the "accommodationists"—was written by . . . William O. Douglas.

But the Everson-McCollum "doctrine" of the high wall of separation was *not* overturned in Zorach; to the contrary, it was explicitly reaffirmed. So the establishment clause, applied to every unit of government, still theoretically meant no "aid" to religion. And in the New York prayer case in 1962, and the Bible-reading cases from Pennsylvania and Maryland in 1963, it was so applied, to strike down those prayers and Bible readings in the public schools.

But remember the method of that Colombian finance minister. In 1970, when the weighty issue of tax exemption for church property came to the Court, with many claiming that such exemptions, though carved into the law of every state, were nevertheless obvious "aids" to religion violating the establishment clause, an almost unanimous Court found such tax exemptions constitutionally permissible.

There was only one dissent, the strictest of the strict, favoring, despite mountains of American history, taxation of church buildings. This dissent, in order presumably to display yet again a belated alignment with Rutledge's opinion of twenty-three years earlier, included, as Rutledge had done, the entire text of James Madison's *Memorial and Remonstrance*. It was as though perhaps the American public had not quite got the point the first time. That lone dissent was written by . . . Justice William O. Douglas.

THE MYTHICAL PEOPLE SPEAK, AND MYTHICAL LAWYERS

Let us return now to the comforts and liberties of fiction. It would be the combination of these twentieth-century interpretations by the Court, all of them still standing in the real world, that would create the legal pincers movement closing in on our offending water fountain: that the Fourteenth Amendment incorporates the First, and that that incorporation includes the establishment clause, and that the establishment clause means no governmental support whatever for religion. To the Reverend Billy Bob and his followers, whose spiritual ancestors were on something like the opposite side of such battles in Virginia in the 1770s, inscribing John 3:16 on the water fountain would not seem to be at all the same as setting up an established church. The only infringement of anybody's "religious liberty" or "free exercise" in the whole matter, it will seem to him, is the infringement of his own, and that of his flock and townspeople, by the Court's intervention. "The atheists and communists have plenty of places to drink," the Reverend Billy Bob will say.

But it will seem quite otherwise to Susan B. Murchison, who will claim that when her son refused to drink at the fountain he was so embarrassed that he could not field ground balls at third base, that he felt left out, and also thirsty. She will refer to the high and impregnable wall that the founders erected between church and state, and claim that the inscribed fountain is an obvious breach—the field, fountain, and water belong to the state; John 3:16 belongs to the church; and there they were, mingled on the softball field. Advocacy groups will agree, and enter the case not only to defend young Eugene V. Tom Paine Walt Whitman Murchison—"Butch" to his friends—and all other softball players "similarly situated," but the constitutional principle they find to be embodied in the establishment clause.

As our case—*Murchison*, as it will come to be called in the law schools—works its way through the layers of the courts, battalions of lawyers will develop all the arguments, contradictory though they be with one another. On the one side, it will be said that no one is forced to play softball; that no one playing softball is required to drink at that fountain; that anyone drinking at that fountain can perfectly well close his eyes and not read the inscription; that the inscribed fountain is *passive*, not spraying its water willy-nilly on passersby and soaking them with unsought belief, but flowing quietly in its own unassuming place. It will be said that the inscription itself was paid for by funds raised voluntarily by Billy Bob's citywide fund-raising campaign; no unbelieving taxpayer had to pay a cent. There is therefore no compulsion, no infringement of religious liberty. It will be argued, further, that though the inscription was originally religious, it has come through the passage of the agitated months to have a constitutionally permissible secular function as the town's leading tourist attraction and source of business for the motels along the highway: the Holy Fountain in the Sage Brush. It will be argued that the inscription is *speech*, the Reverend Mr. Smathers's contribution to the civic dialogue, and therefore *protected* by the First Amendment's provision for free speech. It will be noted that the city fathers of South Mesa Bluffs, on advice of the corporation counsel, affixed to the fountain below John 3:16 the statement that this inscription is intended solely for the secular purpose of encouraging orderly behavior on the softball field. It will be argued that every single one of our American presidents, from George Washington to the present incumbent, has invoked God as do the Reverend Mr. Smathers and his softball players. And beyond that it will be argued that the nation has a long religious tradition which the Court should not lightly disregard—that when it accommodates the religious feelings of our people, movingly set forth in this symbol, it follows the best of our tradition.

On the other side, it will be argued not only that the inscribed fountain gives unfair advantage to evangelical teams over the teams of dehydrated atheists, but also that the municipal softball field is city property, owned by *all* the citizens, not just those who believe in John 3:16; that every youngster—Jew, atheist, Buddhist, secular humanist—has a right to play in softball leagues set up under the town's recreation department. ("How many Buddhists do those lawyers think we've got in South Mesa Bluffs?" Billy Bob will ask.) But the central argument will have to do not with anyone being disadvantaged or coerced, but with "establishing" a religion: The recreation department and municipal softball field rest upon the compulsory machinery of government, and the First Amendment in its establishment clause forbids exactly this kind of aid to religion by that governmental machinery. Another important interpretation by the twentieth-century courts—perhaps it is a part of the "no-aid" reading of the establishment clause—is the holding that it is not necessary to show that any specific person (Butch Murchison, for example) has been compelled or coerced or has had his free exercise of religion infringed in order for there to be a violation of that clause. It is enough that religion and the state be mingled. If this imaginary case is taking place in the late 1940s or 1950s the lawyers opposing the inscription will argue that it represents a breach in the high and impregnable wall between church and state; in the 1960s that it violates the "neutrality" that the government should exhibit; in the 1970s and 1980s that it violates the Court's threefold test of constitutionality under the establishment clause. First, these lawyers will argue, the inscription serves a religious purpose and not a "secular" one, despite the help to motels and the city fathers' disclaimer and Billy Bob's claim that the purpose is to "inculcate good morals"; second, it does use a religious instrument—John 3:16—where a secular one would serve—a quotation from Benjamin Franklin, or Shakespeare, or the Boy Scout Handbook; and third, it does lead to an undue "entanglement" of religion and government, in the constant supply of city water to the religiously inscribed but municipally owned fountain.

AN UTTERLY FICTIONAL CONCLUSION

Let us assume—fiction gives us such liberties—that this imaginary case has come to the Supreme Court at some period in an imaginary time floating up over recent decades when the Rutledge "majority" is intact and that the Court has found the inscription constitutionally impermissible, and struck it down.

In the aftermath of the case, Mrs. Murchison will go on to challenge the town's practice of having both members of the South Mesa Bluffs police force direct traffic in front of Christian churches on Sunday morning; and having the volunteer fire department put out the fire, without charge, at the last big Christian Bar-B-Q; and leaving the property of the town's seventeen churches off the tax rolls. (In the great cities they will ask, "What sort of town is it with seventeen churches but only two policemen?") Mrs. Murchison will point out that one of the Reverend Mr. Smathers's parishioners who teaches in the junior high school unconstitutionally opens his after-school activity in the sheet metal workshop with a prayer. She will protest the painting by Mr. Smathers and his group of a huge red, white, and blue cross on the big rock (the South Mesa Bluffs Plateau) that looms over the city and cannot be avoided by the eyes of any resident, or any tourist, believing or unbelieving. (The city council will respond by deeding exactly that piece of the plateau to a private nonprofit association.) All of these things she will claim to be in violation of the constitutional principle enshrined in the establishment clause of the First Amendment. Not one inclined to let well enough alone, she will object to the study of *Paradise Lost* in the state college, because God's ways are being justified to man with taxpayers' dollars; she will object to the use of tax funds by the state arts council to support an exhibit of regional paintings in which there are several with religious themes (including a rendering of the South Mesa Bluffs Fountain by a painter called the Picasso of Peyote County). She will bring suit against the reading of the Bible from outer space by tax-supported astronauts, and against the school principal who, dropping the word *God*, allows pupils to begin their lunches with the words, addressed to whom it may concern, "We thank you for the flowers so sweet / We thank you for the food we eat / We thank you for the birds that sing / We thank you for everything."

When news of the result of *Murchison* v. *Municipal Softball League* gets back to South Mesa Bluffs, the Reverend Billy Bob will explode against all these secular humanists way off in Washington who tell us here in South Mesa Bluffs that we can put Balzac or somebody on our fountain, but not the Bible. He and his followers will mount a defiant campaign, lining up cadres of supporters for a drink-in at the fountain, singing, "There's Power in the Blood" and other hymns, so that nobody else can drink. "We will cut their water off!" the Reverend Billy Bob will say, in one of his more stirring sermons, and "If Martin Luther King and all of those people could do it, so can we!" There had been a time when he would tell his followers to shun politics because politics and government were of this world, and this world would soon come to an end; he even had a multicolored chart with boxes and arrows showing the National Council of Churches down in the lowest corner, *below* the Devil, because it denied the truth of the Bible and engaged in worldly politics. But now he abruptly changed, and told his followers they must become active in politics, and register, and vote. The BEAST of Revelation is loose! he will exclaim. The BEAST is *government*, and especially the Supreme Court!

Murchison v. *Municipal Softball League* will of course come to the attention of commentators among the intelligentsia in the great cities of the East. About the location of these events, some thousands of miles away, it will be said that they take place in "one of those states you fly over," in one of those "pockets of bigotry," those "enclaves" of the credulous.

In the carpeted halls of the great law firm in the nation's capital, Stale, Phlatt, and Unprofitable, Attorneys at Law, Attorney Stale, straining to understand so inexplicable a phenomenon, will say to Phlatt: "What is the matter with these people? Why do they persist? Millions of those people out there believe what nobody believes any more."

Phlatt, summoning all his compassion, will respond, "I pity them."

Stale, out of his overarching sense of the responsibility of people like himself to keep the nation straightened out, will remark, thoughtfully, "We must find some way to get the animals back in their cages."

In the Faculty Club at Ivy League University it will be agreed, "It is pretty clear. It is the responsible people against the rednecks."

Up on the twenty-first floor of Thrown Rock, the headquarters of

SpectaPictaVistaRama Broadcasting Company ("A Picture Is Worth a Thousand Ideas") the vice-presidents will contemplate the inundation of angry mail received on their coverage of the aftermath of the Murchison case. "It is all these rednecked fundamentalist women," one of the vice-presidents will remark. "They are all such bigots."

All People for Non-Sectarian American Freedom for Drinking Water, the upper-middle-class advocacy group, will send out a very successful fundraising mailing, with large type and many exclamation points: "Thirsty? Want a Drink? Don't Count on It. If Smathers Gets His Way You'll Have to Pray Before You Can Get a Drink of Water. Act Before It Is Too Late. Send Your Check in the Enclosed Envelope TODAY."

A columnist in *The Daily Superior* will discern a great deal in the faces of Billy Bob's supporters, as he saw them in a clip on the TV evening news. "Looking into the faces of mindless, yammering zealots, one gets a dispiriting jolt of *déjà vu*. Where have we seen those faces before? Of course—it was in the newsreels during the days of violent opposition to school integration. The dogma changes somewhat, the hate is masked in demonstrative piety (even cries of 'Amen'), but it's the same ugly mindset all over again."

Billy Bob and his followers will not be unaware of all this, and will make remarks of their own about the shape of metropolitan heads and the capacity of the learned to park bicycles and the convenience of holding advanced views while riding in limousines, and will draw up new charts linking every organization with the word "humanism" or "humanities" in a web with the Supreme Court and the Soviet Union holding hands at the center. Municipal water fountains all across the country, in defiance of law, will sprout Bible verses; fellow members of Television for God will join Billy Bob in a national movement.

In America Only, the conservative political action group that proposes to solve the world's problems by eliminating all other countries, and America's by eliminating the undesirable people (the forthright slogan is "Nuke the Others"), the giant computers registering every citizen's political itch will turn red across great sections of the country, and strategies will be devised, and portentous meetings held.

When a presidential candidate appears in front of the religious telecasters, he will be asked to describe his experience as a born-again Christian.

"Well...," he will say, "we didn't use exactly those words when I was a boy, but my mother always went to church, and she was a saint... " He will deplore the shocking interpretation of America's great tradition of religious liberty as meaning "freedom *from* religion."

There will be a giant Bombs for Jesus rally on the Capitol steps, and Billy Bob Smathers, who in the old days circulated pamphlets explaining that the Roman Catholic Church is the Whore of Babylon and the pope wants to run America, will link arms with a Roman Catholic bishop who says that where there is a *moral* issue at stake, all Christians should stand as one. Billy Bob and the bishop will then join together to tell the throng that this is not at all a political meeting, but a service to morality and America, and that they should vote for candidates on the *Christian* checklist.

Four days before the election, in which the most prominent candidate on that list has insisted that religion has always been the foundation of this nation's government, the nonprofit Belch Beer Foundation, which sponsors nonpartisan research on the elimination of all taxation and the drowning, for their own good, of all persons with an annual income of under $100,000, will publish full-page public service advertisements:

> RELIGION'S INFLUENCE ON PUBLIC POLICY
> HAS HAD A LONG AND DISTINGUISHED HISTORY
>
> Over the past 200 years religion has been a stabilizing force in this country. Suddenly Americans are being told that religion and morality were never meant to influence politics. To believe this would require a disregard for our history—even the desertion of the principles of our forefathers.
>
> The values of religion and morality have influenced public policy from our beginning to the present. Do we now separate religion from politics and ignore our nation's heritage? Think about it.

Around this prose there will be sketches of American Founders, each one accompanied by a quotation in which there is some reference, however slight, to the Deity. Prominent among them will be Thomas Jefferson ("I have sworn on the altar of *God*...") and James Madison ("It is the duty of every man to render to the *Creator*..."). Thus these Founders will be pressed into a somewhat unlikely service in behalf of the candidate who—Billy Bob will expansively claim—will appoint *moral* judges and get this country back to God.

THE HOME GROUND OF
THE MODERN COURT

The situation with respect to the establishment clause seems to deserve a touch of satire, partly because of the disproportion to which we have alluded earlier: heightened passions about symbols that do not deserve that passion, or that investment of symbolic power; heightened recourse to principles of great importance in their time and place in circumstances where they are not; the tendentious flattening and distorting of a complex history; the bald assumption by each side that questions long ago plainly settled are just now unsettled only by the others; religious belief that expresses itself not in generosity but in fanaticism; constitutional democratic principle, sometimes spiced with snobbery, that generates not wisdom but absolutism; the two sides—or the several sides—acting upon each other in a reciprocating escalation; the whole thing generating a passionate division out of all proportion to its usual objects. And much definitional imperialism, with assertions, and counterassertions, about what the nation *is*. Much of the argument is this symbolic kind, pulling and tugging on alternative definitions of the nation—secular, Christian, religious, pluralist—with contestants trying to settle the unsettleable matter by apodictic insistence. There are, of course, considerations of a high order, principles and important goods, distantly connected to the disputes—but *very* distantly.

It should be perceived that the criticism implied in the facetious passages above, with all their license of satirical exaggeration, is to be directed toward both, or all, sides. This is a situation that we have collectively got ourselves into. Part of it is just...America. What did one expect, after all, from a Jeffersonian nation? An immense, diverse, continental community composed exclusively of Jeffersonian rationalists? It may be that Jefferson himself *did* expect just that, but on that point, as perhaps on some others, he was wrong. Some of the modern religious tangle is just the result of the American "pluralism" that the founding structures helped to create, the fundamental diversity that grows from liberty and is part of the price a new kind of nation pays for that great good. A price—and also in some degree a benefit and a protection (this diversity is) though not so unequivocally a protection as Madison sometimes argued nor so completely a benefit as some moderns seem to believe.

What then of the role of the Court? One dislikes adding to the contemporary criticism of the U.S. Supreme Court, of which the nation has had in recent decades an oversupply, but surely it is only just to include the Court, on this particular issue (the little establishment clause and how it grew), for a quite considerable share of the blame.

Note that it is specified here that the criticism extends to this particular issue alone. On other matters there were, in exactly the years the Court was making the interpretations described above, very strong reasons for respecting the Court. A general reason, stretching across much of the twentieth century, is that the Court had to face the music, morally and intellectually. At a time when reductionistic and relativistic outlooks came to hold a central place in the nation's intellectual life—including the law, where lawyers in cynical moments joked about decisions based on what a judge had for breakfast—the courts had to keep on making reasoned judgments in real cases, based upon explicit principles. Although technically they were constitutional judgments rather than "moral" ones, they were in fact loaded with moral substance. The Court had to keep giving *reasons* for deciding as it did. Where disagreement persisted—as again and again it did—the judges had to exhibit the differing *argument* in opinions. In other words, even in an environment in which there was no longer much trust in a role for reason and conscience acting in society, the courts, and above all the U.S. Supreme Court, nevertheless had to keep on performing such a role.

Moreover, the Court in exactly the years that it made the foundational decisions about the establishment clause was distinguishing itself, and distinguishing the nation's whole institutional structure, by some of the most worthy decisions of its entire history. Many of these did, incidentally, rest upon that application of other parts of the First Amendment, and of the others of the so-called Bill of Rights, to the states, by way of the Fourteenth Amendment, in the way we have laboriously described above. In the early 1960s—a good time to make the remark—Edmund Wilson wrote that the U.S. Supreme Court had become "morally the most impressive of our original institutions."

Presumably one would not have said that after the Dred Scott case, or *Plessy* v. *Ferguson*, or in the early 1930s, or earlier in the twentieth century. There certainly have been many times in the past when one would scarcely have assented to such a statement; perhaps there have been moments of doubt since. It may be that Wilson's remark said more about the flatness of the other candidates than about the elevation of the Court. But after the Court reshaped the focus to feature civil liberties and civil rights and made itself the prime guarantor of the social-moral ground rules and the personal rights that stand beyond the reach of popular majorities, remarks like Wilson's, for a time, had a convincing ring.

The moral logic of American democracy rests, of course, not alone upon the rule by the demos by means of majorities, but also upon the protection of the processes of liberty by which majorities may be continually altered, today's overthrowing yesterday's, to be overthrown by tomorrow's. Only majorities achieved under such conditions—in liberty, with liberty retained—have moral dignity. The American republic rests on "majority rule," as the way the people rule; it rests at the same time, necessarily joined to such rule, on the protection of freedoms out of which its only morally legitimate expression arises. The grounding of the American republic on both "majority rule" and "minority rights," as it is sometimes put, may imply a complete opposition between the two, when in fact they are integrally related. The Court has become in modern times a principal protector of the ground rules of such democratically ordered liberty, such freely achieved popular rule. It has become in addition the protector of inherent rights that transcend society.

Among the arenas in which the Supreme Court has exhibited, in these years in the middle of this century, its honorable role, the most important of course is that of racial segregation. What a remarkable story that has been—the long, long difficult chipping away, or sometimes blasting away, at this "one huge wrong" of the American nation, slavery and racial discrimination.

An aristocratic Virginia politician-lawyer with radical ideas, a philosophic turn of mind, and a felicitous style, in an historic moment in Philadelphia, before he went home to fix things in Virginia, wrote a paragraph with an enormous, universal sweep to it, affirming human equality. As it happens, he was himself the owner of slaves, and although he was much bothered in his conscience by human slavery he was capable of writing in his *Notes on the State of Virginia* passages about the inequality of Negroes that would prove embarrassing to his subsequent admirers.

Fourscore and seven years later an Illinois lawyer and politician, whose political beliefs, he said, derived entirely from that Declaration of Independence (who was to represent an extraordinary combination of the nation's Enlightenment and Biblical traditions, of rational and of poetic power), rose to national leadership as the remarkably cogent expositor of the strongest position opposing slavery ("ultimate extinction," no expansion) that had a chance of winning national office, a position beginning with a clear-cut, explicit, and unequivocal moral condemnation of slavery grounded in the original national commitment to equality. Behind him there was a powerful national movement, begun in the 1830s, in which the Protestant religious world had played a very large role: the Finney revivals, the abolitionist evangelist Theodore Weld, the New England Reformers, Harriet Beecher Stowe (the daughter, wife, and sister of Protestant clergymen, producing, with Weld's tract under her pillow, as though God had written it, the most potent reformer's book ever written in this country).

But Lincoln too made statements, politically defensive, rejecting full "social" equality, and the American public acquired its commitment to equality, even in the very limited sense of ending human slavery, only after being carried to it by the rolling passions of war.

Common sense and America's experience with this "one huge wrong" suggest that there is nothing automatic in the working out of this interplay of ideals, institutions, law, a popular movement, and the public will. After the Civil War there had been a retrogression. The northern white public turned its mind to other matters with an abrupt swing of mood of a sort with which America's religious ethos is not unconnected. (Both what is worthy and what is not in America's long coping with her "dilemma" reflect the political character of the Protestant base.) Check off that "moral" problem—on to the next. Human nature in any "ethos" had a lot to do with it, too. Jim Crow was born; legal segregation was instituted eventually (not right away) in the formerly slave states. The condition of the freedmen declined, reaching a nadir at the turn of the century. A hundred years was to be "lost" in the achievement of the equality promised in the post–Civil War amendments.

And the Supreme Court was an important actor in that national tragedy. That same Fourteenth Amendment, intended to protect newly freed blacks, is sometimes said to have been, through the U.S. Supreme Court's interpretation, of more aid to corporations ("persons," not to be deprived...) than to blacks. And in 1896, of course, the Supreme

Court gave constitutional vindication to the system of segregation by law in *Plessy* v. *Ferguson*.

But the remarkable mid-twentieth-century sequence of events that turned that around had at its beginning and center decisions by the Supreme Court. With many anticipatory decisions, and a long follow-up, the climactic moment, of course, was May 17, 1954, when the Court, applying to the states the "equal protection" clause of that Fourteenth Amendment—its original and home ground meaning—found racially segregated schools inherently unequal, a denial of rights guaranteed by the U.S. Constitution. Then there came a remarkable counterpoint of institutional acts—on the part of the president, in 1962 and especially in 1964 and 1965, and of Congress, especially in those same years. These actions by the formal institutions of federal law—anticipated and accompanied by actions of some states and cities, in the sometimes usefully complicated federal system Madison and his colleagues devised in Philadelphia—had been stimulated by a long history of social movements, of speaking and preaching, and, beginning with the Montgomery bus boycott in 1955, of direct nonviolent action (the Protestant ethos in another mode—actually not beginning then; there was a long anticipatory history of that, too) which stimulated a powerful popular movement (itself a quite unusual embodiment of the national idealism, and the national religious idealism), in the end led by the chief victims of the inequality themselves, that from 1954 to 1968 turned the law around and realized at least in law and the vote the equality set forth in the original document and the original moral premise.

Of course the accomplishment of the middle of the twentieth century is still quite incomplete, and there has been another retrogression since about 1968, and particularly in the 1980s, and the broad white public, again, denies that this is so and does not want to hear about it anyway.

Still and all, surveying the whole story of those years 1941 or 1948 or 1954 to 1968, one can see that it was important to such progress as can be claimed, which is not small as human history goes, that all of the elements of the American system were available to play their part, very much including the original national commitment to full human equality, of course very much including the "direct nonviolent" action by citizens, black, and black and white together, but also very much including the U.S. Supreme Court, with its unanimous decision in 1954, and the implementing decision of 1955, and the decisions that preceded and followed. And the lower federal courts, where some judges might be described as heroic. It was a triumph for the American system—and the Court.

Is the story of the Court's work on the subject of church and state a triumph of the same kind? There are those who would say so, but they would not meet with the wide agreement that now happily accompanies the other issue, where even those who once opposed the Court's decision now admit that it was just. Not so with the Court's position on the establishment clause. It sits still partly undigested on the nation's stomach. It has its strong defenders, to be sure; but they are partisans in a continuing cultural conflict, not the morally vindicated victors in a settled matter.

What is the difference? The shape and timing and level of the issues. In the one case, the issue was clear-cut, immense, and fundamental, a principle of the moral foundations stored up from the nation's first days working its way through history to be settled in our own: an issue of liberty and equality that went smack to the nation's soul. In the other case, the nearest parallel principle was settled in the first days, or near to them. There was no lasting institution comparable to slavery, lynching, and Jim Crow, continuing an outrageous mockery of the nation's moral pretensions. There were no trials for heresy or bloody persecutions for cause of conscience or institutionalized torment for reasons of religious belief. Religious liberty, the nearest moral analogue to racial equality, was already long since achieved. Where in the small it still was not (as in matters shortly to be considered—the flag salute), the Court could do its valuable work, and, over time, receive the general commendation of the conscience of the community.

Even on that other matter, not so clearly fundamental, of separation of church from state, the issue had also been essentially resolved. The situation, in the last half of the twentieth century, was this. It was not seriously advocated that the United States institute at that late date— the Anglican laymen having failed to pull it off in the 1780s—an established church. It was not seriously advocated that one particular religious group be given some preferred treatment by governments; that, too, having failed in Virginia, and later in other states, was out of the question. It was not seriously advocated that there be confessional statements by governments or financial enactments directly supporting religious groups or religious positions. The remaining issues had really only to do with the vestiges of the long de facto Protestant "establishment" (a metaphor for Protestant cultural domination) like Sunday laws, prayers and Bible reading in schools, and creches on lawns; with the efforts to find ways to maintain education in religious traditions, and—as a special case—the financing of religious schools.

The Court, in its ringing absolutes about the wall of separation, saw the issue not as a matter of the flow of culture, which it should leave alone, but of equality, which it should protect. Perhaps the then dominant centers of political and social commentary saw issues that way, too. (By "then" we mean those years, beginning with the 1940s and running on perhaps into the early 1970s, when the most important shaping decisions of the modern Court were made.) The kinds of issues the Court is, so to speak, best at and most at home with, are those of clear-cut and direct denials of fundamental liberty and/or equality. Matters that entail clear moral principle. Matters of "discrimination." Matters that clearly reach the level of universal human right and the moral core of a free society where there is a foundational principle to be defended, against majorities, across cultures, and across centuries if need be—like racial equality.

Freedom of religion *was* like that, too—still is, in Iran and India and Ireland, and would of course be here now were it still relevant. Some items under the free-exercise clause are like that—the flag-salute cases. Freedom of thought (the real core of Jefferson's statute) is like that. But the institutional arrangements between believers and unbelievers, and among different sorts of believers, in a complicated semisecular, semireligious multireligious modern nation that includes a far-reaching "state"—is not like that. On those matters to many the Court appears, by the grounds upon which it has made its decisions, to be intervening on one side in the politics of culture.

To the reader whose wariness and disagreement rise with the trend of these remarks, it may be said, conceivably somewhat to reassure or persuade, that few of the cases the Court has dealt with need have had a different outcome had they been but reasoned differently. There is a kernel of the matter that may have slipped by in the extended work of facetious imagination above: The distinct point about the Court's present view of the establishment clause is that there need not be a showing that anyone has been *coerced*—that anyone's *religious liberty* was violated; mere wall-breaching, or government entanglement, or un-neutrality, is enough (remember now: This is reaching all the way through all the levels and parts of American life, with an extraordinary non-majoritarian instrument). It need not be shown that any identifiable human being actually had his or her religious liberty directly infringed in order for there to be a constitutional violation of the establishment clause. It need not be shown that our fictitious Butch Murchison had his religious liberty directly invaded. It need not be shown that the real Terry McCollum, sitting there in study hall while his fellow pupils pursue their religious education, has been coerced by the released-time religious education program in the schools in Champaign, Illinois, in order for it to be found that the program violates a great constitutional principle. It is enough that the state has thus "breached" the wall of separation between church and state; it has put its compulsory school machinery in aid of religion, and therefore violated the constitutional provision. (Presumably the school is a great compulsory agent because it is supported by taxes that are collected compulsorily, and because of the compulsory school attendance law.) In making that interpretation the Court's underlying political philosophy implicitly would stress the element of compulsion in the action of the state, in contrast to the element of collaborative purpose and common project—a continuing part of the story.

Suppose the Court retreated on that point, so far as what it held the Fourteenth Amendment to "incorporate." Cases where there was persuasive evidence that an agnostic or Islamic or Catholic or Jewish person—child—was coerced by a governmental instrument—by being enfolded in a prayer he or she did not believe—could still be held to be unconstitutional. But on grounds more likely to recommend themselves to the lasting conscience of the community over time, because more fundamental and therefore more persuasive.

In order for the Court to have concluded, on the basis of history, that the situations we have been discussing were not to be allowed under the establishment clause, it had to line up in exact coordination, like precisely attuned sights on a rifle, the following three historical judgments:

One, that what those Virginia gentlemen who enacted Jefferson's statute in 1786 meant was no "aid" in the modern scrubbed clean absolute sense;

Two, that what was meant both by the First Congress and by the legislators in the states who ratified the First Amendment in 1789–91 was that there be a separable meaning in the "establishment clause" and that that meaning be exactly that no-aid absolute attributed to the Virginians of 1786; and

Three, that what the corresponding congressmen and legislators who put in place the Fourteenth Amendment meant in 1868 was to apply, in its word *liberty*, the establishment clause exactly as so understood now against the states... which means, as we have said, against every unit of government in any place in the United States.

Any wavering in the historical accuracy of any one of those three points will throw off the rifle shot that puts in peril, just to use it one more time as a symbol of much else, our South Mesa Bluffs water fountain. But every one of those historical judgments is subject to challenge.

Of course the "finding" of constitutional law is not done simply out of historical judgments. The question is then where exactly it does come from.

The answer to that is that it comes from a living constitution, expanding and developing in response to the changing life of an actual people. Were the courts in those years in touch with the changing life of an actual people? The answer—is it not true?—is a kind of implicit moral and political philosophizing that lies behind the judicial interpretations of the Constitution, giving them meanings corresponding to, in Justice Holmes's phrase, the "felt necessities of the time."

It is very hard, then, for the citizen to keep clearly in his or her head that what the Court is doing is not straightforwardly setting public policy according to its own reasoning, but rather a much more restricted task: interpreting the constitutional limits on the work of those who do that—that is, all the elected public officials. And it is not determining the wisdom or even the abstract justice of the actions of these officials, but only whether they are allowable under the Constitution. It is altogether possible that unwise and even in certain ways "unjust" policies, properly enacted, may nevertheless be constitutionally permissible. The Court's role is supposed to be a limited one. It is difficult for a citizen to comprehend that. Sometimes it may be hard for judges, too.

One suspects that the Court that made the decisions we are considering, like the communities of thought to which it would have been closest—the people who filled the ballroom of the Shoreham Hotel on Hugo Black's seventieth birthday, a very worthy sort of people, commonly called liberals—subliminally put the issues of church and state, of the establishment clause, in that slot in their mind which was the most familiar and congenial, and on which they had done their best work: equality, nondiscrimination. But the familiar American phrases repudiating "discrimination" because of "race, creed, or previous condition of servitude," or "race, religion, color, or national origin," or "race, sex, creed, national origin, sexual 'preference' or physical handicap"—this list, winding its way through the vicissitudes of America's good-heartedness keeps getting longer—are seriously misleading so far as "creed" or "religion" is concerned. "Creed" and "religion" are not unchangeable givens of a human being's biological makeup or accident of birth, or unalterable past ("previous condition of servitude"), but entail—however theoretically in demographic fact—mind, and will, and choice. Religious belief is not part of the ineluctable externals of a human being's existence, but part of the substance to which he or she has an inner, changing, substantive relationship, and which, individually and communally, provides the frame to guide and shape conduct and define the great issues of living. A human being can become a heretic, a convert, or a backslider, even though in fact most do not. A believer can become an unbeliever; those who come to scoff can stay to pray; Saul of Tarsus and Martin Luther and Roger Williams and Ignatius Loyola and John Henry Newman can alter their beliefs. The young Edmund Wilson—if we may reverse and perhaps descend a little—reading a sentence of Shaw's while riding on the train back to school from Philadelphia, can feel the whole weight of his ancestral Presbyterianism lifted from his shoulders before he reaches Norristown. Religion is culture not nature; belief not biology; mind and spirit not ethnicity. "High religion" is expressed—usually—in communities of belief that differ, in those same ways, from the groupings grounded simply in nature—in biology, force, historical accident. And this is true even though modern American popular understanding, not too sharp on matters of religion anyway, struggling with the difficulties of practical pluralism, is clouded not only by the apparently automatic correlation of birth with "belief" (even among Baptists) but also by the many inextricable mixtures of ethnic and religious identification since the major immigrations. How much is "discrimination" against the Irish, how much against the Catholic? How much against the foreigner, the Eastern and Southern European, the Italian, the Pole, and how much against the Catholic and the Jew? (It is further clouded by the complexity of the group that has been the recipient of the severest persecutions. Historic Judaism combines "religion" in the sense of belief, or rather observance, with peoplehood—"ethnicity," as it would now be called—and as the recipient of the most terrible of persecutions reinforces the perception that "religion" is simply another given or accidental identity about which no one should properly "discriminate.")

One of the moments that revealed that an important part of the Court had fit these matters into the familiar slot of Equality—of non-discrimination, of all individuals being treated the same—came in the passionate opinions in the Zorach case of 1952, when Justice Douglas had for the moment swerved clear over to the accommodationist side of the road. In his dissent from the majority opinion that his erstwhile companion Douglas had written (allowing the New York released-time program), Black wrote with pungent disapproval:

> Before today, our judicial opinions have refrained from drawing invidious distinctions between those who believe in no religion and those who do believe. The First Amendment has lost much if the religious follower and the atheist are no longer to be judicially regarded as entitled to equal justice under law.

One pictures Hugo Black looking sternly, sadly into the eyes of his old companion Douglas.

But—was allowing New York to conduct that religious education program denying an atheist equal justice under the law? Forcing the issue around that way shows what file folders you have in your mind. The issue of a specific atheist's quite specific equal freedom *did* come before the Court, in the Maryland notary public case in 1961, and was forthrightly answered, with little public outcry. (Maryland cannot exclude an atheist from that job.)

The racial segregation decisions did correspond, despite the ferocious segregationist resistance, to a deep strain in the public conscience; thirty years later, people who resisted admit they were wrong, and endorse the decisions. The same did not happen with the absolute separationist decisions, and will not. Can one imagine sending federal marshals to smash a crèche on a public common, or break up eighth-grade prayer groups in the gym? The separationist strain raises issues of the communal expression of religious belief, and the forming and maintaining of cultures, that do not fit very well the Court's categories or its role.

Justice Rutledge wrote, interpreting Madison's views in that dissenting opinion to which we have often referred, that for Madison "religion was a *wholly private matter* beyond the scope of civil power either to restrain or to support.... the realm of religious training and belief remains, as the [First] amendment made it, the kingdom of the individual and his god.... it should be kept inviolately private." That is of course an American commonplace (that religion "is" a private matter)—but also capable of many meanings and much disputed. Does the claim that religion is a "private matter" mean that it is not to be talked about, as a matter of taste or social grace (as it was certainly for the reticent Jefferson, the non-Christian, and for the reticent Jane Austen, the deep but sensitive Christian, but not unreticent others); that it is "subjective," a "projection" (a modern debunking view, rejected by believers—should the Supreme Court adjudicate this philosophical and theological debate?); that the religious should leave politics and public life alone (stay in the sacristry—a view widely held about religious folk who take political positions different from one's own, but immediately dropped with respect to those whose positions agree with one's own); that one's religion is generated by each person in his or her private, solitary communings (hardly true of most religious persons, though of some); or just that religion is not to be supported by the power of the state (in this country that is so, but that point does not and should not entail any of the others)?

There is a potent, and nearly universal, communal aspect to religion, even in this country. Is there not a deep human yearning, in any community, to give symbolic and ritual expression in religion to the commonalities, to the unity and fellow-feeling that make a community? Notice even in *The Federalist* itself, in Two, when John Jay is remarking with pleasure that "Providence has been pleased to give this one connected country to one united people," he observes that united people "professing the same religion." We have already quoted Washington's Farewell Address. And James Madison, whom Rutledge and Douglas regard as Mr. "private matter" himself, was baptized in an Anglican church, brought up in the church, educated by clergymen, educated in religious classics and a religious atmosphere at Princeton, married to Dolley by an Anglican clergyman (Dolley, with some pain, breaking with her Quaker upbringing, leaving one social expression of religion for another), and at the end of his life buried by the service in the Book of Common Prayer. What happens to the ceremonial recognition and preservation of the seriousness of human life? So believers ask. Think anthropologically, outside one's own community. Imagine applying the establishment clause to the Hopi or the Navaho—or the whole picture of "private matter" religion. One lone Navaho sitting by himself, thinking it through: No, it's not the *green* mountain that is sacred, but the *blue* one beyond it. And insisting that the tribe leave all such choices to each private Indian heart.

We live in a different culture, to be sure, but we have the same human predicament. There are many distinctions and definitions to be made, and an endless argument (there is no intention here to try to end it). But that is part of the continuing cultural process, the debate about what this country "is," and what religion in relation to it "is," not properly to be foreclosed by constitutional prohibitions. As the Court should not say, as it did several times in the nineteenth century, as it did (rather offhandedly) as recently as 1932, that "this is a Christian nation" or even a "Christian people," perhaps even a "religious people," so it should not say we are a secular nation, or people, or that the public school is "the symbol of our secular unity." The Court should not decide what America "is," nor what religion "is" either, or any of the points in cultural dispute among a religious-secular nation-people. Leave that to the people's continuing decision. The Court should be no partisan. If the Jeffersonian/Madisonian view that religion is a private matter should come to win out over the contrary views very much alive in American society, if it has its superior "truth," then ought it not come to "prevail," not by judicial fiat, but by . . . free argument and debate?

RELIGIOUS LIBERTY AND
RELIGIOUS CONSCIENCE

In the late twentieth century a certain kind of conservative Christian— let us say he is a Catholic or an evangelical Protestant in a Main Street denomination—angry at the Court because of its decisions about school prayer and religious schools and religion in the schools and abortion and other matters, expecting that his view will find constitutional vindication in the free-exercise clause—the free exercise of religion, meaning the positive affirmation not only of his own beliefs but also of what he holds to be the religious foundation of the country—is astonished then to find out that the litigation of the free-exercise clause is all about . . . the Jehovah's Witnesses! Which is not what he had in mind. It is also about the Mormons; the Amish; the Great I Am; again, the Jehovah's Witnesses; the Navahos; The Fellowship of Humanity; a snake-handling cult; the Seventh-Day Adventists; Timothy Leary's League of Spiritual Discovery; a Tennessee faith-healing group; again, the Jehovah's Witnesses; the Worldwide Church of God; yet again the Jehovah's Witnesses. Where, he may ask, are the Methodists? The Baptists? The Episcopalians, Presbyterians, Congregationalists, Lutherans, Disciples of Christ? Where is Reform Judaism? Where, for that matter, are the Evangelicals? Catholics appear, to be sure, in cases involving aids to parochial schools, but otherwise they, too, are missing. This list distorts the story only slightly.

He may also be disappointed to discover the *kinds* of activities that have come before the courts under the heading of the free exercise of religion: playing an abusive religious phonograph record on the street; distributing argumentative religious literature door to door; declining on religious grounds to salute the flag in school; using peyote in a Native American rite; declining medical help for a sick child; withdrawing one's children from school after the eighth grade—again, not what he had in mind. Of course, he needs to understand that litigation—constitutional jurisprudence—by its nature selects the unusual, the marginal, the extreme, where boundaries are tested. Dealing with such margins does not reflect very well the life that is lived within those boundaries.

But perhaps there is, for all that, something of value about the nation's underpinnings in the Court's decisions under the free-exercise clause. As we have proposed above, that clause fits more comfortably than did the other one both with the Court's role in the society and with the modern Court's preoccupations.

The law about free exercise, like that of the establishment clause, came onto the national stage in a prominent role—after only bit parts before—in the 1940s, and for the same reason . . . that "incorporation" of the First Amendment by the Fourteenth explained above. The incorporation of the free-exercise clause has been, however, much less controversial, and understandably so, because it plainly involves a "freedom," and hence finding it in the Fourteenth Amendment's protection of "liberty" does not appear to be what Huck Finn called a "stretcher," as does the corresponding discovery about the establishment clause. The "incorporation" of free exercise came about in a 1940 case . . . about the Jehovah's Witnesses.

As with the establishment clause, so with the free-exercise clause: Fundamental decisions taken in the first years after the Court's "incorporation" of the First Amendment by the Fourteenth—that is, in the 1940s—set boundaries for what would come after. The most important of these boundary-setting decisions came in the famous flag-salute cases of 1940 and 1943. It came, however, in rather a backhanded way—not in the majority opinion of the second case, which overturned the first, but in the *rejection* of the powerful position set forth in both cases by Justice Felix Frankfurter. (We will try to explain why the point has to be put in that way.) What was carved out by the rejection of Frankfurter's opinion(s) was a distinct space for distinctly religious conscience.

Both of these flag-salute cases involved Jehovah's Witnesses children who refused in school to salute the flag, for religious reasons. It is important to observe that the first of these—*Minersville* v. *Gobitis*, arising in a Pennsylvania town—came to the Court in 1940, in the shadow of the war in Europe and of the isolationist-interventionist debate in the United States, surrounded by all of the patriotic passions that period evoked.

Despite those passions, it had been expected that the Court would uphold the decision of the lower courts, which protected the right of Jehovah's Witnesses children to decline, on religious grounds, to give that salute to the flag in school. But to the astonishment of many, the U.S. Supreme Court—in June 1940—*overturned* the lower courts, and upheld the penalties against the Jehovah's Witnesses. The Supreme Court *denied* their claim of "free exercise." It did so, moreover, by an overwhelming 8–1 majority.

The passionate and powerful opinion of the Court was written by Frankfurter. Presumably his was the most potent voice on this case. Arthur Schlesinger, Jr., then a young aide in prewar Washington, has written of the astonishment and dismay felt by a clerk of Frankfurter's, and by some of his admirers, when they saw the draft of Frankfurter's opinion.

Then second thoughts came, and a civil-libertarian outcry, and in 1943 in a case from West Virginia (*West Virginia* v. *Barnette*) the Court reversed itself. (West Virginia, after the 1940 decision, had instituted required *statewide* public-school flag salutes.) Frankfurter, still holding to his original position, wrote in the second case an opinion—this time a dissent—even more impassioned and powerfully argued than his majority opinion in the first. But the Court had left him, and voted 6–3 the other way.

The composition of the Court had changed somewhat in the interval between the cases, and two of the hitherto majority had been replaced by justices who voted to overturn the earlier decision. But the more startling development was the announcement, in another (Jehovah's Witnesses!) case during the interval, by three of the first case's majority (Black, Murphy—and Douglas!) that they had now changed their minds.

Frankfurter certainly had not changed his. Putting together his opinions in the two cases one has a clear, consistent, strongly argued position—which, in the end, the Court rejected. As we said—that rejection is important, one might even say philosophically important.

Frankfurter's position rested in part on his continuing desire to see the Court not overextend itself—to exercise restraint, and to leave to the decision of popularly elected officials, however foolish those decisions may seem to be, whatever may be left to them. They are elected; we (the justices) are not. Their job is to make policy; ours is not. Our duty—the Court's duty—is only to see whether they have used constitutionally permissible means to obtain constitutionally permissible ends.

In other words, part of his position sprang from his devotion to "judicial restraint," as it had come to be called. Frankfurter's dissent in the Barnette case is a lengthy and powerful summary of the position he had spent his judicial career defending. (One might argue, though, that on the religion clauses of the First Amendment, Frankfurter could have applied his judicial restraint in exactly the reverse of the way that he did. He certainly did not argue for judicial retraint with respect to the decision of the Ewing Township in New Jersey to pay the bus fares of parochial school students. He voted on Rutledge's side, and wrote his own dissent. Nor did he on the released-time program the Champaign Board of Education wanted to conduct, or the New York City program in the Zorach case, either. On all of the decisive early establishment-clause cases he was one of the most consistent judicial *activists*, where some might hold that restraint was appropriate. Now on a free-exercise case: judicial *restraint*, where some might believe "activism" was more in order.)

But that matter of judicial philosophy was by no means the whole of Frankfurter's position on the flag salutes. He put forward an argument about the nature and limits of freedom of religion in the United States, and it is in the rejection of that argument that the aforesaid boundary is drawn.

We must put the matter with this reverse spin on it—that rejecting Frankfurter made the point—because the Court's opinion in the 1943 case, overturning its decision of 1940, did not rest upon the issue of the free exercise of religion. The majority opinion of 1943 is the well-known and often quoted work of Justice Robert Jackson—quoted earlier in this book, as a modern sample of Jefferson's spirit—to which the word *eloquent* is often and understandably applied. But Jackson's opinion—significantly perhaps—defended the Court's rejection of West Virginia's compulsory flag salute not as a matter of religious freedom but rather on the broader basis of freedom of thought and belief: "the action of the local authorities in compelling the flag salute and pledge ... invades the sphere of intellect and spirit which it is the purpose of the First Amendment ... to reserve from all official control."

But though Jackson for the new majority had moved out onto the wings of the mind and spirit, leaving any distinct *religious* liberty behind, the issue had originally, in 1940, been posed, debated—and decided—exactly on the grounds of a claim (and, then, a denial) of a distinct *religious* liberty under the free-exercise clause. Felix Frankfurter had certainly argued the matter in those terms. So, on the other side, had the Jehovah's Witnesses' lawyers. A prophetic lone dissent by Harlan Stone—a very important dissent—in that first case also rested squarely on the free-exercise clause: "by this law the state seeks to coerce these children to express a sentiment which violates their deepest religious conviction." Stone, in his lone dissent—with Black, Douglas, and Murphy all on the other side—is perhaps rather an unsung hero in this story. In the second case the concurring opinions of Black, Douglas, and Murphy—the switchers—also rested upon religious liberty and the free-exercise clause.

Before we go on to look at Frankfurter's position, let us note the possible significance of the shifting of the ground for the majority opinion in the second case—the mind and spirit, presumably whether religious or not. That shift of ground indicates a question that hovers over this whole territory in the modern period: Is there any distinct and separate liberty called *religious* liberty, if one has secured the freedom of speech (and the implicit freedom of thought) that the Constitution provides?

As the discussion moves along in the law school classroom, one can feel—sometimes hear—the question taking form: Why is there any *need* for a distinctive *religious* freedom, if all the other explicit and implicit civil liberties are protected? Is such a provision necessary? Moreover, one can sense, implied in the comments, the further question: Is such a distinct *religious* liberty dangerous? Unfortunate? Mischievous? A wary law student may imply that specific mention of the free exercise of *religion* provides the religious groups the opportunity to claim something *special* and *peculiar* to themselves, some advantage or immunity not available to the unbelieving citizen. So with that invisible ink with which constitutional lawyers and judges can write things into, and take things out of, the Constitution as it was written two centuries ago, some just erase the provision protecting free exercise of *religion*. Just protect thought, speech. Ideas. "Expression."

Now—if something of this unwillingness to grant a distinct *religious* liberty lay behind the shifting of the ground from Stone's dissent in the first case to Jackson's majority opinion in the second—then, ironically, the strong majority opinion (Jackson) and the strong dissent (Frankfurter) have one (strong?) point in common. Because Frankfurter, too, certainly did not want to grant any distinct place to claims of *religious* liberty against the state.

"The lawmaking authority is not circumscribed," Frankfurter wrote. Making reference, as the reader will not by this time be surprised to discover a justice doing, to Jefferson and Madison, he claimed that "it would never have occurred to them to write into the Constitution the subordination of the general civil authority of the state to sectarian scruples."

Here is the essence of Frankfurter's view: "The constitutional protection of religious freedom terminated disabilities, it did not create new privileges. It gave religious equality, not civil immunity. Its essence is freedom from conformity to religious dogma, not freedom from conformity to law because of religious dogma." To take another view— said Frankfurter—would "subordinate the state and law to the sects." Frankfurter cited ominously the great numbers of religious groups in the country—250 by his count. He anticipated—intending his list to be a kind of reduction to absurdity—many further instances of claimed exemptions from general law on the basis of religious conscience. (Most of the instances he anticipated have since appeared in the real world; the Republic has nevertheless persisted.) He warned against cases involving compulsory vaccination, compulsory medical treatment, the reading of the King James Version of the Bible in schools, conscientious objection to war, the Jehovah's Witnesses' violation of the child-labor laws, and more. He included an extended discussion anticipating the history that was to come, about state aid to parochial schools. (The reader should remember that these cases—in 1940 and 1943—*preceded* the New Jersey bus case [1947], and all the subsequent establishment-clause cases and furor.) Frankfurter's point was: "the validity of secular laws cannot be measured by their conformity to religious doctrines. It is only in a theocratic state that ecclesiastical doctrines measure legal right or wrong." What then about religious freedom? "Waving the banner of religious freedom [does not] relieve us from examining the power we are asked to deny the states. Otherwise the doctrine of separation of church and state . . . would mean not the disestablishment of a state church but the establishment of all churches and of all religious groups." (Here is an instance, on this side of the aisle, of that teeter-tooter effect between the two clauses: If you recognize a positive content to free exercise, then you "establish" the free exercisers!)

Frankfurter argued that if a government is pursuing a legitimate object of its secular role—to preserve safety, or order, or to inculcate national unity (as West Virginia claimed to be doing), or to promote domestic tranquility or the general welfare in ways that did not otherwise run afoul of constitutional proscriptions—then no citizen could properly ask to be exempted simply on grounds of his religion.

Now, it should be noted that this position was certainly not peculiar to Felix Frankfurter. On the contrary. It is the position of most states throughout human history. Not only would Creon hold to such a view; Antigone herself would expect nothing else—she would scarcely expect some court to rescue her, on grounds of her religious rights, from Creon's wrath at her disobedience. Even Roger Williams might have stood alongside John Cotton and John Winthrop on *this* question. Though Williams held that a state should not persecute people for reason of *religious* conscience, he meant by that religious *belief*, and *worship*, and "spirituals" only. For all his heroic attack on persecution for cause of conscience, Williams would not, any more than Cotton or Winthrop, permit individuals to be exempt from the common secular tasks on grounds of their religion—for example, from the task of defending Rhode Island against Indians or the northern Puritan neighbors. On that ship of his, even though each one could go to his own different kind of worship without persecution, nevertheless, everybody had to do his duty. You could not claim that the things you learned in your unpersecuted separated worship service on the ship should allow you therefore not to take your turn on the yardarm. To continue Williams's metaphor, and exaggerate the point in the spirit of Frankfurter's opinions: If on the ship of state each sailor has some peculiar religious objection to the common task—God tells one to avoid ropes and another to stay away from heights; one does not believe in being near the water, and the scriptures of another forbid exposure to the sun—it will be impossible to stay afloat. On the other hand (to continue this anachronistic speculation), Williams might join the anti-Frankfurter side when the issue is not one of cooperating in an active shared duty but rather of a state-imposed profession of belief: the captain of that ship, though he can properly insist on your taking your turn on the yardarm, cannot require of you a profession or testimony or symbolic gesture that violates your religious convictions—perhaps that is a separable question, which Williams would answer differently.

The situation, as Frankfurter's opinions make clear, is particularly difficult in a "pluralist" country. The Fund for the Republic's meetings, mentioned earlier in this book, took place in the days when Catholics still had a Friday obligation not to eat meat, and some Protestants—Methodists and others—were teetotalers; many Jews observed the restrictions of the Dietary Laws. John Cogley, the administrator responsible for the nutrition and social life of the mixed group, in many meetings over many days in many places, remarked: "Thank God for the secularists. They eat like Protestants and drink like Catholics."

That resembles Frankfurter's position: Thank God for the public school, the "symbol of our secular unity," amid all these divisions.

Moreover, to return now from anecdotes to constitutional law, the position of the United States of America had been, in a sense, the same as Frankfurter's—not about "secular unity," but about a unity to which one cannot claim exemption on religious grounds. Frankfurter's position, which was to be rejected by the Court, was not unlike the view that had prevailed not only throughout most of human history, but throughout America's distinct history under the Bill of Rights, too.

In the Mormon polygamy cases in the late nineteenth century, Mormons in the federal territories of Nevada and Idaho claimed, on the basis of the First Amendment, an exemption from the laws requiring monogamous marriage because the teachings of "celestial" marriage—plural marriage—were a part of their religion. The federal authorities and eventually the Supreme Court granted that the views were part of the religion, but nevertheless vigorously rejected the claim. The first of these Mormon polygamy cases, in 1878, is also the first Supreme Court case to bring into high judicial literature our friends Jefferson and Madison, and the Virginia Statute, and the *Memorial and Remonstrance*, and the Danbury letter with its wall.

This case, using a sentence of Jefferson's from the Statute, distinguished *belief*, which the First Amendment makes absolutely free, from *action*, which cannot be—certainly not the action of polygamy, which a later case from Idaho called "odious," and a "crime" in "all civilized and Christian countries." Both of these cases cite rampant possibilities, in the way that Frankfurter will do: human sacrifice, suttee, sexual promiscuity, as part of various religions. The Court said in the Idaho case: "crime is no less odious because sanctioned by what any particular sect may designate as religion."

So it was a moment of some significance when in 1943 the Court recognized, in the backhanded way here described, the constitutional possibility of an appeal to religious conscience against the claims of the state—the backhanded double negative way of rejecting (after having earlier accepted) Frankfurter's very strong rejection of that possibility. Except as it may figure, again rather in the manner of a corkscrew, in the decisions about conscientious objection to war—of which more in a moment—the years that have passed since the flag-salute cases have not seen many decisions by the U.S. Supreme Court that were as loaded

with philosophical meat. The group Mark De Wolfe Howe called Jehovah's litigious Witnesses has obtained a series of decisions protecting
their evangelizing, even when a variety of citizens, and towns, have
found it obnoxious. (Not everyone is sure that liberty is well and justly
served by preventing communities from regulating large numbers of
Jehovah's Witnesses going door to door on Saturday mornings awakening Catholic working men and women to try to sell them *The Watch-
tower*, and to explain to them that their church is the Whore of Babylon.)
The Court has struggled, so far in an on-again, off-again way, with
Sabbath restrictions. After Jewish merchants failed to obtain relief from
Sunday closing laws—a decision many see likely to be altered—a
Seventh-Day Adventist was granted unemployment benefits after re-
jecting a job that would have required her to work on Saturday.

In 1976, in the most important of these cases in the years of the
Burger Court, the Yoder case in Wisconsin, the Amish objected on
religious grounds to sending their children to public high schools, because in their tradition the early basic education sufficed, and because
such further training as was appropriate they would provide within
their own community, and because the flavor of the classes and social
life in the public high schools went against Amish upbringing and belief.
Their victory was important because it acknowledged a *communal*
exemption: The Amish as a longstanding and serious religious community were granted the constitutional exemption. In other words, the
Court acknowledged a religious group's communal character, and on
behalf of the state found a constitutional claim of free exercise against
Wisconsin's compulsory school laws above the eighth grade.

But, still, the most important decision was the one that drew the
first line, in the flag-salute cases. Felix Frankfurter said: The lawmaking
power is not circumscribed. The Court said: Yes, it is. Sometimes.
Wisconsin's is, by Amish "scruples." West Virginia's is, by Jehovah's
Witnesses' scruples (so Stone, Black, Douglas, Murphy). South Carolina's is, by Seventh-Day Adventist scruples. Frankfurter said: That means
the "establishment" of all these sects. You cannot run a government
that way. The Court said: Yes, you can. (We are improvising and par-
aphrasing, obviously, for both sides.) Clearly we would all say in our
own right (all Courts certainly would agree) that the free exercise of
religion and religious conscience in *activity* (in "non-spirituals") cannot
be "absolute."

There are conflicting claims of many sorts: of order, of the rights of
others, of other freedoms. There are fraudulent claims. Some of the
most fervent religious libertarians seem to grant anything that labels

itself "religion" a kind of extraterritoriality; but it is not only in the day of Jonestowns, Manson cults, and mail order ministries that the civil order cannot and should not do that. On the other hand, the civil order can recognize the possibility in theory (as it did in those cases) of a claim of religious conscience that the state acknowledges. And in this perhaps slim possibility there is an important part of America's self-understanding: that there is a realm, beyond the domain of the civil order. *This* state, as a democracy, incorporates the principle of resistance to government within government, and puts the burden on itself to explain why not when it cannot honor an honest claim of religious conscience against it.

Curiously, if one put together from these Court opinions two that represented a nationalism that closed the legal system's attic door on Madison's layer number one—that is, on a duty to a universal sovereign *above* that to the civil society—one, Justice Sutherland's in a 1931 case dealing with granting citizenship to a "selective" conscientious objector, would affirm the nation's Christianity ("We are a Christian people ... but we are a nation with a duty to survive") and the other, Frankfurter's in these flag-salute cases, affirms the nation's secularity ("We are dealing with an interest inferior to none. National unity is the basis of national security"). But the Court came around in the second instance to something more faithful both to our secular and to our Christian national selfhood: in an age of rampant nationalism it granted, with however limited an actual practical application, the principle of our legal system's recognition of the superiority of religious conscience over the nation's claims.

And religious conscience has, so to speak, run interference for consciences of other kinds, as the complicated cases of conscientious objectors show.

THE ANALOGY OF
CONSCIENTIOUS BELIEF

Paul Tillich, who was nothing if not a man of "scope," found religion to be the "substance" of culture, and to be expressed by terms like "ultimate seriousness" and "ultimate concern" and "dimension of depth." He said he found more religious meaning in a well-made piece of furniture—a good chair—than in much "religious" art. A philosopher who was supposed to "debate" Tillich from a nonreligious point of view at Princeton complained that though he would try to disagree with Tillich, to reject his presumed view, to draw a line and challenge this theologian to stand on the other side of it, Tillich kept refusing to join the issue, kept *agreeing* with him, kept giving him "an intellectual bear hug."

Irving Howe, in his intellectual autobiography, *A Margin of Hope*, tells this story about life in Princeton in the early sixties:

> At one of Tillich's seminars where the theologian, charming as the devil and at least as slippery, spun out his notions about faith, those of us listening felt that the idea of a personal God—the God we had rejected, the only God we knew—kept fading farther and farther into the distance. I asked Tillich: "You say religion rests upon a sense of awe before the 'fundament of being.' Does that mean that if, on a starry night perhaps out at sea, I find myself overwhelmed by the beauty of the scene, and become acutely aware of my own transience before the immensity of things, I am having a religious experience?" My intent, of course, was to distinguish between mere cultivated sensibility and religious belief; but Tillich, suave dialectician that he was, seized upon my question and said, yes, even though I called myself a skeptic I had provided "admirably"—he

grinned—a description of a religious experience. He had turned
the tables on us, and we sat there uncomfortably—until from
the back of the room there came the [Edmund] Wilsonian rum-
ble: "Mr. Tillich, you're taking away our rights!"

One can understand why, in the complex demands of modern pluralism, the U.S. Supreme Court seized with a certain amusing eagerness
upon definitions of "religion" like that of Tillich. The Court made a
specific reference to that theologian, among others, in cases dealing
with conscientious objectors to war in the period of the Vietnam War—
and its way of doing so may be seen to carry with it a significance
going beyond even that large and important subject.

For most of American history the government recognized the conscientious objection only of members of the historic peace churches.
That recognition was a matter of policy, not of constitutional right. It
will be remembered that when James Madison brought his proposed
bill of rights into the First Congress in June 1789 he included among
his proposals a provision that persons who were "religiously scrupulous
against participating in war" should be excused from doing so. Had
that proposal been successful, conscientious objection to war on religious grounds would have been a constitutionally guaranteed right. But
it was not successful, and therefore conscientious objection to war on
religious grounds has been, throughout American history, a matter of,
as the lawyers put it, "legislative grace." It is granted by Congress, and
in theory could be removed by Congress.

That, at least, has been the way it has been understood. It may be,
though, that the interpretation of the First Amendment is approaching,
in a very complicated way, something else. Suppose that a kind of
freedom of any person's "conscience" must be discovered in the free-
exercise clause—because to grant only religious people free exercise of
their conscience would be an unconstitutional establishment of religion. Suppose that actual history and culture require that exemption
from participation in war, for conscientious reasons, must be extended
to some religious groups (i.e., the historic peace churches) at least. It
must therefore, in order not to violate the establishment clause, be
extended to *all*—and therefore in effect, with an assist from history, is
found in the Constitution. This is complicated, indeed, but as we know
by now we certainly are, on these subjects, a complicated society.

Already in the Second Congress the United States established the
long tradition of allowing conscientious objection to war on the part
of some. The early Americans, like Madison, had in mind the Quakers,

the Mennonites, and others of the sects in Pennsylvania and elsewhere who had as part of their historic understanding of Christianity a refusal to participate in any war. The first twentieth-century selective service act, passed in 1917, continued to extend the grant only to such historic peace groups.

The Supreme Court dealt with the issue of conscientious objection to war a few times while that was the law, but only under rather special circumstances. Once, in the 1930s, there was a case of some university students objecting to having to serve in the ROTC (denied), and three times there were cases involving the issue of citizens of other countries who wished to be naturalized as American citizens but who declined to say they would bear arms in America's defense. Twice, in 1929 and 1931, the Court held that such objectors could be denied citizenship, but with a powerful dissenting group including Holmes and Brandeis. Then, in 1946, just after World War II, in the case of a Canadian Seventh-Day Adventist named Girouard, the Court reversed itself with respect to the requirement that a person be willing to bear arms to become a naturalized citizen of the United States.

Woven through these and subsequent developments there is a particularly intricate counterpoint between Congress and the Court. The Court in these matters was not in the first instance interpreting the Constitution itself, but the legislative intent of Congress—in the light of the constitutional restrictions. And woven through them also was a most earnest effort on the part of the Court—and Congress—to define what "religion" is, in order to know whether its free exercise was being permitted, and whether particular conscientious objections were truly based upon "religious" training and belief in accord with the law.

In 1940, just before World War II, Congress broadened the historic provisions of earlier selective service acts to extend the permitted objection from historic peace churches to all those individuals who objected for reasons of "religious training and belief." It was no longer necessary to belong to a group that itself was pacifist. In 1948, Congress inserted the phrase "Supreme Being." In 1951 it added the last guarded portion (to date) of the definition of "religious training and belief." It means "an individual belief in a relation to a Supreme Being involving duties superior to those arising from any human relation, but does not include essentially political, sociological, or philosophical views, or a merely personal code."

That was the law when the Vietnam-era cases came, in 1965, to the highest court. In the first case (actually three cases, combined into one) there were three objectors, all admitted to be "sincere" and serious.

They were a skeptic who read Spinoza, put *religious* in quotation marks, and "left open" the question of a Supreme Being (Daniel Seeger—the case is known as the Seeger case); a man named Jakobsen whose beliefs were very much of the Tillichian sort (a "supreme reality"); and a third objector (a Mr. Peter) who was a follower of the New York Unitarian minister John Haynes Holmes, believing in a power in nature but not himself willing to use the words "God" or "Supreme Being."

The Court faced a sticky wicket. It was engaging in what lawyers called "statutory construction," and one of the rules of that exercise, understandably, is that the Court should try, if possible, to construe a congressional enactment in such a way as to "save" its constitutionality. In these conscientious-objector cases the Court carried that work of saving construction to heroic lengths, construing as believing in a Supreme Being persons who said they did not use the phrase or left that question open and construing "religious training and belief" to cover persons who put *religious* in quotation marks. Later, in 1970 (in the Welsh case), on the precedent of the Seeger case the Court would extend its construction out somewhere into the world of Lewis Carroll, finding it constitutionally impermissible to deny exemption to an objector who specifically rejected the word *religious* as applied to himself.

The Court faced, on the one hand, this legislation requiring "religious training and belief" and "belief in a Supreme Being," in order for one to be exempt; on another hand, it had before it these impressive and "conscientious" but not conventionally religious objectors; and on—so to speak—still a third hand, there was the establishment clause, which by the Court's own interpretation forbids preference to, establishment of, "religion," even the nonpreferential religion of religion-in-general. Perhaps an adroit lawyer could add still a fourth hand, the free-exercise clause as the Court interpreted it. In fact, in the Seeger case Justice Douglas wrote that to have decided any other way—to have denied these three the privilege granted to the conventionally religious—would have violated that clause. One can see why the Court worked up a good deal of intellectual perspiration dealing with these cases.

The Court theoretically could have found the entire provision for conscientious objection unconstitutional—as Justice Harlan, in his concurrence in the 1970 Welsh case had come to believe they should have done—because the restriction to those with "religious training and belief" was an establishment of religion. But to have done that would have pitched the whole matter back to Congress in a most fundamental way, and cut down the whole history of American conscientious objection until and unless Congress enacted a new law. The Court understandably did not want to cut so sharply against a long and solidly grounded American tradition. But the Court also—reading its mind now—did not want to deny Mr. Seeger's (or Mr. Jakobsen's or Mr. Peter's) conscientious objection (or even, later, that of Mr. Welsh) while upholding that of Methodist, Quaker, Catholic pacifists.

What to do? This is where Paul Tillich came to the rescue—Tillich, Bishop John Robinson (with his book *Honest to God*), and others. They provided a definition of "religion" so inclusive that Mr. Seeger could not escape it, even though he put *religious* in quotation marks, and an understanding of the Supreme Being so broad as to encompass even those, like Mr. Peter, and the other two as well, who did not use any such phrase. By quoting Tillich and others, the Court adroitly managed to impute religion to those who did not know they had any, and a belief in a Supreme Being to those who were not aware of any such belief, and thus managed simultaneously to uphold Seeger's (and Jakobsen's and Peter's) conscientious objection, the congressional legislation, and the no-aid version of the establishment clause.

Although one may mock this slightly, it seems one should do so only in an amiable way, and perhaps even with a certain muted drum roll for an American accomplishment, peculiar as it is: Granting conscientious objection is difficult enough for a nation at war; to grant it not only to believers in pacifist traditions clearly defined by historic religious communities but also to individual believers is harder; to grant it then to individual conscientious philosophers is harder still. That there are enormous practical difficulties with such provisions is obvious. It is an impressive testimony to its moral strength that this society could get itself into shape to make them.

The Court used in these cases what has come to be called the "parallel-belief test": "The test might be stated in these words: A sincere and meaningful belief which occupies in the life of its possessor a place parallel to that filled by the God of those admittedly qualifying for the exemption." Of Seeger the Court said: "Because his beliefs function as a religion for his life, such an individual is as much entitled to a "religious" conscientious objector exemption as is someone who derives his conscientious opposition to war from traditional religious convictions."

The Court noted Seeger's "compulsion to goodness" which informed his total opposition to war, the undisputed sincerity with which he held his views, and the fact that he had "decried the tremendous 'spiritual' price man must pay for his willingness to destroy human life."

It concluded: "We think it clear that the beliefs which prompted his objection occupy the same place in his life as the belief in a traditional deity holds in the lives of his friends, the Quakers." (The parallel-belief test had appeared in a different jurisprudential context in a California state case in 1957 [a decade before Seeger], in which the issue was whether a group called the Fellowship of Humanity, which explicitly rejected belief in God but otherwise behaved very much like a traditional religious group, qualified for a tax exemption on its property. The California court said the group *did* qualify, because it "fills the same place in the life of believers" as do more traditional, theistic groups; to deny such exemption, moreover, would "establish" theistic religion. So the theory of the parallel belief was there in the storehouse of doctrine.)

To return now to the national drama, and the subject of conscientious objection: In 1967, hawkish members of Congress, angered by the Seeger decision, tried to get Congress to amend the selective service legislation to require membership in an *organized* religion, but could not succeed. They then took another route, amending the legislation so as to remove the reference to a Supreme Being, presumably on the ground that such a change would expunge the Tillichian spaciousness about Supremeness and Beingness from the law, and by leaving "religious training and belief" directly connected to the rejections in the last part of the phrase, restrict it firmly to traditional believers. Enough other members of Congress, one would guess for other reasons, went along with this change so that the Supreme Being was dropped and a shortened version of the earlier law substituted for it. It now read: "Religious training and belief does not include essentially political, sociological, or philosophical views, or a merely personal code."

Lower federal courts, in the midst of the national agitation over Vietnam, found that to be unconstitutional, violating not only the establishment clause, but free exercise, the due process clause, and even the "equal protection" clause of the Fourteenth Amendment. And in 1970, the U.S. Supreme Court, without deciding the constitutionality of the provision, did decide the still more challenging question of its application. There came a case of a man named Welsh, who put a line through the word *religious* in the statement in the selective service form that conscientious objectors must sign, forcing thereby a direct challenge. The Court was sharply divided, split 4–1–3, but the one— Justice Harlan—concurred in the result, though not in the reasoning, so despite Welsh's explicit unreligiousness there was a majority granting his objection. The majority opinion cited as precedent its finding with respect to Seeger and the others. One might say, to refer back to that scene between Edmund Wilson and Paul Tillich, that the Court took away Welsh's "right" to deny that he was "religious" in order to grant him his "right" to be a conscientious objector—in order, that is, to keep from unfairly "establishing" the religion of "Religion" by granting only those who did not cross out the word the privilege of conscientious objection under the statute. The Court engaged in Mark De Wolfe Howe's "acrobatics of logic" to the point of risking an intellectual double hernia.

It was, needless to say, a controversial decision, as the Seeger case had been, too; hawks in Congress were angry. But the outcry among the public did not compare to the outcry over, say, the prayer and Bible-reading cases—the establishment-clause cases. And therein may lie a lesson of the sort we have been suggesting, about the role of the Court. Equal treatment for individuals, including the nonreligious, including atheists (as in the case in which the Court insisted that an atheist could not be denied a post as a notary public in Baltimore; indeed that the state of Maryland could not require belief in God as a condition for holding any office), has a power to reach the conscience of the broad American public that religion-denying decisions about cultural symbols and about what we are and can do as a people do not.

Soon after the Welsh case, in 1971, the Court denied (8–1) the claims of two *selective* objectors—those who were not pacifists but were conscientiously opposed to a *particular* war. One of these, Guy Gillette, was a rock musician with a "religion of humanism." The other, perhaps more interesting, was Louis Negre, a French-born Roman Catholic, who appealed to one of the longest and most thoroughly worked out positions in the West: that of the just war. In fact, this issue had come up before, in the 1931 case dealing with granting citizenship to conscientious objectors. The plaintiff, Douglas Clyde MacIntosh, a Canadian professor at Yale Divinity School, was not an absolute pacifist but a selective objector—a "just war" objector. "He is unwilling to leave the question of his future military service to the wisdom of Congress where it belongs," said the indignant majority opinion. In 1971 the majority was still indignant. Here is an issue that awaits the future.

Now back to the larger significance of the parallel-belief test, to which the Court was driven by the exigencies of modern American life. The principle of that "test" may be carried outside the Court and the law and, perhaps with amendments, spread across the spiritual horizon of present-day America. But let us, in making that expansion, effect a change in the metaphor. The differing beliefs in question may not be exactly "parallel," because the lines leading to them converge in the Christian humanism and the secular humanism (Enlightenment humanism) that are intermingled, influencing each other, in our past. Moreover, there is a kind of argumentative priority—a status of first premise—to one of the "parallel" lines—traditional Christianity, and traditional belief in God. (See the way the Court argues in the quotations above.) Perhaps therefore instead of the geometric figure of parallelism we may substitute the literary-philosophical category of *analogy*.

On the one hand this country has a specific tradition—large and complicated, but specific nevertheless. America did not drop down on this planet out of the pure air of abstract possibility, but arose out of a specific history. The nation has, as the saying goes, roots. We came from somewhere. We came not from reason but from Europe. America was born not from Walt Whitman's imagination but from Western Christendom. We have a history and a tradition that has shaped our mind, our nation, our institutions. That tradition has a core of specific belief—the Christian religion, in its expression in the Western (Roman Catholic) church, and especially in the Protestantism that sprang from (and protested against) it, and more especially still English Protestantism; but also then, doubly joined to Christianity in a peculiar American way, Judaism—making the "Judaeo-Christian tradition," as this nation has come to call it. That tradition, and the continuity of large numbers of adherents to many of its forms, furnishes the measure by which religious belief is known, and by analogy to which new varieties of belief—of religious belief, or of "conscience" that is not religious—are identified.

The United States is not a union of individual rationalists, wholly unstained by social context or history, nor the product of a free-standing abstract reason, nor is it yet the full-fledged parliament of world religions and philosophies that it may in some future century, step by step, come to resemble. It is the product of a specific history, a specific religious history, and carries the results of that history inside its culture and institutions.

That history and that culture and those institutions leave a deposit to which even those who reject traditional beliefs orient themselves. In the quotation above, Irving Howe wrote about the personal God, "the only God we knew," whom he (and Edmund Wilson) found disappearing over the far horizon in Tillich's spacious conception—the God they had come to reject. There is something more than humor in Wilson's humorous remark: To take away, as it were, that God, so they could not effectively reject his existence, was to take away their *rights*.

A religious person might get his own back from the memory of many rude dismissals by saying, Yes, it takes away their *crutch*.

Unitarianism makes sense in a trinitarian environment (Judaism was and is "unitarian" without putting it that way). Universalism requires predestinarian doctrines to reject. An atheist of the Western sort requires the theism of the West as an antagonist. The marks of the religious heritage appear on those who have come to be—"grown," they would say—outside it. Where the Italian atheist says there is no God and Mary is His mother, the most influential of twentieth century American philosophers, John Dewey, reflects in his "common faith" his rejection of organized religion, while endorsing the religious *attitude* of his Vermont Congregational upbringing. This obvious and universal point—that religious underpinnings leave their cultural mark even on those who reject them—is in the ideal working out of the American arrangement taken up into norms of the society in a unique way, in religious liberty and the notion of parallel—let us say analogical—beliefs.

John Mansfield of the Harvard Law School, commenting on the Seeger case, criticized the merely *functional* identification of this parallelism—the concept, that is, that the belief under "test" should fill the place in the life of the believer "filled by traditional belief" in the traditional believer. The problem with that simply functional place-filling conception, Mr. Mansfield says, is that all sorts of nonsense fill the central place in people's lives—"believers" as well as unbelievers. What "functions" at the center of life, where to a believer God ought to be? Well, don't ask. As Roger Williams might say, God-belly, God-money, God-self—and, more recently, some less conventional idols. The better way to indicate that characteristic of traditional belief—of belief in God—to which a parallelism or analogy is to be made is not to point to the *function* the belief fulfills in the believer (the subjective side) but to matters the belief deals with (the objective side)—that is, the fundamental matters of life and death, of God, of good and evil and their grounding, of the nature of the universe.

Now, despite our complaint about the Court, let us venture a statement in our own right as to what the United States *is*. About *such* matters—those fundamental ones—this unusually free and unusually religious nation does now have a kind of noncommittal commitment: It knows that such a dimension exists—such a dimension of belief, analogous to the traditional beliefs of the Christian past. The "state" in the United States is now to be impartial toward the differing convictions about those final things as they appear in the society: None is preferred, none is discouraged. But this impartiality or neutrality does not reflect hostility, nor the expectation or desire that the "religious" belief will wither away, nor indifference, nor ignorance, but deference. The state leaves alone the belief about the first and final matters because the shaping of such belief is reserved to the people, and therefore beyond the state's competence. The American nation learned about that dimension, and learned to defer to it, from its own Christian past.

The state as such, despite history and the preponderance of popular sentiment, is not committed to any substantive proposition in the realm of religion—not to Christianity, not to religion-in-general, not to Judaeo-Christian or Biblical religion, and certainly not to any opposite or alternative to any of these. It is not a confessing state. But it is not a disbelieving one either. The official apparatus of power and law is not, despite the many statements by believers through the years and efforts down to recent times to enact some declaration, formally a "Christian" state. It is not, in the conventional pre-Seeger non-Tillich sense, formally or officially a religious state. But it is in the post-Seeger sense a religion-respecting state.

Insofar as is possible in a real society, the state now treats with evenhanded equality not only all religious positions but also nonreligious positions that deal with comparable fundamental matters: parallel or analogous beliefs.

The state is impartial about such ultimate beliefs not because it is ignorant about and unimpressed with them, pursuing its superior secular national goals without any reference to the religious or irreligious opinion of the people—but rather because it defers to the conscience of the people. What this nation *does* know from its history and its people is that there is a "dimension" that the religions out of which it has come have traditionally represented, and the state defers as far as it can to the people's belief in that superior realm, leaving it, insofar as it can, free.

Our state leaves matters in that realm aside not because they are beneath or against its concern, but because they are above it. Our free state is a state that knows itself to be limited—indeed, our society is a society that knows itself to be limited—with respect to the ultimate loyalties of the citizens. These arise from the free action of citizens and not from the direction of government or the official proclamation of society. The free state, the American state, does not seek to generate, promote, protect, or impede beliefs, convictions, or loyalties at the level with which religion deals.

The American tradition is not so indiscriminate as to make now irrelevant any distinct liberty called religious liberty, swallowing up the whole in a general freedom of thought. On the other hand, it is not so strictly construed as to make "Religion"—the positive, organized, and traditional expression—the only recipient of the protection this society extends under that rubric, which is at least in theory most important, most fundamental, most inextricably linked to human freedom: the sources of meaning and/or worth in life. About such ultimate matters of belief, of meaning, of value, the American state respects the people's free decision. The reasons for that respect on the part of the American state—the American civil order—could still, or rather perhaps once again, be stated in something of the way that Madison did in the first points of his *Memorial and Remonstrance* two hundred years ago.

ON THE UNDERPINNINGS
OF REPUBLICANISM

When James Madison set out for Williamsburg in the spring of 1776, and when Thomas Jefferson returned to Virginia in the fall of that same important year, they were, as the course of human events would prove, in the early stages of a weighty historical episode. That episode had a central moment in Philadelphia in the summer that was bracketed by their two trips. Separately just then, later in collaboration, they were attempting to work out, in their minds and in the law, what they saw to be a better relationship than anything that had hitherto prevailed between religion and civil society. But that important project was to be just one part of a much larger one, which they would pursue through the many decades of their long careers: building a form of civil society itself that was superior to those that had gone before, a full-fledged newly designed "republic," a self-governing society, built to last, to coincide with fundamental human characteristics, to gather up aspirations out of the long history of civilization in the West.

The undertaking that began two centuries ago with the efforts of these men and their colleagues, or more than three and a half centuries ago with the landing of the English settlers on the shores of the New World, was then to develop across the years a size and a strength and, at times at least, a moral appeal that has astonished humankind. It has also more recently come to have a physical power that threatens humankind. Perhaps it has a cultural power that does the same; in any case its culture is not insignificant to this and the next stage of human history. The world asks, not without reason, whether, and how, it works, this empire of liberty whose "empire," though not whose "liberty," extends throughout much of the world.

For those who undertook to construct the American Republic, a particular mind and character in the public was an essential requirement: "public virtue," civic virtue, a care for public things. Although James Madison and Patrick Henry debated against each other about the General Assessment in 1784, Madison did not yield to Henry in his caring about this civil moral substance in the people; the two disagreed only about whether tax support for religion would achieve it. George Mason puzzling about what had happened to virtue after the Revolution, Thomas Jefferson constructing educational plans throughout his life and particularly at the end of it, George Washington and Alexander Hamilton composing Washington's Farewell Address, Benjamin Franklin objecting to sermons designed only to make good Presbyterians rather than good citizens, John Adams helping to design the Massachusetts system of local teachers of piety, religion, and morality and worrying in his treatises on governments about the virtue in the public that must undergird a republic, were in their various ways fully aware of the decisive importance—to the institutions of the republic they were devising—of the habits, the mind, the customs, the character, the "second nature" added by social life, the education and nurture, the piety and virtue, in the citizenry.

They would have differing appraisals of the relationship of that public moral condition to religion, and to tax support of religion. Some, like Sam Adams, would hope for a restoration of a "Christian Commonwealth" continuous with the Puritan conception of John Winthrop. His cousin John Adams, a good deal less orthodox in belief, would nevertheless see instruction in "religion," not creedally insistent, a "piety" joined to virtue, as an essential to the republic to be required by law, supported by taxes if need be. Thomas Jefferson and James Madison, as readers of this book cannot have escaped knowing by now, took a very different position about any tax-supported or collectively affirmed religion; they also did not see religion having the importance to the moral makeup of the public that some others did. But across the varieties of convictions on these two issues—collective support for religion, and the relation of public morality to religion—there was wide agreement about the importance of the intellectual and moral condition of the citizenry. These forefathers did want to avoid that cause of the downfall of the republics of the past, a condition they called by terms with an eighteenth-century meaning, "luxury" and "corruption"—the neglect of the public good for private gain, display, advantage, and pleasure: They did want, in their differing ways, to nurture an attachment to the shared human good.

And, two hundred years later, it is not at all clear why that consideration should be any less important than it was then. A republic, built on something more than submission or indifference or sheer self-aggrandizement from its citizens—requiring responsible citizens, not subjects or barbarians—surely still needs to have those citizens nurtured in the social habits and moral understanding that such a polity—such a difficult polity—demands.

The nation these forefathers set in motion has in 200 years improved itself in many ways—especially in bringing the promise of equality in the Declaration of Independence somewhat nearer to realization by ending the ghastly paradox of slavery, by eliminating property restrictions on voting, and broadening the franchise to make a modern "democracy," by creating an extraordinary system of universal free public education, by finally overcoming legal segregation of the races, by providing the "asylum" to great migrations of peoples to which we have alluded, by expanding and refining the original civil liberties, by including women in the voting population, and in many other ways. And that nation has lasted and prospered, under its one Constitution; it has indeed shown to the world that a nation "so conceived and so dedicated" need not perish from the earth. Nevertheless, 200 years later one may not be confident about the "republican" nurture of its citizens.

Project the original republicanism forward from the nation's beginnings, the way economists do with the national debt or demographers with baby booms. Gather up the conception developing in the Puritan ideas of the covenant and in the English Commonwealth debates and in the Enlightenment's hope for humane and rational new societies, and particularly the ideas in the creative moment of the forming of the American republic. Carry that "republican" ideal forward across decades to the present, adding perhaps a few modern improvements. There will still need to be, as part of the bare bones of civic morality, some perception of "truths" we hold, in reason and conscience, sufficient for our common life not to be a pure power struggle of interests but a meaningful civic argument. There will need to be, for the same reason, a perception of the intrinsic goods of human life, including the common goods. Citizens will need to be nurtured in a mutual respect that is not merely a concession, a quid pro quo, a balance, an occasional effort at "compassion" above and beyond the normal run of a self-interested material life; that is, instead, something integral to the self. Such citizens will find the project of continuous shaping of the common life through "free argument and debate" to be itself part of life's fulfillment.

There will need to be a positive and continuous recognition of the worth of statecraft, of the principle of government, of the honorable work of public life and governing—although now in a new way: as the people's instrument. Government is to be the agent of the community and subordinate to it. The governors are themselves to be governed; the combination *The Federalist* describes is called self-government.

Such a republic will require a community of mutually obligated citizens, a public—there cannot be a republic without a public—and a public forum in which that public can do its thing; and a conception of the public good—the *res publica*—which *is* its thing; and a conception of the citizen as a responsible human being, who in reason and conscience can make discernments about that public good; and the freedom to give voice to those discernments in the free argument and debate of the public forum (such freedom being as much a requirement and a good of the community as of the individual citizen); and the absence of any human interposition that would disarm truth about the public good of those her natural weapons, in order that she may prove the proper and sufficient antagonist to its "erroneous" conceptions. And the citizen will need to be nurtured in "public virtue," that is, in the habitual willingness to subordinate, if necessary, personal and group interest to the public good—to give disinterested attention to the commonweal. That is the way in its beginning, at least, government of the people, by the people, and for the people was to work.

These bare bones of republicanism, in the history of the West, and the history of the emergence of this country, have not been disconnected—to put it in this negative way—from "religion," even in its less spacious definitions. There is a piece of the broken body of truth in the assertion by the conservative religionists that the country's institutions "presuppose a Supreme Being," and have underpinnings in the Christian religion. Christianity was the primary teacher to the broad populace—was it not?—of the essential "republican" premises: that there are other human beings, "neighbors," occupying this globe with us; that we form a community with them; and that that community has a good which is also our good: the bell tolls for thee.

These republican institutions, however, did not develop, and would not have developed, *solely* out of that Christian tradition, as one single uninterrupted flowing river. Their development required not only some dams and boulders and obstructing logs and branchings-off within that river—the Reformation and Puritanism and left-wing offshoots and more—but also the abrupt influx of cold water from other streams— the Enlightenment and its successors. That Christian river, the great muddy Mississippi of Western civilization, had, moreover, already taken into itself something of the non-Christian classical world, so that the historical antecedents of American republican institutions had already become broader than the distinctively Christian heritage—had become the broad Western humanist tradition, secular and Christian—before there was an America. And, today as yesterday, it is by no means clear that "Religion" (undifferentiated and capitalized) can by itself provide the full foundation of republican government. "Religion" comes in many varieties. Among other results, it produces indifference on the one side, and fanaticism on the other side, of public life. It has sanctified many cruelties. Patrick Henry and Timothy Dwight, and the broad American public of the nineteenth century, and the conservative religionists and presidents of the twentieth, are surely wrong when they assert—without inquiring any further—that "religion" will supply the republic's requisite "morality." It may or may not. The same, of course, is true of "secularism." So there needs to be an interplay.

As the new nation got itself afloat and the nineteenth century rolled on, and the twentieth century, as is the way with centuries, followed it, American "culture" was certainly not to be spared the intellectually debilitating—morally debilitating—effects of the acids of modernity that put in jeopardy the realization and maintenance of those bare bones of republican government. This country did feel the effects of the thoroughgoing relativism that removed the link between mind or conscience and any objective truth or good. Indeed the United States was to develop its own form of it.

Truth, once said to be mighty when equipped with her natural weapons, free argument and debate, proved not to be so mighty after all. If she exists. And what are those weapons, finally, but shields for the interest and passion of the arguers? And just who was this Thomas Jefferson, to talk about Truth being mighty and prevailing and all of that? A Virginia aristocrat. An owner of slaves. A white Anglo-Saxon male with a big house on a hill and acres and acres of Virginia land. A strictly eighteenth-century mind. Truth, said to be sufficient against all the winds of doctrine, becomes another breeze among them, and, after all, how do you know which is which? And, above all, who is to say?

One may be tempted in a parochially nationalistic mood to say that these relativistic and reductionist winds of doctrine, blowing the mask off the face of reason, came from Europe, from a nineteenth-century and early twentieth-century European intellectual underground—Europe's revenge, as it were, against the late eighteenth-century American success in building a genuine, large, and lasting republic.

The democratic revolutions in Europe—to continue this slightly pouting and self-indulgent American nationalistic view—did not, generally speaking, go as smoothly as the American, bringing on the Terror and Napoleon, fizzling out, coming and going, one regime, one republic, then another, finally in the twentieth century giving rise to monstrous regimes, evil in a new mode. And meanwhile thinkers without civic responsibility, displaced aristocrats, rebellious sons of the bourgeoisie, of preachers, of rabbis, nursing their boils in the British Museum, scribbling away in attics and basements, thinkers with world-encircling ideas in their heads, exiled from power, cut off from an identification with the polity, with what they would call the "masses" (their un-American word), filled the intellectual air with pictures of ineluctable class conflict, of the irrational in humankind, of the triumph of the will, of the superman, of economic determinism, of the decline of the West, of the revolt of the masses, of the "crowd," of the meaninglessness of any statements that cannot meet the test of empirical verification (so much for "truths"), of all of culture being but an epiphenomenal superstructure on the economic substructure, of "value" chopped apart from "fact" and left to vanish in the winds of mere opinion. And when these dark intellectual clouds floated across the Atlantic to the once sunny new land to the west, the much less theoretical people there, busily growing wheat and building schools and congratulating themselves on their great country, eventually felt the sprinkles and, golly whiz, began to lose their grip on what it was they were to do with this American project except for each to feather his own nest.

But the truth is, of course, that we Americans didn't need any help from Europe to arrive at that result. Already by the 1830s, the greatest of European observers of America was noting the combination of a kind of privatism with a soft, standards-destroying populist conformity that was a harbinger, perhaps a warning, of what was eventually to come in Europe. That the American "culture" that was to develop after the Founders was to become as individualistic, as voluntaristic, as libertarian as any that the Western world had seen, is very familiar. The cultural and intellectual currents that then shaped the new United States moved in the same direction: political-social individualism; religious (evangelical Protestant) individualism; and—what would prove after the Civil War to be the most powerful—economic individualism, all going in the same direction, reinforcing each other. The primary social-moral terms for Americans of all political stripes came to be "freedom" and "rights," underlined so heavily and emphasized so exclusively as to diminish the balancing claims—common good, equality, order, justice, duties, responsibility—and to obscure the social context within which freedoms and rights find their place and ground. "Liberty" came to mean not a condition of society but a claim of each person against society. The happiness to be pursued was not thought to be the "public happiness," John Adams's term revived by Hannah Arendt but incomprehensible to modern-day Americans. "Rights" are claimed in an implied social vacuum, restrained if at all only by a counterclaim of some other person's "rights"—heads bumping, with lawyers for each side. The United States, in sum, was to develop into something rather different from the republic that (let us say) young Madison and Bradford, reading their books in the excitements of Princeton, must have envisioned—different from what the Founders in general envisioned, with respect to its ethos. The main religious tradition that developed in the United States was to abet and encourage, more than it was to resist or impede, that development. So what happens now?

Thomas Jefferson expected the new nation to be Unitarian by about 1830; Isaac Backus expected it to be Baptist by then. The expectation of neither was to be realized in the event, although Backus came closer.

Thomas Jefferson, James Madison, and their rationalist colleagues designed institutions to free reason from the ancient impediment of state-enforced religious conformity; those institutions proved to be an encouragement less to Enlightenment rationalism than to aggressive Biblical pietism. Isaac Backus and his colleagues and heirs planted the Voluntary Way in religion in the soul of the new nation in order that it should be a (Protestant) Christian America; they helped create a nation of liberty in which the largest religious body soon came to be the Roman Catholic Church. The fertile climate of America's religious liberty nourished a luxuriant growth of belief, making the nation by the claims of its nineteenth-century enthusiasts the bearer of a new

Christian civilization, a uniquely religious people among modern nations—the true heart's faith of which in the twentieth century is perhaps effectively summed up in that sentence of Flannery O'Connor's
anti-preacher preacher Hazel Motes, after he has acquired his fine jalopy
in a used-car lot: "Any man with a good car don't need no salvation."
But then a twentieth-century intellectual generation, originally confident in its secularity—raised in ignorance of and disdain for Western
religious traditions, which they expected science and education soon
to polish off, with H. L. Mencken meanwhile providing laughs at the
Bible Belt—was hit by successive shocks of monstrous evil that defy
the myths of progress; by a war for a civilization that may not be
"Christian" but is still somehow morally superior to that other one;
by popular revivals of a religion that somehow does not seem to go
away as it was supposed to; for a time by a theological revival even
among intellectuals; and by catastrophic possibilities for the human
enterprise that demand some moral grounding.

History has sobering surprises for us all. Surveying now, after two
centuries, the results of its surprises in the limited sphere of this book's
subject, one can say that a long-delayed outcome is now arriving. Although in its narrower definition religious liberty was achieved fairly
early in the nation's existence, in its broader definitions, and in the
cultural issues it brings in its train, its full complexity is rising into
view, 200 years after the Virginia statute was enacted. Moreover, this
larger significance comes into place as the long de facto Protestant
establishment has clearly ended, and as no other candidate for that
effectively dominant cultural-religious position can successfully take
its place—not any other religious persuasion, nor any combination of
religious groups, but also not, despite the noisily articulated fears of
segments of the conservative religious community, "secular humanism" either. Establishment by law ended in the nineteenth century.
Establishment by cultural domination ended in the twentieth.

That is, "establishment" with respect to religious matters. It is certainly not to be denied that there are other forms of cultural domination,
weightier perhaps than anything that ever accompanied established
churches in this country. But with respect to the role of religion, and
the effect of religion on political culture, Jefferson's country has come
at last into a remarkable configuration, as the European immigrations
mature; as in particular the Roman Catholic community comes to be
not only a large but also a self-confident participant in the political
community; as the Afro-American world with its different appropriation of evangelical Protestantism—more communal—comes to be a full

partner in the public forum; as other world religions sprinkle themselves upon the scene; as the progressive and conservative applications of religion to the moral questions of common life each come to be more sophisticated in the presence of the other; and—most important—as each side of "pious and secular America" comes to accept the other as a continuing presence, not to be disdained or dismissed out of hand. The United States has come after two centuries to a quite unusual condition with respect to its collective religious stand—a condition sufficiently unusual to make every statement about it subject to challenge, including this one.

We present now to the world a nation endlessly deliberating about first principles, and even about how to state the condition of our deliberation. Must that unusual situation mean shallowness, conflict, chaos? In one aspect a plurality of religious groups does make for a trivial conception of religion's meaning, as a service to civility: You, yours, I, mine; they are all the same at bottom.

Or may it be that each of the weighty participants—the historic high religions, the particular form of American secular social idealism—can find within itself, partly as a result of the deliberation with the others, the resources to contribute to a deeper community.

Republicanism—that is, a citizenry-wide consideration of the public good—requires more of an awareness of the limitations of each person's understanding, and of the distortions of reason by self-interest, than Jefferson perceived. It requires a critical sense of the link—as James Madison put it—between reason and self-love, including in oneself, a sense that is akin to "relativism," but not identical with it. It requires an awareness of each *group's* limitation, and of the magnified effect of self-love on the reason of groups, that was one of Madison's central points. Therefore not only should no man be judge in his own case; no groups should either. The underlying point is not the sheer relativity of all points of view, or the legitimacy of sheer interest-seeking with no self-restraining mind or conscience, no restraint upon them except opposing power—but the endless correction of the limitation of the mind and conscience of each by the reasoning of all, so truth "prevails." They do not simply check and restrain but also illuminate and affect each other. If each is "deep," if each has its own depth, then for the better. Milton's language and metaphor may be better for republican understanding than Jefferson's: truth and error, and good and evil, mixed in this world (as in St. Augustine, too); an endless winnowing, a putting back together of the broken body of truth, with pieces scattered here and there and elsewhere, no one possessing all of them, endlessly trying to reassemble them. Pieces of the true and the good are sometimes to be found in unlikely places: "Precious pearls and jewels, and far more precious truth," wrote Roger Williams, "are found in muddy sheels and places. The rich mines of golden truth lie hid under barren hills and in obscure holes and corners." Williams himself, one might say, represented one of those mines of truth hid in an obscure corner.

One hopes that one has, while at the same time one certainly does not have, truth—"Having and Not Having the Truth" is the title of a chapter by Reinhold Niebuhr. In other words, a twentieth-century American "republican" ("democrat") wants the culture to have taken into itself enough of the relativizing of the thinkers of two centuries to fill in the critical and self-critical aspect that existed incipiently already in a person like Williams, but not so much as to destroy itself—to give over the effort, not to think.

The American democratic society does have metaphysical presuppositions. It is not a wholly empty "process." Even that process—the institutions of liberty and self-government—have implied underpinnings. Those institutions did not come into the world by a total accident out of the air. They arose out of a particular history, and entail presuppositions about human beings and human societies: their nature, their rights, their duties, their goods.

The American republic has such metaphysical underpinnings, but any official, closed, final statement of them violates them. Each explicit statement of those presuppositions is subject to dispute on the basis of other formulations; the argument among these formulations is itself of the essence of the society, and valuable by its lights. The "truths" we have and do not have are potentially corrected by these others. Both H. Richard Niebuhr, in a quotation placed by Sydney Ahlstrom at the head of his last chapter, and Randall Jarrell, in reflections on Wallace Stevens—this citation comes to be complicated, but the doublings-up add to its value, at least for the writer—cite something Santayana wrote about Spinoza: "Say to those little gnostics, to those circumnavigators of being: *I do not believe you; God is great.*"

Coming back from a dialogue of serious theologians of the several faiths, sponsored by that Commission on Religion and the Free Society, the present writer described the gathering to his then editor, a sharp-tongued European. One remark of his was cynical, although with its truth, too. Naming three religious eminences from the same faith groups, he said, "What about them? They're crooks." But he also made a satirical capsule of the writer's own account that might be freed from satire and put forth seriously: "the solidarity of the deep." "Locked in argument," to be sure, as Father Murray would say. Something like that this remarkable nation requires in order to hold both to Truth and to Liberty without allowing either to destroy the other.

APPENDIXES

ACKNOWLEDGMENTS

INDEX

A BILL FOR ESTABLISHING RELIGIOUS FREEDOM
1777

Well aware that the opinions and belief of men depend not on their own will, but follow involuntarily the evidence proposed in their minds; that Almighty God hath created the mind free, *and manifested his supreme will that free it shall remain by making it altogether insusceptible of restraint;* that all attempts to influence it by temporal punishments, or burthens, or by civil incapacitations, tend only to beget habits of hypocrisy and meanness, and are a departure from the plan of the holy author of our religion, who being lord both of body and mind, yet chose not to propagate it by coercions on either, as was in his Almighty power to do, *but to extend it by its influence on reason alone;* that the impious presumption of legislators and rulers, civil as well as ecclesiastical, who, being themselves but fallible and uninspired men, have assumed dominion over the faith of others, setting up their own opinions and modes of thinking as the only true and infallible, and as such endeavoring to impose them on others, hath established and maintained false religions over the greatest part of the world and through all time: That to compel a man to furnish contributions of money for the propagation of opinions which he disbelieves *and abhors,* is sinful and tyrannical: that even the forcing him to support this or that teacher of his own religious persuasion, is depriving him of the comfortable liberty of giving his contributions to the particular pastor whose morals he would make his pattern, and whose powers he feels most persuasive to righteousness; and is withdrawing from the ministry those temporary rewards, which proceeding from an approbation of their personal conduct, are an additional incitement to earnest and unremitting labours for the instruction of mankind; that our civil rights have no dependence on our religious opinions, any more than our opinions in physics or geometry; that therefore the proscribing any citizen as unworthy the public confidence by laying upon him an incapacity of being called to offices of trust and emolument, unless he profess or renounce this or that religious opinion, is depriving him injuriously of those privileges and advantage to which, in common with his fellow citizens, he has a natural right; that it tends also to corrupt the principles of that *very* religion it is meant to encourage, by bribing with a monopoly of worldly honours and emoluments, those who will externally profess and conform to it; that though indeed these are criminal who do not withstand such temptation, yet neither are those innocent who lay the bait in their way; *that the opinions of men are not the object of civil government, nor under its jurisdiction;* that to suffer the civil magistrate to intrude his powers into the field of opinion and to restrain the profession or propagation of principles on supposition of their ill tendency is a dangerous fallacy, which at once destroys all religious liberty, because he being of course judge of that tendency will make his opinions the rule of judgment, and approve or condemn the sentiments of others only as they shall square with or differ from his own; that it is time enough for the rightful purposes of civil government for its officers to interfere when principles break out into overt acts against peace and good order; and finally, that truth is great and will prevail if left to herself; that she is the proper and sufficient antagonist to error, and has nothing to fear from the conflict unless by human interposition disarmed of her natural weapons, free argument and debate; errors ceasing to be dangerous when it is permitted freely to contradict them.

We the General Assembly of Virginia do enact that no man shall be compelled to frequent or support any religious worship, place, or ministry whatsoever, nor shall be enforced, restrained, molested, or burthened in his body or goods, nor shall otherwise suffer, on account of his religious opinions or belief; but that all men shall be free to profess, and by argument to maintain, their opinions in matters of religion, and that the same shall in no wise diminish, enlarge, or affect their civil capacities.

And though we well know that this assembly, elected by the people for the ordinary purposes of legislation only, have no power to restrain the acts of succeeding Assemblies, constituted with powers equal to our own, and that therefore to declare this act irrevocable would be of no effect in law; yet we are free to declare, and do declare, that the rights hereby asserted are of the natural rights of mankind, and that ifany act shall be hereafter passed to repeal the present or to narrow its operation, such act will be in infringement of natural right.

THOMAS JEFFERSON

(The text is taken from the 1784 *Report of the Committee of Revisors.*)

The passages in italics indicate the additions and changes in Jefferson's original text as first proposed in 1776.

TO THE HONORABLE THE GENERAL ASSEMBLY OF THE COMMONWEALTH OF VIRGINIA: A MEMORIAL AND REMONSTRANCE

We the subscribers, citizens of the said Commonwealth, having taken into serious consideration, a Bill printed by order of the last Session of General Assembly, entitled "A Bill establishing a provision for Teachers of the Christian Religion," and conceiving that the same if finally armed with the sanctions of a law, will be a dangerous abuse of power, are bound as faithful members of a free State to remonstrate against it, and to declare the reasons by which we are determined. We remonstrate against the said Bill,

1. Because we hold it for a fundamental and undeniable truth, "that Religion or the duty which we owe to our Creator and the manner of discharging it, can be directed only by reason and conviction, not by force or violence." The Religion then of every man must be left to the conviction and conscience of every man; and it is the right of every man to exercise it as these may dictate. This right is in its nature an unalienable right. It is unalienable, because the opinions of men, depending only on the evidence contemplated by their own minds cannot follow the dictates of other men: It is unalienable also, because what is here a right towards men, is a duty towards the Creator. It is the duty of every man to render to the Creator such homage and such only as he believes to be acceptable to him. This duty is precedent, both in order of time and in degree of obligation, to the claims of Civil Society. Before any man can be considered as a member of Civil Society, he must be considered as a subject of the Governour of the Universe: And if a member of Civil Society, who enters into any subordinate Association, must always do it with a reservation of his duty to the General Authority; much more must every man who becomes a member of any particular Civil Society, do it with a saving of his allegiance to the Universal Sovereign. We maintain therefore that in matters of Religion, no mans right is abridged by the institution of Civil Society and that Religion is wholly exempt from its cognizance. True it is, that no other rule exists, by which any question which may divide a Society, can be

ultimately determined, but the will of the majority; but it is also true that the majority may trespass on the rights of the minority.

2. Because if Religion be exempt from the authority of the Society at large, still less can it be subject to that of the Legislative Body. The latter are but the creatures and vicegerents of the former. Their jurisdiction is both derivative and limited: it is limited with regard to the co-ordinate departments, more necessarily is it limited with regard to the constituents. The preservation of a free Government requires not merely, that the metes and bounds which separate each department of power be invariably maintained; but more especially that neither of them be suffered to overleap the great Barrier which defends the rights of the people. The Rulers who are guilty of such an encroachment, exceed the commission from which they derive their authority, and are Tyrants. The People who submit to it are governed by laws made neither by themselves nor by an authority derived from them, and are slaves.

3. Because it is proper to take alarm at the first experiment on our liberties. We hold this prudent jealousy to be the first duty of Citizens, and one of the noblest characteristics of the late Revolution. The free men of America did not wait till usurped power had strengthened itself by exercise, and entangled the question in precedents. They saw all the consequences in the principle, and they avoided the consequences by denying the principle. We revere this lesson too much soon to forget it. Who does not see that the same authority which can establish Christianity, in exclusion of all other Religions, may establish with the same ease any particular sect of Christians, in exclusion of all other Sects? that the same authority which can force a citizen to contribute three pence only of his property for the support of any one establishment, may force him to conform to any other establishment in all cases whatsoever?

4. Because the Bill violates that equality which ought to be the basis of every law, and which is more indispensable, in proportion as the validity or expediency of any law is more liable to be impeached. If "all men are by nature equally free and independent," all men are to be considered as entering into Society on equal conditions; as relinquishing no more, and therefore retaining no less, one than another, of their natural rights. Above all are they to be considered as retaining an "*equal* title to the free exercise of Religion according to the dictates of Conscience." Whilst we assert for ourselves a freedom to embrace, to profess and to observe the Religion which we believe to be of divine origin, we cannot deny an equal freedom to those whose minds have

not yet yielded to the evidence which has convinced us. If this freedom be abused, it is an offence against God, not against man: To God, therefore, not to man, must an account of it be rendered. As the Bill violates equality by subjecting some peculiar burdens, so it violates the same principle, by granting to others peculiar burdens, so it violates the same principle, by granting to others peculiar exemptions. Are the Quakers and Menonists the only sects who think a compulsive support of their Religions unnecessary and unwarrantable? Can their piety alone be entrusted with the care of public worship? Ought their Religions to be endowed above all others with extraordinary privileges by which proselytes may be enticed from all others? We think too favorably of the justice and good sense of these denominations to believe that they either covet pre-eminences over their fellow citizens or that they will be seduced by them from the common opposition to the measure.

5. Because the Bill implies either that the Civil Magistrate is a competent Judge of Religious Truth; or that he may employ Religion as an engine of Civil policy. The first is an arrogant pretension falsified by the contradictory opinions of Rulers in all ages, and throughout the world: the second an unhallowed perversion of the means of salvation.

6. Because the establishment proposed by the Bill is not requisite for the support of the Christian Religion. To say that it is, is a contradiction to the Christian Religion itself, for every page of it disavows a dependence on the powers of this world: it is a contradiction to fact; for it is known that this Religion both existed and flourished, not only without the support of human laws, but in spite of every opposition from them, and not only during the period of miraculous aid, but long after it had been left to its own evidence and the ordinary care of Providence. Nay, it is a contradiction in terms; for a Religion not invented by human policy, must have pre-existed and been supported, before it was established by human policy. It is moreover to weaken in those who profess this Religion a pious confidence in its innate excellence and the patronage of its Author; and to foster in those who still reject it, a suspicion that its friends are too conscious of its fallacies to trust its own merits.

7. Because experience witnesseth that ecclesiastical establishments, instead of maintaining the purity and efficacy of Religion, have had a contrary operation. During almost fifteen centuries has the legal establishment of Christianity been on trial. What have been its fruits? More or less in all places, pride and indolence in the Clergy, ignorance and servility in the laity, in both, superstition, bigotry and persecution. Enquire of the Teachers of Christianity for the ages in which it appeared

in its greatest lustre; those of every sect, point to the ages prior to its incorporation with Civil policy. Propose a restoration of this primitive State in which its Teachers depended on the voluntary rewards of their flocks, many of them predict its downfall. On which Side ought their testimony to have greatest weight, when for or when against their interest?

8. Because of the establishment in question is not necessary for the support of Civil Government. If it be urged as necessary for the support of Civil Government only as it is a means of supporting Religion, and it be not necessary for the latter purpose, it cannot be necessary for the former. If Religion be not within the cognizance of Civil Government how can its legal establishment be necessary to Civil Government? What influence in fact have ecclesiastical establishments had on Civil Society? In some instances they have been seen to erect a spiritual tyranny on the ruins of the Civil authority; in many instances they have been seen upholding the thrones of political tyranny; in no instance have they been seen the guardians of the liberties of the people. Rulers who wished to subvert the public liberty, may have found an established Clergy convenient auxiliaries. A just Government instituted to secure & perpetuate it needs them not. Such a Government will be best supported by protecting every Citizen in the enjoyment of his Religion with the same equal hand which protects his person and his property; by neither invading the equal rights of any Sect, nor suffering any Sect to invade those of another.

9. Because the proposed establishment is a departure from that generous policy, which, offering an Asylum to the persecuted and oppressed of every Nation and Religion, promised a lustre to our country, and an accession to the number of its citizens. What a melancholy mark is the Bill of sudden degeneracy? Instead of holding forth an Asylum to the persecuted, it is itself a signal of persecution. It degrades from the equal rank of Citizen all those whose opinions in Religion do not bend to those of the Legislative authority. Distant as it may be in its present form from the Inquisition, it differs from it only in degree. The one is the first step, the other the last in the career of intolerance. The magnanimous sufferer under this cruel scourge in foreign Regions, must view the Bill as a Beacon on our Coast, warning him to seek some other haven, where liberty and philanthropy in their due extent, may offer a more certain repose from his Troubles.

10. Because it will have a like tendency to banish our Citizens. The allurements presented by other situations are every day thinning their number. To superadd a fresh motive to emigration by revoking the

liberty which they now enjoy, would be the same species of folly which has dishonoured and depopulated flourishing kingdoms.

11. Because it will destroy that moderation and harmony which the forbearance of our laws to intermeddle with Religion has produced among its several sects. Torrents of blood have been spilt in the old world, by vain attempts of the secular arm, to extinguish Religious discord, by proscribing all difference in Religious opinion. Time has at length revealed the true remedy. Every relaxation of narrow and rigorous policy, wherever it has been tried, has been found to assuage the disease. The American Theatre has exhibited proofs that equal and compleat liberty, if it does not wholly eradicate it, sufficiently destroys its malignant influence on the health and prosperity of the State. If with the salutary effects of this system under our own eyes, we begin to contract the bounds of Religious freedom, we know no name that will too severely reproach our folly. At least let warning be taken at the first fruits of the threatened innovation. The very appearance of the Bill has transformed "that Christian forbearance, love and charity," which of late mutually prevailed, into animosities and jealousies, which may not soon be appeased. What mischiefs may not be dreaded, should this enemy to the public quiet be armed with the force of a law?

12. Because the policy of the Bill is adverse to the diffusion of the light of Christianity. The first wish of those who enjoy this precious gift ought to be that it may be imparted to the whole race of mankind. Compare the number of those who have as yet received it with the number still remaining under the dominion of false Religions; and how small is the former! Does the policy of the Bill tend to lessen the disproportion? No; it at once discourages those who are strangers to the light of revelation from coming into the Region of it; and countenances by example the nations who continue in darkness, in shutting out those who might convey it to them. Instead of Levelling as far as possible, every obstacle to the victorious progress of Truth, the Bill with an ignoble and unchristian timidity would circumscribe it with a wall of defense against the encroachments of error.

13. Because attempts to enforce by legal sanctions, acts obnoxious to so great a proportion of Citizens, tend to enervate the laws in general, and to slacken the bands of Society. If it be difficult to execute any law which is not generally deemed necessary or salutary, what must be the case, where it is deemed invalid and dangerous? And what may be the effect of so striking an example of impotency in the Government, on its general authority?

14. Because a measure of such singular magnitude and delicacy ought

not to be imposed, without the clearest evidence that it is called for by a majority of citizens, and no satisfactory method is yet proposed by which the voice of the majority in this case may be determined, or its influence secured. "The people of the respective counties are indeed requested to signify their opinion respecting the adoption of the Bill to the next Session of Assembly." But the representation must be made equal, before the voice of either of the Representatives or of the Counties will be that of the people. Our hope is that neither of the former will, after due consideration, espouse the dangerous principle of the Bill. Should the event disappoint us, it will still leave us in full confidence, that a fair appeal to the latter will reverse the sentence against our liberties.

15. Because finally, "the equal right of every citizen to the free exercise of his Religion according to the dictates of conscience" is held by the same tenure with all our other rights. If we recur to its origin, it is equally the gift of nature; if we weigh its importance, it cannot be less dear to us; if we consult the "Declaration of those rights which pertain to the good people of Virginia, as the basis and foundation of Government," it is enumerated with equal solemnity, or rather studied emphasis. Either then, we must say, that the Will of the Legislature is the only measure of their authority; and that in the plenitude of this authority, they may sweep away all our fundamental rights; or, that they are bound to leave this particular right untouched and sacred: Either we must say, that they may controul the freedom of the press, may abolish the Trial by Jury, may swallow up the Executive and Judiciary Powers of the State; nay that they may despoil us of our very right of suffrage, and erect themselves into an independent and hereditary Assembly or, we must say, that they have no authority to enact into law the Bill under consideration. We the Subscribers say, that the General Assembly of this Commonwealth have no such authority: And that no effort may be omitted on our part against so dangerous an usurpation, we oppose to it, this remonstrance; earnestly praying, as we are in duty bound, that the Supreme Lawgiver of the Universe, by illuminating those to whom it is addressed, may on the one hand, turn their Councils from the very act which would affront his holy prerogative, or violate the trust committed to them: and on the other, guide them into every measure which may be worthy of his [blessing, may re]dound to their own praise, and may establish more firmly the liberties, the prosperity and the happiness of the Commonwealth.

ACKNOWLEDGMENTS

I owe the largest debt for support of this book to the Lilly Endowment, and to its vice-president, Robert Lynn. Mr. Lynn encouraged the project from the start, and supported it not only with funds to give the writer time to write it but also with significant help as regards both the substance and the mechanics of its development, including three small gatherings of scholars and knowledgeable readers who criticized and commented on drafts in various stages, and discussed the topic to my great benefit. I hope those who attended these gatherings will excuse my not naming them—they would constitute quite a list—and accept my gratitude collectively for their assistance.

Long ago, I incurred a debt that has remained waiting in the womb of time until the publication of this book, to the late John Cogley, and to our colleagues on the Fund for the Republic's group on Religion and a Free Society; in my memory they have constantly circled my desk as I was writing. They were accompanied by the colleagues who asked me to join in teaching, and the students who underwent the grilling about cases, in three courses in the Yale Law School over the years 1961–64, and by many other students in other courses in several other places. I am grateful to them all.

I have sought to acknowledge in the text itself my weightiest specific debts to sources, and to make some commentary on sources a part of it. In the section on the Virginia statute I relied more heavily than the text may convey upon Thomas E. Buckley, S.J., *Church and State in Revolutionary Virginia, 1776–1787*. Mr. Buckley most generously read versions of Parts One and Two, made valuable comments, and saved me from errors; he is of course not responsible for any new ones I may have inserted, or old ones either, or the speculative flights and interpretations. The same exculpation applies to Thomas A. Mason of The James Madison Papers, now located at the University of Virginia, who generously read early versions of the same two parts and made many valuable suggestions and corrections.

I am particularly grateful to my colleagues at the University of Virginia, David Levin, Robert Cross, and David Little, and to Edwin Gaustad of the University of California at Riverside, all of whom read Part

Acknowledgments

Three, and to another UVA colleague, Dorothy A. Ross, who read Part Two, for taking time to read these long sections, comment on them in detail, and help me thereby in many ways.

Several other institutions and agencies, in addition to the Lilly Endowment, supported me while I was working on this book with funds and/ or in other ways, either specifically for this project or for other work as well: the Poynter Center at Indiana University, especially Beverly Davis, David Smith, and Judy Granbois; the Center for the Study of the American Experience at the University of Southern California, where I wish in particular to thank Sheila R. Pierce, Nancy McKay, and Dr. John Weaver, and John Orr and Henry Clark for inviting me to that pleasant, sunny place; the Kennedy Institute of Ethics at Georgetown University, which provided me an office in their car barn filled with less sunshine but more moral philosophy; and the National Endowment for the Humanities, which provided a small grant to support that sojourn in the car barn. I was a guest scholar for two summers at the Woodrow Wilson Center for International Scholars, there in the Castle on the Mall, a wonderful place to work; I wish in particular to thank James Billington, who once in the past gave me more encouragement than he knew, and Michael Lacy, for many helpful conversations, especially about James Madison and republicanism. Finally, my wife and I had the privilege of twenty-eight days at the Villa Serbelloni in Bellagio, the Rockefeller Foundation's answer to Paradise, which surpasses all other places in sunshine and almost every other respect as well. I am grateful to these institutions and their directors and managers.

My colleagues in the Departments of Rhetoric and Communications Studies and of Religious Studies at the University of Virginia, have tolerated my invisibility with an astonishing good humor. I wish to thank the staff of the first of these departments—Margaret Sugerman and, in earlier time and in particular, Joanne Stevens, for word-processing great chunks of the book and for many other kinds of help.

I have the great good fortune to have as an editor Corona Machemer, who has that particular editorial gift of entering sympathetically into the work of someone else's hand and mind, and making it better.

The dedication expresses a debt and friendship that go beyond this book. Finally, I thank Linda Moore Miller, for support that was tangible and intangible, intellectual and practical, not only for the book but for the writer through the time of its writing.

William Lee Miller
Charlottesville, Virginia

INDEX

Index

Index